FROM ANIMISTIC TO
NATURALISTIC
SOCIOLOGY

FROM ANIMISTIC TO NATURALISTIC SOCIOLOGY

William R. Catton, Jr.
Professor of Sociology
University of Washington

McGraw-Hill Book Company
New York
St. Louis
San Francisco
Toronto
London
Sydney

HM
24
.C3

To
Stu
in appreciation of
an intellectual
challenge

The reader of this book is asked to examine very carefully some important roadblocks that have impeded scientific advancement in sociological thought and research. He is invited to explore in detail why they are roadblocks, and why they continue to get in our way even when we genuinely desire to develop sociology as a real science. To surmount these obstacles I shall propose some basic conceptual innovations.

The specific provocation for this book arose from a clash between the neopositivist predispositions with which I entered sociology and some subtle but troublesome flaws that became apparent in supposedly exemplary research already conducted under that persuasion. The neopositivist label, of course, symbolizes a stance toward which few sociologists can remain altogether affectively neutral and when I first became intuitively aware of these research flaws I found my own reliance on intuition distressing. The occasion for my concern was a study in "social physics" that was highly esteemed by some of my mentors and colleagues. Its author happened to use national park travel data in testing an allegedly gravitational model of "interactance" between population aggregates. While I was favorably disposed toward the idea of generalizing the gravitational formula and applying it to interhuman behavior, I happened also to have an aesthetic appreciation of the wilderness areas in national parks. So it bothered me to find that the model in question took population as the social analogue of mass. I could not accept a model of national park travel patterns which implied that the presence of *other people* in them is what attracts visitors to these places. For a devotee of wilderness, it seemed obvious that human crowds in the parks would detract rather than attract.

This anomaly in the supposedly exemplary research confronted me with a complex challenge. First, I felt the need to try to eliminate a patent defect in an otherwise attractive model. Could such a physicalistic model be improved and made sociologically appropriate, or must it be discarded? Second, I felt challenged to reconcile my scientific interests with what now seemed potentially antagonistic aesthetic interests. Could sociologists (and dare they) study spiritual values in a scientific manner? And third, I recognized that despite my predilection for rigorously "positivistic" methods, I was now indulging in an obvious instance of *Verstehende* by this introspective insistence that visitors are drawn to national parks in spite of the presence of other visitors rather than because of it. Was there a legitimate place in scientific sociology for an intuitive and empathic approach?

These are questions of large scope, and it was to answer them that this book was written. In the course of reexamining my own methodological convictions, I found that the term "positivist" (with or without the prefix "neo") ceased to suffice for expressing my position. The reader may likewise come to feel its inadequacy as a reference point for locating himself along the spectrum of sociological perspectives.

In responding to the triple challenge outlined above, I have been aided over the past several years by a number of persons and organizations. My colleagues in the University of Washington Department of Sociology have patiently indulged what must have sometimes seemed to them my rather esoteric interests. My wife Nancy and our sons have enthusiastically shared and markedly enhanced my aesthetic enjoyment of, and pursuit of knowledge about, the national parks—both as a scenic environment and as a sociologically interesting institution in which fortuitously and unexpectedly it became possible for me to explore basic metasociological problems. More than these individuals realize, they have also given me encouragement in the strenuous hours of thought I have put into reconsideration of the physical ancestry of many of the concepts employed in this book.

Various officials of the National Park Service were exceedingly helpful in making data available, including the Chief Ranger at each of several parks, and Mr. Rendel B. Alldredge, Chief of Statistics Analysis in Park Service headquarters in Washington, D.C. Small grants from the Graduate Research Fund and the Agnes Anderson Fund at the University of Washington helped finance both the collection and processing of data. Mr. Gary Barbour and Mr. David Bassett patiently helped with prolonged calculations that could not have been so interesting to them as the implications were to me. Mr. Lennart Berggren wrote a computer program which made possible the comparison of my revised gravitational model and the Stouffer intervening opportunities model. Stimulating discussions with him also helped clarify a number of theoretical problems.

My thanks are also due to Professors Milton Yinger and Ralph Turner, of Oberlin College, for reading portions of the manuscript and making helpful comments. Professor Otto Larsen, of the University of Washington, read the entire manuscript and gave me much encouragement along with many valuable suggestions. None of these people, of course, is necessarily committed to the views I have set down in this book.

A number of publishers have kindly granted permission to quote materials from a variety of sources. In addition to the credit given in footnotes throughout the book I should like to acknowledge at this point the courtesy of the Blaisdell Publishing Company, a division of Ginn and Company, Waltham, Mass., for permission to quote numerous passages from *Social Causation* by Robert M. MacIver; and The Macmillan Co. Ltd., for permission to quote from MacIver's *Community: A Sociological Study*, published in the United States by St. Martin's Press, New York.

Finally, I want to thank the editors of several journals in which substantial parts of Chapters 4 and 5 had previously appeared for granting permission to reprint those materials here in much modified form. Chapter 4 is a revision of an article that originally appeared in *Sociological Inquiry*. Portions of Chapter 5 were revised from articles previously published in the *American Catholic Sociological Review*, the *Pacific Sociological Review*, and the *American Sociological Review*.

William R. Catton, Jr.

The time has come to clarify an issue that has been unclear for too long. Ever since sociology began to claim the status of a science, it has asserted that "man and society are part of nature." The assertion purports to have implications for the choice of methods whereby to study man and society, and it purports to lead to different laws of human social phenomena than those which would follow if man and society were regarded as not a part of nature. Yet controversy persists. A major reason for continued disputes over the adequacy and propriety of "the natural science approach" in sociology is that the implications of calling something a "part of nature" have been only dimly perceived and poorly understood.

Critics of a trend toward naturalistic sociology argue that adoption of the postulates and methods of natural science would "reduce" man to a merely material being and would give inadequate and often spurious explanations of his behavior in terms of purely material forces. They say important aspects of "reality" would be "left out" by this kind of sociology. In particular, they believe that natural science sociology would have to neglect the fact that man is a valuing creature.

Advocates of the naturalistic view, on the other hand, claim to be leaving out nothing that belongs in. In attaching man and society to nature, they say, they are merely excluding from sociology any supernatural and unverifiable explanations of social phenomena.

Important questions are begged on both sides, however. By their glib use of such words as "reality" and "values," critics convey the impression that they are privy to a more adequate method than the one they criticize as inadequate. They imply that their alternative method has given them *knowledge* of a realm of being that is outside "nature." The social scientist who "limits" himself to natural science methods is said thereby to deny himself access to this important additional realm. These critics beg the following questions: *How* do you know there is such an extranatural realm? What do you know about the things in it? How did you learn what you claim to know about them?

But the advocates of naturalistic sociology concede too much when they adopt the language of their critics. In equating naturalism with *exclusion* of something (the supernatural) from the realm of phenomena being studied, they appear to concede the existence of the very outside realm which is at the core of the critics' claims. The advocates have heretofore allowed themselves to be trapped in a verbal dilemma. By asserting that man and society are part of nature, and by implying that the assertion has almost self-evident meaning, they have seemed to say that there are some things that are inside "nature" and some things that are outside it—in which case their claim that man and society are among the inside things could still be moot. Those who have advocated developing sociology as a *natural* science have thus begged these questions: What are the boundaries of "nature"? What lies beyond those boundaries? Are the phenomena of "nature" affected by "nonnatural" phenomena? If so, how can adequate explanations for "natural" phenomena be achieved? Or, is "nature" everything there is? (When the answer to this question is affirmative, then the quotation marks can be dropped.) But if nature is everything there is, then does it mean any more to assert that man and society are part of nature than merely to say that man and society exist?

If we were simply declaring their existence when we say that man and society are part of nature, and if that were all that the so-called "natural science trend" comprised, then (since all sociologists could presumably endorse such an existential postulate) all sociologists would be full participants in the trend. I am under no illusion, though, that paragraphs like these will forever quiet the voices opposing naturalism in sociology. Adoption of naturalistic postulates is more than the mere assertion that we have a subject matter.

Nor is a sociologist, in embracing naturalism, merely denying the existence of a realm of reality outside "nature." What he does deny is the validity for social phenomena of propositions based on certain kinds of assumptions. Clarification of these assumptions and of the reasons for rejecting them is a major requirement for progress in sociology. Sociologists of the past who have inclined toward naturalism have usually left unspecified the characteristics of the nonnatural explanations they were rejecting. The present book seeks to fill this gap in metasociological thought.

For convenience, I will use the term "animism" as an antonym for "naturalism." By saying that man and society are (at least partly) outside "nature," animistic thinkers appear to mean that there are some aspects of human behavior that are exempt from the laws of nature. The exemptions they apparently have in mind are these: man can allegedly modify his actions (or at least change his mind) without cause, and he can act without being acted upon, or he can be acted upon without responding. To the participants in a culture that includes belief in "free will," such propositions seem almost self-evident. That people can act "at will" *seems* to be plain common sense and unquestionable fact. But these notions would clearly set men apart from other entities such as those whose behavior is described in physical mechanics, for example, where unmoved movers are assumed an impossibility, and where action persists unchanged unless modified by a force.

If the animistic views seem like common sense, they can nevertheless be denied, and their denial is precisely what we *should* mean when we say that man and society are natural phenomena. To the thoroughgoing naturalist, the most fundamental epistemological assumption he can make is that *all* phenomena persist unchanged unless acted upon by forces of some kind and that all actions are in fact interactions. Because these axioms of naturalism were first clearly formulated for one particular science, however, which happened to be physical mechanics, rejection of the contrary animistic views is often mistakenly regarded as acceptance of "materialism." The critics of natural science sociology are alarmed at the thought that man, a creature who values, should be studied like a mere lump of matter. One of the aims of this book is to show that man's valuing can be studied naturalistically, and that materialism is not the only alternative to animism. If values are within the reach of naturalistic inquiry, then this should eliminate the usual excuse of animists (that we must avoid "leaving out" essential aspects of the study of man).

Another aim of this book is to disentangle the fundamental issues that divide naturalism from animism and the more superficial issues that have separated various "schools" of sociological thought from one another. I have given special attention to the way the controversy over functional analysis has clouded the fundamental issues; critics of functional analysis have accused it of being teleological without making clear what is wrong with teleology. Functionalists have responded with meticulous attempts to distinguish "functions" from "purposes" so as to repudiate the accusation, but have thereby begged the question how the consequences of a behavior pattern can cause it, especially when unanticipated. The naturalistic sociologist will redefine the issue and take pains to ensure proper chronological sequence in any cause-effect relations he hypothesizes. He need not deny (as the animist supposes the naturalist must) the causal influence of values among human beings.

To deny unmoved movers, as naturalists do, is not to assert that all forces are physical. Nonphysical accelerations will be produced by nonphysical forces; but they will not occur apart from the operation of forces of *some* sort. Nonphysical actions will happen, but they will not happen without equal and opposite reactions of a similarly nonphysical sort. To the extent that we intend to measure and correlate them, nonphysical forces are not entelechies—of which men only make mysteries. For too long, too many sociologists have supposed they had to choose one horn or the other of a dilemma that really doesn't apply. To avoid entelechies, the sociologist does not have to reduce sociology to physics; to avoid reductionism, he does not have to deal in entelechies.

Some sociologists who have advocated what they thought of as a natural science method have stopped short of making it clear that this includes the acceptance of axioms that happened to be articulated clearly for the first time in physical mechanics but which have completely general applicability. A few sociologists who have explored what they or others have called "physical analogies" have badly misunderstood them. In this book I shall try to avoid both kinds of error; I shall try to make my position explicit, and I shall try to be accurate in stating parallels between sociological concepts and those of other sciences. Slipshod use of concepts, whether borrowed or not, has to be avoided.

To the naturalistic sociologist it is evident that man and society can profitably be studied as phenomena that conform to principles which are isomorphic with Newton's three axioms. Neither this isomorphism nor its meaning has been correctly depicted in the past—not even by those who were most receptive to it. For the truly naturalistic sociologist, the assumption that all verifiable sociological laws will be in accord with such axioms should be his point of departure, not his conclusion. It will guide his inquiry, not end it.

Moreover, when the natural scientist asserts that only observable variables (or variables that may at least be inferred from observables) are to be reckoned with, and insists on operational definitions of concepts, this does not mean he is abdicating to the animist all power to inquire into events which scientific theories suppose must happen but which cannot be observed or measured. Too many sociologists imagine they are saying something restrictive rather than creative when they list operationism among the ingredients of the "natural science approach." Operationism stipulates that a process which is theoretically suspected to be going on must not just be taken for granted; if it is important in theory, then it is essential to devise operations for observing (or objectively inferring) it. Whenever such advances in instrumentation or calculation have happened in the history of science they have enlarged the realm of naturalism. They have not at any point resulted in vindicating the antinaturalistic notion that there are events or processes about which we can know by some means other than observation but which we cannot know about through our instrument-aided senses. Operationism should be a challenging rather than a confining doctrine.

The ultimate criterion for acceptance of concepts in sociology, regardless of their origin, must be empirical. Can they be reliably used to classify observations in ways that facilitate increasing recognition of recurrent relations of sequence, concomitance, and contingency? I shall reiterate the importance of empiricism in this sense throughout the book, and I shall therefore assemble varied data by which to test key propositions derived from a naturalistic value theory. The value theory is presented to show that it is not necessary to neglect the fact that man is a valuing creature in order to be naturalistic. It is essential to be fully empirical in studying valuing behavior, though. Accordingly, I have at least begun to test some of the hypotheses generated by this naturalistic approach to value theory. I hope that a few of the readers of this volume may elect to augment this incomplete research.

Animists sometimes adopt an ostensibly generous posture, conceding that naturalism might be somewhat fruitful sociologically, but claiming that it cannot be *adequate* for all sociological questions. Some questions, they say, will always remain unanswered by the naturalistic approach. Possibly so, but discovering the limits of natural science is not tantamount to discovering the powers of some transcendental method or body of thought. Animism usually does not stop with the assertion that science has limits it cannot transcend. Animistic thinkers typically claim more than this. They claim to have transcended the limits by nonnaturalistic means and to know something about an alleged territory beyond. To validate that claim it would be necessary for them to show that by animistic approaches it is possible to predict correctly what free human wills are going to choose to do in instances where naturalistic methods (and common sense) yield either no prediction or an incorrect one. I intend to show in this book that naturalism can carry us a lot further than animists have admitted. But I shall also try to make it clear that the burden of proof must be shared by such opponents of naturalism. They cannot rest their case by pointing to existing deficiencies of naturalistic inquiry. To vindicate their own postulates they must demonstrate, rather than merely contend, that they can succeed where naturalists fail.

When I interpret the views of various sociologists as being more or less animistic, I do not mean to impugn anyone's motives. In fact, an entire chapter will be devoted to showing that there are strong cultural ties that bind us to animistic thoughtways even when we are struggling to become naturalistic. Those contemporary sociologists who find themselves cited in this book on the "wrong" side may be reassured by the conviction that science is a crescive institution. In the future as in the past, it will advance with the aid of contributions from persons who might have wished it to take a different course than it followed in fact. Even the slightest commitment to empiricism is sufficient to ensure that our cultural ties to animism will be gradually but inexorably undone by new theoretical implications of new data. And the commitment of most sociologists to empiricism today is more than slight.

Contents

List of Figures

Chapter One
THE ELEMENTS OF NATURALISM

Growth and Limits of Sociological Consensus

Sociology has changed a great deal since it first began to be recognized as a distinct discipline about a century ago. This change has been markedly accelerated since the Second World War. Most sociologists today probably regard as improvements, or advancements, most of the ways in which sociology has changed. Factual information has accumulated, and new and more effective ways of organizing and augmenting it have been developed. Few sociologists, however, are satisfied that the discipline has reached its goals, can rest on its scientific laurels, and need improve no further. An examination of the progress made so far ought to facilitate further advancement.

There is less debate than there once was among men calling themselves sociologists over whether the discipline is really a science or not. There remains some difference of opinion as to what being a scientific discipline involves. Hardly anyone would contend that sociology is yet one of the "mature" sciences. It is still groping its way toward conceptual clarity. The majority of sociologists now make use of a more or less common body of concepts which are demonstrably useful but not yet adequate to the analysis of interhuman behavior in all its aspects. But these concepts are still designated by varying terms. Though a growing body of propositions about interhuman behavior is fairly widely accepted, there is no

1

large number of well-established quantitative laws, couched in precisely defined and universally used terms.

Bernard Berelson and Gary Steiner have succinctly summarized a list of 1,045 reasonably well-confirmed findings of behavioral science by stating a modern "image of man." The present-day social scientist holds a conception of human nature and human action that is strikingly different from theologically sanctioned notions that prevailed in the Western world prior to the advent of sociology. This conception is also much changed from the overly biological perspectives prevalent in the late nineteenth century. Even with respect to such ostensibly instinctual matters as sexual and maternal behavior, the human being is now seen as an enormously plastic creature, able to live in a wide range of physical environments and to participate in a still wider range of cultural and social systems. But man is also a creature who must simplify reality if he is to cope with it. He is a creature who is subject to the influence of complex forces, so that almost nothing the sociologist studies is caused in a simple way by any one variable. Man is a creature of probability. To him everything familiar is natural, and most unfamiliar things seem unnatural. Given time and social support, however, man is exceedingly adjustable.[1]

It must be noted, though, that in saying man is subject to the influence of complex internal and external forces, Berelson and Steiner put quotation marks around "forces." Thus they seemed to imply that this is not yet one of the concepts on which there is clear sociological consensus. It is nevertheless difficult to avoid using the term in a variety of sociological contexts. As we shall see later, this trepidation about indispensable concepts is indicative of a major weakness in sociological thought.

There are some conspicuous gaps in present-day sociological theory. One of these, it is said, is the lack of a specific, well-developed theory of social change. Because of the extent of change both in sociology and in society in the past few decades, such a gap represents a real theoretical crisis.[2] That we should have come to such a crisis is ironic, in view of sociology's origin as what Don Martindale has called a "science of social motion." Although any science that is barely a century old might be expected to have a number of important gaps in its theories, this particular gap in sociological theory is an additional symptom of fundamental weaknesses in the habitual thoughtways of even those sociologists most earnestly hopeful that sociology is at last approaching scientific maturity.

Maturity is difficult to define, let alone achieve. When a writer says that a scholarly discipline has been maturing, this probably can be taken to mean that he regards with favor certain trends in that discipline. In

[1] Bernard Berelson and Gary A. Steiner, *Human Behavior: An Inventory of Scientific Findings.* New York: Harcourt, Brace & World, Inc., 1964, p. 663.
[2] Don Martindale, "Introduction," in George K. Zollschan and Walter Hirsch, *Explorations in Social Change.* Boston: Houghton Mifflin Company, 1964, pp. xii, xvii.

sociology, a number of writers claim to have discerned something called a "natural science trend." Various alternative names have been used in speaking of it, and these have various connotations. Even when similarly perceived, a trend may be differently evaluated by different observers. George Lundberg was obviously pleased to acknowledge the apparent prevalence of "natural science sociology" a dozen years ago.[3] He agreed that it includes emphases on quantitativism, behaviorism, and pragmatism, which Nicholas Timasheff had said were the ingredients of "neopositivism." Timasheff was obviously not so pleased at finding neopositivism to be the dominant school in mid-twentieth-century American sociology.[4] According to Philip Selznick, as well, there has been a strong trend toward what he simply called "positivism," with a special emphasis on empirical studies and the development and use of sociological measurement techniques.[5] Though he cautioned against certain possible hazards in this trend, Selznick by no means seemed to lament it, and even committed himself strongly to what he termed "naturalism."

The apparent general trend toward minimal differences between sociological procedures and the approaches taken in the natural sciences has not happened without certain eddies and back currents. John C. McKinney, for example, may have had his attention fixed on one of these when he reported that the style of thought customarily designated by the German word *Verstehende* "has assumed an increasingly important role in American sociology in the past two decades."[6] *Verstehende* has not usually been associated with positivism, and is certainly not a common method in the natural sciences. Its potential usefulness as a safeguard against merely spurious naturalism in sociology will be examined in Chapter 6.

Naturalism Displacing Animism

Many kinds of subject matter can be studied in a naturalistic manner, or in some other manner instead. The choice is more than a mere matter of taste; the results achieved depend on the approach taken. When Auguste Comte formulated his so-called "law of three stages" he

---

[3] George A. Lundberg, "The Natural Science Trend in Sociology," *American Journal of Sociology,* 61 (November, 1955), pp. 191–212.

[4] N. S. Timasheff, "Sociological Theory Today," *American Catholic Sociological Review,* 11 (1950).

[5] Philip Selznick, "Natural Law and Sociology," in The Fund for the Republic, *Natural Law and Modern Society.* Cleveland: The World Publishing Company, 1962, p. 156.

[6] John C. McKinney, "Methodology, Procedures, and Techniques in Sociology," chap. 7 in Howard Becker and Alvin Boskoff (eds.), *Modern Sociological Theory.* New York: The Dryden Press, Inc., 1957, p. 196.

contended, in effect, that nonnaturalistic approaches are initially followed in all subject-matter areas, but that these approaches tend in time to be displaced by demonstrably more effective naturalism. It was his hope and his expectation that such displacement was about to occur (in the early nineteenth century) in social thought. At the time he wrote, he felt that he discerned what would later have been called a "cultural lag"—a discrepancy between commitment to study and solution of some kinds of problems in a naturalistic way and a commitment to nonnaturalistic approaches to societal problems. He attributed the postrevolutionary turmoil in his native France to this discrepancy and wished to establish a scientific sociology as a basis for a stable and felicitous social order.

Comte's own writings did not constitute (as the later "religion of humanity" he tried to found would have implied) a finished edifice of naturalistic sociology. Although he gave sociology an identity as an intellectual discipline by coining its name, the naturalistic approach remained inadequately understood both by Comte and his successors. There has been a slowly growing understanding since his time of what is involved in the naturalistic study of sociological topics, but this understanding has grown rather irregularly, and full appreciation of the importance of naturalism has often been missing even when the approach has been clearly glimpsed.

There are several specific elements that distinguish a naturalistic approach from other ways of studying a given subject matter. Each of these elements was more or less absent from the earliest sociological formulations, and subsequent adherence to them has been spasmodic, sometimes unwitting, and often unwilling. It is my view that there has nevertheless been a trend, as others have reported, toward increasingly naturalistic sociology. I maintain that this is a desirable trend, in that the empirical problems that concern sociology are, like the empirical problems confronting other disciplines, *most effectively* studied within a thoroughly and consciously naturalistic framework. When our approach remains only reluctantly naturalistic or is deliberately nonnaturalistic, we tend (1) to ask meaningless questions, (2) to neglect relevant kinds of data, or (3) to subject our data to ineffectual analysis.

For reasons that will be made clear later, I shall refer to the alternative to a naturalistic approach as an "animistic" approach. It is argued in this book that there has been a general tendency to outgrow the animistic mode of thought in sociology. Sociologists who have contributed to and have been affected by this growth have not always perceived it, however. If this trend toward naturalism is deliberately accelerated, by means of a clearer articulation of what is involved, the discipline will profit. More of our research and theorizing will strike scientific pay dirt as we emancipate ourselves from lingering habits of animistic thought.

The Elements of Naturalism

The elements which distinguish a naturalistic study of any subject-matter area from an animistic study of that area are these:

1 A study is naturalistic only to the extent that it asks questions whose answers depend on sensory observation (with the aid of instruments when necessary). Thus naturalism stresses "objectivity"—in the sense that the conclusions of a study are subject to corroboration in parallel research by other investigators.

2 A study is naturalistic only if it seeks to explain given phenomena by reference to data that are or could be available prior to (or at least concurrently with) observations of the phenomena to be explained. It must shun outright teleological explanation. The extent to which so-called "functional explanations" are or are not teleological, and hence may not or may be naturalistic, will be examined in Chapter 3.

3 A study is naturalistic only if it considers change, rather than continuity, to be the problem requiring explanation. This third element of naturalism may be called the "axiom of inertia"; it will be illustrated in the following paragraph, discussed further in Chapter 4; in Chapter 7 the reason it is essential to naturalism will be explained.

4 Finally, a study is naturalistic only if it posits no "unmoved movers"—i.e., never explains a change in terms of something that does not itself change. One of the distinguishing traits of certain forms of animistic thought has been the adherence to the unmoved mover concept. Again, Chapter 7 will elaborate on this.

Whatever the level of complexity of the system being studied, when that system is in a steady state, the naturalistic approach *assumes* continuation of that steady state and deems its interruption to be problematic, whereas the animistic approach seeks explanation for the steadiness of a state of the system, as if assuming its immanent interruption or uncaused modification. An example may clarify the point. If a plant ecologist made successive observations of a biotic community and found that, in spite of turnover in the individual plants living in that community, its ecological structure remained constant, he would take this for granted, under constant environmental conditions. There would only be for him a problem requiring explanation (in terms of some changed circumstance) if later observations revealed an altered community structure, i.e., an altered distribution of plant species. This would prompt him to search for causal changes that might have occurred in soil, climate, or resident fauna. Within even a stable community, however, the germination, growth, reproduction, and death of individual plants would be problematic events (requiring explanation) for the botanist, though not for the ecologist. For the botanist, continued presence of a given plant specimen in a given location under unchanged circumstances would not be problematic, but would be assumed. It would hardly be naturalistic for him to ask, Why is the plant I saw growing in this spot yesterday still growing there today? Some sociologists, however, write as if answers to analogous questions were required of sociology. The kind of question the botanist would be expected to ask would be, Why is the plant I saw growing in this spot yesterday *not* growing there now? or Why is there now a plant where none grew yesterday? etc.

In the naturalistic framework, it would only be meaningful to ask, Why is this plant still growing here? if some event had given cause to expect its demise, so that observing its continued survival implied that some process had occurred which had counteracted the destructive event. Then the effort to discover and analyze the counteractive process which had preserved the plant would be a naturalistic quest. But when it has not been supposed that anything to counteract has happened, the quest for active continuity-maintaining processes is superfluous and nonnaturalistic.

Each of the four elements I have enumerated above has clearly been present in the studies of the various disciplines recognized as natural sciences. The importance of each element in facilitating sound analysis and valid discovery will become increasingly apparent in later chapters. Suffice it to say here that sociologists do not seem fully to have appreciated the importance of any but the first. There is fairly widespread agreement that sociology has been (and ought to be) developing in the direction of naturalism insofar as this consists in reliance on observation of the empirical world. The trend has been somewhat less clear with respect to abandonment of teleology and adoption of the inertial axiom—the second and third elements. The fourth element, the inadmissibility of unmoved movers, has hardly received any notice in sociological literature.

The Trends

Let us look at the reporting of trends in a number of textbooks on the history or development of sociology. In this way we shall see how much explicit or implicit recognition there has recently been of each of these four ingredients of naturalism, and can get some indication of the extent of sociological commitment to them. What I am asking of the sources I will cite is this: How much or how little has each of the elements of naturalism been institutionalized as a norm for sociological work to follow? Of course, not all the literature on this discipline's history is even indirectly addressed to such a question. Some books give little indication of trends of any sort because they are organized primarily along biographical lines (e.g., Barnes, *Introduction to the History of Sociology*), sketching the life and thought of an individual in each separate chapter. Others are mainly concerned with portraying clashing "schools" of thought (e.g., Sorokin, *Contemporary Sociological Theories*). But a number of texts and anthologies, even when they bow in the direction of biographical presentation or classification of men into schools, do suggest trends and are helpful in the present quest.

First Element: Empirical Verification As long ago as 1936, Floyd House reported the emphasis on empirical research to be the most conspicuous trend in sociology in the United States. He said this trend was so pronounced that sociology was sometimes asserted to be a body of research problems and methods almost to the exclusion of knowledge and a system of concepts. Statistical and other quantitative methods were coming into preponderant use, he said, and there was a strong "behavioristic" tendency, represented by such men as Lundberg and Read Bain and, as he put it, less materialistically by L. L. Bernard.[7]

House did not contend that empirical research was pursued to the exclusion of conceptual development, but in connection with it. As concern for methodology came to the fore among American sociologists late in the nineteenth century, the term "methodology" referred not so much to observational procedures, data-gathering operations, and statistical techniques for data processing, but to the "better, more adequate and consistent definition and use of conceptual terms." He noted that the empirical study of actual, concrete social phenomena had been a principal means of achieving conceptual clarification, and he credited the 1921 publication of the well-known *Introduction to the Science of Sociology* by Robert E. Park and Ernest W. Burgess with a major share in the stimulation of interest in concrete research among sociologists of the ensuing generation. It also directly fostered conceptual clarification.[8]

According to Roscoe and Gisela Hinkle,[9] American sociology has, over a half century, diversified the problems it studies, developed specialized methods, and refined its theories. Today it has a body of knowledge, concepts, and theories that are its own, and it is a firmly established discipline. Its research techniques have become specialized without complete resolution of the controversy over quantitative versus qualitative approaches.

They note that it is assumed now as it was in past generations of sociological thought that human behavior involves universal similarities sufficient for codification in a system of laws. Whereas in the first few decades of the twentieth century it was supposed that these laws would emerge

[7] Floyd N. House, *The Development of Sociology*. New York: McGraw-Hill Book Company, 1936, pp. 422–423.
[8] *Ibid.*, pp. 377–379, 382.
[9] Roscoe C. Hinkle, Jr., and Gisela J. Hinkle *The Development of Modern Sociology*. New York: Random House, Inc., 1954, p. 72.

from empirical studies because the laws were inherent in nature, now they are sought by means of logical efforts to *construct* systematic theory—in conjunction with empirical studies, of course. Theory construction is at least implicitly assumed to require explicit relating to empirical data.[10]

By way of urging us to give our intellectual forebears their due, Edgar F. Borgatta and Henry J. Meyer have pointed out that a considerable portion of the attention of students of sociology is given to the accumulated literature of rigorous description and empirical research. There is a resulting tendency, which Borgatta and Meyer wished to restrain, to assume that ideas formulated earlier than the latest research article are to be neglected.[11] Clearly, these authors were concurring with the others already cited that there has come to be a strong emphasis on data in the writings of sociologists.

Lewis Coser and Bernard Rosenberg are convinced that an accumulation of empirical findings is indispensable to the development of sociology as a science. In selecting materials for their reader in sociological theory, they used concepts rather than substantive fields as a criterion. They chose not to try to represent individual writers as such, but to include only those portions of a sociological theorist's work relevant to present-day research.[12] On this basis, though, they were able to put together a sizable volume.

The growth of sociological theory has been divided by Nicholas Timasheff into four periods.[13] The first period, from the beginning of sociology until around 1875, was characterized by largely unrelated efforts of pioneers. The second period, from 1875 to 1900, approximately, was dominated by evolutionism and pervaded with what Timasheff called "the battle of the schools"—between advocates of various single-factor determinisms viewing the evolutionary process in terms of some one preferred explanatory variable. In the third period, about 1900 to 1925, evolutionary theory had been abandoned, and there was a growing concern with empirical studies. The psychological foundations of sociology were emphasized. In the fourth period, about 1925 to the present, there was a growing awareness of a substantial body of empirical findings (resulting, Timasheff said, in some convergence in sociological theories) and a continuing competition between explanatory postulates or frames of reference.

Running through his description of these four historical periods, Timasheff saw competing (rather than complementary) approaches to sociological subject matter—schools of sociological thought. The dominant

[10] *Ibid.*, p. 73.
[11] Edgar F. Borgatta and Henry J. Meyer (eds.), *Sociological Theory: Present-day Sociology from the Past.* New York: Alfred A. Knopf, Inc., 1956, p. x.
[12] Lewis A. Coser and Bernard Rosenberg, *Sociological Theory: A Book of Readings.* New York: The Macmillan Company, 1957, pp. ix–xii.
[13] Nicholas S. Timasheff, *Sociological Theory: Its Nature and Growth,* rev. ed. New York: Random House, Inc., 1957, p. 12.

school at the time of writing was said to be neopositivism, though its dominance has not remained unchallenged. It was possible, he felt, that it might recede in favor of "functional" or "analytic" sociology.[14]

The main contribution made by neopositivism has been methodological, according to Timasheff. It has come to be widely agreed among sociologists that techniques of quantification are quite useful and ought to be employed as research aids wherever possible. Moreover, there has come to be general agreement on the need for supplementing introspective descriptions of social phenomena with behavioristic ones. Careful definition of concepts and avoidance of *a priori* notions now characterize sociological thought, he said.[15] In Timasheff's view, then, sociological work has become thoroughly committed to at least the first of naturalism's four ingredients.

C. Wright Mills, who openly preferred that sociology should be an interpretive rather than an empirically descriptive and predictive discipline, acknowledged in the introduction to his reader, *Images of Man,* that the statistical survey had become one of the leading intellectual features of our times and suggested that we tend to be overwhelmed by the sheer accumulation of facts.[16] There were hints in his writing that facts ought to be considered less important. He referred to thinkers of the "classic tradition," whose interpretive writings appear in his reader, as having done some of the best work of any of the sociologists of the late nineteenth and early twentieth centuries. He stressed its relevance to "the best work" being done now, but then went on to emphasize that most of the classic sociologists' ideas could not be readily shaped for precise testing.[17] Though others might dispute Mills's evaluations of what sociological work now being done is the "best," Mills seemed to be in agreement that the bulk of the work is concerned with observed fact.

In his textbook on *The Nature and Types of Sociological Theory,* Martindale has suggested that sociology originated as a philosophical point of view but could only become established as a science when it developed research methods and sought to verify its theoretical propositions on the basis of its own order of facts.[18] Unless sociological theorists work with data, their efforts will degenerate, he said, into "terminological pyrotechnics."[19]

Heinz Maus, in *A Short History of Sociology,* recognized the prevalence in United States universities of courses in social research techniques, and said this has come to be regarded as the only appropriate scientific form

[14] *Ibid.,* p. 210.
[15] *Ibid.,* pp. 210, 309.
[16] C. Wright Mills (ed.), *Images of Man.* New York: George Braziller, Inc., 1960, p. 6.
[17] *Ibid.,* pp. 2–3.
[18] Don Martindale, *The Nature and Types of Sociological Theory.* Boston: Houghton Mifflin Company, 1960, p. viii.
[19] *Ibid.,* p. xi.

for sociology.[20] The emphasis on research (and its social-psychological aspects) dominates American sociology, he said, but there is also a visible influence of older European sociology in America, though this tends to be looked upon by American sociologists as backward.[21] In Europe, since the Second World War, awareness has grown of the great changes in American sociology, and Europeans have begun to show an eagerness to "make up lost ground." They have thus begun, to Maus's regret, to emulate American research, using American research techniques and neglecting the history of sociology and downgrading older sociological formulations.[22] There were a number of errors in the Maus book (some of which may have been due to faulty translation), and it can largely be dismissed as an attempt by a German author to show that the best sociology has been German and the best influences on American sociology have been German, or at least European. Certainly Maus himself was hardly taking a naturalistic position when he referred to "American" research techniques, as if science had to involve different methods on different sides of international boundaries. He seemed to imply that there was scientific merit in preserving differences between European and American thoughtways. It is interesting, though, that in spite of his apparent attitudes, Maus must nevertheless be credited with recognizing the growing emphasis on empirical research both in the United States and in Europe.

An English sociologist, John Madge, has surveyed our methodological evolution in *The Origins of Scientific Sociology* and stated as the theme of his book the conviction that sociology is at last growing up and is close to attaining the status of a real science. To be such, he said, it must have refined and systematic data-collection methods, appropriate concepts, and suitable modes of analysis. At least to some degree, all these features now characterize sociology, he felt. Though a fully systematic *theory* of sociology still eludes us, our approach toward it is evident in the fact that conceptual development has become manifestly cumulative.[23] The output of sociological research has increased phenomenally in recent decades, with growing interest in and support for sociology. Most major universities now have permanent sociological research centers.[24] These imply appreciable financial commitment to empirical pursuits.

In their respective introductory essays in their large anthology on *Theories of Society*, both Kaspar Naegele and Talcott Parsons indicated that there has been a thorough commitment of modern sociology to the use of empirical data. For Naegele there is no longer any doubt that meaning-

[20] Heinz Maus, *A Short History of Sociology.* New York: Philosophical Library, Inc., 1962, p. 153.
[21] *Ibid.*, p. 160.
[22] *Ibid.*, pp. vii–viii.
[23] John Madge, *The Origins of Scientific Sociology.* New York: The Free Press of Glencoe, 1962, p. 1.
[24] *Ibid.*, p. 4.

ful questions about social life can now be asked and empirically answered.[25] There is no opposition between theory and research, he said, since they are parts of the same enterprise. Sociology has grown by reducing its theoretical aspirations and concerning itself with "making findings."[26] Parsons believed that in sociology today a good deal of implicit consensus is concealed by explicit debate. The greatest consensus, he said, exists in regard to the applicability to sociology of the general canons of scientific method. The erstwhile battles about this are over.[27]

In summary, a varied assortment of authors who have viewed the growth of sociology from diverse perspectives concur in seeing indications of great or growing emphasis on factual knowledge, putting hypotheses to empirical test, making theories empirically relevant. For some this trend is seen as cause for some regret, while for others it is a basis for satisfaction and hope. Opponents and advocates alike report a trend toward naturalistic sociology in regard to at least this first component of naturalism.

Second Element: Temporal Priority of Causes When we turn to the second component of naturalism, we find that indices of either a trend or an existing consensus among sociologists are more obscure. Stark tells us that the modern age is unsympathetic to teleology. Most of us, he says, now tend to prefer explanations of all phenomena in terms of efficient causes behind them rather than the ends or final causes in front of them. However, he maintains that the biological sciences have been unable to dispense with teleology altogether and that reference of actions to goals has the support of common sense. All this is said in defense of Aristotelian thought.[28] The implications of such comments would seem to be that sociology should continue to view its world in Aristotelian terms, which would mean that it *should not* embrace this second aspect of naturalism, but that perhaps it has already done so.

Madge had nothing direct to say in regard to this second component, and one has to be very alert to subtle implications to get even an indirect clue as to his perception of where sociology seems to stand on the issue of teleological explanation. In discussing the use of documents in sociological analysis, Madge noted that the modern tendency is to rely mainly on standardized statements made under controlled conditions which result in materials not essentially different from interview transcriptions or test forms. Then he pointed out that in such materials there is likely to be little sense of history. With contemporary data only, there is no chance

[25] Kaspar D. Naegele, "Some Observations on the Scope of Sociological Analysis," in Talcott Parsons, Edward Shils, Kaspar D. Naegele, and Jesse R. Pitts (eds.), *Theories of Society*. New York: The Free Press of Glencoe, 1961, p. 3.
[26] *Ibid.*, pp. 6, 24.
[27] Talcott Parsons, "An Outline of the Social System," in *ibid.*, pp. 31–32.
[28] Werner Stark, *The Fundamental Forms of Social Thought*. New York: Fordham University Press, 1963, p. 18.

to discern trends or alterations in subjects' attitudes, behavior, or relations
with others. Some social scientists, he said, even *reject* historical perspective as being without scientific worth. Kurt Lewin, for example, Madge
cited as having said that behavior depends on a "present field" rather
than on either the past or the future in any direct way. Others—e.g.,
Robert F. Bales—have shown an awareness of time as a variable, Madge
noted, but not a concern for history as a determinant of the behavior
of their subjects.[29] This discussion was as close as Madge came to the
issue of chronology in relation to causality, and these remarks are quite
ambiguous as to whether teleological analyses are permissible or not.

Martindale was no clearer on this point. In saying that during the nineteenth century there was a reversal of the previously fixed notion that
society is determined by human nature (e.g., through a rationalistic social
contract), he may be construed as remotely suggesting a sociological concern for the time sequence in causation. Sociologists switched from thinking that human nature caused society to thinking that society causes
human nature.[30] Only to the extent that—in order to accomplish this reversal—it was perceived to be necessary also to argue that society actually
exists prior to the given individual could it be said that teleological
analyses were tabooed. Martindale has certainly not said that the taboo
was explicit and had been rigorously followed.

Little conscious attention has been given by historians of sociology to
the question whether sociological analyses have been tending to become
more teleological or less so. What comments have been made have been
mixed, suggesting that sociology has become less teleological but sometimes hinting in the next sentence that it *ought* to be more so, so that
the commentator appears either to reject naturalism or reject as a component of naturalism the concentration on efficient causes and the exclusion of final causes.

At any rate, the material reviewed gives scant indication regarding this
second ingredient. It cannot then be confidently asserted that exclusion
of teleological explanation has been institutionalized as a norm for sociological research. In this respect there seems yet to be room for considerable progress.

Third Element: The Axiom of Inertia   Turning to the third component,
definition of change as problematic, we find that there are more statements
that can be cited, but they seem to indicate a continuing mixture of views
rather than a clear trend in one direction or the other. According to House,
many writers had already asserted prior to the mid-1930s that the fundamental objective of sociology and other social sciences must be explanation
of the facts of social change. Moreover, House noted, social science itself

[29] Madge, *op. cit.*, pp. 528–529.
[30] Martindale, *The Nature and Types of Sociological Theory*, p. 45.

only tends to arise when social change occurs, for in periods of long social stability it is only necessary to know the existing customs and traditions to be as fully knowledgeable sociologically as anyone feels the need to be.[31] Only when customs are changing is it important to develop an awareness, or likely that an awareness will develop, of the dependence of behavior upon convention. In other times the prevalent patterns of behavior merely seem inevitable.

In his introductory essay in *Theories of Society*, Parsons provided a clue in regard to his own position on the inertia axiom. He offered a paradigm for the analysis of social systems which emphasized four basic functions: pattern-maintenance, integration, goal attainment, and adaptation. By the "integration" function he referred to mechanisms of social control, and said this was the "focus" of the "most distinctive properties and processes" of a social system. Therefore, he said, the central core of sociological theory's concerns is the set of problems having to do with this integrative function.[32] Later he spoke of the process of structural change as merely the opposite of this process of social control.[33] It would appear that for Parsons, stability of a social system is at least as problematic as change. In Chapter 7, I will have more to say about Parsons's apparent position in regard to the axiom of inertia, for in *Working Papers* he offered a principle which he felt was tantamount to the axiom of inertia, but which I think actually reflects a basic misconception of that axiom.

Introductory textbooks in sociology usually tack on at the end rather weak and theoretically vacuous chapters on social change, *after* devoting one or two dozen chapters to topics apparently considered more fundamental, or at least on which sociological thought and research have had more to say. That we should have more to say about structure and about static processes within social systems than about social change is ironic, in a sense, if social change was the provocation for the original emergence of sociology. But in another sense this may be understandable. Sociology arose in a time when progress was regarded as inevitable but some of its discomforts were causing concern for the intellectuals. Sociologists saw their task as consisting of the explanation of social stability—the discovery of techniques for restoring stability while progress continued unabated. Even the evolutionary theories of the first generations of sociologists did not then really define change as something to be accounted for; they merely regarded it as an ineluctable phenomenon to be described, welcomed, and either hastened or adjusted to. To the extent that these theories purported to be "explanations" of evolution, they might be said to have defined change as problematic. To the extent, however, that they took evolution for granted and merely sought to describe its "natural"

[31] House, *op. cit.*, p. 3.
[32] Parsons, *op. cit.*, pp. 36–41.
[33] *Ibid.*, p. 70.

course, they can be said instead to have regarded stable norms and continuously recurring patterns of behavior as problematic—in need of explanation. In short, it is not clear that in backing off from the study of
social evolution sociology was rejecting an erstwhile commitment to the
axiom of inertia. It is simply not clear that sociologists had ever embraced,
or even understood, that element of naturalism.

The zeal for publication of piecemeal studies of empirical topics seems
to have been more compatible with research into the structural characteristics of society than with longitudinal studies of prolonged duration.
Longitudinal studies would more clearly contribute to our knowledge of
social dynamics. As social change has accelerated since the Second World
War, renewed theoretical attention has been given to questions of social
development. Both in the histories of sociological thought or syntheses
of contemporary theory that have appeared in recent years and in the
treatises and textbooks on social change, clues can be found as to the
inclinations of sociologists in regard to the inertial principle.

Charles and Zona Loomis, in stating their own synthetic theory as a
basis for presenting condensations, analyses, and appraisals of the theories
of half a dozen contemporaries, offered the premise that "interaction tends
to develop certain uniformities over time, some of which tend to persist."[34]
They then noted that these patterns impinge on each other and are subject
to change, and they argued that "it is important that process or change
itself be made the focus of observation."[35] Insofar as social processes are
not the same thing as social change, however, the Loomises remain ambiguous in regard to this third aspect of naturalism. It would be naturalistic to focus causal inquiry on social change, but only at the social-
psychological (not at the strictly sociological) level would it be naturalistic to focus on social processes. For comparison, recall what was said
above about the plant ecologist taking as axiomatic what the botanist
might regard as problematic. Since the Loomises were interested in theories of *social systems,* they were presumably working on the sociological
level; hence what they said is ambiguous as an indicator of whether the
axiom of inertia has been given appropriate recognition in their
formulations.

Wilbert Moore, likewise, seems partly naturalistic and partly animistic
on this score. He has been critical of the equilibrium model underlying
much contemporary sociological thought, conceding that it is harmless
if construed merely as a sensitizing concept, but arguing that it can be
mischievous if followed too rigidly. In addition to "orderly persistence
of interrelated patterns of action," he said, there are in social systems
"ample sources of disorder." There are conflicts, tensions, and *"intrinsic*

[34] Charles P. Loomis and Zona K. Loomis, *Modern Social Theories.* Princeton, N.J.:
D. Van Nostrand Company, Inc., 1961, p. 2.
[35] *Ibid.,* p. 6.

sources and paths of change."[36] Moore has not quite gone so far as to deny the axiom of inertia, for he has not actually argued for the occurrence of uncaused change. But his predominant interest in "intrinsic" sources of change within the system undergoing change seems perilously close to acceptance of the notion that change could be uncaused.

It is difficult to impute to Moore a clear-cut choice between the position that change is problematic and the alternative view that stability is problematic. He seems to embrace both views. His ambivalence may stem from the ambiguous sociological usage of the word "equilibrium." We sometimes use it to refer to the homeostatic capacity of systems to make equilibrating responses to disturbing stimuli, and we sometimes use it to refer simply to the absence of stimuli (or to the fact that one stimulus is offset by another). This ambiguity is particularly evident in expressions about a disturbance that threatens to "destroy the equilibrium" of a system. Is it the system's capacity for counteracting the disturbance that is threatened, or is it the existing rate of various activities in the system that is threatened with acceleration and hence with departure from its normal magnitude? It would help to separate these two meanings, not signifying both with the same word.

By way of illustration, consider a family in which a death occurs. The activities of the surviving members of that family are likely to be changed by the loss they have suffered. Each of them will make some adjustments in his personal actions, in his interactions with others in the family, and with persons and groups outside the family. Some of these changes will consist of reallocation of roles formerly assigned to the deceased. Thus the changes function as compensation for a previous change—his departure. His death created a disequilibrium; the adjustments of the survivors result in a new (or "restored") equilibrium. The capacity of the surviving portion of the family to make the adjustment is sometimes inappropriately labeled "equilibrium." It should more accurately be called something like "homeostatic capability." In most families, death of a member tends to disturb equilibrium without disrupting homeostatic capability, though in exceptional cases it might do both. If a mother and father were both killed in an accident, for example, it might be impossible for their orphaned children to continue to live together as a family. The fact that a sufficiently large disturbance can upset both equilibrium and homeostatic capability, however, does not warrant equating these two concepts. It is to be hoped that clarification of this ambiguity can obviate the ambivalence felt by such men as Moore toward the axiom of inertia.

Madge differentiated sociology from sciences such as geology, which studies inanimate objects, and astronomy, which studies objects in dynamic equilibrium. (Dynamic equilibrium obviously does not mean to the astronomer anything like homeostatic capability, though sociologists are

[36] Wilbert E. Moore, "Editorial Introduction," in *ibid.*, p. xxiii.

prone to use the phrase as if that *were* what it meant.) Madge said the changes which the empirical sociologist studies are both irreversible and generated internally, at least to some extent. At this point Madge and Moore seem to have shared a common preoccupation. Because it allegedly must study internally generated change, sociology confronts the same problems as the other organic sciences. But Madge acknowledged that such phenomena can be simulated by servomechanisms.[37] Servomechanisms hardly require a nonnaturalistic analysis, yet Madge went on to cite W. I. Thomas and Florian Znaniecki, who had pointed out that sociological theory must focus on social change because it is so characteristic of civilized society (not, apparently, because natural science requires an axiom of inertia). Because social change is so common, Thomas and Znaniecki had said, "sociological laws must be phrased in terms not of 'stereotyped activity' but of 'social becoming.'"[38] It is quite unclear here whether Madge, or even Thomas and Znaniecki, intended to assert that change is normal and to be taken for granted apart from resistive action, or is to be defined as problematic, requiring explanation. The disparaging of laws of "stereotyped activity" suggests a leaning toward the latter, naturalistic position, but the word "becoming"—implying immanence—connotes animism.

In the context of a discussion of the role of evaluative processes in society, Madge referred to Durkheim's analysis of social control, and said, "While stating that social standards are generally stable, being imposed without the need for violence, Durkheim recognizes that they are constantly changing in response to economic fluctuations and the changes occurring in the moral ideas of society."[39] If emphasis is given to the phrase "in response to," then this comes close to imputing an inertial property to norms and recognizing the problematic character of change. But it is not this recognition that Madge was striving for or seeking to convey in quoting Durkheim. Instead he went on to say that Durkheim was anxious to establish a constant and detached standard of normality which could afford an outside criterion for judgment of behavior. To this end, Durkheim pursued the analogy between conformity and health and between deviance and pathology and concluded that frequency of occurrence is the best criterion of normality in both sociological and biological contexts.[40] So Madge missed an opportunity to extract from Durkheim a fundamental metasociological principle, an implication regarding the axiom of inertia.

It is therefore a reasonable inference that Madge did not regard this axiom as a fundamental aspect of contemporary sociological thought or

[37] Madge, *op. cit.*, p. 542.
[38] *Ibid.*, p. 543.
[39] *Ibid.*, p. 544.
[40] *Ibid.*, pp. 544–545.

of the Durkheim heritage. If Durkheim had consistently followed out the notion that the statistically frequent phenomenon is the normal and hence the nonproblematic occurrence, then in a world of abundant social change, change would not be seen as problematic. But this would be analogous to a Galileo saying that since more projectiles follow parabolic trajectories than linear ones, therefore there is nothing problematic about parabolic trajectories. Had Galileo held such an attitude, it would have enfeebled his contribution to science by precluding further analysis of the trajectory into horizontal motion at constant velocity and vertical motion subject to constant acceleration. It would have delayed subsequent generalizing of the attribution of that constant acceleration to gravity.

Madge's optimistic conviction that sociology is within sight of scientific maturity was apparently arrived at without benefit of clear recognition of the third element of naturalistic thought, and hence without clear perception of a trend toward or away from this aspect of naturalism.

Borgatta and Meyer were as mixed as Moore appeared to be on this issue. In their introduction to the section of their *Sociological Theory* reader entitled "The Persistence of Social Structures," they wrote: "Sociological theory must account for the persistence of society and of social structures just as it must account for their development and their changes."[41] They seem not to have been imputing the property of inertia to social structures—as if change could occur capriciously. Later on, in their introduction to the section on "Social Change," they said, "The fact of change, in society as in all nature, is universally recognized. The task of sociological theory is to define the special character of social change and to describe and account for the processes which bring it about." The phrase "processes which bring it about" suggests recognition that change is not merely spontaneous. Implicit in a number of readings included in this section of their book, said Borgatta and Meyer, was the notion that social change "is not capricious." But they credited MacIver's 1937 textbook, *Society*, with an unsurpassed conceptual analysis of social change,[42] whereas I will show in Chapter 4 that this was one of MacIver's more animistic publications.

One writer has asserted that in the equilibrium model widely used in economic and sociological theorizing, social change has to be regarded as an external or accidental phenomenon. This is meant by that writer to be a criticism of equilibrium models. In contrast, he cited the work of Sorokin, containing the fundamental premise that social change is "inherent in social systems," as a preferable approach.[43] Sociology could have

[41] Borgatta and Meyer, *op cit.*, p. 361. Cf. Wilbert E. Moore, *Social Change.* Englewood Cliffs, N.J.: Prentice-Hall, Inc., 1963, esp. chap. 1, "The Normality of Change."
[42] *Ibid.*, p. 445.
[43] Arthur K. Davis, "Lessons from Sorokin," in Edward A. Tiryakian (ed.), *Sociological Theory, Values, and Sociocultural Change.* New York: The Free Press of Glencoe, 1963, p. 3.

been further advanced than it now is, he suggested, had it better learned the lessons of Sorokin's theories.[44] In his view, then, sociology has already gone *too far* toward adoption of the view that continuity is to be expected apart from the operation of change-producing forces. He implied that we have already become too naturalistic for our own good as a discipline.

Confusion of several conceptual issues seems to have retarded sociological acceptance of the axiom of inertia. The fundamental question of whether change is to be regarded as caused or uncaused has been repeatedly confused with the more incidental question whether change is common or uncommon. It has also been confused with ambiguous distinctions between "internal" versus "external" sources of change. And it has been further beclouded by the ambiguous usage of the term "equilibrium," resulting in a partially misdirected attack on "equilibrium models." Among this web of questions, only the assertion that change is never properly regarded as uncaused needs to be taken as a criterion of naturalistic inquiry.

Fourth Element: No One-way Action   The conviction that we have gone too far in the direction of making sociology naturalistic is not surprising, perhaps, in the writings of some authors who misunderstand the axiom of inertia. But it is difficult to take this conviction very seriously when we go on to consider the fourth aspect of naturalism, the rejection of unmoved movers, or the assumption that change can only be caused by something that undergoes change itself. As we shall see in Chapter 7, various writers have presented approximations of this postulate, but have not done much with it after stating it. They have shown varying degrees of understanding of its significance. Actual sociological research seems rather to have ignored this postulate, and some research analysis has even violated it. None of the writers of recent volumes on the history of sociological thought have mentioned it in connection with their assessments of the approach of sociology toward scientific maturity. When they have mentioned the theorists who happen to have formulated some version of this postulate, they have not alluded to that aspect of their work—apparently attaching no significance to it.

There has even been a tendency in sociology to be unconcerned with accounting for changing, or varying, normative patterns by relating them to changing, or varying, conditions. Instead, some sociologists seem especially interested in attributing cultural universals to "functional prerequisites." And those who err in regard to the axiom of inertia seem to err again in regard to the issue of one-way action. In urging the need to account for constancy by studying processes of "pattern-maintenance," they neglect to consider whether the maintenance of one pattern in the

[44] *Ibid.*, p. 5.

face of change-inducing forces would require the compensatory modification of other patterns.

These issues will be explored more fully in Chapter 7. For now, it should be noted that writers of quite diverse opinion as to what kind of discipline sociology *ought* to be tend to agree that it *is* showing increasing resemblance to natural science. Perhaps such agreement is premature. Their impressions of what natural science consists of are not altogether cogent.

Ambiguity of Scientific Canons

Hinkle and Hinkle have written that at least implicitly the methods of sociological research in use today are patterned after those of other social and natural sciences. The use of statistical techniques implies some emphasis on quantification. The construction of research design implies some effort to approximate experimentation. The formulation of explicit research hypotheses often leans on the existing literature of interrelated sociological principles, generalizations, and laws. Historical materials are generally avoided, say the Hinkles, on the assumption that they pertain to unique events rather than to the repetitive and generalizable aspects of social phenomena.[45]

This picture of the nature of modern sociology is in apparent agreement with Sorokin's contention, a decade earlier, that sociological conceptions of causal relationships among the phenomena sociology studies, and its conceptions of time and space, were obtained from the natural sciences.[46] To Sorokin, however, this was not as it should be, so it is odd that an advocate of mathematical sociology, Nicholas Rashevsky, whose own scientific work has been in mathematical biophysics, should have cited Sorokin as an important precedent for his efforts to develop quantitative studies in social science. Sorokin's *Social and Cultural Dynamics*, Rashevsky felt, was "permeated with the quantitative spirit characteristic of natural sciences," and he also made reference to *Social Mobility* and *Contemporary Sociological Theories* by Sorokin, apparently totally unaware of Sorokin's opposition to natural science sociology as expressed in the latter volume and in some of his subsequent publications.[47]

Sorokin himself has set the record straight by conceding that Park had correctly surmised in a review of *Social and Cultural Dynamics* that the

[45] Hinkle and Hinkle, *op. cit.*, p. 73.
[46] Pitirim A. Sorokin, *Sociocultural Causality, Space, Time.* Durham, N.C.: The Duke University Press, 1943, p. vii.
[47] N. Rashevsky, *Mathematical Theory of Human Relations.* Bloomington, Ind.: Principia Press, 1947, p. v.

many statistical tables contained in its first three volumes were put in
as "a concession to the prevailing mentality and the contemporary system
of truth." Sorokin went on to anticipate a day when "there will be much
less need for this kind of evidence" and more demand for evidence of
the type he called "meaningful-causal."[48]

A similar wish that sociology would not become a natural science was
apparent in some comments by Stark. He said it took the natural sciences
many centuries to extricate themselves from the animistic thoughtways
of the primitive mentality,[49] but then he went on to contend that sociology
needs just as badly to extricate itself from the thoughtways of natural
science. In primitive man's approach to nature, according to Stark, the
fatal error was that he substituted for reality a fictional (and anthropomorphic) model which "personified the impersonal." Modern man has committed the opposite error; he has come to see society not as it "really
is" but as it would have to be in order for him to explain it in the same
way he explains nature. Like his primitive ancestors, then, modern man
has, in Stark's judgment, replaced reality with a fiction. This time the
fiction depersonalizes what is personal.[50] Stark seems to have been declaring our conception of society and of social forces not anthropomorphic
enough!

He had, of course, utterly neglected in the midst of this argument the
issue of empirical adequacy. A model is to be accepted or rejected on
grounds of metaphysical propriety, he implied, regardless of data. Even
if he were right in supposing that on some metaphysical basis anthropomorphic models were required for sociology, could they really be accepted
by the sophisticated sociologist without regard for the closeness of fit between hypotheses derived from them and significant bodies of empirical
data?

But these are not the matters that concerned Stark. His interest was
in resolving a sociological version of the old philosophical dispute between
"nominalism" and "realism." Both philosophies, he said, are sound but
one-sided.[51] There can be, in his view, only three fundamental forms of
social thought. One of them is "organicist" thought, which takes the position of philosophical realism. "Mechanicist" thought, which takes the
nominalist position, is another. The third, and in Stark's judgment the
best, is "culturalist" sociology, which synthesizes the first two, and "does
justice, both to the real integration of the social order and to the real
independence of the individuals comprised by it." What is interesting in
this gross oversimplification of the variations in sociological perspectives
is Stark's effort to depict a trend. Though he asserted that the third form

[48] Sorokin, *op. cit.,* pp. 95–96.
[49] Stark, *op. cit.,* p. 256.
[50] *Ibid.,* p. 259.
[51] *Ibid.,* p. 3.

of theory "at once appears superior to the other two" it has, he said, until recently received insufficient attention.[52]

Summary

Many sociologists have aspired to move their discipline closer to the natural sciences, and there are numerous indications that in some respects they have been able to do this. The naturalistic study of any given subject-matter area involves several things, and movement of sociology toward naturalism has not been equally marked in all of these respects. We can summarize these developments as follows:

1 There is a widespread and apparently well-institutionalized commitment to the use of data obtained by some form of sensory observation as the ultimate test of the validity of sociological propositions. Beyond this, recognition of the other aspects of naturalism is unclear, and it would appear that many sociologists either suppose that this is *all* that is required to make a discipline scientific or else do not really expect sociology to become a natural science.

On some aspects of naturalism there is active controversy among sociologists.

2 The temporal priority of a cause in relation to its effect is not yet postulated by a clear majority of sociologists, and the necessity for such a postulate is openly disputed by some. Teleological explanation still tempts us.

3 Change is frequently asserted to be intrinsic in social systems, and the need for postulating the impossibility of uncaused change is little understood by sociologists.

4 The naturalistic refusal to imagine unmoved movers has received little attention from sociologists. As we shall see later, sociologists have not in this respect been true to the general definition of their own subject matter because they have failed to direct their studies consistently toward analysis of *inter*action.

To some sociologists, standards of scientific quality have remained ambiguous and the somewhat sporadic trend toward naturalism has taken place in the face of manifest reluctance.

[52] *Ibid.*, p. 1.

Chapter Two

NATURALISM IN COMPARISON WITH OTHER VIEWPOINTS

A naturalist has been defined as a person who respects the conclusions of natural science.[1] As a philosophical position, naturalism may be regarded as empirical in method, postulating one all-embracing system of nature within which all occurrences result from causes. Causality applies even to those things or events that men commonly designate as spiritual, purposeful, and rational.[2]

To assert that sociology can be, or has been tending to become, naturalistic would be meaningless unless some alternative to naturalism were conceivable. Alternative positions have indeed been taken by philosophers and by sociologists. What I claim, then, is that these alternatives are less fertile and have tended to be cast aside as sociology has advanced.

An appreciable body of philosophical thought has even rejected or sidestepped the postulates of naturalism in the realm of inanimate, nonhuman phenomena—the realm in which naturalism is generally taken for granted today in Western civilization. Such philosophies need only concern us indirectly in this chapter. Of more immediate interest are those doctrines, asserted by sociologists or by philosophers of social science, which insist on a *difference* between the naturalistic postulates applicable to inanimate or at least nonhuman phenomena and some other set of postulates required for the study of sociological subject matter.

[1] John Dewey, "Antinaturalism in Extremis," in Yervant H. Krikorian (ed.), *Naturalism and the Human Spirit*. New York: Columbia University Press, 1944, p. 2.
[2] Sterling P. Lamprecht, "Naturalism and Religion," in *ibid.*, p. 18.

Must Sociology Be Different?

Are there fundamental differences between the social and the natural? If there are, do they entail different fundamental methods of inquiry in the social sciences as contrasted with the natural sciences? A number of writers have answered such questions in the affirmative. For example, Naegele has suggested that we apply the term "natural" to a realm that has a high degree of "impersonal givenness," whose phenomena can be accounted for without recourse to such concepts as "choice" or "intentions" or "meaning." The latter terms are said to be essential in analyzing human social phenomena. This usage would enable us to distinguish natural from social phenomena in degree rather than absolutely, however. Naegele has noted that the distinctions we make between organic and inorganic, between alive and dead, reflect the *graduated* remoteness of the natural universe from our own personal realm.[3] But he concluded that because of its concern with matters of value and meaning, "the human order" has to be distinguished from "the nonhuman order."[4] The situations to be studied by the sociologist involve judgments and sanctions, expectations and consequences, and are thus set apart from natural science's subject matter.[5]

Such views are more or less representative of one side in a long-standing division among sociologists. Alpert has referred to "positivistic" versus "humanistic" conceptions of sociology. The first emphasizes operationalism, quantification, the naturalness of human behavior, and similarities between sociology and the biological and physical sciences. It tends to differentiate sociology from the humanities. The second conception, on the other hand, conceives men as goal seekers and as beings who create values and impute meanings. According to this view, any differentiation of sociology from the humanities is a mere scientistic taboo.[6]

Some writers have flatly asserted that naturalistic approaches to sociological inquiry are misleading or at least sterile. Sorokin, for example, has urged that in order to be adequate for social science, "the prevalent naturalistic conceptions" of causality, space, and time "need drastic modifications."[7] Even Durkheim, whose meticulous researches on concrete sociological topics helped the discipline become more scientific, went out of his way to distinguish the social from the physical and the physiologi-

[3] Kaspar D. Naegele, "Some Observations on the Scope of Sociological Analysis," in Talcott Parsons, Edward Shils, Kaspar D. Naegele, and Jesse R. Pitts (eds.), *Theories of Society*. New York: The Free Press of Glencoe, 1961, p. 10.
[4] *Ibid.*, p. 26.
[5] *Ibid.*, p. 13.
[6] Quoted in Charles H. Page, "Sociology as a Teaching Enterprise," chap. 25 in Robert K. Merton, Leonard Broom, and Leonard S. Cottrell, Jr. (eds.), *Sociology Today*. New York: Basic Books, Inc., Publishers, 1959, pp. 586–587.
[7] Pitirim A. Sorokin, *Sociocultural Causality, Space, Time*. Durham, N.C.: The Duke University Press, 1943, p. vii.

cal. Human passions, he said, have to be limited in order to be harmonized with the faculties and satisfied. This requires *social* constraints. "Physical restraint would be ineffective; hearts cannot be touched by physico-chemical forces."[8]

Perhaps the classic assertion of a fundamental distinction between natural science and social science came from the pen of Wilhelm Dilthey, who concluded that there are three basic forms of thought: objective idealism, naturalism, and subjective idealism. Objective idealism arises from acquaintance with living organisms that comprise a body that is material and a soul that is spiritual. Naturalism, more materialistic in Dilthey's view, stems from acquaintance with phenomena of inanimate nature and construes physical laws as regularities characterizing all existence. Subjective idealism reflects the experience of moral conflict and is basically dualistic.[9] Sociology would, in this view, be misguided if it sought to be a natural science, shunning those aspects of reality dealt with by objective or subjective idealism.

Writers have sometimes merely been classified as "pronaturalistic" or "antinaturalistic," regardless of the preference of the classifier. Popper, for example, termed pronaturalistic those students of social science who favor using the methods of physics. Those who oppose such methods, he termed antinaturalistic.[10] Smith suggested a noninvidious distinction between mechanists, vitalists, and behaviorists, according to their respective interpretations of such phenomena as the experimentally demonstrated capacity of protozoa to learn in simple tube mazes. The mechanist, according to Smith, could claim that the concepts of physics and chemistry would suffice to explain such apparently purposeful behavior and learning. The vitalist could argue that these results call for applying to these simpler forms the concepts of intention and intelligence usually applied only to more complex forms (e.g., man). The behaviorist could disregard the problem of how the organism achieved learning and be concerned only with the observable results.[11]

Assigning the Burden of Proof

Such ostensibly neutral attempts at classification, however, can themselves give the misleading impression that any of these approaches or systems

[8] Emile Durkheim, *Suicide* (tr. John A. Spaulding and George Simpson). New York: The Free Press of Glencoe, 1951, pp. 248–249.
[9] On Dilthey's views, see Werner Stark, *The Fundamental Forms of Social Thought.* New York: Fordham University Press, 1963, pp. 7–8.
[10] Karl R. Popper, *The Poverty of Historicism.* Boston: Beacon Press, 1957, p. 2.
[11] F. V. Smith, *Explanation of Human Behaviour,* 2d ed. London: Constable & Co., Ltd., 1960, p. 10.

of postulates is as fruitful as another. It seems necessary, before going further, to reject unequivocally the notion that the choice of a naturalistic or nonnaturalistic mode of inquiry is arbitrary and a matter of mere taste. Inquiry leads to different conclusions depending on the approach taken. In physics, chemistry, biology, etc., naturalistic thoughtways have demonstrated their superiority over nonnaturalistic assumptions and methods. I see no reason why those who advocate naturalism in sociology should bear a larger burden of proof than those who insist that sociology must be nonnaturalistic. Why should animism be any freer of the need to justify itself than naturalism?

If there is a substantial commitment to naturalism among present-day sociologists, what were its antecedents? Has sociology a naturalistic heritage of some duration, or has it only recently shown signs of studying social phenomena naturalistically? Opponents and advocates of naturalism seem to agree that a number of the sociological pioneers held naturalistic orientations. Ward, Giddings, Small, and Sumner, despite obvious and important differences, have all been considered essentially naturalistic in outlook by one writer whose own persuasion is nonnaturalistic.[12] He attributes their adoption of naturalism to their intellectual descent from Comte and Spencer.[13] Other American social scientists who have been considered distinctly naturalistic in outlook include Morgan, Veblen, and Beard, suggesting the diffusion of naturalism, in America at least, into all of the social sciences in varying degrees, not just into sociology.[14] Of course not everyone who has had naturalism attributed to him has necessarily given full commitment to all four of the elements of naturalism outlined in Chapter 1.

There were diverse expressions of naturalism in the first few generations of sociological writing. The analogy between the social organism and biological organisms, of which Spencer made so much and which was a central theme in the writings of many of his followers, was in some respects pursued with naturalistic intentions, however false the hypotheses this analogy suggested. Equally inadequate, but just as naturalistically intended, were the doctrines of social forces and social mechanism, as formulated by Ward. From a naturalistic standpoint, such doctrines should be criticized in terms of their empirical adequacy; instead, an opponent of naturalism has criticized them merely for being naturalistic and for leading to the neglect of supernatural principles.[15]

Antinaturalists are continually assigning sociology tasks with which the

[12] William T. O'Connor, *Naturalism and the Pioneers of American Sociology.* Washington, D.C.: The Catholic University of America Press, 1942, p. 210.
[13] See *ibid.* Cf. James Bissett Pratt, *Naturalism.* New Haven, Conn.: Yale University Press, 1939, p. 87.
[14] On this diffusion, see Harold A. Larrabee, "Naturalism in America," in Krikorian (ed.), *op. cit.,* p. 350.
[15] See O'Connor, *op. cit.,* pp. 72–73.

natural sciences are not burdened. One critic of "scientism" (as he terms
naturalistic sociology) has acknowledged that the physicist is not required
to state what form of matter is best. But the social scientist, he feels,
is inevitably confronted with the problem of discerning the best form of
society.[16] Moreover, according to Dewey, by claiming that human social
behavior is extranatural, antinaturalism has insisted that radically different
methods are required for its study. Antinaturalism has thus impeded application of scientific methods of inquiry to social phenomena. It was Dewey's
conviction that incalculably many undesirable features of the plight of
modern man arise from the resulting backwardness of social science.[17]

Two Clusters of Thoughtways

By now a number of different "isms" have been alluded to. There are
hazards in using such language. We tend to reify categories, and it is
easy to fall into the error of supposing that we know all about a man
by tagging him with the label designating which of these isms he belongs
to. A good many men, including numerous sociologists, are too complex
to be so neatly categorized. Later, particularly in Chapter 4, I will try
to show that we mislead ourselves if we imagine that a sociologist has
to be either a clear-cut naturalist or a clear-cut something else. The sociologist can as easily as his fellow citizen be a marginal man, transitional
in his allegiance between two or more intellectual subcultures. In the
hope, therefore, that it will help to avert rather than to foster rigidity
in thought, I want now to discuss explicitly two clusters of thoughtways.
The first cluster comprises an array of somewhat varied isms which share
the common conviction that "there is something more" in the world than
the things that can effectively be studied naturalistically. I will contrast
with these another varied array of isms sharing the common conviction
that this "something more" is illusory. For clarity, the two sets of isms
are listed in Table 1. The lists are not meant to be exhaustive.

It is important to note that I do *not* mean by naturalism the sum of
all the doctrines asserted by all the isms in the right-hand column of
Table 1. It should be clear, however, that the eight positions listed there
have *tended* to be more naturalistic (in the sense explained in Chapter
1) than the nine positions listed in the left-hand column. It would not
be accurate to regard the terms in a given column as synonyms for each
other, just as it would be inappropriate to suppose that they label wholly
discrete philosophies with no concepts or doctrines in common. I am not

[16] A. H. Hobbs, *Social Problems and Scientism.* Harrisburg, Pa.: The Stackpole Company, 1953, p. 195.
[17] Dewey, *op. cit.*, p. 3.

Table 1 Assorted metascientific positions, classified by their apparent relation to naturalism

Tend to be antinaturalistic	Tend to be naturalistic
Vitalism	Physicalism
Philosophical idealism	Mechanism
Voluntarism	Determinism
Spiritualism	Monism
Supernaturalism	Behaviorism
Transcendentalism	Materialism
Rationalism	Positivism
Indeterminism	Empiricism
Historicism	

trying to delineate wholly antagonistic schools of thought. But when all these disclaimers are stated, it remains clear, I think, that the nine isms in the left-hand column can be meaningfully grouped together and contrasted with the meaningfully grouped list of eight in the right-hand column. The basic difference between the two clusters seems to me clearly to be a pro-con difference on the "something more" issue.

I want to emphasize that my purpose in presenting Table 1 and discussing the terms listed therein is to safeguard the reader from any misunderstanding of what I intend the term "naturalism" to convey. It is not so commonly used by sociologists as various other words, and its meaning is not unambiguously standardized. When confronted with a word one has not often employed, one may be tempted to replace it mentally with a supposed synonym. The substitution could be misleading, however. I want to make it clear, therefore, that I will *not* use the word "naturalism" to mean any one of the isms listed in the right-hand column of Table 1, nor all of them in combination. I will *not* equate animism with any one or all of the isms listed in the left-hand column. But I will note some of the resemblances between the styles of thought denoted by the labels in each list and will also point out their differences.

1 Positions That Tend to Be Antinaturalistic

Vitalism Without necessarily becoming doctrinaire vitalists, some sociologists have shown vitalistic leanings. MacIver, for example, although never an extreme vitalist, insisted that social causation includes something more than correlation and implied that the something more had to do with the subjective feelings we have when we bring about an event of some sort.[18] MacIver's concern for these subjective feelings of nexus between

---

[18] On this aspect of MacIver's views, see Donald W. Calhoun, Review of *Social Causation*, *American Sociological Review*, 7 (October, 1942), p. 715.

action and result is quite different from the statistician's recognition that a correlation can be "spurious" in a way that can be detected by calculating partial correlations. It is instead a conviction that the behavior of living entities is subject to different causation than the actions of dead entities, and in turn can cause phenomena differently. Likewise, Stark has asked rhetorically how we can compare what is dead with what is alive, asserting that the social order is only superficially similar to a mechanical system. He epitomizes this view with the truism, "A man is not a molecule," and insists that they cannot be effectively subsumed under one concept.[19]

Vitalists assert that life is "autonomous" and that living things therefore do not behave entirely in accordance with mechanical laws.[20] Human life, especially, is viewed as partly exempted from the laws of mechanics.[21] In the seventeenth and eighteenth centuries one of the staunchest advocates of the independence of the human mind from biochemical determinism was the German, G. E. Stahl, who also originated the phlogiston theory of combustion.[22] But vitalism has more ancient roots than this; Aristotle has been called the first great vitalist.[23] The Greek term "entelechy," which Driesch used to designate the something more of vitalism, was taken from Aristotle's description of the soul as "the first actuality."[24] Modern vitalism, insofar as it has pretensions to scientific stature, dates from Driesch's experiments in 1895 with fragmentation of the sea-urchin embryo.[25] From his experiments and from studies of the restitution of animal parts, Driesch concluded that organic growth was no simple mechanical process—since it could apparently be accomplished in more than one way—and therefore construed it as involving some extranatural influences. He also argued that mechanical theories are incapable of accounting for reproduction of a whole organism from a single cell produced in an ovary, with the offspring organism so nearly an exact copy of the parent.[26] Recent advances in genetics and biochemistry, of course, make his argument far less impressive today than it seemed at the end of the nineteenth century. But sociologists who find vitalism attractive are neither deterred by the implications of modern biochemistry nor dependent on the misconceived experiments and reasoning of Driesch.

Other phenomena said to be inexplicable mechanistically, and hence requiring vitalistic assumptions, included the *esprit de corps* of such human groups as school teams, army battalions, ship's crews, etc. Since

[19] Stark, *op. cit.*, pp. 250–251.
[20] See, for example, L. Richmond Wheeler, *Vitalism: Its History and Validity*. London: Witherby, 1939, p. 155.
[21] *Ibid.*, p. 152.
[22] *Ibid.*, pp. 24–27.
[23] *Ibid.*, p. 6.
[24] *Ibid.*, pp. 7–8.
[25] *Ibid.*, p. 162.
[26] *Ibid.*, p. 145.

groups of a given type, with equal numbers of equally well-qualified individual members, may vary so markedly in performance, morale, and discipline, a vitalistic something more seemed required to explain their variation.[27] Learning—i.e., reflex conditioning—was also said to require vitalistic explanation, since no matter how often a book is opened at the same time a magnet is brought near a compass, the compass needle will never come to be deflected by the mere opening of the book. To have refuted vitalism, it was argued, Pavlov would have had to teach a compass needle to associate the sound of a bell with the approach of a magnet.[28]

Vitalists also tended to insist that the burden of proof was on their opponents. As long as it had not been fully demonstrated that vital and physicochemical processes were identical, "we are not forced to deny the existence of that mysterious thing we call life." And failure to produce life in the laboratory was cited in support of vitalism.[29] Some naturalistic writers, however, had already refused to accept this burden of proof. As long ago as 1912, one of them had put it this way:[30]

The problem of the beginning and end of individual life is physicochemically clear. It is, therefore, unwarranted to continue the statement that in addition to the acceleration of oxidations the beginning of individual life is determined by the entrance of a metaphysical "life principle" into the egg; and that death is determined, aside from the cessation of oxidations, by the departure of this "principle" from the body. In the case of the evaporation of water we are satisfied with the explanation given by the kinetic theory of gases and do not demand that—to repeat a well-known jest of Huxley—the disappearance of the "aquosity" be also taken into consideration.

Latter-day defenders of vitalism have acknowledged that some of the specific arguments on its behalf have been too narrow or have been refuted, and have lamented the consequent rejection of vitalism even by those who see inadequacies in more naturalistic alternatives.[31] On the other hand, some have apparently clung to vitalism as a faith in spite of their own growing commitments to at least some aspects of naturalism—possibly because of the descent of vitalism from philosophical rationalism, which has not wholly given way yet to empiricism.[32] For the most part, in the philosophy of biology it can now be said that substantive vitalism, such as Driesch advocated, is a dead issue. It was not so much killed by criticism as by its own heuristic sterility.[33]

[27] *Ibid.*, p. 190.
[28] *Ibid.*, pp. 150–151
[29] See, for example, O'Connor, *op. cit.*, p. 229.
[30] Jacques Loeb, *The Mechanistic Conception of Life*. Chicago: The University of Chicago Press, 1912, pp. 14–15.
[31] See, for example, Wheeler, *op. cit.*, p. 258.
[32] On vitalism's descent from rationalism, see Hans Reichenbach, *The Rise of Scientific Philosophy*. Berkeley, Calif.: University of California Press, 1951, pp. 202–203.
[33] Cf. Ernest Nagel, *The Structure of Science*. New York: Harcourt, Brace & World, Inc., 1961, pp. 428–429.

It persists in social thought, however, perhaps partly because it some-times has assumed a more subtle form. One might suppose that any analy-sis of social processes and trends which employed the term "forces" would tend to be mechanistic, but vitalism has acquired this masquerade. Ran-dall has pointed out how often our explanations of historical events have relied on "forces," such as "democracy," "fascism," "nationalism," "collec-tivism," etc., which "grow," "threaten," "triumph." He regards this as a typically vitalistic approach.[34] Some (but not all) of our insistence in so-ciology that we are dealing with "emergent" phenomena not in principle explicable by theories of a lower level may likewise represent a vestigial vitalism. A full discussion of "emergence" versus "reductionism" appears in Chapter 9.

The major weakness apparent in vitalism, in either biology or sociology, has been its inability to define precisely the characteristics of the some-thing more it insists is there to distinguish vital phenomena from natural phenomena. It thus suggests an inner sanctum whose door must remain forever barred to systematic research and explanation.[35] Vitalistic sociol-ogy can hardly be anything but mere tychism unless it can begin to state determinate propositions about vital behavior. Since this is seldom attempted, vitalism can perhaps best be defined in a wholly negative way; it is merely the insistence that natural science is not enough.[36] It never seems to succeed in specifying *what else* is needed.

Idealism   Though I have imputed vitalistic views to MacIver, he has by no means been thoroughly and exclusively committed to a vitalistic orien-tation. What he did insist upon as a distinction between the kind of causal nexus characteristic of human actions and the kind characterizing me-chanical phenomena was the occurrence of "dynamic assessments." This concept was roughly equivalent to the "definition of the situation" empha-sized by Thomas.[37] To stress this sort of concept is less antinaturalistic than a truly vitalist outlook would be, for it at least begins to specify the nature of the something more to be invoked by the social scientist. Since the suggested additional element is primarily mental, this orientation can be called "idealist."

It was illustrated in MacIver's attempt to explain the prevalence of di-vorce by attributing it to the devaluation of family continuity. Calhoun has raised the question whether MacIver wasn't virtually insisting that subjective factors are to be treated as *privileged* data, to be not only invoked when needed, but invoked unskeptically. After all, MacIver's ex-

---

[34] John Herman Randall, Jr., *Nature and Historical Experience*. New York: Columbia University Press, 1958, p. 88.
[35] Cf. Pratt, *op. cit.*, p. 77.
[36] Such a definition is suggested, in fact, by Wheeler, *op. cit.*, p. 196.
[37] Cf. Calhoun, *op. cit.*, p. 717

planation could be construed as a mere tautology, asserting that family instability is prevalent where families are unstable.[38]

An idealist orientation can result in question begging. O'Connor, in the course of criticizing naturalistic sociology, argued as follows:[39]

The mind is the subject of many spiritual, immaterial activities, and since everything acts according to its own nature, it follows that the mind must be immaterial. These major immaterial operations of the mind are the formation of concepts, judgments, and reasoning processes, along with the capacity for reflection and self-consciousness. Each operation necessitates an immaterial principle of activity.

Clearly, such an argument makes sense only if one begins with the *assumption* that "everything acts according to its own nature." This is a distinctively Aristotelian postulate and can hardly serve to prove to a non-Aristotelian the validity of an idealist orientation.

An opposing argument has been succinctly stated by Reichenbach. Because no verifiable difference can occur between a person with a mind and the same person, similarly constituted physicochemically at another moment and behaving without a mind, therefore "mind" and "bodily organization" have to be regarded as two labels for the same phenomena. Reichenbach compares with the person who wishes to insist that the mind is more than physicochemical organization and behavior, a man who disassembles the engine of a 130 h.p. car and fails to find the 130 h.p.[40] Such a failure would certainly not refute the applicability of naturalism to automotive engineering. The naturalist would be the first to insist that a heap of unorganized engine parts will generate fewer horsepower than an organized engine. And I doubt whether even the staunchest idealist would care to insist that those 130 h.p. must "still exist" in some other place or in another form.

Voluntarism If not mind, some writers would invoke *will* as the extra ingredient that must distinguish human behavior from natural phenomena. Comte pointed out long ago that the theological concept of will implied an arbitrariness in human actions. He noted that in practical affairs men had increasingly found it useful instead to conceive of invariable laws.[41]

In indicating his own voluntaristic attitude, Stark has recently imputed voluntarism to Sumner by suggesting that the concept of folkways was firmly based on recognition of the moral dilemma of a human species living on marginal ground "between freedom and determination." To Stark, this is the "essence of society."[42]

[38] *Ibid.*
[39] O'Connor, *op. cit.*, pp. 222–223.
[40] Reichenbach, *op. cit.*, p. 272.
[41] Auguste Comte, *A General View of Positivism.* (tr. J. H. Bridges). New York: E. P. Dutton & Co., Inc., 1908, p. 10.
[42] Stark, *op. cit.*, p. 265.

If men could, by willing, influence events in the physical world, but it could be shown that no physical event influenced their wills, naturalistic sociology would fall, and voluntarism would replace it. Voluntaristic writers hardly care to assert such an extreme view, however. Usually only *some* autonomy is accorded the will, and even that is often only accorded it implicitly. The issue is commonly just not faced. Granting that men act as they will, if their will is shaped by experience, education, propaganda, etc., the concept of will is not sufficient to demonstrate and fulfill the need for something more than a naturalistic approach can yield.

However antinaturalistic MacIver may have seemed in other things he wrote, it is to his credit that he saw weaknesses in the doctrine of "free will." Where it denies causality, he noted, it is based on a misconception. While he felt the advocates of freedom of will tended to advance a somewhat less specious argument than the extreme vitalists offered, he maintained that the controversy over the concept had been confused by partisans for both sides. It had been widely imagined that freedom versus constraint was equivalent to capricious versus determined, but that was not MacIver's way of defining the issue.[43]

Spiritualism   If his evident preference for ideational and idealistic cultures over sensate cultures were not enough to cause Sorokin's sociology to be marked as spiritualist in flavor, it has been so labeled on somewhat more specific grounds. It has been said that Sorokin, without treating directly of the supernatural, at least has recognized (more so, by implication, than other sociologists) that man requires higher gratifications than those of his senses. Sorokin "demands something besides oscillating relative standards as a basis for right human conduct. While his 'Divine Absolute' may not reach the Godhead as St. Thomas knows It, the fact that he admits the existence of Divinity and absolute values, sets him apart from the other sociologists. . . ." In short, Sorokin is said to have a "regard for the primacy of the spiritual."[44] The implication seems to be that sociologists are supposed to define the phenomena they study as primarily spiritual, and thus should recognize the inadequacy of any approach that overemphasizes nonspiritual aspects of human behavior.

Supernaturalism   Whenever a sociologist is given credit, as O'Connor gave credit to Giddings, for correctly insisting that supernatural causation should not be postulated "where natural causation has been demonstrated," then by implication it is postulated that there is another realm with which sociologists are concerned in which causation *is* super-

---

[43] Robert M. MacIver, *Social Causation.* Boston: Ginn and Company, 1942, pp. 234–242.

[44] Sister Roberta Snell, *The Nature of Man in St. Thomas Aquinas Compared with the Nature of Man in American Sociology.* Washington, D.C.: The Catholic University of America Press, 1942, p. 164.

natural.[45] It may even be supposed by some that *wherever* natural causation has not been demonstrated, events must be supernaturally caused rather than just not yet explained.

Transcendentalism   When a sociologist is tempted to suppose that he can learn about societal phenomena by studying the way men *think* about them, he is substituting transcendentalist for naturalist methods of inquiry. A transcendental conception of knowledge has been characteristic of speculative philosophy.[46] To the extent that modern sociologists tend to use "philosophy" as a pejorative term, especially by putting the word "armchair" in front of it, they imply at least some commitment to naturalism. It should be noted, however, that by no means all philosophers disdain observation as the criterion of nonempty truth.[47]

Rationalism   Plato, and many philosophers since his time, supposed that human reason could actually *perceive* ideas as "existing" entities. He resorted to picturesque mythology to "explain" how this could occur. Tangible objects were taken to be mere shadows of the more real *ideas* from which they derived their form. Reichenbach suggested that there is an irresistible temptation for philosophers to use picture language in place of explanation when confronted with a question that cannot be answered by reference to valid information.[48] Just as he contrasted such rationalist philosophy with empiricist philosophy, it might be suggested that sociologists, instead of properly acknowledging ignorance in the face of some sociological question, are now and then tempted to formulate hypotheses. To formulate hypotheses is not in itself antinaturalistic, but if we then take them for granted on the basis of their plausibility or their inclusion of cogent concepts, this is not at all naturalistic.

Few sociologists would go so far as Plato and actually deny that observation could contribute to knowledge. To Plato, one must learn through "the natural gift of reason." One should explore cosmology, he suggested, by sheer ratiocination, and "let the heavens alone," i.e., not bother with making observations of celestial phenomena. Reichenbach attributes this antiempirical attitude to the desire for certainty and an impatience with mere probabilities.[49] Most modern sociologists seem to be more patient.

Only when sociologists begin to write as if their postulates were truly self-evident are they courting rationalism in lieu of naturalism. As shown in Chapter 1, sociologists today give little credence to the notion that the reasoning mind has direct access to ultimate truths and can dispense with sensory observation. But occasionally, when we make assumptions

[45] This implication is apparent in O'Connor, *op. cit.*, p. 94.
[46] Reichenbach, *op. cit.*, p. 252.
[47] *Ibid.*
[48] *Ibid.*, p. 24.
[49] *Ibid.*, p. 31.

whose plausibility arises from their anthropomorphism, as animistic
philosophers have done in the past,[50] we may be in danger of regressing
into rationalism.

There is another reason why rationalism is still tempting. Rationalism
has understandably had a close connection with theology, whose doctrines
have, of course, required extrasensory validation because they are not formulated in terms of observables. Thus, philosophers of a rationalist persuasion were natural allies of theologians. But this alliance has given the
rationalist a basis for feeling morally superior to the empiricist.[51] Accordingly, the sociologists who would reject on empirical grounds some hypothesis in which someone has a vested moral interest can expect to be
castigated as a clan of doubting Thomases, and conversely, those sociologists who without data will accept the hypothesis on the basis that it
is "reasonable" will be deemed more virtuous. The naturalist can only
answer that *in the long run* he who accepts and acts upon the seemingly
reasonable but empirically false hypothesis will come to grief.

Indeterminism   In a sense, this form of antinaturalism does not exactly
contend that there is an essential something more that shapes human
social behavior. Instead, it virtually says such behavior is shapeless. It
assumes uncaused events, orderless sequences, occurrences without consequences. It embraces the old notion that something can be created out
of nothing. But as MacIver naturalistically pointed out, the notion of spontaneous generation is quite unscientific.[52] Nagel has gone further and
argued that the conception of absolute and unqualified disorder is self-
contradictory. Hence, any assertion that some event was completely fortuitous or uncaused must be evaluated in terms of the fact that the disorder implied in the sequence of events to which that particular event
belongs can only be relative.[53]

Historicism   According to historicists, the methods of natural science are
inapplicable to sociology because of the historical relativity of social laws.
In short, the uniformity-of-nature principle from physics is regarded as
alien to sociology.[54] It is hopeless for the sociologist to attempt to discover
laws of social change, for example, because after a time the laws themselves will have changed.

[50] On the tendency to make anthropomorphic assumptions, see William S. Beck,
Modern Science and the Nature of Life. Garden City, N.Y.: Anchor Books, Doubleday
& Company, Inc., 1961, pp. 38–41.
[51] Reichenbach, *op. cit.,* pp. 77–78.
[52] Robert M. MacIver, *The Challenge of the Passing Years: My Encounter with Time.*
New York: Trident Press, Inc., 1962, p. 89.
[53] Nagel, *op. cit.,* p. 334. Cf. Melvin L. DeFleur and William R. Catton, Jr., "The
Limits of Determinacy in Attitude Measurement," *Social Forces,* 35 (May, 1957),
pp. 295–300.
[54] Popper, *op. cit.,* p. 6.

In particular, the historicist sees the self-fulfilling prophecy in social affairs as an insurmountable obstacle to naturalistic prediction by social scientists. Awareness that social predictions may influence social actions destroys objectivity in social science, according to historicist thought.[55] An astronomer's prediction of an eclipse or a conjunction of planets will not be undermined by being publicized; the sociologist's predictions are subject to self-destruction, however. Hence, sociology cannot be scientific, the historicist contends. It might instead be argued simply that sociological predictions which are self-refuting are not stated on an appropriate level of abstraction. Simon has shown, for example, how an opinion poll could theoretically take into account a bandwagon or antibandwagon effect so as to avoid self-refutation.[56]

Anyway, such problems would not be sufficient to compel the historicist conclusion. Historicists take the antinaturalistic view that the social sciences, in contrast to the natural sciences, must use the method of intuitive understanding to get at the purpose and meaning of historic events.[57] I will show in Chapters 6 and 7 that *Verstehende* methods can be helpful to sociologists, but this is not the same as the claim of historicism that this must be the sole way of acquiring social knowledge.

There are limited respects in which historicism recognizes common features of sociology and natural science. For instance, it regards sociology, like physics, as a branch of knowledge that is both theoretical and empirical. Otherwise historicism is fundamentally antinaturalistic.[58]

2   Positions That Tend toward Naturalism

Physicalism   Because the science of physics has succeeded so well in constructing adequate descriptions and workable explanations of a wide variety of phenomena involving matter and energy, the temptation has been strong for a long time to use its generalizations as well as its concepts as models in other areas. The conviction that nature is a unity strengthens this temptation for some. Such specific breakthroughs as the development of workable theories of electromagnetism, for example, have stimulated naïvely literal emulation by some sociologists.[59]

Direct imitation of physics has never gone unchallenged. One of the more interesting criticisms has been offered by Sorokin. He has suggested that if the claims of physicalistic sociologists could be realized, sociology would merely be absorbed into the physicochemical sciences and cease to

---

[55] *Ibid.*, pp. 13–14.
[56] Herbert A. Simon, *Models of Man.* New York: John Wiley & Sons, Inc., 1957, Chap. 5.
[57] Popper, *op. cit.*, p. 20.
[58] *Ibid.*, p. 35.
[59] Cf. Stark, *op. cit.*, p. 155.

exist as an independent discipline.[60] As will become increasingly evident
in later chapters, I do not believe this to be a necessary consequence of
patterning sociology along naturalistic lines. But even if it were true,
the merging of sociology into physicochemical science need not be
feared unless the independence of sociology is valued as an end in itself.
I happen to believe that a certain amount of disciplinary autonomy is
useful in the quest for valid knowledge, but it is the knowledge that
justifies the autonomy, not vice versa.

Mechanism In some respects, a more specific way in which sociologists
have been tempted to emulate the physical sciences has consisted in the
borrowing of concepts and formulas from one sector of physics—the science of mechanics. The term "mechanism," however, has come to mean
not only the narrowest attempts to explain everything by the laws of
mechanics, but also in a broader usage signifies universal explanation in
terms of nonteleological causal relations (i.e., invariant correlations)
among physicochemical entities.[61]

In the seventeenth century, philosophers had largely convinced themselves that the appropriate conception of the universe was a huge machine. Its behavior was regarded as following laws that could be discovered. Although the existence of the universe and the nature of the laws
by which it operated were attributed to God, the new view of how it
operated within those divinely ordained laws was essentially mechanistic.[62] That view, of course, prevailed as a part of the intellectual climate
in which sociology arose less than two centuries later.

The naturalism advocated in this book partakes of that intellectual heritage. Its postulates are in accord with certain aspects of the mechanistic
conception of the universe. But it is not by any means limited to the
view that only the *presently known* principles of *physical* mechanics can
be invoked in the scientific explanation of social phenomena. Such a narrow view is what is sometimes meant by the term "mechanism," and it
indeed merits much of the criticism it has received from Sorokin and
others.

Determinism If a number of the isms discussed above have been fraught
with ambiguity, certainly the word "determinism" excels them in this respect. One meaning that has often been attached to the word is flagrantly
nonnaturalistic and needs to be clearly disavowed before going on. When
I speak of determinism as one of the viewpoints that tends toward naturalism I do *not* have in mind any of the numerous single-factor theories
of human history that have been called "determinisms." I do not mean

[60] Sorokin, *op. cit.*, p. 3.
[61] Yervant H. Krikorian, "A Naturalistic View of Mind," in Krikorian (ed.), *op. cit.*,
p. 244.
[62] Beck, *op. cit.*, pp. 50–51.

such theories as "geographic determinism," "racial determinism," "cultural determinism," etc. Obviously, the import of the word "determinism" in such phrases is that the factor mentioned is taken to be the *sole* determinant or at least the overwhelmingly most important determinant of the variables for which explanation is being offered.

Physical mechanics is, of course, a deterministic science in quite a different sense. In this latter, more useful sense, determinism characterizes any theory that asserts that the values of the several variables by which the state of a system is described can be predicted for some time t_1 if we are given the knowledge of their values at another time t_0 and if we know the interval between t_0 and t_1.[63] It is precisely because deterministic theories of this sort have been found workable that we are able to see the futility in the single-factor theories that are misleadingly called "determinisms." For the state of a system at a future date to be predictable from knowledge of the values of its state variables at the present, the list of state variables taken into account must be *sufficient* in number. Even in the relatively simple field of physical mechanics, sufficiency is never attained with only a single variable.

Physical mechanics so clearly constitutes a deterministic theory and is so conspicuously successful that it has been easy to regard it as canonical for other fields of inquiry. But it is a mistake to assume that it is the only instance of genuine determinism or that to be deterministic a theory must be readily reducible to physical mechanics.[64] It is also erroneous to suppose that a theory cannot be deterministic if it is stated in statistical terms; statistical determinism is strict determinism with respect to a system whose state variables are statistical.[65] An empirical system of this type will be studied at length in Chapter 8.

There are questions that can be asked which cannot be answered within a deterministic framework. That is to say, there are questions which appear profound within some frames of thought which simply have no meaning in a deterministic framework. For example, in a deterministic framework it would be meaningless to ask what caused the universe. Given the existence of the universe, however, we can postulate a deterministic framework according to which future states of the universe can be accurately predicted by knowing the values of its state variables at present.[66] It is the office of a deterministic theory to list and define the required state variables and to elucidate their interrelations.

Two characteristics suffice, then, to state as precisely as possible what is meant by determinism. First, a theory is deterministic if it expects "lawful" sequences, rather than arbitrary ones. That is, it must expect that less than all conceivable combinations of events could actually occur. Sec-

[63] Nagel, *op. cit.*, p. 292.
[64] *Ibid.*, pp. 285–286. Cf. Mario Bunge, *Causality*. Cleveland: Meridian Books, The World Publishing Company, 1963, p. 12.
[65] Nagel, *op. cit.*, p. 291.
[66] Reichenbach, *op. cit.*, pp. 208, 214.

ond, to be deterministic, a theory must at least implicitly embrace "the genetic principle" which rejects any supposition that there could be an event wholly devoid of antecedent conditions or wholly without consequences.[67]

Approximately equivalent to the notion of determinism in this sense is the term "causalism." This refers to the assumption of the universal validity of the causal principle, which is the conviction that under like circumstances, like results can always be expected to occur. The word "causality" is sometimes used as a synonym for "causalism," but it also sometimes is used just to mean the fact of a particular causal connection.[68] Thus it is not clear how much is being affirmed when a sociologist professes to believe in causality. He may be affirming determinism, or he may only be acknowledging a particular determinate sequence.

Probably few sociologists would be willing explicitly to reject causalism or determinism when the latter is taken to mean simply the two broad notions, the principle of lawfulness and the genetic principle. Yet the extent to which such viewpoints as voluntarism, historicism, rationalism, and even indeterminism have pervaded sociological thought suggests that not all sociologists have thus far actually accepted these two principles or made them the foundations of their conceptualization of human social behavior. Early in the history of sociology, Ward tried (apparently without successful impact on those who came after him) to clarify these issues. Looking back on four books he had published prior to the appearance in 1906 of *Applied Sociology*, Ward wrote that he had been trying "to point out a remedy for the general paralysis that is creeping over the world, and which a too narrow conception of the law of cosmic evolution serves rather to increase than to diminish." His sociology was meant to proclaim "the efficacy of effort, provided it is guided by intelligence. It would remove the embargo laid upon human activity by *a false interpretation of scientific determinism,* and, without having recourse to *the equally false conception of a power to will,* it insists upon the power to act."[69]

For Ward, determinism was a framework within which knowledge could be acquired that would augment the power to act effectively; determinism was not a conclusion but a starting point. It was not a theory, but a basis for theorizing. Too many others have mistaken it for substantive knowledge.

Monism All systematic thinkers, including those of naturalistic inclination, wish to be parsimonious with their concepts. Monistic doctrines, whatever their other attributes, are at least more parsimonious than dualis-

[67] Bunge, *op. cit.*, pp. 13, 25–26.
[68] *Ibid.*, pp. 3–4.
[69] Lester F. Ward, *Applied Sociology.* Boston: Ginn and Company, 1906, p. iii. (My italics.)

tic doctrines. To be naturalistic, however, the desire to be monistic rather than dualistic or pluralistic must be tempered with rigorous commitment to the empirical.[70] Sociology may be insufficiently naturalistic if it allows its hypotheses to presuppose a dualism between society and nature. Assumed "great gulfs" between social and natural phenomena imply an "essential difference" between social causation and natural causation or between social scientific method and natural scientific method. But if this is insufficiently naturalistic, it is not merely because it is dualistic rather than monistic; it is only so if there are *empirical* reasons for rejecting the great-gulf hypothesis. To paraphrase a cliché, unity of science is all right in its place; its place is one of subordination to empirical validity.

Behaviorism While there is still controversy over whether sociology should or should not be a science of behavior,[71] reference to it as a "behavioral science" has become increasingly common. Increasingly, when concepts are employed whose referents are subjective, there is insistence that assertions about them be supported with data referring to behavioral indices of the implied subjective states. In sociology, then, behaviorism may be regarded merely as a methodological tenet. It comprises the rule that scientific work in sociology requires verifiable data obtained through the instrument-aided senses, and the postulate that social phenomena are of such character as to make such data in principle obtainable.[72]

Materialism Critics of naturalistic sociology may refer to it as a "nothing but" discipline. It has been charged, for example, that in order to encourage moral relativism, sociologists have described man as "*nothing but* a particular arrangement of chemical substances."[73] Not many sociologists affirm materialism to such an extent, and if they did, their motives would not be at issue here. It appears to be more common, however, to assert, imply, or come close to implying that man is nothing but a product of interaction between genetic endowment and social experience. Inclusion of the latter factor should go far to exempt this common view from being labeled "materialistic," while the fact that it has no need to employ any unobservable or capricious concepts of something more tends to align it with naturalism.

Some writers, both pro and con, have equated naturalism with materialism.[74] For example, the eighteenth-century French philosopher, Diderot,

---

[70] Cf. Pratt, *op. cit.*, pp. 100–101.
[71] See, for example, Charles D. Bolton, "Is Sociology a Behavioral Science?" *Pacific Sociological Review*, 6 (Spring, 1963), pp. 3–9.
[72] George A. Lundberg, "Is Sociology Too Scientific?" *Sociologus*, 9 (September, 1933), pp. 300–301.
[73] Hobbs, *op. cit.*, p. 66.
[74] See, for example, W. H. Sheldon, "Critique of Naturalism," *The Journal of Philosophy*, 42 (1945), pp. 253–270.

insisted that nature was fundamentally an ensemble of material particles, and it was because of this that we could know the laws according to which events occur. Many of his contemporaries, too, meant by naturalism the expectation that ultimately all psychological, moral, or social questions could be transformed into questions of physics and biology.[75] Diderot saw pitfalls in being dogmatically materialist, but his naturalism at least gave the sciences of material nature a role in human understanding that was at the time revolutionary.[76]

One of the themes in the development of sociological thought has been the effort to disentangle naturalism from flagrant materialism. While recognizing the organic basis for human personality, for example, sociologists generally wish to study human beings as actors with personalities, holding positions in social structures, playing parts in social systems, etc., rather than study them just as physical bodies. Durkheim set the pace by insisting that social life consists of "natural facts which are explained by natural causes," and then also adamantly stating: "Nothing is wider of the mark than the mistaken accusation of materialism which has been levelled against us."[77]

Positivism Here is another word that is troublesome because of its varied meanings. Naegele has referred to it as a faith. As such, it consists of "belief in science's ultimate adequacy as a mode of knowing and as a guide for action." It sees in history the progressive vindication of the human mind, conquering magic, superstition, and theology. Differences between social and natural sciences are minimized, with positivists holding a firm conviction of the possibility of systematic, quantitative study of both natural and human phenomena.[78]

Martindale has described positivism as the elevation of the procedures of science to being the norm of all sound thought. He traces positivism's origin to the Greek atomists and Sophists, ancestral to modern naturalism. Positivism, he says, tries to explain all phenomena in terms of facts, forces, energies, etc.[79] For Martindale, sociology began as "positivistic organicism," which, in his view of the history of the discipline could not cope with certain issues and hence broke down. Positivism became divorced from organicism.[80] Among the works of nonorganismic positivism, then, he cites Dodd's *Dimensions of Society* as "an example of the danger

[75] Aram Vartanian, *Diderot and Descartes: A Study of Scientific Naturalism in the Enlightenment.* Princeton, N.J.: Princeton University Press, 1953, pp. 20–21.
[76] *Ibid.,* p. 32.
[77] Emile Durkheim, *Sociology and Philosophy* (tr. D. F. Pocock). New York: The Free Press of Glencoe, 1953, p. 34.
[78] Kaspar D. Naegele, "Social Change: Introduction," in Parsons, Shils, Naegele, and Pitts (eds.), *op. cit.,* p. 1210.
[79] Don Martindale, *The Nature and Types of Sociological Theory.* Boston: Houghton Mifflin Company, 1960, p. 76.
[80] *Ibid.,* chap. 5.

always facing pure positivism of degenerating into an empty formula."
He describes Lundberg as the "most able and influential" positivist,[81] and
relies most heavily on his *Foundations of Sociology* in portraying Lundberg's position. In view of the close association between Dodd and Lundberg as colleagues, and the cross-references in each book to the other
as a "companion volume," it is ironic that Martindale should evaluate them
so differently.

For O'Connor, positivism was "just another sensist or sensationalist theory of epistemology," denying that we can have any valid knowledge
transcending our senses.[82] His objection to it was that it excluded philosophical and theological methods of knowing, and he indicated that such
pioneer sociologists as Ward, Giddings, Small, and Sumner had contempt
for philosophy, metaphysics, and theology. Since Small was an active
layman in his church and Sumner was an ordained clergyman, it is undoubtedly an exaggeration bordering on error to attribute to them contempt for theology. If O'Connor had had in mind the modern version
of positivism associated with the work of the Vienna Circle, it would certainly have been apt to characterize it as antimetaphysical.

Yet another interpretation of positivism, as applied to fields beyond sociology alone, is Bunge's statement that it is a reaction against causal
explanation. In place of explanation, causal or otherwise, positivism confined itself to straightforward description.[83] It rejected "why" questions,
and considered nothing beyond "how" questions. It is this interpretation
of positivism that MacIver had in mind when he found positivism an
unacceptable viewpoint. Not content with correlations, he wanted to go
beyond them in search of a "nexus" between correlated variables. Correlation was seen as only a first step in the search for causation.[84] Moreover,
he accused positivists of effectively choosing darkness by rejecting an imperfect light when demanding complete objective verification. By
allegedly rejecting subjective phenomena, positivists rendered themselves
incapable of dealing with the issues of major concern to sociology, he
said, and they certainly made no headway in the quest for causation when
they used this tactic.[85] It was this version of positivism, too, that Radcliffe-Brown said was fundamentally fallacious. He criticized the substituting of correlation for causation on the ground that it provides no basis
for believing that a law true today must also hold tomorrow.[86] The sophisticated positivist, of course, does not confine his attention to zero-order
correlations. He is more inclined to review a whole matrix of intercorrela-

[81] *Ibid.*, p. 119.
[82] O'Connor, *op. cit.*, pp. 215–218.
[83] Bunge, *op. cit.*, p. 282. Cf. O'Connor, *op. cit.*, p. 214.
[84] MacIver, *Social Causation*, pp. 91–92.
[85] *Ibid.*, p. 383.
[86] A. R. Radcliffe-Brown, *A Natural Science of Society*. New York: The Free Press
of Glencoe, 1957, p. 13.

tions among variables and to draw conclusions from partial and multiple measures of association, and he might insist that there is little else one can do to assess supposed causal linkages.

The varied meanings of positivism, then, include at least these: faith in the adequacy of science; normative regard for scientific procedures; sterile formalism; antitranscendentalism; antisubjectivism; unconcern for causal connections. It is therefore not very informative to say that a certain thinker is a positivist, for the label falls far short of telling which of these views is being imputed to him. It should be apparent, however, that all but one or two of these kinds of positivism would have a close affinity for naturalism as the latter was outlined in Chapter 1.

Empiricism As I noted earlier, philosophy was predominantly rationalistic until only a few centuries ago. Then it began to show increasing concern for empirical information about the observable world. As modern science arose, empiricist philosophical positions were articulated by such men as Francis Bacon, John Locke, and David Hume.[87] Valuable as this new line of thought was to be, it had its own pitfalls. Its "original sin" has been described by one writer as the identification of truth with the criterion by which truth is ascertained.[88] There may be some point in distinguishing knowledge from the means of knowing, and most sociologists probably have colleagues whom they regard as long on methodology and short on sociology. I doubt, however, that we are in as much danger from erring in that direction as from the deep-seated habit of mistaking hypotheses for knowledge through inadequate concern for their empirical verification, or insufficiently precise formulation and insufficiently sensitive tests. It can hardly be anything but a healthy naturalistic attitude to regard science as a method rather than a closed body of knowledge.[89] At any rate, the commitment of sociology to concern for the empirical is strong and thorough, as we saw in Chapter 1.

The various isms that have been briefly described in the preceding pages have not been in any sense discrete schools of thought.[90] The purpose in presenting and discussing such an array of terms has been to safeguard the reader against misconstruing naturalism as I intend it in this book. By naturalism I do *not* mean any one of the quasi-naturalistic isms discussed above, nor do I mean merely the negation of any one of the generally antinaturalistic views presented. And, as noted earlier, naturalism cannot be defined simply as the composite of physicalism, mechanism, determinism, monism, behaviorism, materialism, positivism, and em-

[87] See Reichenbach, *op. cit.*, p. 78.
[88] Bunge, *op. cit.*, p. 45.
[89] Cf. Homer W. Smith, "Forward," in Beck, *op. cit.*, p. xv.
[90] This is shown, for example, by the fact that MacIver has had affinities for several of these isms. Wheeler, in opposing mechanism, even tried to conjoin vitalism and empiricism; see Wheeler, *op. cit.*, p. 141.

piricism. There are affinities between each of these and naturalism, but naturalism does not consist of any one of them or all of them. Naturalism would not be adequately defined, either, by the negation of all the following: vitalism, idealism, voluntarism, spiritualism, supernaturalism, transcendentalism, rationalism, indeterminism, and historicism. (Perhaps few people could reject *all* these views *unless* they had embraced naturalism, but even so I would not be content to define naturalism in that way.)

Whether one's predilections are favorable or unfavorable to naturalism, there is a tendency, as I have found in discussions of the subject, to equate naturalism with, say, positivism, or materialism, or determinism, and as a consequence to misevaluate its heuristic utility. It was to afford some protection against such misevaluation that I wished to delineate explicitly several familiarly named, quasi-naturalistic views, and a similar array of more or less antinaturalistic views.

Rise of the Term "Naturalism"

When the philosophic movements of the nineteenth century linked men and nature, removing the great gulf that had formerly been supposed to separate them, a name was needed for this new viewpoint. "Naturalism" came to be used in that context. In addition, with discovery of the principles of natural selection and the formulation of hypotheses regarding the descent of man, evolutionary thought came to be regarded as the epitome of naturalism. It was not in the nineteenth century or in the work of the evolutionists, however, that naturalism originated. Only the popularity of this name to refer to that style of thought is so recent. Naturalistic thought dates back at least to the seventeenth century and has important antecedents in Greek thought.[91]

In American thought, the foundations for naturalism were laid by the anticlericalism and Deism which prevailed during and after the Revolutionary War. There was some regression following the French Revolution, for the Reign of Terror in France made American public opinion more hostile to unbelief, and religious fundamentalism flourished between then and the Civil War. When the industrial North triumphed over the plantation South, and at the same time Darwin put forth his evolutionary theory, the foundations of supernaturalism were again shaken. If transcendentalism was undermined by these events, so idealism in American literature had to yield to a vigorous naturalism after the First World War.[92] While academic philosophy in America has had a lingering attachment to ideal-

[91] John Herman Randall, Jr., "Epilogue: The Nature of Naturalism," in Krikorian (ed.), *Naturalism and the Human Spirit*, pp. 356–357.
[92] Larrabee, *op. cit.*, pp. 331–351.

ism, naturalism was said to have been "a major unreflective assumption of everyday existence in America. . . ."[93]

The word "naturalism" has been used, as have the other isms surveyed in this chapter, with varied meanings. One common usage has been to regard it as simply the antithesis of supernaturalism. O'Connor, for example, has said that naturalism consists essentially of "negation of the supernatural" and can be reduced to one of three basic types—materialism, evolutionism, or positivism.[94] Other writers have at least contrasted naturalism with supernaturalism, even if they have not defined it merely by that difference.[95] Nagel has provided an example by writing that in the naturalist's conception of nature there is no place for immaterial spirit or disembodied forces.[96]

Though Nagel did not mean to equate naturalism and materialism, it was this sort of statement which O'Connor apparently had in mind when he said that materialism was one of the three basic types of naturalism. In the last analysis, O'Connor wrote, materialism asserts that all events in the space-time universe are matter in motion.[97] His view of positivism makes it closely parallel to such materialism, for he said it limits truth to the tangible and concerns itself only with the discovery of natural laws, using evidence that is physically measurable.[98] Even evolutionary thought seemed, for O'Connor, materialistic; he noted that Spencer had regarded society as a purely natural phenomenon, evolving like other entities in a way that was to be explained in terms of matter, motion, and force.[99] Though hardly a mere materialist himself, A. R. Radcliffe-Brown advocated a natural science of society in almost these terms. He regarded society as a "natural system." Natural systems are the subject matter of natural science. Therefore, there can be, in principle, a natural science of society. By "natural system," he meant a set of entities (events or systems of events) whose relations consist of phenomenally real interconnectedness.[100] That is, they are not just joined in thought by the person studying them.

One does not become naturalistic, however, just by rejecting notions of the supernatural. A method of inquiry is involved.[101] Naturalism defines nature as universal, so that there is nothing outside of it, and thus there are no real phenomena not accessible in principle to experimental

[93] *Ibid.*, p. 319.
[94] O'Connor, *op. cit.*, pp. 8, 23.
[95] See, for example, Pratt, *op. cit.*, pp. 2–17.
[96] Ernest Nagel, *Logic without Metaphysics.* New York: The Free Press of Glencoe, 1956, pp. 7–8.
[97] O'Connor, *op. cit.*, p. 8.
[98] *Ibid.*, pp. 13–16.
[99] *Ibid.*, pp. 16–17.
[100] Radcliffe-Brown, *op. cit.*, p. 43.
[101] Nagel, *Logic without Metaphysics*, p. 41.

method.[102] (There may be, of course, great practical obstacles to experimentation—or even to systematic observation—in the given case.) It is only as a result of these convictions that supernatural or transcendental conceptions are rejected. Their rejection is a result, not a defining characteristic, of naturalism.

Historically, "naturalism" has referred to those movements of thought which have extended, or at least have endorsed or promoted the extension of, the methods of science into areas of inquiry from which they had been barred.[103] Perhaps it has been this recurrent invasion of previously inviolable realms which has led some to regard the word as an epithet. In religious circles, at least, naturalism has often been seen as an evil conspiracy against all that is ideal and spiritual. Hence the tendency to equate it with materialism or mechanism.[104] Of course, a good deal of the work of natural science has *seemed* materialistic and antispiritual. Descartes, for instance, regarded animals and plants as mere automata, entirely unconscious, with all their vital processes being mere cases of chemical or physical phenomena, ultimately reducible to geometry and the laws of motion. He was some three centuries premature with such hypotheses, but much research since then has given support to similar conceptions.[105]

Others have seen in naturalism a protest against *both* supernaturalism and crass materialism.[106] Nagel has insisted that naturalism does not amount to reductive materialism. It is acknowledged by naturalists, he says, that thought, feeling, and emotion are characteristic of men and that, because of these characteristics, men can perform actions which bodies not organized as human bodies are cannot perform. But men's actions are by no means those of *disembodied* minds.[107] It is certainly not in an overly materialistic sense that Berelson and Steiner used the word "naturalistic" when they anticipated that the behavioral sciences "will make a distinctive, indeed an indispensable, contribution to the naturalistic description of human nature. . . ."[108] Among the 1,045 propositions of behavioral science reviewed in their book were many that dealt with beliefs, wants, values, learning, attitudes toward persons, etc., and not merely with the physical requirements of human survival.[109] Nor could

---

[102] Krikorian, "A Naturalistic View of Man," p. 242.
[103] Thelma Z. Lavine, "Naturalism and the Sociological Analysis of Knowledge," in Krikorian (ed.), *Naturalism and the Human Spirit*, p. 185; in the same book, also see Abraham Edel, "Naturalism and Ethical Theory," p. 65.
[104] Cf. Pratt, *op. cit.*, p. 2.
[105] *Ibid.*, p. 59.
[106] E.g., Santayana, as indicated by Randall, *op. cit.*, p. 363.
[107] Cf. Nagel, *Logic without Metaphysics*, pp. 24–27.
[108] Bernard Berelson and Gary A. Steiner, *Human Behavior: An Inventory of Scientific Findings*. New York: Harcourt, Brace & World, Inc., 1964, p. 667.
[109] *Ibid.*, p. 665.

Selznick be accused of mere materialism in professing a commitment to naturalism, since he implied only that his thinking is consistent with the logic of science (in the sense of Dewey's pragmatism, not a narrower positivism).[110]

Its reliance on observation does not reduce naturalism to materialism, either. The first step any science must take is taxonomic; this is true also of social science, but here the work has been said hardly to have begun.[111] The development of an appropriate set of concepts for sociology is a trial-and-error process, and it is still in a state of some confusion. In addition to concepts with which observable phenomena can be classified, a natural science requires higher-order concepts to connect them. The relationships between these different orders of concepts need to be understood more clearly than has heretofore been the case in sociology.

Reichenbach noted that in order to construct a consistent system of relations among observables it is often necessary to assume that they are being affected by other entities we cannot observe directly. For such inferred things he suggested the term "illata." These differ not only from "concreta" which can be directly observed, but also from "abstracta," or combinations of concreta—not so directly observable, because they are collective. Illata are not collective; they are inferred from concreta, but they do not subsume an array of concreta, as do abstracta.[112] To illustrate these categories, we might say that a set of approved acts fall under the heading of concreta (they are observable), while their clustering around a position in a social structure leads to the concept of role, and roles are therefore abstracta. The basis for approval of the acts may be a value, and values are illata. It is my impression that the difference between concreta and abstracta is less troublesome and more likely to be recognized than the distinction between abstracta and illata.

It should be clear that a natural science which deals with illata and abstracta is neither materialistic nor positivistic in the narrow sense. Materialism would deal only with concreta; positivism would at least exclude illata.

Naturalism and Its Antithesis, Animism

Naturalism cannot be satisfactorily defined in negative terms. It is more than merely the antithesis of supernaturalism. It is more than the mere rejection of the hypothesis of "something beyond." At the same time it

[110] Philip Selznick, "Natural Law and Sociology," in The Fund for the Republic, *Natural Law and Modern Society.* Cleveland: The World Publishing Company, 1962, p. 156.
[111] Radcliffe-Brown, *op. cit.,* pp. 32–33.
[112] Reichenbach, *op. cit.,* pp. 263–264.

is more than materialism or empiricism or positivism. To be naturalistic in the pursuit of knowledge means working in accord with the four precepts stated in Chapter 1: (1) insistence on empirical verification of propositions; (2) explanation in terms of antecedent causes or concomitant conditions; (3) acceptance of the axiom of inertia—defining change rather than continuity as problematic; (4) regarding every action as an interaction.

If a negative definition of naturalism is unsatisfactory, it would be almost as inadequate to define its opposite in merely negative terms. Instead of speaking of "antinaturalistic" or "nonnaturalistic" views, we need a word which denotes the ideas *affirmed* by those who remain unsympathetic to naturalistic sociology. It might have seemed sufficient to refer to "vitalistic" sociology in opposition to naturalistic sociology. But, as we saw earlier, vitalism almost reduces to the *negation* of naturalism because it never clearly specifies the nature of the something more it insists on postulating, and it utterly fails to specify the nonnaturalistic modes of analysis allegedly required. It rests its case by standing for the vague "whatever" inorganic or abstract science has thus far left unexplained.[113] A better term, therefore, seems to be "animism." This book is about the differences between animistic sociology, as I call it, and naturalistic sociology.

When used to refer to a certain pattern of heathen religious belief, "animism" means the belief in spirits, including those of nonhuman origin along with those of deceased or absent humans.[114] Religiously animistic peoples impute to such spirits the power to control events and to bring about good or evil results, and are therefore concerned with placating them. In choosing the term for use in the present context I do not mean to imply that such views are held by the opponents of naturalistic sociology. A thoroughgoing animism of the sort characterizing many preliterate peoples imputes spirits to rocks, trees, mountains, jungles, etc.—objects we would call "inanimate." But apart from this, the animist regards these spirits as having the traits he perceives in persons.[115] He assumes the spirits can be influenced, primarily by appropriate use of words.[116] These features are not altogether alien to the sociological thoughtways I propose to call "animistic," but they are not crucial to them.

What I mean by animistic sociology is this: (1) the assumption that our common-sense notions about the nature of human nature are valid; (2) the conviction that these common-sense notions can and should serve as the premises from which more elaborate sociological formulations are to be derived.

[113] See Wheeler, *op. cit.*, p. 260.
[114] Eugene A. Nida and William A. Smalley, *Introducing Animism*. New York: Friendship Press, 1959, p. 5.
[115] *Ibid.*, pp. 17–18.
[116] *Ibid.*, p. 22.

Included among the common-sense notions that I have in mind here are a number of the concepts central to the various antinaturalistic isms previously surveyed. It is a matter of common sense to many people that human nature involves something more than the material traits of our bodies. It is widely assumed that this extramaterial part includes a "will." More specifically, when we say that we can act "voluntarily," we seem to mean that our actions do not exhibit invariable causal sequences, that they are to some degree "independent" of stimuli, that "future" goals sometimes cause our actions, and that we can act without always being acted upon. Because we are capable of apparent caprice, we suppose that steadfastness is problematic. In short, the common-sense assumptions which the animistic sociologist tends to take seriously as valid descriptions of human characteristics are the antithesis of the basic elements of naturalism.

Animism tacitly assumes that the difference between the "animate" and the "inanimate" is fundamental—rather than there being more or less continuous gradations between extremes. Since we are "animate" and our social systems must therefore also be, sociology must differ from the sciences of "inanimate" phenomena in fundamental ways. Societal events, animistically interpreted, happen because of the volition of agents.[117] The whole history of science, as MacIver has correctly observed, attests to the persistence of animistic notions. Our conception of "force," for example, though it is central to the first clearly naturalistic formulations of the science of mechanics, arises from the sensation of strain or effort in doing work with our muscles. We tend toward a "pathetic fallacy," too, by which we attribute benign or hostile qualities to our environment. We are tempted to view the universe teleologically.[118] All these things sociology has had to struggle to outgrow, and it has not entirely shed them yet.

Outgrowing Animism

Sociology became possible only after certain foundations had been laid by philosophy and history. Though sometimes viewed in recent times as an obstacle to enlightened thought, Greek logic and Greek mathematics gave us, as Martindale has pointed out, the idea of rational proof. Historiography, beginning with the Greeks, temporarily subordinated to the purposes of moral instruction in medieval times, but revived and refined since the Renaissance, fostered precision in the investigation of social

[117] F. V. Smith, *op. cit.*, pp. 36–37.
[118] MacIver, *Social Causation*, p. 37.

facts.[119] These developments were essential prerequisites of sociology. So was the separation of natural science from philosophy, which set a precedent and provided motivation for the subsequent departure of social science. Experimentation developed to serve science as rational proof had served philosophy. The transition from philosophy to science was, according to Martindale, mediated by art, wherein prestige attaches to craftsmanship and originality. Hence, artists of the caliber of Leonardo da Vinci could also be experimental scientists. Art was also relatively free from religious control.[120] With the meticulous manner in which he conducted his research, Galileo provided a paradigm for experimental science. Newton, in the later decades of the seventeenth century, came to exemplify the interweaving of science's warp and woof—rational proof and experimental or observational evidence.[121]

The emphasis on evidence was strongly reinforced when philosophers in the twentieth century formulated the verifiability theory of meaning—declaring a sentence meaningless if its truth cannot be ascertained by observation, direct or indirect.[122] Insistence of scientists upon objectivity, or verifiability, often entails ignoring factors which might seem important to the layman but for which no adequate observational techniques yet exist. The advancement of science, however, often depends on technical improvement which brings additional variables within the purview of observation.[123]

Before a genuine social science could emerge, two basic conditions had to be met, according to Martindale. It had to become possible and respectable to look at social phenomena naturalistically, and it had to become possible to suspend ethical judgment so that social phenomena could be studied cognitively rather than evaluatively.[124] There is still resistance to both these activities. In addition to all the repugnance naturalistic sociology seems to have for those who think animistically, ethical neutrality is difficult to achieve, even if it does not encounter hostility. One of the defenders of vitalism in biology, for example, has said that biology of a mechanistic sort is "pitifully biased and restricted in scope" and has asserted that this is objectionable because such biology leads to sociological and moral inferences that are "misleading and potentially productive of evil."[125] Before any discipline (including sociology) could hope to become a natural science, it had to outgrow the tendency to appraise its theories in terms of their moral impact rather than their empirical validity.

[119] Martindale, *op. cit.*, pp. 6–17.
[120] *Ibid.*, pp. 19–24.
[121] *Ibid.*, p. 24.
[122] Reichenbach, *op. cit.*, pp. 256–257.
[123] Cf. Lundberg, *op. cit.*, p. 303.
[124] Martindale, *op. cit.*, p. 29.
[125] Wheeler, *op. cit.*, p. 262.

Extrascientific reasons for accepting or rejecting theories are not easily excluded. Occasionally there may be some congruence between empirical evidence and such extrascientific considerations, so that theories are accepted when true and rejected when false, but only partly because of their truth or falsity. One advocate of vitalism, for example, though contending that sound biological knowledge could compel adoption of vitalist views, acknowledged that such adoption would come easier if one were already influenced by certain religious or psychological assumptions.[126]

It was part of Ward's aim, at the end of the nineteenth century, to persuade his readers that nature was morally indifferent, but that man could increasingly take his destiny into his own hands if he increased his knowledge of how nature operated.[127] The transition from the habit of evaluative inquiry to the ability to keep inquiry purely cognitive is incomplete and has always been difficult. It was facilitated, just prior to the advent of sociology, by the style of religious thought known as Deism. According to Martindale, Deism was an important precursor to sociology because it extended quasi-naturalistic thought into the social world. It asserted that even man's spiritual life was subject to natural laws, and thus, with its emphasis on human rationality, it implied that this subject matter could be studied scientifically.[128]

Since the Renaissance, and especially in the early twentieth century, European philosophy has become increasingly naturalistic.[129] An important exception to this trend, of course, was the widespread literal acceptance of the Genesis account of creation up until the Darwinian revolution. That revolution, as even an advocate of vitalism has felt required to admit, augmented the earlier naturalistic impact of the work of Newton, Leibniz, etc.[130] In the century that has elapsed since, sociology has developed and has shown a sufficient tendency toward naturalistic thought to be evident even to writers primarily concerned with final moral values.[131] Empiricist philosophers, meanwhile, have articulated their views to the point where they can look with favor upon naturalistic developments in sociology and can provide logical support for the insistence that a single method must characterize social sciences and other natural sciences.[132]

In a sense, it would be tempting to define naturalism negatively as refusal to regard the word "nature" as a term distinguishing something from something else. All being is included in nature. Naturalism not only rejects supernaturalism through this refusal, however, but it also rejects the kind

[126] *Ibid.*, p. 226.
[127] Lester F. Ward, *Outlines of Sociology*, New York: The Macmillan Company, 1897, p. 25.
[128] Martindale, *op. cit.*, pp. 31–32.
[129] Pratt, *op. cit.*, p. 1.
[130] See Wheeler, *op. cit.*, pp. 46–47, 51–64, 225.
[131] See, for example, Theodore Hemelt, *Final Moral Values in Sociology*. Washington, D.C.: Sulpician Seminary Press, 1929, pp. 30–34.
[132] See, for example, Reichenbach, *op. cit.*, p. 309.

of reductionist thinking that would equate nature with *any* less-than-universal category. If there are mental, cultural, moral phenomena, naturalism says these must be included as part of nature, and sociology must be included as part of natural science. All areas of human experience are asserted to be amenable to scientific study.[133]

The Issue of Supraempirical Postulates

In this regard, it may be instructive to consider the attempt by Paul H. Furfey to sketch a series of choices sociologists might make among alternative "supraempirical postulates." Furfey's work has the merit of articulating with unusual clarity the contention that "natural science" is a narrower category than "science." His argument challenges naturalism, and the challenge deserves a response, although I think Furfey misperceived the nature of the challenge he presented.

Having admitted that a natural science of sociology is possible, Furfey went on to advocate a sociology that would instead come under the heading of a "moral science." He distinguished his preferred kind of sociology from the "positivistic" kind by contrasting five supraempirical postulates which he endorsed with five others supposedly embraced by positivism.[134]

1 *Metaphysical Postulates:* (*a*) Dualism is Furfey's preference as a metaphysical postulate. He would recognize both material and immaterial existence, the one not being considered reducible to the other. (*b*) Materialism is an alternative postulate, rejected by Furfey. Positivist sociology, he said, asserts that only matter exists and that all phenomena can be explained in terms of matter and motion. (*c*) Idealism is another logically possible alternative, then, and it is also rejected by Furfey. It would assert the half of his preferred duality other than the half allegedly taken by positivism. By the idealist postulate, reality could be identified with mind, thought, idea, or spirit, or at least these could be considered prior to matter in importance.

My comment: Furfey failed to note that one is adopting a postulate in even posing these alternatives and implying that these terms are meaningful. Instead, one might assert their meaninglessness. In my view, genuinely naturalistic sociology would simply say that there is no operationally verifiable meaning to the dichotomy "material reality" versus "immaterial reality." It would insist that there is an unwarranted *presumption* of dualism in even conjoining the words "immaterial" and "reality." This conjunction gives specious plausibility to the ensuing disjunction between

[133] Randall, *op. cit.*, pp. 357, 361, 374.
[134] Paul Hanly Furfey, *The Scope and Method of Sociology*. New York: Harper & Row, Publishers, Incorporated, 1953, pp. 219–220.

the two phrases "material reality" and "immaterial reality." To the naturalist, the postulate of dualism is merely a symptom of careless use of words.

The operationally real is the observable; to be observable, a phenomenon must be capable of sensory detection. It must thus at least *involve* matter and energy. Furfey has falsely defined the issue (unintentionally, I am sure). The issue is not which of his metaphysical postulates to adopt, but whether to consider any of them meaningful at all.

2 *Postulates on Mind:* (a) Furfey assigned no name to the postulate he preferred, which is the opposite of the one he called "behaviorism." His preferred postulate asserts a distinction between moral and natural sciences. (b) Behaviorism. According to Furfey, positivistic sociology embraces this view which denies the existence of mental phenomena, or at least denies the relevance of motives in determining behavior.

My Comment: Again, it is a postulate that there is a meaningful difference between mental or motivated acts and acts that are not mental or not motivated. An alternative would be to assert that no such distinction can be sustained. Naturalistic sociology, I believe, would simply say that mental events and motivation can only be inferred from observable behavior, so that it is meaningless to assume the dichotomy on which Furfey predicates the pair of allegedly alternative postulates. One can, as modern psychology has shown, be mistaken about even one's own thoughts and motives. But even if we granted that at least in the case of oneself, there could be direct access to mental phenomena and to motives, the patent necessity for relying on inference in all cases other than oneself reduces Furfey's postulate either to meaninglessness or to incipient solipcism. This is *not* to say, however, that naturalistic sociology has no concern for thought or motivation. I am only saying that when we do use these concepts they must refer to what Reichenbach called illata, or at least to abstracta, but certainly they cannot refer to concreta. The real issue, then, is the animistic sociologist's pretension that he has direct access to these illata; this pretension contrasts with the naturalistic sociologist's recognition of the inferential status of illata.

3 *Postulates on Will:* (a) Furfey embraced indeterminism, which he said asserts that there are circumstances under which human beings are "free to make choices" and are not constrained by necessity, either internal or external. The term "free" can be troublesome; Furfey seemed to mean by it that human action is not always patterned in accord with principles analogous to Newton's axioms. In other words, human action is either not assumed to remain constant unless acted upon by a social or psychological force, or it is not assumed to entail an equal and opposite reaction. (b) According to Furfey, positivism accepts determinism. Furfey defined this as the assumption that all events, including human acts, are completely determined by laws that are essentially uniform whether they refer to physical phenomena or human behavior.

My Comment: To say that action is "determined" by laws can be taken to mean either that (1) it is *patterned in accord with* propositions called "laws," or that (2) it is *controlled by* such propositions. Furfey seems to have supposed that the issue between determinism and indeterminism is in terms of the latter meaning, but a more salient issue would be in terms of mere patterning in accord with certain principles. Thus, taking the word "free" as used by Furfey to mean what I have suggested he might have meant by it, his preferred postulate is quite animistic. In Chapter 8, I shall present an empirical case against this aspect of animism. For the present, however, I will only point out that the naturalistic postulate opposed to it asserts that *changes* in human action are what require explanation in terms of social or psychological forces, and that there are no unmoved movers.

The animistic sociologist will probably feel that I am here simply denying the existence of "will"—or at least "free will." So be it. Of course I have "chosen" to write this book, but I am under no illusion that this volition was uncaused. In my view, no scientific gain can come of attempting to create such an illusion.

4 Ethical Postulates: Furfey said these are implicit (though seldom explicitly acknowledged) in almost all sociological classifications of human activities, especially in the area of social problems. (*a*) Ethical absolutism is the postulate preferred by Furfey. It asserts changeless norms, existing independently of human opinion. (*b*) Ethical relativism is the postulate imputed by him to positivism. It is said to make the group's consensus the basis for norms. If group attitudes change, norms change—to Furfey's regret.

My Comment: It is a postulate to assert that a person must be either an ethical absolutist or an ethical relativist *altogether.* An alternative postulate, based on sociological recognition that each of us is normally able to perform many roles and keep them rather distinct from one another, would assert that we may take a relativistic position in some circumstances and may not do so in others. In my role as sociologist, scientifically studying and accounting for the behavior I observe in various groups, it is important to me to have my observations as undistorted as possible. I therefore adopt a position of cultural relativism *in that role,* so that the biasing effects of my personal preferences may be minimized. Cultural relativism forces me to see the values of others as values, rather than as deviations from my values. When I revert to my other roles—father, husband, voter, etc.—I am expected to allow my values to influence my actions (and even my perceptions).

Furfey seems to have imagined that cognition and evaluation are always inextricably bound together, so that our only alternatives are between different evaluative frameworks. Naturalistic sociologists assert the contrary, that when proper precautions are taken, cognition and evaluation can be separated to some degree and that, whatever our values may be, it behooves us in the quest of valid knowledge not to let them distort our cognitive efforts. If the insulation between our roles is less than perfect, this hardly justifies removing what insulation there is, as Furfey's statement of the issue would require.

5 *Theological Postulates:* (*a*) Furfey wished to incorporate into sociology certain postulates from Christian theology. (*b*) Positivism, he said, rejects Christian doctrine as irrelevant to sociology.

My Comment: Sociology certainly may study human responses to theological symbols and doctrines. It may also study the social conditions which seem to shape such doctrines and influence the coming and going of such symbols. But behind Furfey's adoption of specific postulates from Christian theology there lies a more general postulate that should be made explicit and examined. It is this general postulate which differentiates animistic and naturalistic sociology—not the specific assumptions from Christian doctrine which Furfey wished to inject into sociology. This implicit postulate asserts that theological symbols have referents to which men respond and that human responses to the referents are distinguishable from human responses to the symbols. Only by assuming this postulate can one assert that theological assumptions containing such symbols ought to be included in sociology.

An alternative postulate is that the responses of human beings to theological symbols cannot be operationally distinguished from the responses the same people would make to the supposed referents of those symbols. Hence, while sociology properly includes propositions about symbolic processes, it does not require theological assumptions as part of its postulate system. Naturalistic sociology is nominalistic as far as theology is concerned. For instance, it must equate God with "God," until it has found some empirically meaningful distinction between the responses to the symbol and the responses to what the symbol is said to stand for. Furfey, quite obviously, would take the philosophical realist's position (i.e., the opposite of the nominalist's position) in this respect and would maintain that God is not the same as "God." But again he has unwittingly misstated the issue. The issue is not whether doctrines involving theological concepts are required in an adequate postulate set for sociology. The issue is whether *any* propositions are admissible which involve concepts that are not at least illata, and hence derive their meaning at least indirectly from observation of concreta.

The five postulates attributed by Furfey to what he termed "positivism" are not the postulates that characterize naturalistic sociology. The moral science of sociology which he advocated would certainly not be naturalistic, but it would differ from naturalism in other respects than the differences he described between it and positivism. The reader who dissents

from the postulates of Furfey's moral science need not accept the postulates he ascribed to positivism. Nor must the dissenter from positivism
embrace Furfey's postulates. Naturalistic sociology presents more
adequate alternatives.

In arguing for the admissibility of supraempirical postulates in sociology, in particular those implicit in Christian social thought, Furfey ad-
duced certain "metasociological propositions." One was this: "Every
supra-empirical postulate should be factually true." Otherwise it should
not be admitted into sociology.[135] Elsewhere he had distinguished "factual
truth" from "formal truth." The former was said to correspond to reality,
whereas the latter merely asserts that conclusions follow rigorously from
assumptions.[136] Thus, Furfey seems to have asserted a self-contradiction,
for postulates that are "factually true" can hardly be "supraempirical."
While one might justifiably accept as factually true some proposition that
had been demonstrated empirically in, say, psychology or biology, and
take this proposition as a postulate for sociology, it would be a much
bolder step to take into sociology as a postulate some proposition so alien
to naturalism as to be not empirically demonstrable at all. The postulates
of sociology may be supraempirical in the special sense that they are not
at issue empirically *in sociology*, but if they are said to be "factually true"
then they cannot be supraempirical for natural science taken altogether.

In insisting that sociology should be a moral science rather than a natural science, Furfey was apparently advocating that sociologists give attention to "why" questions, and not confine themselves to formulating and
answering "how" questions. In particular, he wanted some of the "why"
questions to be concerned with ethical imperatives. Sociological explanations of social phenomena would thus include propositions of the following form: "This happens because it is meant to happen," or "This cannot
occur because it would be evil." In contrast, MacIver (who had, as we
shall see in Chapter 4, his own somewhat different inclinations toward
animism) correctly pointed out that the "whys" of science invariably resolve themselves eventually into "hows." When he has succeeded in explaining some problematic phenomenon by reducing it to invariant sequence and concomitance of basic properties, the scientist does not go
on to ask why the sequence and concomitance are invariant. MacIver
knew that such a question is meaningless in science.[137]

But it is the irrepressible urge to ask "why" questions that characterizes
animistic thought, and these questions lead to "explanations" that consist
of the imputation of anthropomorphic desires as the causes of impersonal

[135] *Ibid.*, p. 223.
[136] *Ibid.*, p. 114.
[137] MacIver, *Social Causation*, p. 12. When the natural scientist does permit himself
to use the word "why?" he never means by it, "for what purpose?" but only "as
an instance of what more inclusive generalization does this pattern prevail?"

phenomena. Those sociologists who still succumb to the urge to ask such questions and who resist efforts to transform them into "how" questions, thereby reveal their lingering animistic predispositions.

Summary

Through the ages there have been many arguments that social science and natural science are fundamentally different. Acceptance or rejection of this contention is more than a mere matter of taste; inquiry leads to different conclusions when it is naturalistic than when it is not. The superiority of naturalistic thoughtways in producing verified knowledge has been amply demonstrated in those disciplines which are universally recognized as natural sciences. Those who advocate naturalism in sociology should not have to bear a larger burden of proof than those who oppose it.

Sociology has a naturalistic heritage, but it is often obscured by contentions that sociology must answer questions and use concepts from which the natural sciences have been exempted. Most sociologists have been "marginal men" in transition between once prevalent animistic thoughtways and the emerging naturalistic conceptions. We do ourselves an injustice when we thrust ourselves into reified pigeonholes, labeling ourselves as adherents of supposedly discrete isms or schools of thought. A number of these hypothetical schools have tended toward naturalism, and a number of others have tended toward animism. Neither naturalism nor animism should be defined as being equated with any one of these imperfectly distinguishable philosophical emphases, however. Naturalism resembles and partakes of, but is not coterminous with any or all of, the following: physicalism, mechanism, determinism, monism, behaviorism, materialism, positivism, empiricism. It is thus contrasted with animism, which resembles the following: vitalism, philosophical idealism, voluntarism, spiritualism, supernaturalism, transcendentalism, rationalism, indeterminism, historicism.

The term "naturalism" arose to label the nineteenth-century philosophical movements linking men and nature, though the origins of naturalistic thought were far earlier. The word has been used with varied meanings, just as have the names of the other philosophical isms. Its widest usage implies that nature is universal; there is nothing outside of it. There are thus no real phenomena not accessible (in principle at least) to experimental method. It is as a result of belief in the universal fertility of scientific modes of inquiry that supernatural or transcendental conceptions are rejected. It is not their rejection that defines naturalism, but the positive conviction that the methods of science can fruitfully be extended into areas of study from which they have in the past been barred. Naturalism is not crass materialism; it acknowledges that men have thoughts and feelings and wishes, and only insists that these are not inscrutable or unlawful. Because it recognizes the necessity of invoking illata and abstracta and does not confine its attention to concreta, naturalistic sociology is neither materialistic nor positivistic in the narrow sense.

Naturalistic sociology affirms these precepts: (1) propositions must be subject to empirical verification, directly or indirectly; (2) phenomena are to be explained in terms of antecedent causes or concomitant conditions rather than teleologically; (3) change rather than persistence requires explanation, by the terms of the inertial axiom; (4) every action is an aspect of an interaction.

Animistic sociology, by contrast, affirms these precepts: (1) our common-sense notions about the nature of human nature are valid; (2) these common-sense notions can and should serve as premises for the derivation of more elaborate sociological propositions. To many people it is a matter of common sense that human nature involves something more than the aspects science can study, and this extramaterial part includes a "will"— thought to be intrinsically immune to scientific analysis and prediction because it allegedly does not conform to the principle of inertia and now and then it does act as an unmoved mover.

A major obstacle to the abandonment of these animistic beliefs in favor of those affirmed by naturalism has been the habit of appraising theories by their supposed moral impact rather than their empirical validity. Fictions that seem to sustain traditional values are often preferred to truths that might corrode them. The struggle in sociology to separate cognition from evaluation has been difficult and has not been fully accomplished, though it has had some religious and philosophical as well as scientific precedents.

For the sake of cognitive accuracy, the naturalistic sociologist seeks to insulate his scientific role from his other roles. He strives to be thoroughly relativistic in his role as scientist, but he willingly lays aside the methodological tool of cultural relativism when acting in his nonscientific roles which entail value commitments. He believes it is not necessary to choose once and for all between ethical absolutism and ethical relativism as all-pervasive stances, though others have postulated the necessity of this choice.

The naturalistic sociologist is equally skeptical of other supraempirical postulates. For him, all that is real is observable or inferrable from observation. Observation is by means of the human senses, aided if necessary by appropriate instruments, so there is nothing real that does not involve matter and energy. On the basis of observation, naturalistic sociologists make cautious inferences. When they speak of such illata as "thought" or "motivation," they recognize the inferential character of these concepts. They do not avoid such concepts, but they reject the pretensions of the animistic sociologist to some kind of direct access to knowledge of illata. Naturalistic sociology assumes that human action, like all other events in nature, is patterned in accord with discoverable laws. The laws sociologists formulate are more or less accurate descriptions of invariant sequences. Laws do not cause events, but events are not uncaused—not even human choices.

If one dissents from sterile positivism, the conception of sociology as a "moral science" is not the only alternative. It is possible to seek explanations of social phenomena that do not involve the futile wordplay of animism.

Chapter Three

FUNCTIONAL ANALYSIS AND CAUSAL ANALYSIS

Sources of Confusion

The doctrines of functionalism tend to create confusion in regard to two of the points at issue between naturalistic and animistic sociology. These have to do with the second and third elements of naturalism—the temporal priority of causes and the axiom of inertia. Animism expects teleological explanations, at least of some classes of phenomena, whereas naturalism requires that events be explained in terms of antecedent or concomitant conditions. Functionalism beclouds the issue by speaking of "functions" in terms which at least seem to make final causes of them, though often they can be resolved into efficient causes if the language is carefully analyzed. Animism attributes change to the operation of will, which it defines as "free" or capricious, thereby making continuity problematic, whereas naturalism accepts the axiom of inertia and regards change as problematic. Functionalism confuses the issue by seeking to explain processes such as "pattern-maintenance" without always stipulating that social and cultural patterns require *active* maintenance only because of their exposure to disruptive forces.

The term "functionalism" has various shades of meaning, of course, and it would be well to sort them out before proceeding. In an extreme form, it can refer to the doctrine which denies "cultural survivals." By this doctrine, every practice and every social structure is assumed to be "functional," and if the function they serve is not obvious, then the doctrine may require attributing to them some subtle solidarity-maintenance function. I shall not be concerned directly with this type of functionalism here.

A milder kind of functionalism would have only a legitimate heuristic significance. By assuming that usually and in the long run, structures do not survive unless functional, one obtains the following broad paradigm for research: observe a structure and then be alert for its possible function(s) in the system of which it is a part. If this paradigm is tempered with the expectation that the quest may occasionally be abortive, then it may be relatively harmless and quite useful in leading the investigator into a heightened awareness of the interconnectedness of the parts of a social or cultural system. It might be better to speak of "functional analysis" rather than "functional*ism*" when this meaning is intended.

A third meaning of the term may or may not be linked to this second one, namely, the assumption that no explanation of social phenomena is complete without reference to their functions. Such an assumption is common among sociologists, even when they do not apply to themselves the label "functionalist." For some, it may derive respectability not only from the fact that it has been repeatedly articulated by renowned sociologists but also from the appearance of moderation. Less moderate is the assumption which may occasionally tempt those sociologists of animistic inclination, that explanation wholly in terms of functions is the *sine qua non* of sociology.

The Aristotelian Heritage

It will be recalled that Aristotle, over two thousand years ago, described four different kinds of "causes" to be sought in formulating a complete explanation of anything. These were: (1) material cause, (2) formal cause, (3) efficient cause, and (4) final cause. To explain, for example, this book, Aristotle would have said that we must know the nature of the materials of which it is manufactured, we must have an idea of the structure of the book, we must know of the acts of men which imposed that structure on those materials, and we must also know something of the purposes which caused them to do so.

With the advent of modern science, however, interest became focused on just one of these four categories—efficient causes. Formal and final causes were discarded as being inaccessible to experiment insofar as they might not be reducible to efficient causes, and material causes were taken for granted (i.e., not defined as "causes"). Only efficient causes were regarded as meriting scientific research.[1] From the point of view of naturalism, this change represents an abandonment of chimerical concepts.

For others less naturalistic in outlook, however, it has seemed to be an unwarranted narrowing of the range of inquiry. Since modern science has confirmed the validity of Aristotle's interest in efficient causes, it is felt that his other three types of cause ought not to be dismissed too lightly. Final causes, for example, deserve attention because in them Aristotle was merely "recognizing the seemingly teleological facts of life and mind" which require *some sort* of explanation. Any theory which ignores these is simply unrealistic, it is argued.[2] Whatever his early Platonic training, Aristotle in his later years was merely being legitimately empirical, so it is said, in refusing to shut his eyes to nature's purposiveness.[3]

If one does not begin with perception-slanting allegiance to Aristotelian thoughtways, however, the subject takes on quite a different aspect. What Aristotle seems to have done was this: he developed some concepts which were rather cogent for understanding the behavior of living things—as he and his contemporaries knew them. Then he made these concepts canonical for all inquiry. Nonliving things, too, were explained in teleological terms. Final causes were focal in Aristotle's theories. No cleavage between biology and other natural science was assumed in Greek science; *all* phenomena required explanations in terms that included final causes.[4] As a purposive being himself, Aristotle projected purpose onto the inanimate cosmos. It was easier to do this in his day, and harder to recognize that this was what one was doing, because so much less valid knowledge of the inanimate world then existed. Whereas modern science would describe the thermonuclear reactions occurring in the sun and would then include among the consequences of these reactions the warming of the earth by radiant energy, an Aristotelian type of explanation would consist of asserting that the sun shines "in order to" warm the earth. Or instead of saying that when rain falls on plowed land it tends to make crops grow or to erode away the topsoil, the Aristotelian would give an explanation in terms of final causes, attributing growth or erosion to the rain as its purposes (or to the heavens from which the rain "was sent"—rather than from which it descended).

Most of us today are sophisticated enough to reject such explanations of warmth, growth, or erosion. But there are still strong temptations to cling to this mode of thought in regard to human actions and the activities

[1] Mario Bunge, *Causality*. Cleveland: Meridian Books, The World Publishing Company, 1963, p. 32.
[2] For such an argument, see James Bissett Pratt, *Naturalism*. New Haven, Conn.: Yale University Press, 1939, p. 24.
[3] *Ibid.*, pp. 27–28.
[4] Ernest Nagel, *The Structure of Science*. New York: Harcourt, Brace & World, Inc., 1961, p. 401.

of human social organizations. Proposals to treat these areas, too, in naturalistic terms, abandoning final causes and concentrating on efficient causes, tend to be viewed as radical and misguided. The irony is that the perpetuation of animistic thoughtways in this area is taken to represent caution. Where inquiry has been pursued to great lengths along scientific lines, animistic thoughtways have been clearly discredited. Yet it is those thoughtways we "cautiously" fall back on in the areas of which we know too little. It has been suggested that we must be content in sociology with functional explanations for the time being because we do not yet know enough about certain social phenomena to go beyond functional analysis and formulate deterministic explanations.[5]

Sociologists were warned of the folly in this several generations ago. Ward said we should no longer regard as "wise conservatism" the dualistic tendency to assign natural and genetic explanations only to those relatively simple phenomena whose causes have been ascertained, while insisting on supernatural or teleological explanations for all else. Rather than discretion, he regarded this as "intellectual deficiency, by which the grasp of truth is enfeebled by the fear of consequences and the voice of reason muffled by conventionalism."[6] Where we don't yet know efficient causes we have no warrant for imputing final causes.

There remain to this day those who imagine they are being generous in conceding to naturalism that it has an appropriate but restricted place, and then demanding that it leave certain other domains of inquiry untouched. Stark, for example, has admitted that Aristotle may have overreached himself in interpreting nature teleologically, but insists he was right and reasonable in such interpretations of man. The influence of purpose on human behavior "cannot be doubted," he says.[7]

Similarly, Furfey decries the identification of cause in general with efficient cause alone. He insists that sociologists can and do investigate all four Aristotelian causal types. Demographic studies tell us of the raw material of society. Studies of social structure reveal the formal causes. Research on social change, he feels, is often concerned with efficient causes. And he regards social psychological studies of motivation as largely concerned with final causes.[8] Were there no misunderstandings here of the

[5] See, for example, Harry Johnson, *Sociology: A Systematic Introduction.* New York: Harcourt, Brace & World, Inc., 1960, p. 647.

[6] Lester F. Ward, *Dynamic Sociology.* New York: D. Appleton & Co., 1883, vol. 1, p. 412. Cf. Don Martindale, *The Nature and Types of Sociological Theory.* Boston: Houghton Mifflin Company, 1960, p. 537. Martindale gives the appearance of caution which Ward decried, by assuming that sociological functionalism is pregnant with theoretical significance when he says, "Sociological functionalism is too recent a development to have revealed the full panoply of its potentialities."

[7] Werner Stark, *The Fundamental Forms of Social Thought.* New York: Fordham University Press, 1963, p. 19.

[8] Paul Hanly Furfey, *The Scope and Method of Sociology.* New York: Harper & Row, Publishers, Incorporated, 1953, p. 71.

actual content and import of the work of demographers, organizational analysts, students of social change, or social psychologists, Furfey's concern for distinguishing the four types of cause would apparently have led anyway to an absurd conclusion. For he claims that sociology:[9]

is actually in a better position to study causality than most of the natural sciences. Sociologists have the enormous advantage of studying their subject matter, so to speak, from within. We are ourselves the stuff of which society is made, the material cause of social groupings. We have a peculiar appreciation of the structure of society because it is our own creation. We can, and often do, function as efficient causes of social entities. A man may organize a debating society, for example. Above all, we are peculiarly at home in the realm of final causes. When a physicist is asked why a stone falls to the ground, he may talk of gravitation or quote the law of falling bodies or discuss Einstein's relativity, but the intimate nature of the phenomenon eludes him. The sociologist is in a much better position when he is asked why this individual is socially mobile upward or why this pathological thief steals as he does. We understand human motivation by experience. It is our peculiar territory. We know it at first hand.

To take Furfey's contentions seriously, one would have to conclude that physics must indeed be scientifically retarded in comparison with sociology! With our "enormous advantage" we must surely have amassed a far greater wealth of verified propositions than the disadvantaged physicist who finds the "intimate nature" of his phenomena eluding him.

Instead, the truth of the matter would seem to be that it is precisely this firsthand knowledge of human motivation that has misled us. It misled Aristotle. It took two thousand years for scientific thought to become emancipated from the Aristotelian misconceptions which mistook the obvious for the truth. So far the emancipation is incomplete, too. It is no longer obvious to us, as it was to Aristotle, that the stars are "motivated" to move in "perfect" (i.e., circular) paths because that is their "nature" as celestial objects. But we have not completely outgrown the tendency to elevate to the status of sociological postulates certain propositions about human nature that seem obvious to us because we are "inside our subject matter." Surely we ought to have gained since Aristotle's time a healthy respect for the fallibility of human perception and conceptualization.

Even in those branches of natural science where quasi-teleological language persists, the meaning has changed so that less and less attention is paid to final causes in the strict Aristotelian sense. There are still explanations in biology and psychology that sound teleological. It cannot be stressed too strongly, though, that such formulations do not vindicate animism. They merely show that rather than discard familiar linguistic forms, modern science has altered their meaning and made them effectively naturalistic. Teleology has begun to be deprived of its overtones

[9] *Ibid.*, pp. 72–73.

of supernaturalism. It has been shown to be often insufficient, and sometimes replaceable by other types of explanation.[10] Moreover, even where
concepts of "purpose" have been retained, their study need not be confined to philosophical analysis. Recent biological work shows that for total
organisms as well as for isolated chemical or physical systems, rigorous
mathematical analysis of their behavior is possible. Goal-directed behavior
is not a mystical process but a property of material systems organized
along certain lines. As such, it is subject to scientific study.[11] Its study
has been facilitated by the translation into nonteleological terms of biological statements using such phrases as "the function of," "so as to," or
"in order that."[12]

The idea that causes may be of four types, and in particular that final
causes have commensurate status with efficient causes, may be put another
way. From antiquity men have felt that whatever happens happens for
a purpose, and the concept of causation has been confused by this conviction of universal purposiveness.[13] In sociology, it is often taken for
granted that without a purpose, no action would occur. Therefore, to know
why an action occurred, we must know the actor's purposes. MacIver,
for example, admitted that "why" questions in the physical sciences always
get resolved into questions of "how" things happen, but insisted that sociological "why" questions, concerned with objectives or goals, cannot be
so resolved. Because they can't, the juncture of why and how remains
enigmatic, he said.[14]

In contrast to Furfey's claim that sociologists enjoy a peculiar advantage, MacIver pointed to peculiar difficulties besetting the sociological
investigation of causes. "The factors we invoke embarrassingly combine
the universal elements of physical causation and the human elements of
teleological causation."[15] It is not clear why such a combination had to
be deemed embarrassing, unless MacIver meant that the task of the sociologist is more complex and hence more difficult than the task of the
physical scientist. Durkheim apparently felt no embarrassment in stating
a similar methodological maxim, and was not misled by it into accepting
animistic assumptions. He noted that in explaining a social phenomenon
"we must seek separately the efficient cause which produces it and the
function it fulfils."[16] Since writing this, Durkheim has come to be regarded
as something of a patron saint of functionalism. It seems likely, however,

[10] Bunge, *op. cit.*, p. 303.
[11] William S. Beck, *Modern Science and the Nature of Life*. Garden City, N.Y.: Anchor
Books, Doubleday & Company, Inc., 1961, pp. 277–278.
[12] Nagel, *op. cit.*, p. 403.
[13] Beck, *op. cit.*, p. 188.
[14] Robert M. MacIver, *Social Causation*. Boston: Ginn and Company, 1942, p. 16.
[15] *Ibid.*, p. 74.
[16] Emile Durkheim, *The Rules of the Sociological Method* (tr. Sarah A. Solovay and
John H. Mueller; ed. George E. G. Catlin). New York: The Free Press of Glencoe,
1950, p. 95.

that he intended an approach quite different from that which has come to be called "functionalist." He was *not* saying that we must explain a social phenomenon by claiming it to be caused by the function it serves. Just the opposite: he was saying that we should *distinguish between* efficient causes on the one hand and functions on the other. We must seek the efficient cause which produces a social fact *separately* from the function it fulfills. By being made to seem less naturalistic than he was, Durkheim has been done an injustice by those who persistently distort his methodological views in the belief that they are adhering to them.

Functionalism and Biology

From Comte's time to the present, repeated attempts have been made to build sociology on the basis of biology. This has been one of the sources of functionalism's plausibility. Among the reasons Comte thought sociology must be allied to the older science of biology, he included what he called "the positive version of the dogma of final causes." If the study of purposes was important in the analysis of individual behavior, he felt it was all the more significant for *social* science. The word "necessary" could have two philosophical meanings, he noted. It could mean "inevitable" and it could mean "indispensable," and in sociology he thought it should deliberately be taken to mean both.[17] Thus Comte took what amounted to a functionalist position, and in his quest for models in biology to incorporate into his new science of sociology, he apparently proceeded on the basis of Aristotelian assumptions.

Again, MacIver justified his insistence that social causation involves something more than the processes amenable to naturalistic analysis by pointing out that we are studying living organisms. It is through the interdependent functioning of its parts that an organism can function as a living unity. Therefore, he argued, what we must be interested in discovering is the *functional significance* of components and actions, and our questions cannot be usefully put in physicalistic terms. In addition to sequence, concomitance, and interaction, we are interested in function—which he conceived as a distinct category.[18]

Organicist thought acquired its justification in Stark's mind also from the resemblance between social systems and biological entities. An organism and a society are both "systems of differentiated and integrated structure and function."[19] Whether these more recent writers would have been so drawn to biological models without the nineteenth-century use of the

[17] Auguste Comte, *The Positive Philosophy* (tr. Harriet Martineau). New York: Calvin Blanchard, 1856, p. 489.
[18] MacIver, *op. cit.*, pp. 13–14.
[19] Stark, *op. cit.*, p. 34.

organismic analogy by Herbert Spencer we cannot know. But if there is less tendency now to say, as Spencer virtually did, that society *is* an organism and *because of this* the laws of biology can be generalized to sociology, still there are hazards. The appeal to biology is often made with insufficient biological sophistication. Animistic propositions in sociology are thought to be supported by parallel propositions in biology not because biological science really does support them, but because animistic concepts are more easily projected by social theorists into biology than into physics.

This becomes evident when some social theorists begin to talk about evolution, and reveal their misunderstanding of it even in the biological realm. Stark, for instance, argues that there is a natural affinity in sociology between organicist thought and evolutionism because growth is characteristic of living things. If society is a living thing, he says, it must be subject to processes of growth.[20] It ought to be obvious that evolution is not the same thing as the growth of an organism, but it is not obvious to Stark. Nor is he the first to commit this error. The Social Darwinists often supposed that evolutionary principles must apply to society *because society is an organism.* They thereby revealed their failure to understand that Darwin had not formulated a principle by which organisms change as they pass through their life spans, but a principle by which species change as they pass through a series of many generations. All organisms exhibit processes of maturation, and some organisms even go through processes of metamorphosis, but neither of these is what biologists mean by evolution. The Social Darwinists were less guilty of injecting biology into sociology than of projecting false sociological assumptions onto biology, to be used as a basis for their ostensible legitimation in social thought.

Objections are sometimes raised against borrowing models from other sciences on the ground that they just have nothing to offer to sociology. Sociology is *sui generis*, we are told, and only wastes its time when it looks to older disciplines for concepts or hypotheses, let alone for conclusions. In Chapter 9, I shall examine the antireductionism taboo more fully. Suffice it to say here that I do not believe a rigid sociological embargo on concepts or hypotheses of extrasociological origin is called for. In the case of biology, there have been problems analogous to some which confront sociologists; examining the manner in which biologists have solved them may offer useful guidance to sociological research and theory construction. More misguided than such a universal embargo, however, is the notion that if sociology is going to import concepts and hypotheses at all, it can only legitimately do so from certain specified sciences and not from others. A concept borrowed from biology is just as truly borrowed as one obtained from physics or chemistry, yet the biology concept is looked upon with kindlier receptivity by many sociologists. Scientifi-

[20] *Ibid.*, p. 56.

cally, it must gain acceptance or be rejected ultimately on empirical grounds. It should not be accorded privileged status just on the assumption that biology is "closer" to sociology than is physics.

Arguments for functional analysis sometimes commit precisely this fallacy. They seem to assume a privileged status for concepts of biological origin. We must not seek to eliminate final causes from sociology, we are told, because the biologist has not been able to eliminate them from his discipline. Living beings are said to be "biased toward self-maintenance," and though they can also be studied as physicochemical systems, their study is incomplete without recognition of the purposive aspects of their behavior.[21] Perhaps so, but it *does not follow* that social systems must therefore also be studied in terms of a self-maintenance bias and that all social behavior must be attributed to purposes. It does not, of course, follow that purpose and self-maintenance are *absent* from social behavior either. The point is that whatever concepts and hypotheses we borrow from biology (whether they have or have not remained central to biological thought) must gain acceptance in sociology through their utility and not through their ancestry.

We ought to be particularly cautious about this because some of the notions incorporated into sociology from biology have since ceased to have their original meaning or importance in biology, so that the pedigree which gained them entrée concealed their illegitimacy. This seems to be the case with respect to the doctrine of final causes. As biology has advanced, its apparently teleological explanations have increasingly been reduced to other terms; yet it has often been their supposed indispensability in biology that justified their retention in sociology.

The impetus to erect sociological superstructures on biological foundations has come not only from social scientists but from biological scientists as well. While the latter may not make some of the errors of projection that have been committed by sociological importers of ostensibly biological concepts and hypotheses, their own conceptual exports may contain other errors based on mistaken sociological notions. An example of a biological scientist seeking to export biological ideas to sociology was Walter B. Cannon, author of the well-known book on *The Wisdom of the Body*. In an epilogue he suggested some tentative sociological lessons to be drawn by analogy from his studies of homeostasis. Some of them were in general accord with conclusions that had been reached by Durkheim in his analysis of division of labor, though Cannon did not say so, and may not have been aware that any of his tentative hypotheses had already been explored by sociologists. It is to Cannon's credit that he did not argue that certain things *must* be true of social systems because they

[21] See Yervant H. Krikorian, "A Naturalistic View of Mind," in Yervant H. Krikorian (ed.), *Naturalism and the Human Spirit*. New York: Columbia University Press, 1944, pp. 250–251.

are true of organisms.[22] He only suggested more cautiously that what he had shown to be true of an organism *might* also be true of a society, and that the possibility was worth investigating.

If it is unwise to argue too single-mindedly from similarities between social and biological phenomena, it may be just as unwise to exaggerate the differences. One of the facts of social life that has most impressed modern sociologists and anthropologists is the conspicuous variety of mores from one culture to another. Sumner asserted that "the mores can make anything right," and the literature of anthropology often appears to be an endless string of anecdotes showing how infinitely varied human behavior may be in different places on earth. Nagel has suggested that this is a point of sharp contrast between social and biological entities. One is unlikely to find, he says, that the lungs of one organism perform the functions performed by the stomach in another, or vice versa. In societies, however, exchange of functions by different structures is common and can be very nearly as extensive as this, he claims.[23] I will not discuss here the tendency of sociologists to exaggerate the extent and overstress the importance of cultural variability, but when we look to biology for our models we may fall into the opposite error by assuming a closer correspondence between structure and function than is true even in biology. While one organism may not *entirely* turn over to its stomach the functions performed in another organism by the lungs, *some* substitution of this sort does occur. Witness, in man, the occasional substitution of esophageal speech in cases where vocal cords have been damaged or surgically removed. Here the stomach rather than the lungs must supply the sound-producing air. Or apart from such culturally contrived substitutions, witness the grasping function being variously performed—by hands (in apes and monkeys), by forepaws (in squirrels), by noses (in elephants), by prehensile tails (in opossums), and by jaws (in a wide variety of animals). The point is that there is no biological warrant for a sociological assumption that a given structure must always have the same function or that a given function must always involve the same structure. If any such hypothesis were entertained by sociologists, it would have to stand or fall on its empirical sociological merits and not on the basis of biology.

It might be argued, of course, that in order to grasp things, an appendage must be able to wrap itself around them, whether the appendage be attached to a forelimb, the face, the posterior end of the spine, or elsewhere. But if such a consideration were cited in support of the notion

[22] Walter B. Cannon, *The Wisdom of the Body*. New York: W. W. Norton & Company, Inc., 1932, pp. 287–306. However, Cannon's epilogue was cited by Merton as an instance of "the fruitless extremes to which even a distinguished mind is driven once he sets about to draw *substantive* analogies and homologies between biological organisms and social systems." See Robert K. Merton, *Social Theory and Social Structure*, rev. ed. New York: The Free Press of Glencoe, 1957, p. 48.
[23] Nagel, *op. cit.*, p. 534.

that there are intrinsic connections between a given set of structures and a given set of functions, it would not be an argument from biology but an argument from mechanics. Those who insist that sociology *must* use certain concepts because biology has allegedly found them indispensable are usually out of sympathy with mechanical explanations. Apparently it is not possible to practice a *consistent* preference for importing concepts from biology while excluding any from such other disciplines as physical mechanics.

Functionalism and Anthropology

No attempt will be made here to give a full account of the development or prevalence of functional thought in anthropology. I do want to consider, however, the possibility that anthropologists are susceptible to the same theoretical shortsightedness as sociologists and could thus reinforce rather than correct our conceptual errors.

Social anthropologists have been described by Stark as a group of researchers who are "realistic" and who have felt a strong attraction to organismic conceptions of the social and cultural systems they study. Though he does also use the word "realistic" to mean merely the opposite of "nominalistic," the full context seems to indicate that here Stark means to say that social anthropologists are empirically oriented.[24] There is no doubt that the concept of function has been widely used in anthropological literature, and that literature is certainly based on observation, though it has generally not been concerned with niceties of sampling or with problems of quantification and measurement. Even the distinction between firsthand observation by a trained observer and secondhand acceptance of the verbal reports of a native informant is often neglected. It is possible that the lack of concern with these matters has facilitated the popularity of functional analysis among anthropologists. At any rate, Stark commends Malinowski and Radcliffe-Brown for abandoning materialism, and he generalizes to the effect that the soundness of functionalism depends on its being pursued in the spirit of Aristotle and St. Thomas Aquinas, rather than in the manner of Spencer and others.[25]

Because he deals with exotic cultures, the social anthropologist is forced, Stark says, to be meticulous and detailed in his descriptions. He is, therefore, more scientific than other social scientists, in Stark's judgment. This, together with the anthropologist's skeptical reaction to the premature system building of the nineteenth-century theorists, leads Stark to the view that anthropological adherence to the functional approach justifies it and

[24] Stark, *op. cit.*, p. 76.
[25] *Ibid.*, pp. 83–84.

ought to motivate other social scientists to emulate the anthropologist in this respect.[26] Stark has not shown that anthropology has been able to make important discoveries by using functional concepts that could not have been made with another conceptual schema. What needs to be noted, then, is that Stark has presented a thinly veiled argument *ad hominem.* It legitimates a conceptual scheme not in terms of its successful solution of theoretical problems or its demonstrated empirical relevance, but in terms of the merits of other persons who have used it.

Because the boundary between anthropology and sociology is nebulous, there is some plausibility to the argument that the sociologist should seriously consider adopting a methodology *found useful and workable* by anthropologists. But it remains to be demonstrated that anthropology has made discoveries by using functional concepts that it could not have made at least as readily without them. The possibility ought to be considered that instead of this, the basis for anthropologists' preference for such concepts, like the preference of some sociologists, arises from the spurious affinity for biology. If sociologists have been fond of borrowing concepts from biology because anthropomorphic meanings could be projected into them, perhaps their adoption by anthropologists has had a similar basis. It would do sociology little good to increase its caution regarding the importation of concepts from biology only to have them freely enter in disguise through the anthropological back door left incautiously open.

The Issue of Chronology

The question whether events can be caused by antecedent or concomitant circumstances only or can also be influenced in the present by future states (final causes) has been obfuscated by functional analysis. The term "function" refers to the consequences of an act or of an institution which are adaptive for the system in which that act or institution is included. A "functional explanation," then, purports to account for acts in terms of their effects rather than in terms of efficient causes. In some instances this is an innocent confusion of terminology, as I will show later, arising from a misunderstanding of the mechanism of evolution. But sometimes it has been deliberately stated by functionalists that causes need not be temporally prior to their effects.

Radcliffe-Brown contended that one general obstacle to the development of what he deemed a natural science of society was "the historical fallacy." By this he meant the assumption that historical explanation is the only valid kind of explanation. Such an assumption was widely held, he said regretfully, by anthropologists in America and elsewhere in the

[26] *Ibid.,* p. 91.

world.[27] Of course, it is true that the way in which an institution is now operating can be studied apart from any attempt to trace its history all the way back to its origin as a recognizable entity, and it is true that this has not always been understood. But Radcliffe-Brown seemed to be claiming something more. He seemed to be saying that we ought not to be preoccupied with the past tense in seeking the causes of present phenomena. One can hardly account for present phenomena, however, without taking into account at least the *immediate* past.

A natural science of anthropology or sociology could hardly dispense with causality—the assumption that all phenomena are determined by antecedents in a lawful (i.e., regular) manner.[28] MacIver said that causation "always expresses a relation of antecedent and consequent."[29] Functional analysis sometimes at least *seems* to deny this, by saying that some things are caused by their consequences rather than by their antecedents. Merton has quoted Malinowski as holding that functional theories try to explain anthropological facts "by their function, by the part which they play within the integral system of culture, by the manner in which they are related to each other within the system. . . ."[30]

In spite of efforts to guard against it, functional analyses seem to degenerate into teleological explanations. This appears to be one of the hazards in using functionalist terminology. To illustrate: Bredemeier and Stephenson have pointed out that one consequence of the incest taboo is the prevention of sexual rivalry between nuclear family members. Noting that this could be called a "function" of the incest taboo, they went on to caution that nothing has necessarily been implied about people's ideas and attitudes when the sociologist has described some function of their ways of behaving. People avoid incest without giving any more thought to preventing rivalry among family members than the heart gives to its task of pumping nutriments to the body's cells.[31] Yet later in the same book, Bredemeier and Stephenson "call attention to one matter that seems probably a sufficient explanation" of the incest taboo. They seem to assume that laws only forbid acts that are otherwise tempting, and argue that prevention of incest is highly dependent on normative and legal proscription in the absence of any instinctive horror of it. Then they note that the incest prohibition has the additional function for society of providing individuals with an incentive for establishing emotional ties with some group other than their own nuclear family.[32] The social impor-

[27] A. R. Radcliffe-Brown, *A Natural Science of Society.* New York: The Free Press of Glencoe, 1957, p. 146.
[28] Cf. Jacques Rueff, *From the Physical to the Social Sciences* (tr. Herman Green). Baltimore: The Johns Hopkins Press, 1929, p. 6.
[29] MacIver, *op. cit.*, p. 43.
[30] Merton, *op. cit.*, p. 22.
[31] Harry C. Bredemeier and Richard M. Stephenson, *The Analysis of Social Systems.* New York: Holt, Rinehart and Winston, Inc., 1962, pp. 43, 45.
[32] *Ibid.*, p. 180.

tance of interfamily ties is thus said to "explain" the rule from which such ties result.

Parsons's functional explanation of the same taboo was almost obviously teleological. He argued that erotic gratification was indispensable as a factor in the socialization process, but would be highly disruptive if unregulated. Noting the occurrence of an incest taboo in all societies, he suggested such a taboo is universal "because it constitutes a main focus of the *regulation* of the erotic factor."[33] This amounts to saying it occurs because of what it does. He went on to admit that this was a functional argument and left unsolved the question of "how incest taboos come into being," but claimed that after functional analysis has illuminated the manifold involvement of a norm in the life of a going society and has shown the interdependence of social systems and personality processes, the significance of "the problem of origins" is lessened.[34] In short, explicit attention to final causes was presumed to lessen the salience of efficient causes.

George Peter Murdock has provided another instance of a preoccupation with final causes which tends to foreclose consideration of efficient-cause hypotheses. In an analysis of patterns of cross-cousin marriage in various societies he cited tabulations which can be stated in the following form. Among 11 societies permitting premarital sex relations between a young male and his father's sister's daughter, none forbid marriage between them. Among 39 societies forbidding premarital sex relations between them, 37 forbid them to marry each other. Similarly, among 13 societies permitting premarital sex relations between a young male and his mother's brother's daughter, none forbid them to marry, while among 38 societies forbidding them to have premarital intercourse, 35 forbid them to marry.[35] In efficient-cause terms, such findings might be explained by noting that premarital sexual contacts may lead to marriage; if premarital intercourse between certain persons does not occur, marriage between them is rendered less likely than if it did occur and when marriage between two categories of persons is very rare such marriage comes to be deemed abnormal. But instead of relating the events to each other in their natural temporal sequence, Murdock offered the formula: "Future marriages may be said to cast their shadows before them."[36]

Only if it is assumed that all causes can in principle be analyzed into efficient causes can the flow of time have any meaning. If we insist that living things are subject to a different kind of causation than nonliving things, being influenced by the future as well as by the past, then we

[33] Talcott Parsons, "The Incest Taboo in Relation to Social Structure and Socialization of the Child," *British Journal of Sociology*, 5 (June, 1954), p. 115.
[34] *Ibid.*
[35] George Peter Murdock, *Social Structure*. New York: The Macmillan Company, 1949, p. 272.
[36] *Ibid.*, p. 271.

deprive time of its directionality.[37] This could be disastrous for our science. If we destroy the directionality of time we destroy one fundamental basis for deciding whether A caused B or not. If we have found A and B correlated, and still wonder whether A has caused B or B has caused A, one factor in deciding this issue is an inspection of their time sequence. If A occurred later than B, we ordinarily suppose that it could not have been a cause of B. If we are trying to discriminate between various alternative hypothetical causes of B, one way to eliminate some of them and reduce the list of candidates is to consider chronology. If A occurred after B, while C preceded B, this does not suffice to prove that C caused B, but we ordinarily do take it as sufficient evidence that at least A did not cause B. If our choice had been narrowed to just A and C because of other considerations, then chronology would suffice for the remaining decision.

Only in the case of so-called "purposive" behavior, where we are still in the habit of invoking teleological explanations, do we deprive ourselves of this tool. But this deprivation is unnecessary. A number of writers have noted that the "purposes" which motivate human action consist of *present images* of future states, not the future states themselves.[38] Some who admit this at one occasion fail to remember it at another when they are arguing for the necessity of something more in social science than is required in natural science. MacIver, for example, notes that it is only as a "projection" prior to the physical process from which it arises that an "effect" can cause the behavior that causes it. Yet this does not stop him from citing such foresight as indicative of a fundamental distinction between causal connections in the social world and causal connections in the physical world.[39]

Strictly speaking, functionalists deny that "functions" are equivalent to "purposes." They thus claim *not* to be delving into the Aristotelian realm of final causes. Nevertheless, the language of functionalism at least strongly suggests that in a special domain inhabited by social scientists, consequences somehow cause preceding events, rather than vice versa as elsewhere. The attempt to distinguish functions from purposes, commendable as it may be on other criteria, is largely beside the point as far as this issue is concerned. According to Kingsley Davis, who has tried to show that functional analysis and good sociological analysis are one and the same thing, functionalists regard teleology as either alien to their point of view or as an accidental fault. The language functionalists use makes it difficult for them to defend their work against the charge that it is

[37] Cf. Hans Reichenbach, *The Rise of Scientific Philosophy*. Berkeley, Calif.: University of California Press, 1951, p. 194.
[38] For example, see *ibid.*, and MacIver, *op. cit.*, pp. 8–9.
[39] *Ibid.*, p. 8.

teleological, though in Davis's view they do try hard to avoid the teleological fallacy.[40] He has pointed out that the distinction between manifest and latent functions is contrary to the dictionary definition of teleology. In functional theory, he claimed, incest taboos or magical rites are not said to occur as a result of *perception* of their functions by their practitioners.[41] But I think Davis has it just backward; he has defended functional theory by emphasizing one of its chief confusions.

Functional explanations of magical rites or of incest taboos remain virtually teleological if they fail to specify *how* these phenomena can be caused by their unperceived social consequences. Davis tried to solve this problem by attributing to functional analysis the principle that "the unrecognized social consequences of an action [lead], by their unrecognized effect on conditions, to the continuous reinforcement or minimization of that action in the society. . . ."[42] What he meant by "reinforcement" is not altogether clear. If he had psychological learning theory in mind, then he has put the functionalist in the position of saying that people are more likely to repeat acts that are rewarding to the society even if as individuals they are not direct beneficiaries and are oblivious of the societal benefits. This represents severe stretching of the theory of operant conditioning.

Two things can be said of this interpretation. First, if stated with due care, it would restore efficient causation to the center of the stage. The reinforcing consequences of an act make its recurrence in the future more likely, not its occurrence in the past. But the functional terminology does more to obscure than to reveal this. Second, there is at least one conspicuous instance in which a sociological study has shown that the unrecognized consequences of an act fall far short of fostering its recurrence in the way that recognized consequences do. I have in mind Lindesmith's study of opiate addiction.

Like some of the functionalists, Lindesmith took pains to distinguish "cause" from "motive," and said he was not investigating motives.[43] By the method of analytic induction applied to intensive case studies of opiate addicts, he came to the conclusion that informed recognition of withdrawal symptoms followed by renewed use of the drug with the intention of relieving these symptoms were the factors invariably associated with the onset of addiction.[44] Addiction does not occur, he said, when the withdrawal symptoms are experienced but remain unrecognized by, say, a hospital patient after morphine injections are medically administered

[40] Kingsley Davis, "The Myth of Functional Analysis as a Special Method in Sociology and Anthropology," *American Sociological Review*, 24 (December, 1959), pp. 758, 765.
[41] *Ibid.*, p. 765, and Merton, *op. cit.*, p. 51.
[42] Davis, *op. cit.*, p. 766.
[43] Alfred R. Lindesmith, *Opiate Addiction*. Bloomington, Ind.: Principia Press, 1947, p. 16.
[44] *Ibid.*, pp. 69, 139, *et passim*.

and then discontinued. It is recognition followed by renewed use that quickly brings on addiction.[45] The addict's desperate preoccupation with maintaining access to his drug arises from his "apprehension of the consequences of deprivation." The physiological consequences themselves are not sufficient without social definition to make him organize his life around the process of acquiring the drug.[46] To suppose that a *social* system can be organized around certain high-priority activities whose functions are not recognized by the participants is a large supposition.

It appears, then, that functional analyses *can* be translated into efficient cause explanations, but preference for functionalist terminology appears to be associated with predilection for explanation by final causes. As Davis has acknowledged, words like "function," "latent," etc., "are treacherous for the same reason that they are handy." This is because the language of functionalism "is peculiarly close to the purposive and moralistic reasoning of ordinary discourse. . . ."[47]

Functionalism and Evolution

If functional analysis were admitted to be an aspect of evolutionary theory, it would be important to distinguish function from purpose. Natural selection is not purposive; it does not involve final causes, but it does discriminate between more functional and less functional traits. Structural change in successive generations can be accounted for by noting differences in the relative effectiveness of alternative structures in the performance of functions for the system in question. The functionally less effective structure tends to be eliminated, and natural selection increases the proportionate prevalence of the more effective structure in subsequent generations. This happens because of the environmental circumstances to which the system must adapt if it is to survive. Environment provides the efficient causes by which evolution occurs in a manner which we call "natural selection."

There is a limited and elliptic sense, then, in which a thing can be "caused by its consequences." By filling in the ellipsis, a naturalistic explication of this limited case ought to make it quite clear that no final causes are involved, as such. It should also become clear that the tendency of functionalist literature to sound as if events are being explained in terms of final causes stems from neglect by the functionalists of the connection between functional analysis and evolutionary processes. For a going system, the function of a given structure or pattern of behavior

[45] *Ibid.*, p. 165.
[46] *Ibid.*, p. 81.
[47] Davis, *op. cit.*, p. 763.

may be said to be the consequences of that structure or behavior which contribute somehow to the system's survival. If the system survives, then either *it* continues to manifest that structure or behavior, or its progeny do. Such *later manifestations* of the given structure or behavior pattern may correctly be said to have been *caused by the consequences of earlier instances of such structure or behavior.*

Survival of the system has to have been included among the consequences of the earlier instances of a given structure or behavior for present instances to be explicable in functional terms. Only by taking account of its survival and *assuming that a surviving system continues to behave in the way that it has been behaving* (from which survival resulted), or *tends to bring forth progeny like itself,* can we arrive at an explanation of structural features or behavioral tendencies in functional terms. Thus, correctly understood, functional explanations require the inertial axiom of naturalism, as well as a frame of reference that is longitudinal with regard to time. Functional analysis is truly explanatory only for evolutionary sequences. The evolutionary sequences may be only implicit; that is, a present structure may be explained in an abbreviated way by describing the contribution it makes to the survival of the system containing it *now,* without referring explicitly to the past survival of that system or systems ancestral to it. But if, in addition to omitting explicit mention of the evolutionary sequence, the longitudinal character of functional explanation is actually denied, then functional explanation becomes patently non-naturalistic.

There have been such denials. Davis has said that functionalism was born of rebellion against evolutionism.[48] Malinowski, in particular, was fighting against both evolutionary theory and the analysis of culture trait diffusion. These two approaches had dominated anthropological thought, leaving little room for investigations of societies as going concerns. Malinowski used the name "functionalism" to carve out such a niche in anthropological inquiry, and it was quickly adopted by sociologists as well as anthropologists.[49] But it is more important in the present context to examine whether functional analysis continues to reject or sidestep the evolutionary framework than to know whether such avoidance was its birthright. Merton's work may be inspected with this question in mind.

There is a clear naturalistic inclination in Merton's writing. In challenging the postulate that every existing cultural item performs some vital function and is thus indispensable, Merton wrote that this was "a problem for investigation, not a conclusion in advance of investigation."[50] Such assertions crop up again and again in his chapter on "Manifest and Latent Functions," and even provide one of his justifications for paying explicit

[48] *Ibid.,* p. 761.
[49] *Ibid.,* p. 769.
[50] Merton, *op. cit.,* p. 32.

attention to functions that are unrecognized or latent.[51] If, in spite of this inclination, the connection between functional analysis and natural selection eluded Merton, this would suggest that there is something misleading in the concepts employed in such analysis.

Merton noted that the postulate of universal functionalism (all cultural items serve vital functions) was a rejoinder to the idea of cultural survivals. The postulate had sometimes led to imputing to seemingly functionless survivals nothing more than the function of "preserving the familiar, of maintaining a tradition." Kluckhohn had imputed such a function to coat-sleeve buttons in Western societies. Merton regarded such imputations as worthless. When all that is being said is that the function of conformity to an established pattern is to enable the conformist to avoid sanctions for nonconformity, the statement is true but trivial. It is a sterile use of the concept of function. It does not add anything to a mere straightforward description of the practice or the artifact in question.[52]

The inertial axiom, of course, would dispel this issue. Survivals would not be regarded as problematic. Patterned action would simply be expected to persist until altered by some social force. Functional analysis denies that survivals are just that—survivals. It regards the persistence of any culture trait as problematic, requiring explanation. Naturalism asks why an item stops surviving, rather than why it continues.

One of Merton's contributions to functional analysis has been a strong emphasis on the search for functional equivalents or functional alternatives. In every discipline that has employed functional analysis, he said, the concept of functional alternatives has repeatedly emerged.[53] Apparently the postulate of indispensability of existing forms, rejected by Merton, has been tacitly held *at first* by all such disciplines, each of which has subsequently found it misleading. Has the initial error each time been due to the nebulous boundary between teleology and functionalism? The common frontier with teleology was acknowledged by Merton, along with the reduction to absurdity which threatened sociology if the border were to be crossed by adopting the indispensability postulate.[54]

Merton himself seemed inadvertently to cross the boundary by another route. In explaining political bossism in functional terms, he noted the existence of constitutional blocks to the centralization of political power in the United States, but pointed to social needs for such concentration. Then he generalized that "the functional deficiencies of the official structure *generate* an alternative (unofficial) structure to fulfill existing needs somewhat more effectively."[55] His choice of a verb implying determination rather than facilitation suggests that this hypothesis involves final causes.

[51] *Ibid.*, pp. 63ff.
[52] *Ibid.*, p. 31.
[53] *Ibid.*, p. 34.
[54] *Ibid.*, p. 38.
[55] *Ibid.*, p. 73. (My italics.)

Merton further amplified it by saying that "in a prevalently market society, we should expect appropriate enterprises to arise whenever there is a market demand for certain goods or services."[56] Such a statement presupposes the technical feasibility of such enterprises. It is tantamount to saying that necessity (rather than a reservoir of knowledge) is the mother of invention.

Two pages later, Merton offered as "a basic theorem" the following: ". . . any attempt to eliminate an existing social structure without providing adequate alternative structures for fulfilling the functions previously fulfilled by the abolished organization is doomed to failure."[57] Inadvertently (I suppose) he had reaffirmed the postulate of universal functionalism which he had earlier rejected and called unnecessary to functional analysis. That is, he had implicitly assumed that the abolished structure *had* a function. With the best of intentions, then, it appears that functional analysis can shade into doctrinaire functionalism—with the functional sociologist remaining unaware that he has crossed the line between them.

According to Merton, the heuristic utility of the concept of latent function lies partly in its capacity to alert us to unintended consequences of practices which persist even when they clearly do not achieve their manifest purpose. Without the concept, Merton felt, the tendency would be to attribute such items to "superstition" or to "so-called inertia," both of which he regarded as derogatory terms. Such attribution is merely ethnocentric and "in no sense accounts for" these seemingly irrational social patterns, he said. It would be better, in his view, to extend our inquiry in search of unrecognized functions—which presumably *would* "account for" the patterns' persistence.[58]

Merton cited Hopi rainmaking rituals as an example. In the light of modern meteorological knowledge we are confident they did not really affect the weather; in terms of their manifest function, then, they were failures. Why did they persist? Merton's argument was that they performed a latent function for the group—reinforcing group identity by bringing the scattered members of the group together periodically to participate in collective activity.[59] It may be quite true that periodic participation by the entire group in some collective activity has survival value (in the natural selection sense) for the group. So Merton's functional analysis, if viewed in the context of evolutionary theory, helps account for the *survival of Hopi society*. But that is as far as it went; to account for *persistence of the rainmaking ritual* in the face of its manifest failure and the latency of its group identity reinforcement function, it is still necessary to assume that existing social practices have inertial properties. A practice

[56] *Ibid.*, p. 79.
[57] *Ibid.*, p. 81.
[58] *Ibid.*, p. 64.
[59] *Ibid.*, pp. 64–65.

whose functions are entirely unrecognized may promote group survival, but continued adherence by the group to that practice can hardly be accounted for by what it does for them since they don't recognize that it is doing anything for them. In spite of the fact that Merton thought inertia was an ethnocentric term, the concept remains essential in the full explication of functional analysis. Functionalist terminology obscured this and kept Merton from seeing it.

According to Merton, sociologists have made their most distinctive and important contributions precisely where they have shifted attention away from analysis of manifest functions to the analysis of latent functions.[60] As an example, he cited Thorstein Veblen's analysis of conspicuous consumption. Veblen saw that it is often not the superior quality of expensive goods but the very fact that they are high priced which motivates people to buy them. Costliness is equated with high social rank, independently of its imperfect correlation with quality of merchandise.[61] High prices can thus attract as well as repel purchasers, when quality is held constant. But in citing this as an example of fruitful analysis of latent functions, Merton overlooked his earlier effort to separate the analysis of functions from the analysis of motivations. Moreover, even granting that individual motivations are legitimate subject matter for such analysis, the latent function only *explains* conspicuous consumption by ceasing to remain latent (becoming recognized by the conspicuous consumer) or else by invoking a further assumption. It would have to be assumed either that (1) psychological reinforcement theory applies to rewards-without-awareness, or (2) ostensible possession of high social rank has survival value. In the latter case, the inertial principle would once again have to be assumed if the persistence of conspicuous consumption (rather than just the survival of conspicuous consumers) is to be explained.

Throughout several examples given by Merton, the link between functional analysis and natural selection theory remained unmentioned. Merton cited *The Wisdom of the Body* by Walter B. Cannon as a good example of the logic of functional analysis, but neglected to mention Cannon's explicit references to the way homeostatic mechanisms had evolved by natural selection. He reduced Cannon's logic to four "steps," which he gave in the following sequence: (1) establishment of the survival requirements of the organism; (2) description of the structures and processes by which such requirements are met in normal cases; (3) quest for compensating mechanisms in cases where the normal ones have been impaired; (4) detailed description of the structure for which the functional requirements apply, and of the arrangements by which these requirements are met.[62] Merton's reference to certain functional

[60] *Ibid.*, p. 66.
[61] *Ibid.*, p. 69.
[62] *Ibid.*, pp. 48–49.

requirements "if the organism is to survive" is as close as he came to recognizing the evolutionary time span and natural selection mechanism required to make functional analysis compatible with naturalism. It suggests that he was at best quite vague on this matter. Apparently the functionalist terminology is not conducive to clarity.

Writers whose sympathy for functional analysis arises from their wish to invoke final causes are perhaps especially prone to deny the evolutionary basis of functional explanation. Stark, for example, regarded functionalism and evolutionism as competitors. They are alternatives, between which a choice must be made. Whereas functionalism stresses coexistence and coordination, according to Stark, evolutionism stresses succession of phenomena and their mutual displacement. What these allegedly antithetical approaches have in common, for Stark, is their heritage of organicism or sociological realism.[63]

This kind of confusion misses the real contribution to naturalism that was made by Darwin's evolutionary theory. Since evolution looks progressive, it has always been tempting to construe it teleologically. What Darwin made clear, however, was that the teleological conceptions were superfluous. The combination of chance variation with statistically biased survival rates produces ordered change in the distributions of species traits. Natural selection, then, is a process in which the causes precede the effects as truly as they do in the case of any other phenomena investigated naturalistically.[64] Darwin replaced final causes by efficient causes, and thus departed quite radically from the world view of theology. What has been said in the foregoing paragraphs is equally true even if the evolutionary model underlying functional analysis is relaxed somewhat (as often advocated by functionalists) by substituting "success" for "survival."

As if Darwin's accomplishment were not sufficient to settle the issue, more recent studies of cybernetic phenomena have yielded a growing understanding of equilibrating processes and "feedback" mechanisms.[65] There is less and less excuse any more for supposing that causes must precede effects only in the realm of inanimate nature and not in the world of biology or at least sociology.

Statics and Dynamics

Further confusion has been apparent in assertions that functional analyses are "dynamic" rather that "static." Such assertions imply that some alterna-

[63] Stark, *op. cit.*, p. 77.
[64] Cf. Reichenbach, *op. cit.*, pp. 199–201.
[65] See Abraham Kaplan, *The Conduct of Inquiry*. San Francisco, Calif.: Chandler Publishing Company, 1964, p. 366.

tive kinds of analysis (e.g., structural as distinct from functional) are less dynamic and more static. Such confusion is unnecessary. It seems to arise from attempts to construe as antithetical those pairs of concepts which might better be regarded as complementary.

The confusion was penetrated long ago by Ward, but his sound insights have been widely overlooked in later years. Ward saw what were the crucial implications of Darwin's work and, in warning against the misconceptions of the Social Darwinists, he dispelled the apparent antithesis between structural analysis and functional analysis and correctly appraised their relation to statics and dynamics, respectively.

In both the organic world and the social world, Ward noted, it is less a question of individuals of varying degrees of fitness struggling against each other for survival than a question of survival of the best-adapted structures. Evolution, he wrote, was a "struggle for structure."[66] The emergence of structures from collections of previously unorganized elements, and the alteration of existing structures by adaptation to changed circumstances or by selective survival constitute dynamic occurrences, he said.[67] For Ward, then, "structural" was not the opposite of "dynamic." He carefully avoided invoking final causes in explaining such dynamic phenomena. Both in human beings and in unintelligent beings it was false to suppose, he said, that functional effects are necessarily understood by the agents whose acts produce them. Even for rational communities, functional results are not only undesired; they are automatic. This is why function tends to be static. Only when automatic actions fail to satisfy desire or need is modification of structure likely.[68] "Functional" was no synonym for "dynamic" in Ward's vocabulary, as it has been for some writers since.

Ward saw function as inherently static, but Parsons and Bales argued half a century later that it was inherently dynamic. As will become apparent, this difference results from different usage of the term "dynamic." Virtually acknowledging the connection between functional analysis and evolutionary frameworks, Parsons and Bales wrote that there has to be a certain amount of structural compatibility of the patterns of organization of the different components of the system. This was stated in what Parsons and Bales called "dynamic terms" by attributing the *survival* of a pattern element within a system of action to that pattern element's *contribution* to the system's integration.[69] This was about what Ward meant in calling function static; as long as an element is functional, it won't change.

As noted earlier, adequate functional explanations require use of the

---

[66] Lester F. Ward, *Pure Sociology*. New York: The Macmillan Company, 1903, p. 184.
[67] Lester F. Ward, *Outlines of Sociology*. New York: The Macmillan Company, 1897, p. 176.
[68] *Ibid.*, p. 177.
[69] Talcott Parsons and Robert F. Bales, "The Dimensions of Action Space," chap. 3 in Talcott Parsons, Robert F. Bales, and Edward A. Shils (eds.), *Working Papers in the Theory of Action*. New York: The Free Press of Glencoe, 1953, p. 101.

inertial axiom. Parsons has apparently felt this need and has expressed
it by referring to "pattern-maintenance." Some of the things he has said
about pattern-maintenance, however, indicate confusion in regard to just
what is involved in the inertial axiom. In describing the "function of pattern-maintenance" as the "imperative" of keeping stable the institutionalized culture patterns that define a system's structure, Parsons seems
to have had in mind something like survival value for the system.[70]
Pattern-maintenance is imperative insofar as it has survival value; thus
Parsons has implicitly adopted a natural selection schema. But he went
on to say that the part played by pattern-maintenance in action theory
is "comparable to that of the concept of inertia in mechanics."[71] But in
mechanics, inertia is not an "imperative." The inertia exhibited by a physical object today is no resultant of any survival value accruing to the object
in the past or to its antecedents from their inertia. It is merely a property
of material bodies which they exhibit when analyzed according to the
axioms of Newton. To say that in the absence of forces a body in motion
continues to move without acceleration has different connotations than
to say that it "maintains" its motion. The latter connotes action to prevent
change, rather than the mere nonoccurrence of change.

Parsons not only overlooked the subtly animistic connotations of his
vocabulary, but he gave his emphasis to a misperception of the relation
of statics and dynamics. Pattern-maintenance, he said, serves as the most
fundamental point of reference to which we can relate the analysis of
other more variable factors. "Properly conceived and used it does not
imply the empirical predominance of stability over change."[72] Neither does
inertia in mechanics imply that instances of constant velocity are empirically more frequent than instances of acceleration, but it would hardly
have been supposed that this was an issue unless it had been made an
issue by animistic language. It has long since been recognized in mechanics that the axiom of inertia does not imply an "inert" universe in
the sense of a universe where nothing happens. It is not necessary to
go out of our way to *deny* that the term "inertia" implies such a universe.
Why, then, is it necessary to deny that in the social world the concept
of pattern-maintenance implies the absence of change? In my judgment,
it is because of animistic overtones in Parsons' use of the phrase "pattern-
maintenance." His denial that change is disallowed by his concepts involves an assertion that the concepts pertain to the social dynamics division of sociology.

By speaking of pattern-*maintenance*, rather than of the mere *continua*-

---

[70] Talcott Parsons, "An Outline of the Social System," in Talcott Parsons, Edward
Shils, Kaspar D. Naegele, and Jesse R. Pitts (eds.), *Theories of Society*. New York:
The Free Press of Glencoe, 1961, p. 38.
[71] *Ibid.*, p. 39.
[72] *Ibid.*

tion of patterns in the absence of net forces, Parsons himself has created the misleading impression that social systems never allow themselves to be changed. Then, since social change does occur, he had to go out of his way to deny that he had denied it. This is the result of a choice of words that was, I think, more than merely unfortunate. Because of the pervasive element of voluntarism in his action theory, it seems likely that the implication of *active undoing* of incipient change that is conveyed by "pattern-maintenance" would have been more attractive to Parsons's way of thinking than the more truly inertial phrases, "pattern persistence," or "pattern continuation." Though attractive to him for this reason, the term he adopted did confront him with the problem already indicated. In his attempt to extricate himself from the conceptual predicament in which animistic terminology had placed him, Parsons referred to functions as "the link between the structural and the dynamic aspects of the system,"[73] as if "dynamic" were the obverse of "structural" rather than of "static."

Later in the same work, Parsons repeated the denial that any static connotations were intended by the concept of pattern-maintenance.[74] Evidently the possibility that he would seem to be preoccupied with statics and insufficiently involved with dynamics was of some concern to him. He had distinguished morphological (i.e., structural) notions from dynamic ones, and had divided the latter into problems of equilibrium and problems of structural change.[75] Without using the terms, he had lumped the sociological counterparts of *physiology* and *evolution* under the heading of dynamics. This is questionable usage. The issue ought not to be just the question whether Parsons's theories are inherently static, but whether social physiology belongs to social statics or to social dynamics. Parsons apparently supposed he was studying dynamics when he studied the sociological equivalent of physiology—i.e., social processes. But the study of continuing social processes might be more appropriately assigned to statics, and the task of dynamics could be said to consist of the study of social change—accelerations or decelerations of various social processes.

Both statics and dynamics have to be concerned with structure. Shifting attention from structure to physiology is not tantamount to shifting from statics to dynamics. Shifting from physiology to evolution would be. Though Parsons's functional analysis implicitly entails a natural selection schema, his terminology and his definition of issues suggests that he has not escaped the error of the Social Darwinists who confused the metamorphosis or even the maturation of an organism with the evolution of species. If that error persists, then the functional explanations that accompany it will not benefit from Darwin's buttressing of naturalism, and

[73] *Ibid.*, p. 38.
[74] *Ibid.*, p. 57.
[75] *Ibid.*, pp. 36–37.

may continue to deny the temporal priority of cause. Moreover, there will be a persistent tendency to assume that stability rather than change is what is problematic. The concern with pattern-maintenance implies just such an assumption. Parsons seems to be saying that social patterns would change *unless actively maintained.* What valid meaning this might have will be examined in a later section of this chapter.

The confusions committed by Parsons were quite unnecessary. Ward had seen through them long ago, and sociologists could have followed his lead had they been emancipated earlier from their predilection for animistic points of view. Ward wrote that no organic change would result unless something took place besides routine performance of function. Function alone could not modify structure. This was plain and obvious to Ward, who therefore expressed astonishment that numerous sociologists who base their discipline on biology should regard anatomy as statical and physiology as dynamic. He ascribed this confusion of thought "to the failure to analyze the phenomena of structure and function, but still more to the utter chaos that reigns among sociologists as to what constitutes statics and dynamics in the concrete sciences."[76]

To Ward, the evolution of social structures was describable in the same terms as the evolution of celestial objects and of organisms. It went on naturally and as a result of antecedent causes. It was only necessary to use teleological terminology because of "the great poverty of language," but this terminology should, he felt, "convey no false implications to the well-informed." Every social structure, he said, had a function, which is the work it does. He cited a long list of biological and social structures or mechanisms and stated the function of each, and then declared, ". . . all considerations of structure and function are statical. The investigation of structures is anatomy, that of functions is physiology, and in all sciences, including sociology, the study of both anatomy and physiology belongs to the department of statics."[77]

Effects of Emphasizing Dynamics

Whether functional analysis is *inherently* static or not (and Parsons has had company when he has insisted that it is not), in the twentieth century more sociological attention has certainly been directed to questions of "anatomy" and "physiology" than to questions of "evolution." Among anthropologists, especially, the whole notion of cultural evolution became quite unfashionable for a time, and sociologists have long tended to dismiss as naïve the doctrine of progress that seemed to be implicit in evolutionary theories. Only since the Second World War, in an era of political

[76] Ward, *Pure Sociology,* pp. 181–182.
[77] Ward, *Outlines of Sociology,* pp. 170–175.

ferment, heightened culture contact, and unprecedentedly rapid economic development, has sociological interest in theories of social change reverted to anything like the intensity that characterized the beginnings of sociology.

As has already been pointed out, the earliest sociological theories of societal evolution were naïvely founded on mistaken biological analogies. In some respects, then, it was necessary to accumulate a body of empirical *sociological* knowledge as a prerequisite to a more fruitful attempt to formulate theories of social change. That is to say, before adequate theories of succession among social facts could be stated, some social facts had to be rather firmly known. Given an accumulation of social facts, however, there is no real warrant for assuming that their static interrelations must be studied before we can investigate their dynamic sequences. Both statics and dynamics deal with interrelations among facts. There is no reason why laws of succession can only be formulated after laws of coexistence. We may just as well first read across the rows of a matrix as down its columns.

Still trying to shake off the stigma of preoccupation with static theories, Parsons continued to confuse the issue by identifying morphology with statics in insisting that morphological premises are required for dynamic analysis lest it be completely disoriented.[78] Plausible as his assertion sounds, it not only does not prove that statics must precede dynamics, but it also overlooks the revolutionary consequences that have arisen in other sciences from shifting the emphasis to dynamic problems. In biology, for example, it was the shift of emphasis to evolution that rendered biological thought vastly more prolific. Even the physiological mechanisms that resemble "pattern-maintenance" were discovered (and subsequently explained) *after* this shift of emphasis. In short, Darwin preceded Cannon. Biology was on an intellectual plateau until boosted off by evolution. Still earlier, in physical science, the approximately circular motion of celestial objects led to few important scientific concepts or theories as long as it was viewed in static terms. A scientific revolution followed Newton's redefinition of orbital motion in dynamic terms, however.

After Darwin, biology ceased to be merely a static discipline concerned with classification of its phenomena into named categories. It became dynamic and autonomous, and it acquired its own philosophical foundations. Tremendous changes ensued in physiology and biochemistry, and in psychology, and the new science of ecology emerged when dynamic biology required recognition of the interconnected web of life.[79] New scientific questions were asked that would not have been conceived previously. Explanation by inscrutable unknowns collapsed, though thinkers of supernaturalist persuasion regrouped and continue to challenge the basic in-

[78] Parsons, "An Outline of the Social System," p. 70.
[79] Beck, *op. cit.*, p. 118.

sights of the new biology.[80] It would be false to claim that because this revolutionary expansion of thought happened in biology it *must* happen in sociology, but it would be foolish to ignore the apparent likelihood of parallel developments.

Can functional analysis be concerned with dynamics? Durkheim evidently thought so. He argued that the explanation of phenomena was not complete without determination of their functions, for if the usefulness of something is not the cause of its existence, at least when a thing is useless, this suffices to make it harmful, because then it costs effort without yielding any returns. Patterns that are dysfunctional will tend to be displaced by patterns that are functional.[81] This is a statement in dynamics. What is important to note about it is that for Durkheim, evidently, functional explanation was not an evasion of the search for efficient causes. Insofar as it was concerned with dynamics, Durkheim's functional analysis took functions as one type of efficient causes, rather than as final causes.

In biology, naturalism is not compromised by the continued interest in functions which is so often cited as sufficient basis for insisting that sociological explanation must be couched in functional terms. According to Cannon's accounts of the body's "wisdom," an organism is freed to undertake more complicated tasks by the fact that it lives in a self-contained fluid matrix in which constant conditions prevail through automatic regulation which counteracts environmental inconstancy. Cannon noted that these regulative devices had resulted from evolution through many generations.[82] Unlike some sociologists who suppose functionalism and evolutionism to be competing alternatives, Cannon recognized the dependence of functional analysis on an evolutionary background. Moreover, he was unimpeachably naturalistic in attributing the organism's freedom to its homeostatic fluid matrix rather than vice versa. It would have been more like the modern sociological functionalist (forgetful of Durkheim's clear methodology, but superficially mindful of his concern with functions) to have said something like this: The organism lives in a fluid matrix that is automatically kept in a constant condition because this liberates it for its more complicated tasks; it evolved regulatory devices so that it could be liberated. Durkheim would not have said this, but his followers make statements very much like it and imagine they are thereby honoring his methodological precepts.

In contrast, Cannon consistently let the evolutionary horse walk in front of the functional (homeostatic) cart. In the introduction to his book he began by noting that a long evolutionary process had produced self-regulatory mechanisms. He noted how unstable is the material of which the

[80] *Ibid.*, pp. 130–131.
[81] Durkheim, *op. cit.*, p. 97.
[82] Cannon, *op. cit.*, p. 285.

body consists, how easily it could be disturbed by relatively slight external forces but for the operation of such self-regulatory arrangements.[83]

Cannon's interest in homeostasis was in no sense a disregard for dynamic relationships and cannot justify sociological preoccupation with statics. In "open systems" such as our bodies, which consist of unstable materials and continually encounter disturbing conditions, he insisted that "constancy is in itself evidence that agencies are acting, or ready to act, to maintain this constancy."[84] If Newton's redefinition of orbital motion in dynamic terms seemed subtle to his Aristotelian-minded contemporaries who were accustomed to take the constant centripetal acceleration of planets as no acceleration at all (because circular motion was expected of celestial bodies), Cannon's recognition of the dynamics implied in homeostasis was subtle enough to be readily misunderstood by sociologists. In their ostensibly analogous formulations, sociologists have animistically rejected the inertial axiom of naturalism, as will be seen in Chapter 4. But for Cannon it was clearly not constancy as such that was problematic (as it is for animistic thinkers). It was constancy in the face of environmental change—and in the face of entropy—that required explanation. Like Newton, he sought to explain accelerations rather than velocities: *changes* of oxidation rates, *changes* of pulse rates, *changes* of perspiration rates, etc., rather than the rates themselves.[85]

Cannon was apparently concerned lest his dynamic analyses be mistaken for theories in statics. Rather than referring by the term "equilibrium" to the constant states automatically maintained in the body, he chose another word not so closely identified with the known balance of forces in relatively simple, closed, physicochemical systems. His preferred term was "homeostasis," which he said "does not imply something set and immobile, a stagnation." It was intended to mean a condition that might vary a little, but was relatively constant—in comparison with variations the environment would have produced apart from the operation of regulatory mechanisms.[86]

Despite Cannon's efforts to define the term clearly, however, even his own usage of "homeostasis" was beset by certain minor ambiguities. In his discussion of the role of the autonomic nervous system, for example, it was not clear whether "homeostasis" referred to (1) the system's internal economy, (2) the stability or constancy of that economy, or (3) the preservation of its stability or constancy.[87] When explaining the fact of constancy in terms of survival value, however, he seemed to use "homeostasis" and "constancy" as synonymous terms.[88] Elsewhere this syn-

[83] *Ibid.*, pp. 19ff.
[84] *Ibid.*, p. 281.
[85] This is evident in *ibid.*, pp. 253–254.
[86] *Ibid.*, p. 24.
[87] *Ibid.*, p. 247.
[88] *Ibid.*, p. 249.

onymity was manifest,[89] and occasionally he even used the expression "homeostatic conditions."[90] His phrase "homeostasis of temperature," on the other hand, occurred in a context which made it seem to refer to the stabilization of body temperature rather than to the stability of it.[91] Again, the expression "homeostatic regulation," which he used repeatedly,[92] made it seem that the regulatory process rather than the end result, constancy, was what was meant by "homeostasis." Regardless of these confusions (which have their counterpart in the ambiguous sociological usage of "equilibrium"—sometimes meaning balance of forces and other times meaning the capacity for or process of restoring such balance), Cannon was quite naturalistic, however, in regarding constancy as problematic only in the face of disturbing forces. It was only because the environment was variable that regulatory mechanisms had to be invoked to account for constancy.

In current biological usage, the ambiguity seems to have been resolved so that homeostasis is defined now as the tendency toward, or process of, restoration of equilibrium in an organism when it has been disturbed.[93] The point to be noted in such a definition is that "homeostasis" refers to an equilibrium-restoring response to disequilibrium. It does not simply mean equilibrium itself. It is thus a term in biological dynamics rather than biological statics, and cannot be properly used by sociologists as a weapon for repulsing the naturalistic axiom of inertia, nor as an excuse for disregarding dynamic problems.

Obstacles to Naturalistic Functional Analysis

It ought to be possible in the study of social systems, as it evidently is in the study of organic systems, to be concerned with the *dynamics* of pattern persistence in the face of pattern-disruptive forces. "Pattern-maintenance" becomes a reasonable term insofar as it is applied to *responses* of systems to situations of disequilibrium. But Parsons, it will be recalled, likened it to the axiom of inertia. When the forces impinging on a system are in balance, if it is still assumed that change would occur but for active processes of pattern-maintenance, then we have lapsed back into animism. In that case our theoretical endeavors are likely to be as sterile as were the animistic formulations of the pre-Newtonian cosmologists.

To get on with the study of social change, careful and explicit recognition must be given to the subtle distinction between the inertial properties of social patterns and the homeostatic properties of the systems in which

[89] *Ibid.*, p. 253.
[90] *Ibid.*, p. 268.
[91] *Ibid.*, p. 284.
[92] *Ibid.*, pp. 272, 277, 278.
[93] Beck, *op. cit.*, p. 270.

they occur. When some form of social action is occurring at a given rate, social forces of different magnitudes can be expected to change that rate by different amounts, and it will not change at all if it is subjected to no force at all. That is the principle of inertia. But when a force is applied and a change of rate that would have been expected is prevented by the system's compensatory action, that is homeostasis, or what we *should* mean when we use such a term as "pattern-maintenance." It is misleading to confuse inertia and homeostasis.

Almost invariably, the terminology of functional analysis fosters such confusion. Parsons has done so by calling pattern-maintenance an imperative and yet describing it as the action theory equivalent of the axiom of inertia. Even when users of the term "function" attempt to eliminate unwanted connotations and be explicit regarding its denotations, "function" remains a troublesomely ambiguous term. Radcliffe-Brown, for example, sought to use the word only with reference to the problem of "the way in which [society] manages to persist."[94] This seems at least to avoid Aristotelian implications of final causes, but it can embrace both inertia and homeostasis. These two concepts are so fundamentally distinct that no term which obscures the distinction should be retained in our working vocabulary, at least not without strenuous efforts to refine its usage and separate these meanings.

For this reason, at least, I am inclined to agree with Nagel's appraisal of functional explanations in sociology when they are modeled after physiological processes. He says they are of dubious cognitive worth.[95] In physiology, functional statements can be recognized by their distinctive phraseology, but those which are cognitively valid can be "exhaustively rendered by nonfunctional formulations," according to Nagel. The latter are more conventional in other sectors of natural science.[96] Even where biologists still employ the language of functional analysis, they have long since dispensed with vitalistic forces. Moreover, they are aware of recent developments in the knowledge of servomechanisms. Such knowledge makes it clear that "purposive" behavior can be mechanically accounted for without invoking such concepts as "volition."[97] (Ironically, however, servomechanisms were known to the vitalist Driesch, but they did not dissuade him from his vitalistic convictions.[98] To what extent, then, his persistent vitalism reflects the inertia of his beliefs and to what extent it reflects the homeostatic character of his mind, must remain a matter of speculation.)

Since there are systems, both natural and man-made, that are "directively organized" (i.e., have homeostatic properties), it is important to

---

[94] Radcliffe-Brown, *op. cit.*, p. 85.
[95] Nagel, *op. cit.*, pp. 534–535.
[96] Ernest Nagel, *Logic without Metaphysics*. New York: The Free Press of Glencoe, 1956, p. 250.
[97] *Ibid.*, p. 367.
[98] Hans Driesch, *The History and Theory of Vitalism* (tr. C. K. Ogden). New York: St. Martin's Press, Inc., 1914, p. 4.

spell out the necessary steps in their analysis. In such analysis, we have to be as specific as we can be about the following items: (1) the trait or traits with respect to which the system is self-maintaining; (2) whether the system which is directively organized with respect to a given trait is or is not part of a more inclusive system which may or may not be directively organized relative to that trait; (3) whether the system is directively organized in regard to several traits rather than just one, and whether these form a hierarchy.[99] No system can be self-maintaining with respect to all its traits equally and simultaneously; it can only minimize the environment-caused variation of a particular trait by undergoing compensatory change in one or more of its other traits. For a thermostat to minimize the variation in room temperature it must produce variation in the rate of fuel consumption by the furnace to compensate for variation in the temperature of the outside environment. My body cannot keep its temperature constant as the warmth of the environment changes unless it alters its rate of metabolism or its rate of perspiration, etc. A social system cannot arm to maintain its political independence when threatened with military invasion without interrupting its routine of "business as usual." *The process of pattern-maintenance necessarily entails some pattern modification,* but the language of functionalism often obscures this fundamental principle of equal and opposite action and reaction. The necessity for denying unmoved movers is less readily recognized when one is habituated to functional modes of explanation.

In studying the developing mentality of the child, Piaget found that youngsters under seven years old had a tendency toward "nominal realism." By this he meant that they supposed that in learning the name of a thing they were somehow reaching its essence and discovering its explanation. A similar thoughtway is commonly observed in adults, whose curiosity shows some abatement when an unfamiliar object or process has been tagged with a name that is vaguely familiar.[100] The appeal which functional analysis has for many minds may be akin to this. When we can state the part played in a system by one of its components, then we feel that we understand that component. Knowing what it does seems to tell us what it "is," and that seems to explain it.

If that is the kind of understanding sought, perhaps this accounts for the imprecision so characteristic of functional analysis. As Nagel has pointed out, functional analyses ordinarily do not define with sufficient precision the state of the system that is allegedly maintained. Thus their explanations of how it is maintained lack substantive content. Glib generalizations about such concepts as "pattern-maintenance" are of little avail unless there is explicit specification of *what patterns* are maintained and *by means of the modification of what other patterns.* Specification

[99] Nagel, *Logic without Metaphysics*, pp. 253–254.
[100] F. V. Smith, *Explanation of Human Behaviour*, 2d ed. London: Constable & Co., Ltd., 1960, p. 36.

can be more easily done for relatively small groups than for a whole society, but this does not seem to inhibit the use of functional terminology in describing the behavior of whole societies.[101]

In practice, functional analysis tends to put the cart before the horse. Instead of identifying a system trait whose constancy is conducive to system survival, and then looking for the mechanisms by which it might be kept constant in the face of disturbing forces, functional analysis in social inquiry typically starts with a social structure or practice and then a search is made for the function(s) it performs. It is because of this reversal of the appropriate analytic sequence that we commonly neglect the fact that mechanisms which maintain a pattern in one system may interfere with its maintenance in a more inclusive system, or may interfere with the maintenance of other patterns in the given system. It is also easy to neglect the fact that *various* structures or practices may contribute to the maintenance of a given state variable in a given system. Thus we tend to conclude erroneously that some particular structure or practice is functionally indispensable.[102]

In many realms it is true that the same process may lead to a variety of consequences, under varied circumstances. One hazard in the use of functional explanations is that this may be overlooked. Some one consequence is more likely to be singled out and treated as if it were the only effect of the given process when the description is in the quasi-teleological terms of functionalism than when it is not. A part is more likely to be seen in relation only to a given whole, and its involvements in other wholes is likely to be neglected.[103]

If all the above pitfalls are assiduously avoided and if the connection between functional explanation and an evolutionary framework is borne in mind, then functional analysis can certainly be of heuristic value, and functional concepts may even acquire rigorous theoretical import. What the biologists have shown us is not that functional analysis is indispensable to sociology (as one of the sciences of living entities), but that *if* we indulge in functional analysis we must be *especially* alert to the requirements of naturalism. By adopting a functional approach we expose ourselves to special temptations to revert to animism, and special precautions become necessary if the benefits of naturalism are to be retained.

A Precautionary Maneuver

One way to be reminded of the animistic errors that are latent in functional formulations is to take some common proposition from natural sci-

---

[101] Nagel, *The Structure of Science,* pp. 530–531.
[102] *Ibid.,* pp. 532–533.
[103] *Ibid.,* p. 424.

ence and restate it in functional language. For example, Boyle's law—that at constant temperature, a gas under varying pressure varies in volume inversely with the pressure—might be restated as follows: Under constant temperature, when the pressure on a gas varies, it changes its volume in order to hold constant the product of the pressure and its volume. Or, even more flagrantly: Under constant temperature and varying pressure, the function of a gas's changing volume is to keep the product of pressure and volume constant.[104]

Why are we skeptical of such versions of this familiar scientific generalization? They would have been taken seriously by Aristotle. One reason we shun them is that variations in gas pressure can have many consequences, while the functional formulations purport to assign special importance to a particular consequence. We are reluctant to concede it paramount significance. For another thing, when Boyle's law is restated in functional language it implies that an enclosed volume of gas is a directively organized system, which we are not inclined to believe.[105] This suggests, then, the need for caution in the use of functional language in sociology. It behooves us to be sure the system under study is in fact a self-regulating system before we undertake its functional analysis. It might not be, or at least its capacity for pattern-maintenance might be cruder than the language would indicate. It might be directively organized but not with respect to the trait in question. The absurdity that is so obvious when Boyle's law is put in functional terms would not always be so obvious in an equivalent sociological proposition because of habits of anthropomorphic thought.

Yet even in sociology, the naturalistic inclination may have already been sufficiently institutionalized that we can at least apprehend the difference between a nonfunctional generalization and a functional one. Consider, for example, the familiar hypothesis of the "demographic transition." It is assumed that a stable population first has high fertility balanced by high mortality. Then it experiences a decline in mortality as it begins to undergo modernization. The ensuing excess of births over deaths results in population growth. Eventually, as the growing population approaches saturation of its enlarged ecological niche, the changed way of life (urbanized and industrialized) reduces fertility, or else death rates rise again as a direct result of congestion, contagion, starvation, etc. In one way or the other, then, population stability is again attained, according to the theory, at an increased density. The theory regards the renewed population stability as more probably resulting from the reduced fertility that is once again commensurate with mortality at a lower level than prior to the transition period. All this is stated in nonfunctional terms. Conventionally we say that the birth rate comes down near the level of the death

[104] Adapted from *ibid.*, p. 406.
[105] *Ibid.*, pp. 408, 421.

rate *because of* the changed way of life, or the death rate goes back up *because of* saturation of the ecological niche. We thus invoke efficient causes only, not final causes. We do not usually say that the death rate goes back up "in order to" restore population stability. And the obstacles encountered by those who are alert to the dangers of overpopulation and who are trying to reduce fertility (quite literally *in order to* restore population stability) so as to avert disaster certainly indicates that in this respect our societies are not yet directively organized systems. The pattern-maintenance concept is belied in this instance by the fact that there is inertial resistance to efforts to make the system directively organized.

By now it ought to be clear that human fertility and mortality are social and not merely biological phenomena. They are shaped, that is, by innumerable social and cultural factors. Some readers may nevertheless object that the above demographic example is not sufficiently sociological to be relevant. The objection is without weight unless one has already rejected all the arguments previously discussed by which it is commonly claimed that final causes must be invoked in sociology because they have remained indispensable in biology.

If we turn to a more obviously sociological proposition, we may again compare its naturalistic version with a functional restatement of it. In studies of mate selection, it has been found repeatedly that marriages exhibit a tendency to residential propinquity. That is, persons of opposite sex residing short distances apart are more likely to marry each other than those residing far apart. Nearness begets acquaintance, facilitates courtship, and thus enhances the chances of marrying. That is a causal explanation of distance gradients in marriage rates. I doubt that any sociologist would give serious consideration to the following reformulation of the propinquity principle, however: People select mates in order to produce a distance gradient in marriage rates, and thereby to hold as constant as possible the product of premarital residential separation and probability of marriage. The phrase "in order to" has been designated an earmark of functional explanation.

Surely no sociologist supposes that suitors distribute their attentions with the intent of establishing such a distance gradient. They have other goals in mind entirely. But, as Nagel has pointed out, it is not necessary to impute conscious intent to the things and activities for which functional explanations are given.[106] The reformulation of the principle of propinquitous marriage can be considered a functional proposition without interpreting it to imply conscious intent. It may be taken to suggest that the social system in which mate selection is occurring and being studied is rendered more viable by the constancy of the product of premarital residential separation and marriage probability. It is the phrase "in order to" that has this implication. If it could be shown that the more propin-

[106] *Ibid.*, p. 24.

quitous marriages are more stable, and that societal viability depends on the marital stability of society's constituent families, as is sometimes claimed, then such a functional reformulation of the familiar generalization could be considered valid. Even so, the functional version would be an elliptical statement. Until such additional generalizations are not only stated but substantiated, scientific caution favors the more conventional version of the principle of propinquitous mate selection. That it happens to be the more conventional form is a sign that naturalistic tenets currently have some adherents in the sociological profession.

On the other hand, such phenomena as the incest taboo are commonly explained in functional terms, with little or no awareness of the intervening links in the implied causal chain that are thereby omitted or possibly denied. It is commonly said that incest taboos exist universally in order to prevent the confounding of statuses in a kinship structure. Clearly this would be an effect of an incest taboo, but is it truly the cause of the taboo? Could it not be instead that the nonerotic role relationships between brother and sister or between son and mother have an inertial tendency to persist, so that the probability of a spousal or sexual relationship arising between the same two persons is very low?

Even closer to the propinquity example is the common sociological explanation of assortative mating. Rather than attributing assortative mating to the fact of ecological segregation and the tendency to mate propinquitously, we say that assortative mating is practiced "so that" homogamy will prevail. Assuredly, homogamy is a result of assortative mating, but we don't really know that a need for homogamy (or a desire for it) is actually the cause of assortative mating. Sociology has really not yet determined whether heterogamous marriages tend to be stigmatized because they are rare or tend to be rare because they are stigmatized. When we use the language of functional analysis we tend to overlook the necessity for raising such questions.

Summary

Two issues distinguishing naturalistic from animistic sociology tend to be confused by the doctrines and vocabulary of functionalism. Functions are often spoken of in a way which seems to make final causes of them, so that the issue of the chronological relation between cause and effect is beclouded. And the axiom of inertia which makes change problematic, as opposed to the concept of will which makes continuity problematic, is beclouded by unrigorous usage of terms such as "pattern-maintenance."

Functionalism draws upon the Aristotelian heritage which made anthropomorphic notions canonical for all explanations of all kinds of phenomena. It is often justified by the argument that teleological explanation remains indispensable in biology and must therefore be necessary to sociology. In fact, however, all sound functional explanations in biology refer at least implicitly to an evolutionary time scale and are reducible to explanations by efficient cause. The present manifestation of a trait can be considered caused by the consequences of earlier instances of that trait, where those consequences contributed to the survival of the system possessing the trait. To say that the trait is caused by *its* consequences, however, is either false or elliptical.

Though its modern proponents regard functional analysis as part of dynamics and contrast it with the study of structure as statics, when the evolutionary framework is neglected, functional analysis belongs thoroughly to statics. The excuse that we must study structures before we can study change misses the real division between statics and dynamics, for there is no reason why laws of coexistence of social facts must be stated before we can state laws of succession of social facts. Moreover, in other sciences, thought was markedly accelerated by a shift in emphasis from statics to dynamics, and this might be expected in sociology, too.

The use of functional terminology is beset with many special pitfalls. Though in principle it is possible to conduct a thoroughly naturalistic inquiry in functional terms, special efforts to avoid regressing into animism are required. Careful distinction between inertia and homeostasis is essential. Functional language tends to muddy this distinction. The particular traits maintained and the specific systems exhibiting homeostasis in regard to those traits must be precisely indicated. The fact that pattern-maintenance entails pattern modification must be recognized, though functional analysis ordinarily obscures it.

The use of functional language in biology no longer indicates that biology is basically teleological, and it does not warrant insistence that sociology must be. There are areas of sociological study in which functional reformulations of conventional empirical generalizations can be readily recognized as unorthodox. Their omissions of intervening variables and their implications of final causes can be readily seen as defects. To this extent, naturalism has a following among sociologists. There are other sociological generalizations, however, whose conventional mode of analysis is in functional terms. The omitted variables and the questionable validity of the teleological implications are not always acknowledged. To correct these oversights, a stronger commitment to naturalism would be useful, and its attainment would probably be facilitated by abandoning the functional vocabulary.

Chapter Four
SOCIOLOGISTS IN TRANSITION

Cross Pressures

Evidence was presented in Chapter 1 that there has been a somewhat irregular trend toward naturalism in sociology, with our having attained varying degrees of commitment to the several tenets of naturalistic inquiry. Sociologists are thoroughly committed to reliance on empirical data as the ultimate test of the validity of their generalizations, but they are less clear in their understanding of and less firm in their adherence to the principle that causes must precede effects and in their adherence to the principle of inertia. There is very little acknowledgement, and frequent violation, of the principle that nothing unchanging can explain change.

In Chapter 2, we saw that the issues between animism and naturalism have been confounded with other and less important distinctions between various isms. In particular, naturalistic explanations have often been supposed to entail metaphysical assumptions that were too materialistic to suit the tastes of some sociologists. In opposition to the apparently materialistic implications of positivism, Furfey proposed to incorporate into sociology a series of supraempirical postulates. These were examined and shown to assert false issues. Naturalism, then, was said to maintain that (1) there is no operationally verifiable meaning to the dichotomy "material reality" versus "immaterial reality"; (2) there is no sustainable distinction between natural sciences and so-called "moral sciences"; (3) not constancy but *changes* in human action require explanation, and change cannot be accounted for by reference to unmoved movers; (4) cognition and evaluation can and must be separated in the quest for valid knowledge; (5) no propositions are admissible into sociology which involve concepts that are not at least illata, deriving their meaning from observation of concreta, at least indirectly.

In Chapter 3, the language of functional analysis was shown to be analyzable in keeping with naturalism but likely in practice to pull the investigator who uses it back into animism. Safeguards against this were suggested. Readers with strong sympathies for functional terminology might be inclined to conclude that I have really shown in Chapter 3 that the distinctions between naturalistic inquiry and other styles of inquiry are of no great importance, since functional language can bridge the gap. But the gap is not worth bridging, for I insist that animism is essentially sterile and that naturalism opens the way to new knowledge. In showing the marginality of functional explanations between sterile animism and scientific naturalism, I meant to suggest that the practitioners of functional analysis are truly marginal men—influenced by two cultures. It is for this reason that I had to make such frequent use in Chapter 3 of the words "confused" and "confusion." A marginal man, being cross-pressured, experiences ambivalence and expresses confusion. Because he is ambivalent, his writing is often ambiguous.

In the present chapter, I want to examine the phenomenon of marginality in somewhat greater depth. Those sociologists who may occasionally apply to themselves the functionalist label are by no means the only ones exhibiting such marginality. *All of us* are caught to some extent in the interstices between two cultures. We stand between the humanistic culture, which used to prescribe the guidelines for legitimately conducting social inquiry, and the modern scientific culture, whose different standards have come to seem increasingly more relevant to our quest. The humanistic culture has given us predilections toward animism, while the scientific culture impels us toward naturalism. The scientific culture has begun to claim the allegiance not merely of the avowed positivists, but of others, too, somewhat less conspicuously.

Nagel has said that a "latent naturalism" can be discovered in the everyday actions and in the common beliefs of most people.[1] But it has been latent for a long time. The ambivalence resulting from exposure to two cultures goes back several centuries. In France, during the Enlightenment, there were two distinct orientations among intellectuals. One emphasized experimentation and induction as the principal avenue to knowledge, and revered the names of Galileo, Bacon, Pascal, Boyle, and Newton. The other orientation had a religious heritage, of course, but was also represented in the philosophy of such men as Descartes. It emphasized the

[1] Ernest Nagel, *Logic without Metaphysics.* New York: The Free Press of Glencoe, 1956, p. 40.

a priori, deductive approach to knowledge. In many minds these two approaches were intermingled, but there was a tension between them, and
they were generally referred to as the "Newtonian" and the "Cartesian"
approaches. Diderot, for one, has been described as oscillating between
these two positions.[2] Even the writing of Descartes himself, however, contained seeds of incipient naturalism in spite of a heavy surface of spiritualist metaphysics.[3]

When he launched a new discipline and coined the name "sociology"
for it, Comte was in large part concerned with overcoming just such philosophical marginality. As long as thought was still divided between the
theological, the metaphysical, and the positive orientations, and was not
yet wholly positive, Comte felt that the opportunities for political zealots
to promote their various supposedly immutable regimes would not be
checked by valid knowledge of societal mechanisms. Chaos would remain
the only alternative to tyranny.[4] Positivistic sociology was offered by
Comte, then, as an antidote to political, philosophical, and moral confusion
resulting from a broad intellectual marginality.

The proffered antidote has not relieved the malady (perhaps partly because it has not been taken by the patient who has never fully accepted
the diagnosis, but also partly because it is not that powerful a nostrum).
The aims of sociologists have since become less grandiose. But at any
rate, the marginality still exists, if not quite in the terms of Comte's description, and the work of twentieth-century sociologists reflects the transition still under way from animism to naturalism. I want to examine the
work of Robert M. MacIver as a particularly cogent case in point.

Processes of perception and thought are such that anyone who reads
a book is necessarily selective in absorbing the author's meaning. What
one reader thinks the author was saying may not coincide with what the
author intended to say nor with another reader's perception of what the
author meant. The first time I read MacIver's *Social Causation,* the parts
which most caught my attention made the book seem at best an uncon-
vincing defense of the *Verstehende* approach in sociology or at worst a
thoroughly animistic and antiscientific treatise. After a number of years
I reread it, following exposure to some epistemological literature which
provided me with a different perspective. The facets I had missed the
first time reflect what I now take to be MacIver's genuine involvement
in the efforts to advance the scientific quality of sociology. A third reading
convinced me that *both* of the first two perceptions were correct, though
incomplete. It is my intention here to demonstrate that MacIver's book,
like some of the works of other sociologists, is in fact such a mixture,

[2] See Aram Vartanian, *Diderot and Descartes: A Study of Scientific Naturalism in
the Enlightenment.* Princeton, N.J.: Princeton University Press, 1953, pp. 137–138.
[3] *Ibid.,* p. 3.
[4] Auguste Comte, *The Positive Philosophy,* 3d ed. (tr. Harriet Martineau). New York:
Calvin Blanchard, 1856, p. 455.

to explain how this happened, and from this explanation to shed further light on the requirements of naturalistic sociology.

Although MacIver will be cited more often than any other author, this chapter is not intended as mere exegesis of one man's thoughts. MacIver is taken as a specimen, more or less representative (in the ways to be described below) of others. The interpretations offered are intended to apply to sociology rather than to just this particular sociologist.

MacIver—Conflicting Interpretations

1 First Impression: Animistic

My first impression of *Social Causation* happened to focus mainly on MacIver's assertion that the kind of causal nexus pursued by the physical scientist was not the only kind there is,[5] and that the phenomena studied by social science exhibit "a special type of causal process" importantly different from "the causality of external nature."[6] Arguing that it was pointless to try to apply the causal formula of classical mechanics to social systems, MacIver went on to contend that the sociologist has the advantage of dealing with causal factors that are *understandable,* whose causal character is directly experienced.[7] In this, of course, he sounded like Furfey, who claimed the sociologist has an important advantage over the physical scientist by virtue of being "inside" his subject matter and knowing it firsthand. The fallacy of such notions was examined in Chapter 3.

Aware that these views would incur the charge of animism, MacIver sought to rebut the accusation, but he did it in a way that seemed to me only to validate it. He acknowledged that it would be animistic to explain the phenomenon of lightning striking a tree by imputing anger to the lightning. Here, according to MacIver, the concept of angry intention would be *illegitimately extended* to a sphere in which it is inappropriate. He took animism to mean such illegitimate extension. I have defined it more generally. Then he asked rhetorically what it could possibly mean to dub the language of motives and goals animistic when it is applied to angry men rather than to angry lightning bolts. Experience *entitles* us to apply concepts like angry intention to people, he argued.[8] But experience can be misread, as it was misread by Aristotle. I have shown in what sense Aristotle was animistic. MacIver was here giving expression to that supposedly cautious view that Aristotelian assumptions may not apply to physical phenomena but cannot be ruled out in social science.

[5] Robert M. MacIver, *Social Causation.* Boston: Ginn and Company, 1942, p. 13.
[6] *Ibid.,* p. 371.
[7] *Ibid.,* pp. 263–264.
[8] *Ibid.,* p. 206.

Explanation of interdependence of parts in organic unities, he contended, cannot be adequately formulated in terms of interaction, concomitance, and sequence, but requires the concept of function.[9] Not ordinarily assigned to a functionalist school, MacIver nevertheless showed an affinity for the terminology of functional analysis. In the study of social causation, he said, statistical analysis is only a preliminary screening that any hypothesis must pass before it merits further investigation. "If it meets this requirement we *continue the search on another level*. We seek to discover whether the association or correlation of phenomena is *meaningful.* . . ."[10] This requires "projecting ourselves by sympathetic reconstruction into the situation as it is assessed by others. . . ."[11] MacIver spoke of operationalism as a blind alley.[12]

Having mainly perceived these facets of the book in my first reading, I could not agree with Page's feeling that MacIver had "found the golden mean" between neopositivist identification of social causation with natural causation on the one hand and Sorokin's denial of the applicability of the concept of cause to social phenomena on the other.[13] Nor did I agree with Furfey that MacIver's was the best existing treatment of the subject.[14]

2   From Another Perspective: Naturalistic

When I had read such other books as Brown's *Explanation in Social Science*[15]—which covers much the same ground as MacIver's book, though less readably—and Bunge's *Causality*,[16] I was prompted to reread and reconsider *Social Causation*. As pointed out in Chapter 3, with the advent of modern science, the Aristotelian four categories of cause were reduced to one. Formal and final causes were discarded as inaccessible to experiment, and material causes were simply taken for granted. Only efficient causes were regarded as meriting scientific research.[17] The difference between social and physical causation urged by MacIver seems to consist of insistence on looking for the final causes natural science has abandoned.[18] And yet there was a hint in MacIver's book that the teleology he deemed necessary to sociological explanation can be reduced

[9] *Ibid.*, pp. 13–14.
[10] *Ibid.*, p. 390. (My italics.)
[11] *Ibid.*, p. 391.
[12] *Ibid.*, pp. 156–157.
[13] Charles H. Page, "Robert M. MacIver," in Nicholas S. Timasheff, *Sociological Theory: Its Nature and Growth*, rev. ed. New York: Random House, Inc., 1957, p. 254.
[14] Paul Hanly Furfey, *The Scope and Method of Sociology*. New York: Harper & Row, Publishers, Incorporated, 1953, p. 69.
[15] Robert Brown, *Explanation in Social Science*. Chicago: Aldine Publishing Company, 1963.
[16] Mario Bunge, *Causality*. Cleveland: Meridian Books, The World Publishing Company, 1963.
[17] *Ibid.*, p. 32.
[18] For an indication of this, see MacIver, *op. cit.*, p. 8.

to a special case of efficient cause. He wrote: "The effect, dimly adumbrated or clearly conceived, exists as projection in advance of the physical process from which, as actuality, it emerges."[19] As actuality, the effect follows the process that brings it about. It is only as a "projection" or image or anticipation that it causes that process, and MacIver was acknowledging that the image antedates the process. Thus he was not quite invoking final causes in the full Aristotelian sense.

In Bunge's book, the general determinism assumed by natural science was defined as consisting of the principle of lawfulness combined with the genetic principle.[20] The principle of lawfulness states that nothing ever happens in an unconditional, altogether irregular, or arbitrary way. The genetic principle simply says that nothing can arise out of nothing or pass into nothing. This definition provided my revised perspective for re-reading *Social Causation*, and in the light of it I discovered that MacIver had made many statements compatible with such general determinism. It even seemed now that one of his purposes in writing the book might have been to advocate such a position. I had previously read the book as if its aim were just the opposite—to refute ideas like the genetic principle and the principle of lawfulness.

I now discovered that in addition to the various antipositivistic assertions I had noticed before, MacIver had also written in the same book such things as the following: he said, for example, that behavior cannot be explained by referring "to the subjective alone." Human motivations, he felt, have to be interpreted with regard for the objective situations toward which they are directed.[21] (In Chapter 5, I will attempt to elucidate ways in which this can be done, and show their compatibility with naturalism.)

I found that, while MacIver spoke of the difficulty sociologists face in seeking to bring motives under scientific study and noted that the attempts so far to do so were rudimentary, he had argued that science must not therefore merely renounce such efforts.[22] He seemed here to be emphasizing the need for studying motives scientifically as much as he was stressing science's need to study motives. Moreover, he rejected the notion that any principle of indeterminism or any concept of free will constituted an insurmountable obstacle to the scientific analysis of causal connections among human actions.[23] He spoke of ways to "bring the social phenomena within the universal formula of causal investigation,"[24] and asserted the axion that "whatever happens has a cause,"[25] which is close to being simply the principle of lawfulness. He regarded the doctrines of vitalism (as

[19] *Ibid.*, pp. 8–9.
[20] Bunge, *op. cit.*, pp. 25–26.
[21] MacIver, *op. cit.*, pp. 202–203.
[22] *Ibid.*, pp. 207, 216.
[23] *Ibid.*, pp. 235–236.
[24] *Ibid.*, pp. 333–334.
[25] *Ibid.*, p. 26.

exemplified by Bergson) as an even more specious basis than free will for denying the universality of causation.[26] Wherever we find order in nature, he said, we vindicate our trust in the causal axiom, and we renew our faith in it by seeking to extend the realm of science.[27] If he had seemed before to be attempting to restrict the realm of science, he now appeared to be enlarging it, or working for its enlargement. He insisted that order, sequence, uniformity, law were both a condition of science and a datum of experience.[28]

Ambivalence and Marginality

Admittedly my perception of MacIver's book had been slanted each time I read it. The first time, I failed to notice the phrases and statements that were compatible with naturalism. The second time, more deliberately, I overlooked the animistic passages and sought out the naturalistic earmarks. What matters from the point of view of the present chapter is not the fact that my reading was selective but the fact that *both* kinds of statements were actually there. It would be unfair to MacIver not to try to discern the causes that impelled him to mix together in one book such opposite notions.

We may begin by assuming that this mixture reflects a genuine ambivalence in MacIver at the time he wrote *Social Causation,* early in the 1940s. One common source of ambivalent attitudes is marginal involvement in two cultures,[29] and I will presently explore the hypothesis that such marginality can and does account for MacIver's apparent ambivalence.

It has been suggested that all of us are more or less marginal personalities as a result of living in a rapidly changing society.[30] The norms we internalized early in life tend to be out of phase with the social structure and the culture we experience later in life after change has proceeded a bit further. More specifically, it has been suggested that our intellectual life is being increasingly polarized between two cultures, with the literary intellectuals at one pole and the physical scientists at the other.[31] In sociology, the naturalistic orientation has not completely won out yet over animism. The competition between them can be traced back through the

[26] *Ibid.,* p. 31.
[27] *Ibid.,* pp. 33–34.
[28] *Ibid.,* p. 48.
[29] For a brief and representative discussion of this point, see George E. Simpson and J. Milton Yinger, *Racial and Cultural Minorities,* rev. ed. New York: Harper & Row, Publishers, Incorporated, 1958, pp. 207, 212.
[30] *Ibid.,* p. 206.
[31] C. P. Snow, *The Two Cultures and the Scientific Revolution.* New York: Cambridge University Press, 1959, p. 4.

division between positivism and humanism. The positivistic orientation allied sociology with naturalism, while the humanistic orientation resisted what it has always regarded as specious scientism.[32]

There are conflicting views as to which orientation is gaining ascendancy. McKinney believes the *"verstehende* line of thought has assumed an increasingly important role in American sociology in the past two decades."[33] He includes MacIver among its foremost proponents. In contrast, as we saw earlier, Lundberg claims to have discerned a trend toward natural science sociology.[34] There is considerable evidence to support such a view, as I showed in Chapter 1. The hypothesis that sociologists such as MacIver are ambivalent would allow both McKinney and Lundberg to be correct in their perceptions; the trend could be going both ways at once, though we would then have to suppose that sociological ambivalence was increasing.

Lundberg has suggested that the attempt to declare social phenomena essentially different from physical phenomena (and thus erect a barrier between social and physical science) is a last desperate effort to preserve what is taken for human "dignity" against the naturalistic trend that followed Darwin.[35] It would be quite remarkable, he has argued, if social thought remained uninfluenced by natural science which looms so important in Western civilization.[36]

There can be little doubt that the kinds of explanation accepted as valid have been different in different cultural epochs. There is evidence, too, that the types of explanation acceptable to an individual at an early age differ from the types he accepts as he advances in age, there being generally an apparent trend from animistic to more naturalistic ways of thought.[37] In what follows, evidence will be presented for the thesis that the ambivalence reflected in *Social Causation* was the result of a transition then in progress in MacIver's thinking, from animism toward naturalism.

His ambivalence was apparent to various reviewers of the book. Nagel described it as "meandering and frequently repetitious" and "provocative and informative" even when not carrying conviction. He saw the book as "an obvious challenge" to the social science trends toward positivism

---

[32] Charles H. Page, "Sociology as a Teaching Enterprise," chap. 25 in Robert K. Merton, Leonard Broom, and Leonard S. Cottrell, Jr. (eds.), *Sociology Today*. New York: Basic Books, Inc., Publishers, 1959, pp. 586–587.

[33] John C. McKinney, "Methodology, Procedures, and Techniques in Sociology," chap. 7 in Howard Becker and Alvin Boskoff (eds.), *Modern Sociological Theory*. New York: The Dryden Press, Inc., 1957, p. 196.

[34] George A. Lundberg, "The Natural Science Trend in Sociology," *American Journal of Sociology*, 61 (November, 1955), pp. 191–212.

[35] George A. Lundberg, "Is Sociology Too Scientific?" *Sociologus*, 9 (September, 1933), p. 304.

[36] *Ibid.,* p. 315.

[37] The work of Piaget and others pertaining to this trend is summarized in F. V. Smith, *Explanation of Human Behaviour*, 2d ed. London: Constable & Co., Ltd., 1960, pp. 30–40.

and behaviorism.[38] But he found MacIver less than convincing in his contention that social inquiry requires a special logic, essentially different from naturalism.[39]

Though Martindale credited MacIver with developing his social-action theory to its fullest precision in *Social Causation*, and compared its emphasis on processes of "dynamic assessment" with Weber's *Verstehende* analysis of "meaningful social actions,"[40] another sociologist appraising the book said its major weakness was a tendency to fall back on common sense as scientific evidence.[41] Another reviewer found himself generally agreeing with MacIver's position but dissatisfied with its development and exposition.[42] MacIver was accused of never quite facing the question whether subjective factors really have any causal autonomy.[43] The book was said to give the impression that MacIver had indulged in "a kind of vain twisting and turning, almost a squirming, through four hundred pages, in an effort to 'have it both ways,' in the conception of reality."[44] But the reviewer exposed a similar ambivalence in himself when he said that "the only tenable position is to recognize that causality always has both aspects; it is at once an empirical and a dynamic concept. Yet the two principles are logically opposed, even antithetical, in meaning."[45] Perhaps the reviewer was a product of the same two cultures that were, if I am correct, competing for MacIver's allegiance.

MacIver in Transition

The hypothesis that MacIver was moving from one intellectual culture to the other is compatible with his own acknowledgement, at the age of thirty-five, that on another issue he had had a fundamental change of attitude. Having once asserted that there was no definite science of

[38] Nagel, *op. cit.*, p. 369.
[39] *Ibid.*, p. 375.
[40] Don Martindale, *The Nature and Types of Sociological Theory*. Boston: Houghton Mifflin Company, 1960, pp. 406, 411.
[41] Donald W. Calhoun, Review of MacIver's *Social Causation*, *American Sociological Review*, 7 (October, 1942), p. 719.
[42] Frank H. Knight, "Social Causation," *American Journal of Sociology*, 49 (July, 1943), p. 46. Similarly, Lundberg wrote: "I am in fundamental agreement with MacIver's theory of causation" as set forth in *Society: Its Structure and Changes*. New York: Ray Long and Richard R. Smith, Inc., 1931, chaps. 1, 2, 3, and 26. Lundberg felt that MacIver "brilliantly expounds" the view "that the set of relations which appear as a result of the interaction between a thing and its environment cannot be explained in terms of either pole of the duality taken by itself." But MacIver was mistaken, in Lundberg's view, in imputing any such "mechanical" notion of causation to the physical sciences. Lundberg, "Is Sociology Too Scientific?" p. 305.
[43] Calhoun, *op. cit.*, p. 718.
[44] Knight, *op. cit.*, p. 47.
[45] *Ibid.*

society other than such specific studies as economics and politics, he prefaced one of his early sociological treatises by saying he now believed that view to be completely mistaken.[46] It would thus seem *possible* for MacIver to have changed so fundamentally as to move also from animism toward naturalism. A comparison of samples of his writing over a forty-five-year span after he had moved from political economy into sociology makes it seem *probable* that he did undergo such a transition, though in a letter to me recently he claimed to be still "unreconstructed" and did not perceive his own growth quite as I describe it below. He discounted some of the clues which prompt me to credit him with progress toward naturalism.

In a sociological analysis of the development of human community, published in 1917, MacIver cited Plato's *The Republic* as "the first and greatest of sociological treatises."[47] In Aristotelian fashion he proclaimed that there is a different kind of law for each different kind of reality, and specifically distinguished "material" law from "vital" law. Material law is "the law of invariable concomitance or sequence, the fixed order of material nature." Vital law, however, is "revealed in the *will* of the living, unstable, relative, *riddled with changefulness* and imperfection."[48] Vital law, unlike material law, can only be understood in terms of purposes, needs, and passions.[49] The primary social facts to be studied by the sociologist are "willed relations."[50] All this sounds far more animistic than the things he said twenty-five years later in *Social Causation*.

In *Community*, MacIver's emphasis was, then, in 1917, on the vast difference between vital law, with which sociology would have to be concerned, and the material law of invariable concomitance or sequence discovered by the natural sciences. Hence sociology could not aspire to be a natural science. Dressed up in more elaborate language, this is an instance of the argument that sociology cannot dispense with final causes because the biological sciences have had to retain them.

At this point it would be well to clarify which aspect of naturalism was most conspicuously missing from MacIver's thought in the beginning. It was the inertial axiom which, in effect, he was limiting to the material world and explicitly repudiating in the supposedly separate realm of "willed relations." It was this axiom which more and more was infused into his later publications.

In this connection, it is illuminating to compare MacIver with an earlier figure in another discipline who struggled with the transition from old to new thoughtways—Johannes Kepler. Kepler's notions of physics

[46] Robert M. MacIver, *Community: A Sociological Study*. New York: St. Martin's Press, Inc., 1917, p. viii.
[47] *Ibid.*, p. 51.
[48] *Ibid.*, p. 12. (My italics.)
[49] *Ibid.*, p. 59.
[50] *Ibid.*, p. 5.

straddled the great divide between Aristotelian and Newtonian conceptions. Absent from Kepler's writing was the essential concept of impetus or momentum, the property by which a moving body persists in its motion without help from an external force. Though accurate in describing planetary orbits as ellipses, Kepler could only explain planetary motion by imagining that somehow by some solar force the planets were "dragged through the ether like a Greek oxcart through the mud."[51]

The following account of the scientific revolution is condensed and adapted from Cohen.[52] Aristotle had explained celestial motions (which he, of course, perceived to be geocentrically circular) by postulating that heavenly bodies were not made of any of the four terrestrial elements. They were instead made of ether, a fifth element with an intrinsic tendency for circular motion; hence they moved in circles. Galileo, like Kepler, was transitional between this Aristotelian view and the ideas of Newton. After observing sunspots, Galileo explained their observed rotation around the sun by postulating a kind of circular inertia, maintaining that physical bodies set in motion in a circular path would continue to move in the same path at the same speed unless acted upon by an external force.

Later, one of Newton's crucial insights was the analysis of circular motion into an inertial component along a straight line (tangent to the circle) combined with constant centripetal acceleration. Thus, for Newton, circular motion was not inertial as such. A centripetal force is required to explain its departure from linearity. It was in this respect that Newton redefined as a problem in dynamics phenomena that his predecessors had assumed to be a problem in statics.

In Aristotelian science it was motion as such that was problematic, whereas Newtonian science regards *change* of motion as the problem to be explained. The Aristotelian explanation for motion of a body consisted of identifying the kind of motion (upward, downward, linear, circular) characteristic of the element of which that body was composed. The Newtonian explanation for acceleration is the application of a force.

Galileo succeeded in shifting part way from the Aristotelian view toward the conception which was to be formulated by Newton.[53] Recognizing the effect of air resistance on falling bodies, Galileo said this resistance would increase as a function of the speed of falling, until eventually it would equal the downward force of the body's weight. When this condition was reached, Galileo concluded there would be no further increase in velocity. He was well ahead of his time in inferring that every body falling through the atmosphere would have a finite terminal velocity. But

[51] Arthur Koestler, *The Watershed*. Garden City, N.Y.: Anchor Books, Doubleday & Company, Inc., 1960, p. 151. By permission of Harold Matson Company, Inc.
[52] I. Bernard Cohen, *The Birth of a New Physics*. Garden City, N.Y.: Anchor Books, Doubleday & Company, Inc., 1960, pp. 26, 125, 128.
[53] *Ibid.*, pp. 115–116.

what is more significant is that he did *not* conclude that the body would cease falling when air resistance equaled the downward force of gravity. By avoiding that conclusion, he made a major departure from Aristotelian thought, since Aristotle had asserted motion would be zero when resistance is not less than force. (This mistaken notion of Aristotle's will be compared with hypotheses of Parsons and Stouffer in a later section of this chapter.) But Galileo's conclusion was not yet Newton's principle of inertia, for Galileo only applied it to downward motion (bodies falling a finite distance to the earth) and did not assert that *in general* uniform motion would continue unchanged as long as the net force was zero.

In this analysis of MacIver's sociological writing, then, I shall try to alert the reader to one aspect of animism, namely, the assumption that action (whether physical or social) would not continue unless maintained by a continually applied force. Likewise, I shall focus on one aspect of naturalism, the contrary assumption that the speed or direction of some action would change only if the action were accelerated by some force. In short, I take as animistic any statements implying that action as such is problematic, and I take as naturalistic any statements implying that it is the acceleration of action that is problematic.[54] By these definitions, it should be clearly apparent that MacIver's earlier sociological writing was more animistic and his later writing more naturalistic.

In 1917, MacIver wrote that associations have to be created to *uphold* communal interests by pursuing these interests in specific ways.[55] He referred to "the great forms of social unity that, though pierced by endless forces of division, cohere victoriously in communal life. How they so cohere, how the various common interests (or wills) which create associations are coordinated into community, this we must next consider."[56] By way of explaining this persistence of social unity, he called the state an association "men as social beings have willed to create and now will to maintain," and added that there would be no state if that will should cease.[57] "Every association, every organization of men, came into being through a covenant of men to establish it, and exists in *a covenant of men to maintain it*."[58] Again and again, in the 1917 book, MacIver seemed clearly to be assuming that social patterns would spontaneously fall apart *unless actively maintained*. It was as if Galileo had said a body would cease falling if air resistance came to equal the force of gravity so that there was no net force. At the very least, MacIver was stumbling along with the same ambiguities that would later characterize Parsons's use of the term "pattern-maintenance"—mixing up inertia with the quite different

[54] Cf. Ernest Nagel, *The Structure of Science*. New York: Harcourt, Brace & World, Inc., 1961, p. 214.
[55] MacIver, *Community*, p. 107.
[56] *Ibid.*, p. 125.
[57] *Ibid.*, p. 127.
[58] *Ibid.*, p. 128. (My italics.)

concept, homeostasis. At worst, he could be regarded as flatly rejecting
the application of the inertial principle in sociology.

Twenty years later, in *Society: A Textbook of Sociology,* there were
still strong indications of such animism, though some hints of growing
naturalism had begun to intrude. Unlike physical phenomena, he wrote,
"social phenomena are aspects of a total nonmechanical, *consciously up-
held* system of relationships."[59] The well-known assertion of an essential
difference between the causation of a paper flying before the wind and
a man flying from a pursuing crowd appeared in this volume, too.[60] And
here he also wrote that "culture changes in accordance with its own principle, . . ."[61] which sounds animistic as I have defined the term, though
it occurs in conjunction with the possibly naturalistic assertion that "therefore it must be regarded as an initiator of social change." The latter clause
may be construed as naturalistic insofar as it implies that changes in social
action (acceleration) can be attributed to cultural changes (external
forces). A similarly mixed statement is the assertion that "anti-evolution-
ary forces always resist the evolutionary trend."[62] This seems to imply
(animistically) that social action would change spontaneously except insofar as forces operate to prevent change. Yet if it were assumed that Mac-
Iver would have attributed the evolutionary trend to a force, then it would
be consistent with naturalism to conceive of antievolutionary forces decelerating the trend.[63] Elsewhere in the 1937 volume MacIver remained
more unambiguously animistic; for example: "Every social phenomenon is
an event . . . [that] does not endure an instant longer than it is maintained by the contemporary attitudes and activities of social beings."[64]
There was not much point in making such an assertion as this unless
he meant to deny the inertial axiom.

To emphasize and clarify his contention that the very nature of sociology's subject matter impedes unconditional prediction because society is
"a process, not a product," he contrasted a physical object (such as a
rock) with a social institution. Over a considerable span of time the rock
may remain to all intents and purposes unchanged, without a history.
But institutions cannot exist apart from their history. "If people no longer
observe a custom, the custom no longer exists on the face of the earth,"
he wrote, and "a social structure cannot be placed in a museum to save
it from the ravages of time. . . . It lives only as it is maintained by the

[59] Robert M. MacIver, *Society: A Textbook of Sociology.* New York: Holt, Rinehart
and Winston, Inc., 1937, p. 476. (My italics.)
[60] *Ibid.,* pp. 476–477.
[61] *Ibid.,* p. 469.
[62] *Ibid.,* p. 509.
[63] But he wrote that we cannot properly speak of evolution "when an object or system
is changed merely by forces acting on it from without. The change must occur within
the changing unity, as the manifestation of forces operative within it, so as to constitute
a fuller revelation through time of its own capacities." *Ibid.,* p. 409.
[64] *Ibid.,* p. 465.

will of social beings in the present."[65] Thus conceived, institutions, customs, and social structures would seem exempt from the principle of inertia.

A very similar statement to this last one by MacIver was made some time later by Radcliffe-Brown, who was advocating what would have been, in his judgment, a natural science of society. He said that while there could be a science of society, there could not be a science of culture. Culture could only be studied "as a characteristic of a social system." It could not "exist of itself even for a moment; certainly it cannot continue."[66] The similarity of Radcliffe-Brown's statement to MacIver's indicates that no matter how much MacIver's 1937 position contradicted naturalism, it represented serious thought regarding basic concepts. MacIver still opposed positivism but not for reasons that were merely negativistic.

In taking up social change specifically, the 1937 text began rather definitely to sound naturalistic. MacIver referred to "the transformations of the social structure and the forces that bring them about" and sought to show "how the social system changes in response to the changing conditions on which it depends."[67] The hypothesis that he was feeling an obligation to be scientific is supported by his statement that technological advance "is concrete, measurable, demonstrable, and therefore the study of its influence on society seems to offer greater prospects to the scientific mind" than an alternative he had considered and rejected. His next sentence sounds thoroughly naturalistic: "In so far as we can establish a clear relation between its [technology's] changes and corresponding social changes we seem to be on scientific ground." And he seems almost self-conscious of the transition from animism to naturalism in the next sentence: "In fact it was when sociology began to follow this road that it emerged from the realm of philosophy."[68] It is social change that is problematic, and sociology began to be scientific when it began to try to relate social change to causative changes in other variables, he was saying.

Considering demographic change as an element in social change, MacIver noted that birth rates began to decline continuously in England from 1878, the year after the trial of Charles Bradhaugh and Mrs. Annie Besant for publishing a book on birth control. He reported that 125,000 copies of the book sold in the three months between arrest and trial, compared with sales of only 700 copies per year before the incident and its attendant publicity. Clearly, MacIver seems to have been implying that the accelerated sales of the book could be attributed to the trial publicity—a naturalistic kind of interpretation (whether or not true). He also seems to

[65] *Ibid.*, pp. 394–395.
[66] A. R. Radcliffe-Brown, *A Natural Science of Society*. New York: The Free Press of Glencoe, 1957, pp. 106–107.
[67] MacIver, *Society*, p. 396.
[68] *Ibid.*, p. 439.

have been implying that sales of the book constituted *a force that decel-erated the birth rate,* though he was cautious about saying so, claiming only that "it seems a reasonable assumption that these episodes, with this sudden impact on the public mind, helped to precipitate attitudes which more deep-moving forces were fostering."[69]

The animistic assumption that patterned social action is itself problematic seems to have been forgotten in the statement that custom is sustained by its common acceptance without prescription by constituted authority, and in the statement that in comparison with a law with which it conflicts custom has an advantage in that it is obeyed spontaneously.[70]

In *Social Causation,* published in 1942, there were again some statements reflecting lingering animism. "A social situation . . . implies a system of sustaining forces." This was followed by a sentence that could be meant either animistically or naturalistically, asserting that a social situation "is possible only on the postulate that certain forces are dominant and others incidental, weak, or absent."[71] MacIver's thought was clearly animistic when he said, "We cannot assume that a trend manifested prior to the eruption of some disturbing factor would have continued to pursue its previous course had it not been for the disturbance."[72] That sentence is a flat denial of the axiom of inertia.

Elsewhere in the book, however, he contradicted this denial and *implicitly affirmed* the axiom of inertia when he said:[73]

. . . in assigning the decisive role of precipitant to any act or event we are in substance claiming to know, not only what actually happened, but what *would have happened* had not this act or event occurred. Like every causal imputation, this is an inference, not a datum. . . . It implies that we know, not merely the immediate operation of the forces inherent in the situation, but the mode in which, but for the precipitant, they *would have continued* to operate.

It is precisely to permit such inference that Newton's first axiom (or "law" of motion) is required by natural science. MacIver postulated a sociological equivalent of Newton's first law, though not without some misgivings, as will be seen below.

Whereas he had earlier claimed that a trend could only be evolutionary if it was determined by forces internal to it, he now maintained that "the dynamic of social institutions or social systems is not, as it were, internal to them."[74] Evidently he had at last recognized the important difference

[69] *Ibid.,* pp. 435–436.
[70] *Ibid.,* pp. 359, 361.
[71] MacIver, *Social Causation,* p. 176.
[72] *Ibid.,* p. 358.
[73] *Ibid.,* p. 180.
[74] *Ibid.,* p. 111.

between growth or metamorphosis and evolution. Having missed this distinction at first, it is to his credit that he did later become aware of it.

Naturalism reigns in his statement that we are challenged to seek causes "when a situation ceases to conform to our expectancy, when it no longer reveals, as before, its typical activities and its typical chances. Then we must presume that the hitherto dominant pattern of sustaining forces has suffered a serious change. And we look for some intruding force."[75] His concept of "precipitant" is clearly naturalistic: "any specific factor or condition regarded as diverting the pre-established direction of affairs, as disrupting a pre-existing equilibrium, or as releasing hitherto suppressed or latent tendencies or forces."[76] He seemed about ready to offer naturalistic translations of his formerly animistic assumptions when he said, "If some action or event thwarts or balks the operation of the intrusive factor we may speak of it as an anti-precipitant."[77]

MacIver's marriage to naturalism seemed almost consummated when he wrote, "We postulate a social law roughly corresponding to the physical law of inertia, to the effect that every social system tends to maintain itself, to persevere in its present state, until compelled by some force to alter that state." His next sentence, however, suggests lingering attachments to animism, after the manner of Kepler and Galileo: "Every social system is at every moment and in every part sustained by codes and institutions, by traditions, by interests." Either he was shifting attention from inertia as such to something more like social homeostasis (Parsons's "pattern-maintenance" again), or continuity of action had not altogether ceased to be problematic for MacIver. His next sentence was a brave attempt to have it both ways: "If a social order or any social situation within it, suffers significant change we think of some insurgent or invading force, breaking as it were this 'inertia,' the status quo."[78] The gist of the sentence is naturalistic but some of the language is animistic—e.g., the description of the force as "insurgent" or "invading," the notion that it "breaks" the inertia (which is a definitely Aristotelian conception), and possibly the notion that the social order "suffers" change—though this might have been merely an anachronistic synonym for "undergoes." Even MacIver's enclosure of the word inertia in quotation marks suggests that he was not yet at ease in embracing naturalism.

Twenty years later, philosophizing about the development of his world view in a little book entitled *The Challenge of the Passing Years: My Encounter with Time*, octogenarian MacIver said some things that indicated a nearly complete adjustment to naturalism. He now rejected his earlier phrase "the ravages of time" and said we should not assume that

---

[75] *Ibid.*, p. 176.
[76] *Ibid.*, p. 172.
[77] *Ibid.*, p. 179.
[78] *Ibid.*, p. 173.

"time's hand cannot be stayed" or picture time as carrying a scythe to mow down all things. Time is not a force. It creates nothing and destroys nothing. "The rocks are worn down, and stars grow old, empires decay and men pass from childhood to age—not because time works on them but because energies . . . conspire to that effect. The wheel, once set in motion would turn, and the top would spin forever, if no forces impinged on them."[79] Though this statement clearly seems to define change rather than constancy as problematic, and contains a forthright affirmation of the inertial axiom, in a letter to me about it MacIver professed to be unable to see why I would quote it as evidence for a shift toward naturalism.

Change, he now said in this book, "is experienced only against the background of what endures."[80] "Everyone welcomes change when it is in accord with his desires, but it requires a particular type of disposition to accommodate itself to change no matter what it brings."[81] (Here he seemed to be regarding an inertial resistance to change as a normal personality trait; only a few people are so lacking in this inertial property as to be able to change readily in any given way.) And institutions, which he once had contrasted with ageless rocks, "do not pass away like mortal men. They have an indefinitely long and always renewable tenure."[82] (This suggests that inertia is also a normal attribute of culture, which he had earlier denied was possible.) Organizations persist, too, having "a tendency to outlive their usefulness and . . . a way of clinging to existence without too much regard for the need for them."[83] (Apparently he was now willing to impute inertia to social structures, too.)

"The notion that there can be creation out of nothing is . . . wholly at odds with the scientific approach."[84] This is a strong endorsement of the genetic principle. And his earlier dualism had vanished when he wrote, "The line from the inorganic to the organic is continuous. The line therefore from the nonliving to the living is continuous and among the living from the simplest forms of vegetative existence to the highest of the ani-

[79] Robert M. MacIver, *The Challenge of the Passing Years: My Encounter with Time.* New York: Trident Press, Inc., 1962, pp. 3–4.
[80] *Ibid.,* p. 128.
[81] *Ibid.,* p. 60.
[82] *Ibid.,* p. 30.
[83] *Ibid.,* p. 97. This rather thoroughly naturalistic statement constrasts with his earlier assertion that "a social structure is a nexus of *present* relationships. It lives only as it is maintained by the will of social beings in the present." *Society,* p. 395. In *Social Causation,* p. 320, he presented a mixed view: "Men build organizations, and they find that the frame of organization somehow holds them in its grasp. They develop institutions to serve their particular purposes, and they sometimes end by worshipping them. Seeking to preserve institutions from change men turn them into sanctuaries of bureaucrats. Or they overthrow the established order, and something else comes into being than the shining goals they sought." This seems to deny voluntarism, but it is not clearly an affirmation of naturalism, in comparison with the 1962 version.
[84] MacIver, *The Challenge,* p. 89.

mal world."[85] It is evident that MacIver's youthful passion for an essential distinction between physical science subject matter and laws and the subject matter and laws of social science had now subsided. Whether he knew it or not, he was wed to naturalism.

Scientists and Somnambulists: An Interpretation

According to Nagel, clear ideas regarding the true character and requirements of scientific method have never been necessary for its correct use. Habits of good workmanship get developed from the force of example and by participation in the scientific tradition. This is fortunate, he suggests, as the working scientist may be too preoccupied ever to articulate clearly or ever to comprehend consciously the procedures by which he makes his valid contributions to knowledge.[86] Comte, too, once noted that only in action could the positive method be adequately judged. Regardless of how clearly we stated the method, or how long we discoursed upon it, he said, we might not know it as well as the man who has carried out actual research and has implemented that method—with or without explicit philosophical intention to do so.[87]

In short, the transition from animism toward naturalism may involve fortuitous drift as much as it involves deliberate progress. In the case of MacIver, some of his basic assumptions seem to have been modified in ways he was not altogether aware of.

To understand the cultural significance of MacIver's transformation, consider again Johannes Kepler. Kepler's thinking, like MacIver's, showed no sudden break with the past. Kepler did not refute medieval superstitions all at once. Instead, there was evident a gradual transformation from mythology to mathematics and from the conception of a moving *spirit* controlling the planets to the conception of a moving *force*. But this moving force, as Kepler conceived it, was not yet gravity. It was "rather like a whip which lashes the sluggish planets along their paths."[88] It accounted for motion rather than for acceleration.

To Kepler himself there was no apparent reason why an orbit should be an ellipse (as he had discovered it to be) rather than an oval. He and his contemporaries, including Galileo, therefore attached less value to this scientifically pregnant discovery than to his mystically fascinating but scientifically sterile fitting of the five regular solids between the planetary spheres.[89] Kepler's descriptive laws of planetary motion were empirically

[85] *Ibid.*, p. 91.
[86] Nagel, *Logic without Metaphysics*, p. 317.
[87] Comte, *op. cit.*, p. 34.
[88] Koestler, *op. cit.*, p. 57.
[89] *Ibid.*, p. 148.

true, but it was only *after* the development of Newtonian mechanics that they made sense. Signs of MacIver's ambivalence were noted by the reviewers of his *Social Causation* when it first appeared, but these reviewers did not look for the sources of his mixed commitments. The mixture became fully explicable only after comparison of his work with similar books by other authors appearing twenty years later.

Kepler has been likened to a sleepwalker, making correct use of facts he failed to recognize.[90] After six years of prodigious effort, he fitted an equation to Tycho Brahe's data for the Martian orbit, but failed to recognize the equation as the formula for an ellipse. Trying to represent it geometrically he made errors which led to a curve he knew was too bulgy. In despair he discarded his equation because he wanted to try another hunch—an ellipse. Only later did he discover that this was the curve he had already fitted to the data.[91] Perhaps there is a tendency toward sleepwalking in all who are marginal between the two intellectual cultures. In the same book in which MacIver insisted that it was pointless to apply the causal formula of classical mechanics to social phenomena, he postulated a law of inertia for sociology! Although in *Social Causation* he had nearly crossed the divide between animism and naturalism, his understanding of the distinction between these two kinds of thought was still far from clear.

Comte long ago suggested that theological conceptions had been *necessary antecedents* to positive science. The mind could make no progress without indulging in a great deal of irksome labor, and theological philosophy gave it the impetus for that labor. It was "the chimeras of astrology and alchemy" that gave rise to "the long series of observations and experiments on which our positive science is based," Comte wrote. "Kepler felt this on behalf of astronomy, and Berthollet on behalf of chemistry."[92] In the same way, Boring has described phrenology as an important precursor of scientific psychology. It was essentially wrong, but "was just enough right to further scientific thought." It correctly asserted the brain to be the organ of mind, helping to end metaphysical speculation on that issue, and it suggested the localization of functions within regions of the brain.[93] Its other errors, glaring as they were, could not destroy these contributions.

MacIver had expressed a willingness in 1917 to abandon the label "science," which some writers had already said could only apply to sociology if its laws could be formulated with the same exactitude as the laws of physics. "It is unprofitable to quarrel over names. If men care to reserve the title of science to those subjects which admit of quantitative state-

---

[90] *Ibid.*, p. 109.
[91] *Ibid.*, pp. 146–147.
[92] Comte, *op. cit.*, pp. 27–28.
[93] Edwin G. Boring, *A History of Experimental Psychology*, 2d ed. New York: Appleton-Century-Crofts, Inc., 1950, pp. 57–58.

ment, they may be permitted the reservation."[94] But MacIver did not quite actually abide by this concession, for he continued in all his books to refer to sociology as a science. His commitment to the conception of sociology as a science made him, like a sleepwalker, continuously susceptible, then, to the scientific culture in spite of gross misconceptions of the actual character of that culture's norms.

In 1917 these misconceptions were evident when he flatly stated that his laws of communal development were indeed necessary laws which would help to give sociology a place among the sciences. They were laws, he said, in that they revealed "the real nature of communal development. . . ." Communities must conform to them in passing from one stage to a higher stage "because these rules are what development at these stages *means*."[95] As late as 1937 he again displayed a serious misunderstanding of the term "law" as used in science when he suggested that "society is distinct from physical reality in that the laws which sustain it are, at least in part, *prescriptive* or *normative*. Unlike the laws of nature, they can be disobeyed and they can be changed. They have not the inexorable character of natural laws."[96] He seemed here to be imagining that "laws of society" was an expression synonymous with "laws of sociology." Behavior can, of course, depart from the normative prescriptions (or laws) enacted by legislative bodies, but these are not the laws which the sociologist seeks to formulate.

Social laws, MacIver said, differed from natural laws in carrying a sense of obligation and being addressed to the heart and will of those they govern. MacIver was seemingly oblivious of the fact that the laws of a science don't "govern" the phenomena studied by that science. Scientific laws describe, predict, and explain. They are not "addressed" to the phenomena they describe, but to the human mind. MacIver's confusion on this point can be taken as precedent for Parsons's notion that pattern-maintenance was both an "imperative" and a parallel to the axiom of inertia. MacIver was neither the first nor the last great mind to be confused by the unfortunate coincidence that in our language both scientific generalization and custom or legislative statute are designated by the same word.

Other Marginal Men

If MacIver's writing was influenced by the transition from animism to naturalism, so was that of other sociologists. Several men will be treated

---

[94] MacIver, *Community*, p. ix.
[95] *Ibid.*, p. 166.
[96] MacIver, *Society*, p. 328. (My italics.)

from this perspective somewhat more briefly than I have examined Mac-
Iver. No attempt will be made to trace their growth in any longitudinal
way, but indications of their confounding of animistic and naturalistic
elements will be cited.

1 Radcliffe-Brown

In a book entitled A *Natural Science of Society,* in which he argued that
societal phenomena were as amenable to genuinely scientific study as
other phenomena, Radcliffe-Brown seemed to include certain rather animistic notions among the concepts and procedures proposed for his societal science. In some instances, what he said simply left it unclear
whether he retained vestiges of animism in his approach or not. One
would suppose that had he been 100 percent naturalistic, he would have
been able to indicate it more clearly than he did.

He described three sorts of problems a social science would have to
cope with. The first two, problems of classification of social systems and
problems of persistence of social systems, could not be separated, he said.
But a third kind of problem must be studied separately. Problems of persistence may be called "synchronic" problems and must be distinguished
from problems of how societies change their type, which may be called
"diachronic" problems.[97] This sounds rather like Comte's division of sociology into social statics and social dynamics, but if so, then it is astonish-
ing to read Radcliffe-Brown's opinion that synchronic problems (statics?)
are more fundamental than diachronic ones (dynamics?).[98]

There are hints in Radcliffe-Brown's book that he was oscillating toward
and away from the axiom of inertia. "In studying a society synchronically,"
he said, "one treats it as though it were persisting relatively unchanged."[99]
But he added, "Fundamentally societies do not remain unchanged."[100] It
is the word "fundamentally" that makes this sentence difficult to interpret;
I am not sure what he meant by it. If he meant "intrinsically" or "essentially," then the statement could be taken as a denial of the axiom of
inertia. If he meant "empirically," then the statement only amounts to
an equivalent of Parsons's repeated denial that he was denying the occurrence of social change when he spoke of pattern-maintenance.

The assignment of social processes to statics and of acceleration or deceleration of social processes to dynamics, suggested in Chapter 3, had
a rough parallel in Radcliffe-Brown's book. He described the marriage
of two individuals as change *within* a social structure that leaves the structure itself unchanged. Such events were to be studied as synchronic rather

[97] Radcliffe-Brown, *op. cit.,* p. 88.
[98,99] *Ibid.*
[100] *Ibid.,* p. 89.

than diachronic problems. He noted their resemblance to physiological changes in an organism. He called them "readjustments." They were to be sharply differentiated from "changes of type" in which the structural form of a society is modified.[101]

While implying that there do occur instances of diachronic "changes of types," Radcliffe-Brown also said, "A social structure is a natural persistent system. It maintains its continuity despite internal changes from moment to moment, year to year, just as a living organism remains the same living organism in spite of metabolic changes; it is dynamic."[102] In such a statement it is not clear whether he saw change as problematic or constancy as problematic. The concepts of inertia and homeostasis seemed confounded here. At least no conscious effort seemed to have been made to disentangle them. But it sounded as if Radcliffe-Brown was declaring stability to be the problem requiring explanation when he said that social science would have to cope with the question of "*how* social systems perpetuate themselves,"[103] (unless he meant "perpetuate themselves in the face of pressures toward change").

As if arguing that in sociology change was not problematic, he said that one important distinction between human societies and organisms was that societies change type whereas organisms do not. "If an animal gets sick, it either dies or recovers, but if a society gets sick, it makes in due course a recovery, in which, however, it is likely to change its type. A pig does not become sick and recover as a hippopotamus; but that is what a society does."[104] This amounted to drawing a sociological conclusion from biological premises, and the dangers that were cited in the description of such procedures in the previous chapter should be recalled here. Radcliffe-Brown projected onto biology an assumption he wanted to sustain in sociology, but it is questionable even for biology. He had forgotten the biological phenomenon of metamorphosis, whereby a caterpillar becomes a butterfly, or a tadpole a frog. In the guise of asserting an empirical difference between organic and societal phenomena, he merely revealed the indefinite meaning of the phrase "the same type." If it is not altogether clear when a society can properly be said to be "sick," then it is hardly obvious that it does not usually recover as the "same type" of society. A clumsily used metaphor is not a sufficient consideration for ruling out of sociology the inertial axiom.

Radcliffe-Brown suggested the term "dynamic continuity" to refer to the fact that a social system wards off or takes remedial action in response to structural damage.[105] This term, not unlike Parsons's "pattern-maintenance" again, suggests the notion of homeostasis. But he almost seemed

[101] *Ibid.*, p. 87.
[102] *Ibid.*, p. 55.
[103] *Ibid.*, p. 85.
[104] *Ibid.*, p. 83.
[105] *Ibid.*, p. 81.

to be going beyond the affirmation that homeostasis characterizes social systems and might have been denying that social systems have any strictly inertial properties when he said that "the system persists only as long as there is . . . dynamic continuity."[106]

Possibly he did recognize a difference between inertia and homeostasis, for Radcliffe-Brown sought to distinguish "mechanical or temporary systems" from "dynamic and persistent" systems. Mechanical systems comprise relations of mass and motion, and he gave as an example the falling bodies studied by Galileo. A persistent system was one that "maintains through a certain lapse of time its structural continuity." The word "maintains" connotes compensatory activity to undo change, yet the examples given hardly accord with the implication that by "persistent system" he meant a homeostatic system. His examples: an atom, a molecule, a crystal, as well as a living cell, or a multicelled organism.[107]

In short, Radcliffe-Brown seemed quite unclear in regard to the inertial axiom of naturalism. While his attitude toward scientific study of societal phenomena was basically sympathetic, he still exhibited a tendency to argue for an essential something more in social systems that would require them to be studied with different assumptions than natural phenomena entail.

2 Moore

The sleepwalking simile may apply to the ambivalent attitudes of Wilbert Moore in regard to social change and the properties of social systems. He seemed correct in stating in a small book on social change that the equilibrium model of a social system (which, as he described it, may be taken as animistic) "either forecloses questions about the sources of change, or if discordant internal elements are brought into the analysis, the theoretical model will predict one direction of change, and one only—change that restores the system to a steady state."[108] In viewing society as a tension-managing rather than a self-equilibrating system, so as to make "*both* order and change problematical," he seemed to be moving sociology toward naturalism. This declaration that both order and change are problematical could be tantamount to recognizing the distinction between the inertia of social patterns and the homeostasis of social systems. I think this is the insight toward which Moore has been working, and it is a very important one. Yet, as though he were compulsively animistic, Moore went out of his way to "underscore the normality of

[106] *Ibid.*
[107] *Ibid.*, pp. 24–25.
[108] Wilbert E. Moore, *Social Change.* Englewood Cliffs, N.J.: Prentice-Hall, Inc., 1963, p. 10.

change,"[109] when naturalism would require that he define change as problematic.

For another of his books, Moore received the MacIver award. He delivered his MacIver Award Lecture, "Predicting Discontinuities in Social Change," before the Southwestern Sociological Association, and again showed signs of ambivalence in regard to the inertial axiom of naturalism. He spoke of studying "changing *rates* of change" and of "acceleration" in such forms as exponential growth curves, and thereby sounded quite naturalistic. Yet he sounded animistic in asserting that "anthropologists and sociologists have tended to cultural conservatism based on the supposed integrity of time-honored values and customs" and in suggesting that "the resistances are exaggerated and the implied slowness of change simply wrong."[110] This comes close to expecting change regardless of the presence or absence of accelerating forces, and is close to defining constancy as problematic. Worse yet, he justified his tension-management conception of social systems on the ground that it "makes order itself problematical rather than assumed, . . ."[111] as if simply discarding the idea of inertia.

I don't think he fully meant to discard it, though, for his lecture included naturalistic statements like this: "Resistances to change are of course real. Some may be based on a simple preference for the known over the unknown, some on a failure to perceive prospective benefits, some on clearly perceived prospective loss."[112] Both inertia and homeostasis can be read into such a statement, though I do not mean to imply that Moore is again confounding them—only that he acknowledges here the salience of both concepts for sociology.

Like Radcliffe-Brown, or MacIver, then, Moore appears ambivalent in regard to a basic difference between animism and naturalism and can plausibly be regarded as a sociologist in transition. He seems to make naturalistic statements without fully appreciating just how naturalistic they are.

3 Parsons and Naegele

In the preceding chapter I pointed out symptoms of animism in Parsons's writing, though these have for the past decade or so been combined with indications of an apparent desire to be naturalistic at least by association. The claim that pattern-maintenance does for sociology what Newton's first axiom does for physics is an instance of that desire. In an analysis of

[109] *Ibid.*, p. 5. Chap. 1 is entitled, "The Normality of Change."
[110] Wilbert E. Moore, "Predicting Discontinuities in Social Change," *American Sociological Review*, 29 (June, 1964), pp. 333–334.
[111] *Ibid.*, p. 337.
[112] *Ibid.*, p. 334.

the trend in Parsons's writing, Scott perceived an important contrast between Parsons's output prior to the Second World War, about, and his
output after that time. In his early work, Parsons thought that a materialistic determinism was essential to the metaphysics underlying naturalism, and since he did not feel that mental phenomena such as cognition
and evaluation could be explained in such terms, he shied away from
naturalism. He was strongly voluntaristic in his orientation at that time,
according to Scott.[113] More recently, Scott found, Parsons has backed away
from metaphysical dualism, and his terminology has become ambiguous
at points where it was quite clear in his earlier work. The ambiguities
recur in such a way as to seem to Scott to warrant the label "crucial
equivocations"—as if Parsons were striving to maintain a terminological
continuity with his earlier work while moving toward a more naturalistic
orientation.[114] The autonomy of mental activity has been toned down.[115]
But his writing has continued at least to leave ajar the door into voluntarism.[116] Surely these tendencies represent ambivalence.

With respect to the issue of adopting or rejecting the inertial axiom
in sociology, Parsons has candidly confessed to anthropomorphism. He
has described the socialization of a child as comprising structural change
in the child's role patterns, and then has acknowledged that this serves
as his model for the study of social change. In the light of such a model,
he has listed several factors that make change probable, including: (1)
adequate mechanisms to overcome vested interests; (2) occurrence of new
combinations with adequately adaptive effects; (3) a model to be emulated; (4) a pattern of sanctions tending to inhibit former practices and
reward the new pattern.[117] What is significant about this paradigm is that
it makes change seem automatic and hardly problematic, and it is frankly
based on an anthropomorphic analogy. To Parsons, of course, it may have
seemed that he was offering an *explanation* of change, thus implying naturalistically that change *required* explaining. At best, however, he was ambiguous on this, and seemed to go on to regard constancy as problematic
because of the prevalence of the factors in his paradigm. It is a reasonable
conjecture that his ambiguity reflects ambivalence.

There is a similar mixture of animistic and naturalistic elements in
Parsons's close associate, Kaspar Naegele. In his contribution to a collaborative work with Parsons and others, Naegele referred to Newton as
authority for the idea that neither persistence nor change require explana-

---

[113] John Finley Scott, "The Changing Foundations of the Parsonian Action Scheme,"
American Sociological Review, 28 (October, 1963), p. 718.
[114] *Ibid.*, pp. 718–719.
[115] *Ibid.*, p. 716.
[116] *Ibid.*, p. 725.
[117] Talcott Parsons, "An Outline of the Social System," in Talcott Parsons, Edward
Shils, Kaspar D. Naegele, and Jesse R. Pitts (eds.), *Theories of Society*. New York:
The Free Press of Glencoe, 1961, pp. 75–76.

tion in the immediate present. It is their alternation that requires explaining.[118] Cultures do undoubtedly change, he wrote, but why and how they change is what is problematic.[119] These statements sound naturalistic enough, but they seem more or less at variance with such other expressions as the following: Social analysis has the task of providing a verifiable account of "the aliveness of social arrangements," which "lies precisely in their transformation."[120] Every account of collective activities or the impersonal trends of history requires "a relatively detailed sense of human motives."[121] Social change involves changes in "the configuration of motives and dispositions characterizing the members of that society."[122] And the inertial axiom appears to have been rejected in his statement that "forms of change can also be formulated on the basis of their being inherent in social arrangements as distinct from their being imposed on them. . . ."[123] Perhaps it could be said of Naegele, as of Parsons, that he is somewhat reluctantly naturalistic.

Even in those statements in which it seems most likely that Parsons has tried to be thoroughly naturalistic, the Aristotelian assumptions of animism are evident. For example: "Structural change is possible only when a certain level of strain on institutionalized structure is reached."[124] If this proposition is subjected to careful analysis it turns out to reflect a sociological version of Aristotle's laws of motion, rather than Newton's. According to Aristotelian physics: (1) force F must exceed resistance R for motion to occur; (2) velocity V will be inversely proportional to resistance; (3) velocity will be proportional to force.[125] Hence, in modern notation, for all positive values of $F - R$,

$$V = k \left(\frac{F - R}{R} \right) \tag{1}$$

or

$$V = k \left(\frac{F}{R} - 1 \right) \tag{2}$$

4 Stouffer

But Parsons was not alone in bringing such Aristotelian axioms into sociology. Stouffer, who was not usually considered a devotee of voluntarism or of the anthropomorphic or *Verstehende* approach, unwittingly remained

[118] Kaspar D. Naegele, "Introduction" (to part V, "Social Change") in *ibid.*, p. 1208.
[119] *Ibid.*, p. 1218.
[120] *Ibid.*, pp. 1208, 1221.
[121] *Ibid.*, p. 1212.
[122] *Ibid.*, p. 1216.
[123] *Ibid.*, p. 1220.
[124] Parsons, *op. cit.*, p. 75.
[125] See Cohen, *op. cit.*, pp. 27–30.

precariously close to such axioms in his theory of intervening opportunities.[126] Though generally regarded as devoted to quantification and operationalism, Stouffer sought to explain distance differentials in migration in terms of a social variable (intervening opportunities) rather than the physical variable, distance. The formula representing his theory has nearly the same form as Equation 2, above. Stouffer's hypothesis asserts that the migration rate (velocity) varies directly with opportunities at a given distance (attractive force, e.g., available jobs, etc.) and inversely with intervening opportunities (resistance). Thus,

$$V = k \frac{F}{R} \tag{3}$$

Though Stouffer's hypothesis fits certain data reasonably well it is nevertheless very nearly parallel to the Aristotelian laws of motion—except for the latter's subtraction of unity from the ratio of force over resistance. In a limited way, too, the Aristotelian formula seemingly holds for certain classes of physical phenomena, e.g., solid bodies of various weights and degrees of buoyancy falling through fluids of various density and viscosity. Physical science nonetheless could not make much headway until it ceased to regard motion as its problem and became concerned instead with accelerations. There is no adequate reason for supposing *a priori* that sociology would not similarly profit from the abandonment of animistic postulates and the adoption of naturalistic ones.

Stouffer's hypothesis may seem reasonable in asserting that two destinations equidistant from a starting point will attract different numbers of migrants depending inversely on the number of intervening alternative destinations. But it would seem rather less reasonable if it were noted that it also implies that when there are *no* intervening alternatives, a destination's power to attract migrants from a given source is not at all dependent on its distance from that source. In Chapter 9, I shall have more to say about the taboo against reductionism. Here I need only say that Stouffer's theory overlooks (and thus implicitly denies) the fact that distance *as distance* is a deterrent to travel.

Moreover, if Stouffer's hypothesis were amended to make it fully Aristotelian—by including the minus 1 within the parentheses on the right side of the equation, it would become incapable of disconfirmation and hence empirically meaningless. That is, Equation 2 amounts to

$$(V + k) \frac{R}{F} = k \tag{4}$$

It is easy to see that Equation 4 becomes true regardless of the values of V, F, and R, if we merely take $k = \infty$. Later, in Chapter 8, it will

[126] See Samuel A. Stouffer, "Intervening Opportunities: A Theory Relating Mobility and Distance," *American Sociological Review*, 5 (December, 1940), pp. 845–867.

be instructive to compare Equation 4 with various other equations somewhat similar in form that are intended to account for variation among certain social "velocities." For the present it is sufficient to note that, given matrices of values of any two of the three variables *V*, *F*, and *R* for an assortment of sources and of destinations, it would be impossible to solve this equation to obtain a matrix of the values of the third variable. This is because *k* remains a free parameter. Neither Aristotle, nor Parsons or Stouffer, did anything to specify its magnitude. None claimed it to be a constant of nature, like the *G* in Newton's gravitational formula, whose fixed magnitude could be discovered empirically. Since *k* appears on both sides of Equation 4, it would have to be specified in order for the equation to become empirically testable.

Thus, when stated in quantitative form, and made as closely parallel to a naturalistic counterpart as possible, the Aristotelian approach remains predictively sterile. It should be discarded by sociology. Stouffer fell back too far toward it in his efforts to avoid being reductionist while working in a way that was otherwise sympathetic to naturalism.

Summary

We are still in an era of intellectual transition, and sociologists, among others, are cross-pressured by the humanistic culture which draws them back toward animism and the modern scientific culture which would guide their inquiry along naturalistic lines. Various sociologists have displayed an ambivalence in their writings which it is reasonable to suppose has resulted from their marginality between these two cultures. Specifically focusing on the inertial postulate as a basic feature that distinguishes naturalism from animism, we find such men as MacIver, Radcliffe-Brown, Moore, Parsons, Naegele, and in a way even Stouffer, either showing a continuous trend toward naturalism or oscillating between the two orientations. Part of the confusion with which these men have struggled lies in the superficial similarity of homeostasis and inertia. For many sociologists the subtle but fundamental difference between these concepts has been obscured, though there has apparently been some progress toward its clarification. When clarification of this issue has finally been achieved, it will be apparent that the great longevity of Aristotelian assumptions was unwarranted and unfortunate. Their firm rejection by sociology is overdue.

Chapter Five
NATURALISTIC STUDY OF VALUES

Two Barriers to Knowledge

When it is naturalistic, the sociological investigation of social phenomena proceeds according to the same logic followed by the natural sciences, and explanations for observed social regularities are sought in accord with the tenets of natural science stated in Chapter 1. Animistic sociology, on the other hand, would insist that naturalism "leaves out" something essential in human behavior that distinguishes it from the phenomena studied by the natural sciences. As we saw in Chapter 4, in his earlier writings MacIver insisted on a fundamental distinction between "material law" and "vital law." The latter was what sociology must seek to formulate for its subject matter, he argued; it could not aspire to be a natural science because its phenomena were not patterned in accordance with material law. MacIver felt that sociology, to be true to its subject matter, must not fail to take into account the "dynamic assessments" performed by men in interaction.

The something more that is alleged to remove sociology from the category of natural science has been called by various names. In addition to MacIver's dynamic assessments, the concepts of will, function, final cause, and vital principle have all had one attribute in common: they purport to be immune to analysis by naturalistic means. Man is said to be a creature with *values*, and hence different from the creatures and objects science can effectively study. He chooses, he has aims and intentions, he seeks goals, his behavior is purposive.

The purposiveness of man's actions has sometimes been cited as an explanation for the observed regularities in human behavior. At other times it has been offered as the ultimate excuse for human inexplicability. Man's behavior is not predictable, the latter view maintains, because it is willful. To refute this extreme position, it ought to be sufficient to show (as sociological studies over the years have repeatedly done) that there are clear and important regularities in human activity and especially in the interaction of human groups. Those who continue to believe in the essentially unpredictable character of human beings have simply refused to accept the first axiom of naturalism, namely, the reliance on empirical evidence as the test of truth. I do not hope to reach such persons with this book.

I do hope, however, to reach some of those who take purposiveness to be the distinguishing human characteristic and who give it explanatory significance. I hope to enable them to see that little is accomplished by merely insisting (as some often do) that "you can't explain human behavior without reference to values." It is up to them, I think, to assume some burden of proof, and *demonstrate* that the value concept does contribute to the explanation of human behavior. It needs also to be demonstrated, not merely argued, that values can be reliably and validly known. We need to be confident that in predicting actions from values we are predicting from data and not just from unverifiable revelation.

I think most sociologists whom I would regard as moderately animistic would accept such a burden of proof. Extreme voluntarists and vitalists probably would not. They insist on injecting *concepts* of value and will into the analysis of human social experience, but withhold any hope of linking such concepts with *data*. In their view, values and acts of will remain fundamentally inscrutable. Science they say, is inadequate without them, but it cannot get at them to incorporate them into its battery of predictor variables. Such thinking brings down an iron curtain between the scientist and the information he is told he can't do without.

To illustrate this doctrine, which would frustrate science, I will quote MacIver—the early MacIver who insisted that vital law was absolutely distinct from material law. He wrote:[1]

Those who would make sociology a "natural" science, unconcerned with values, would leave out of account the special characteristics of the world of which it treats, in a vain attempt to ape those sciences where such characteristics are unknown. We are overmuch inclined to see in physical science the type and model of all science, and to imagine that measurement alone is knowledge. Purposes are incommensurate; the movements of thought among a people cannot

[1] Robert M. MacIver, *Community: A Sociological Study.* New York: St. Martin's Press, Inc., 1917, pp. 56–57.

be estimated by counting heads; the power of personality is not to be measured like the power of an engine; institutions are ideal constructions without quantitative length or breadth.

MacIver was simply mistaken in supposing that as a natural science sociology would have to be unconcerned with values, but he was equally mistaken in supposing that values can never be measured.

On the other side, another barrier is put in the way of social science by the extreme positivist viewpoint that inferential constructs are taboo. Data are sought, and correlations among data, but these correlations must not, according to extreme positivism, be "explained" by invoking illata as links between concreta. In Chapter 2, I listed positivism in association with naturalism, but I said the two should not be equated. Whatever the positivist might insist, it is not a foregone conclusion that the value concept is alien to sociology any more than it is a foregone conclusion that it is essential to sociology but unmeasurable.

Many sociological propositions can be stated in the form: The probability that behavior pattern Y will occur is greater (by some specified amount) if behavior pattern X occurs than if X does not occur. The quest of sociology is in part for statements of contingent probability. Doctrinaire positivism would stop with this, or would even require that such propositions say no more than that the probability that behavior pattern Y will *be observed* is greater (by some specified amount) if behavior pattern X *has been observed* than if it has not. Not all the generalizations in the current literature of sociology can be reduced to this form, but various sociologists from time to time—beginning with Comte—have advocated this as the ideal. I contend that this is no more the ideal of naturalistic sociology than is the avoidance of the value concept.

In the strictly positivist framework, the question *why* pattern Y is statistically contingent upon pattern X is regarded as meaningless and unscientific. Such "why" questions were abjured by Comte as metaphysical or theological, and many sociologists since his time have tried to be similarly positivistic. Others, however, while wishing to be rigorously scientific, have refused to equate science with positivism and have persisted in asking, Why does X lead to Y? or What is the nature of the connection between them? or How do we know X would again be followed by Y?

A common answer to such questions involves the concept of values. Human behavior is patterned as it is, supposedly, because men hold certain *conceptions of the desirable* which motivate them to act in certain ways and in certain sequences. For example: In a certain population let us suppose we observe a four-year cycle in the proportion of mass communications content that consists of vituperative discussion. This proportion rises to a peak around the end of October each leap year. Early in November it virtually disappears and is immediately replaced by messages of congratulations from one small group of persons to another and by innumerable analyses (not necessarily in agreement with one another) as to why these congratulatory messages flowed from left to right, say, rather than from right to left as they had four years earlier. Suppose we have recorded a number of successive cycles of this type. We predict their continued recurrence. Why? Not from mere statistical extrapolation of an observed trend, but because we *infer* that the American electorate desires to uphold the Constitution and conform to the expressed will of the majority more than it desires the election of particular candidates. That is, we assume the efficacy of certain *values*—conceptions of the desirable—in the American political system.

If those who advocate use of the value concept in sociology do not show that values can be studied scientifically, naturalistically, then they invite the response of the doctrinaire positivist who rejects the concept altogether. He has felt constrained to dismiss the value concept as nothing but sociopsychological phlogiston, without any empirical referent and hence devoid of any genuine explanatory power.

If the principal thing a writer says about values is that they constitute an essential difference between humanity and the other categories of phenomena in the universe so that the method of natural science so successfully applied to obtaining knowledge of those other entities is inapplicable to persons and societies, then that writer invites his readers to label him a "vitalist." More important, he unwittingly invites his readers to conclude that science must resist the intrusion of the value concept, which is just the opposite of what he presumably intends. He won't gain adoption of his favorite concept by science just by preaching that the concept is indispensable, if he allows it to retain occult connotations. In *Social Causation*, MacIver repeatedly asserted the *necessity* of the value concept as an element in the causal nexus of one social event with another. But its *utility* was largely left to the reader's inference. Just *how* it would facilitate prediction, or explanation (the subsuming of one predictive proposition under another of greater generality), was not made clear.

It is my contention that we do not need to reject the value concept in order to make sociology a natural science. It does not need to remain an occult notion. I disagree with Franz Adler's assertion that "the natural science sociologist . . . has no real need for a value concept," although I agree with him that "valuations . . . can be known only from . . . actions" of one sort or another.[2] (I would include verbal responses under the rubric "actions.") To say that values have to be inferred from behavior is not the same as saying that values can be "equated with action" as Adler did.[3]

Caught, as it were, between the Scylla of vitalism and the Charybdis

[2] Franz Adler, "The Value Concept in Sociology," *American Journal of Sociology*, 62 (November, 1956), p. 275.
[3] *Ibid.*, pp. 276–277.

of positivism, the advocate of naturalistic sociology, it seems to me, must do one of two things. He must either show that he can get along nicely without the value concept, or that it is no mere entelechy. Actually it seems to be possible to do some of each. Human actions can be shown to be less value-determined than vitalists suppose, and to the extent that they *are* shaped by values, if enough ingenuity is applied in designing studies, these values can be investigated naturalistically.

If values could *not* be studied within a naturalistic framework, but *were* essential elements in social causation, then the vitalist would be right in his claim that the domain of natural science is severely circumscribed. The naturalistic sociologist does his own cause a disservice, however, when he seems to concede this point. He sometimes appears to do so when he goes out of his way to assert that values are "merely" inferential constructs. Of course, they are inferred rather than observed, but there is a legitimate place in scientific thought for inferential constructs, so long as they are truly inferential and not simply metaphysical or *a priori*.

It is true that in studying values, a sociologist studies illata rather than directly observable phenomena (concreta). These illata must, of course, be inferred from preferential *behavior*. What doctrinaire positivists suggest is simply this: the illata are not worth the effort of inferring them. I contend that they are and that it is within the bounds of naturalism to do so.

The extreme positivist's prescription for a healthy science is reminiscent of the old-fashioned almanac. Its daily weather forecasts (a year in advance) were simply assertions that the weather most often observed on a given date in past years would be the most probable weather on the corresponding date in the coming year. We could, if we wished, build an almanaclike sociology. Alternatively, we could emulate the meteorologist who tries to ascertain the forces which produce specified changes of weather. His forecasts tend to be more accurate (and more specific) than those of an almanac. Even when they are in error we still regard them as more sophisticated, with greater prospects for refinement and improvement.

Sociology must concern itself always with empirical regularities. It does not follow that we must *confine* our work to discerning and recording such empirical regularities. How are we to know that the regularity is more than an artifact of our preconceptions as reflected in our choice of sample and our method of observation?

The sun, moon, and planets exhibit patterned movements in the sky, and man has (I presume) nearly always expected these regularities to persist. I doubt if he has often been content to leave it at that, however, and I don't believe he is well advised by positivism to do so. Man has sought explanations for the observed regularities. His explanations have varied from time to time. Theologically oriented people have attributed such regularities to Divine Providence. This was, of course, a kind of animism: celestial bodies moved as they did because God had ordained it. Sometimes such motions have been explained in terms of essences. Celestial bodies being composed of ether, whose essential property was perfect (i.e., circular) motion, consequently moved in circles. Since Newton, we have attributed the recurrences of celestial events to movements of the Earth and other planets in orbits around the sun—under the influence of their mutual gravitation. Gravity is, however, an inferential construct. It cannot be directly observed; only the movements of falling objects or of celestial bodies are observable. Nevertheless, the gravity concept has been of great importance in the advancement of science.

We could continue to specify, as Adler would have us do, those "situations in which people who have experienced certain specifiable kinds of interaction behave differently from those who did not experience them."[4] We might produce a large catalog of rather clear empirical regularities. This is worth doing, but it is not all that we can do in naturalistic sociology. I believe that the value concept as I define it below can enable us to go beyond such almanac compilation. By knowing something about the *forces* that produce observed regularities we know how to go about looking for previously unobserved patterns. We know how to relate one regularity to another.

Parsimony is not served by refusing to invoke illata, but by choosing them wisely so that they can connect many concreta and abstracta in one theory. The remainder of this chapter presents a theory of valuing behavior which will permit the study of values within a naturalistic framework. It is compatible with existing social-psychological theory and knowledge in the Cooley-Mead-Faris tradition. It is mainly a synthesis of selected contributions by various sociologists, psychologists, and value theorists from other disciplines. It should help to clarify some of the difficulties that have heretofore beset the study of values and have made the clash between the vitalistic advocacy of the value concept and the naturalistic inclination to reject it seem perpetual. Variations in preferential behavior can be accounted for in naturalistic terms that will actually help to make clear how the illusions of vitalism are sustained. Then they can be laid to rest.

Some Definitions

Let a "desideratum" be anything some person desires at some time. It may be a material object, a social relationship, an item of information—in

[4] Franz Adler, "On Values and Value Theory," *American Sociological Review*, 25 (February, 1960), p. 85.

general, anything tangible or intangible denoted by the words "object of desire." "Valuing" may then be defined as actions which show a person's intensity of desire for various desiderata,[5] or the amount of his "motivation"[6] to pursue them.

Every personality, and every social organization, is confronted at frequent intervals with the task of choosing among alternative desiderata. As MacIver put it, "No abstract measuring-rod can be found, but no person can act at all unless he can choose; the necessities of life and character are necessities of choice. . . . the whole social situation implies that [desiderata] are comparable, that they are forms of a single value. That is the pre-condition of the co-ordination of community, that is also the pre-condition of the unity of life."[7] Certainly energy that is expended to obtain one desideratum is not available for the pursuit of others. Preferences must thus be expressed among diverse objects. Typically, such preferences are not random, but patterned. The patterns they exhibit are relatively stable.[8]

Although such valuing behavior exhibits a certain amount of regularity within a given society or group, it may differ systematically from one group or society to another.[9] This indicates that valuing (or preferring) is partly a function of socially acquired characteristics of valuers. Much of the early struggle to formulate sociological theories consisted of hesitant but growing recognition of the fact of cultural variability and of the implications of this for cultural relativity. Such recognition was impeded, for a time, by the ethnocentric insistence on the notion of unilinear cultural evolution, which regarded diverse existing cultures as representing different stages in a fixed sequence. Even today, some of the resistance to naturalistic sociology comes from those who are unwilling to consider any challenge to the notion of a single, transcultural, objectively valid system of values. But only after variation between cultures is acknowledged can substantial uniformity of preferential behaviors within each separate culture be recognized and analyzed.

If preferential behavior exhibits certain regularities, to what may these be attributed? The noun "value" has usually been used to imply some code or standard which persists through time and provides a criterion by

[5] Stuart C. Dodd, "On Classifying Human Values: A Step in the Prediction of Human Valuing," *American Sociological Review,* 16 (October, 1951), p. 646.
[6] For an operational definition of "motivation" that could serve naturalistic value theory, see L. L. Thurstone, "The Indifference Function," *Journal of Social Psychology,* 2 (May, 1931), pp. 141–142.
[7] MacIver, *op. cit.,* p. 301.
[8] See William R. Catton, Jr., "Exploring Techniques for Measuring Human Values," *American Sociological Review,* 19 (February, 1954), pp. 49–55: William R. Catton, Jr., "A Retest of the Measurability of Certain Human Values," *American Sociological Review,* 21 (June, 1956), pp. 357–359; Hornell Hart, "A Reliable Scale of Value Judgments," *American Sociological Review,* 10 (August, 1945), pp. 473–481.
[9] See Charles Morris, *Varieties of Human Value.* Chicago: The University of Chicago Press, 1956, chap. 3.

which people order their intensities of desiring various desiderata. To the extent that the people of a given society are able to place objects, actions, ways of life, and so on, on a continuum of approval-disapproval with some reliability, it appears that their responses to particular desiderata are functions of culturally acquired *values*.

In investigating the values of a person or group, a sociologist studies inferential constructs—which need not always resemble verbal statements that have been or can be made by the persons whose behavior is being studied. The sociologist may simply regard it as useful to try to infer from the patterned choices of persons or groups some "conception . . . of the desirable which influences the selection from available modes, means, and ends of action."[10] The desiderata are usually concreta, but may sometimes be abstracta. The choices the sociologist observes are concreta, but if they are repeatedly observed so that an inductive inference is made that "this person *typically* chooses that desideratum in such and such a situation" then the preferential *patterns* are abstracta. Finally, the values which are presumed to motivate the expressions of preference are illata, not directly observable, but connected to observations by certain repeatable operations.

The values inferred will depend, of course, upon what sort of expressions of preference are used as data. If we study a person's *actual* preferences among an array of desiderata, any discerned regularities may cause us to speak of what Charles Morris has called "operative values." If we emphasize those preferences which seem to be based on a person's *anticipation* of the outcome of alternative behaviors (where anticipation is possible through symbolic representation or covert imagery), then the regularities to which we refer may be called his "conceived values." If we assume that, apart from his actual preferences or his anticipatory preferences, he *ought* to prefer certain things and disprefer others, then we are speaking of "object values"—those things which "are in fact" preferable, whether or not preferred, and whether or not conceived as preferable by the subject. As Morris noted, however, all three usages of the term "values" have in common some association with the concept of preference. Value may refer to the preferred, to what is conceived as preferable, or to the "actually" preferable.

According to Morris, "operative values" can be found through a study of preferential behavior. What is conceived to be preferable (conceived values) can be studied through the symbols employed in preferential behavior and the preferential behavior directed toward symbols.[11] In effect,

---

[10] Clyde Kluckhohn, "Values and Value-orientations in the Theory of Action: An Exploration in Definition and Classification," in Talcott Parsons and Edward A. Shils (eds.), *Toward a General Theory of Action*. Cambridge, Mass.: Harvard University Press, 1952, p. 395.

[11] Morris, *op. cit.*, p. 12.

then, Morris has *operationally defined* two concepts: (1) "Operative values" are operationally defined as factors to be found through an analysis of preferences among nonsymbolic desiderata. (2) "Conceived values" are operationally defined as factors to be found through an analysis of preferences among symbolic desiderata (that is, preferential behavior directed toward symbols employed in other preferential behavior).

His category of "object values" remains without operational definition, perhaps implying that Morris relegated it to a nonempirical universe of discourse. If the naturalist would really join issues with the vitalist, here is the ground for it. The naturalist need not get into a position of denying *all* values; he only has to adopt an agnostic position regarding the "object values" asserted by the vitalist. The vitalist has no business maintaining that all values are scientifically inscrutable. He can only claim this for his alleged "object values."

Morris's operational definitions, and the general suggestion that axiology can be defined as the science of preferential behavior,[12] can greatly help to penetrate the confusion in the literature on values. Confusion arises because "value" is given several different meanings in the literature, and it is not always clear which meaning a given writer intends.[13] But this hardly warrants the conclusion that the value concept is superfluous.[14]

According to Clyde Kluckhohn, we should restrict the use of the term "value" to something combining the characteristics of "conceived values" and of "object values." He defines a value as "a conception of the desirable" that is regarded as "justified."[15] But if, as Morris seemed to imply by not attempting to define them operationally, "object values" lie outside any empirical universe of discourse, how can we hope to study, by the methods of science, values so conceived?

In attempting to study values naturalistically, let us tentatively adopt Kluckhohn's definition, subject to revision as our analysis proceeds. If a

[12] See Charles Morris, "Axiology as the Science of Preferential Behavior," in Ray Lepley (ed.), *Value: A Cooperative Inquiry.* New York: Columbia University Press, 1949.

[13] Franz Adler, "The Value Concept in Sociology," pp. 272–279. "Concepts of value can . . . be reduced to about four basic types: (A) Values are considered as absolutes, existing in the mind of God as eternal ideas, as independent validities, etc. (B) Values are considered as being in the object, material or non-material. (C) Values are seen as located in man, originating in his biological needs or in his mind. Man by himself or man in the aggregate, variously referred to as group, society, culture, state, class, is seen as 'holding' values. (D) Values are equated with actions."

Adler would study only type (D) which approximates "operative values" as defined by Morris. Type (C) perhaps is equivalent to "conceived values." Types (A) and (B) together amount to what Morris called "object values." Despite the apparent researchability of "conceived values" as Morris operationally defined them, Adler contends that type (C) values are "inaccessible to the methods of the natural sciences (at the present state of our knowledge concerning internal mental and emotional phenomena) . . . ." This statement seems unwarranted if we are willing to adopt the general position that preferential behavior, both symbolic and nonsymbolic, can be observed, recorded, and studied.

[14] See *ibid.*, pp. 275 and 279.

[15] Kluckhohn, *op. cit.*, p. 396.

value is a *"conception* of the desirable," then clearly we must study it, following Morris, by analyzing preferences among *symbolic* desiderata. Basic value variables we might discover through such analysis need not, by any purely logical necessity, bear any relation to the variables we might discover by analyzing the preferences of the same population with respect to *nonsymbolic* desiderata. As Adler has pointed out, "All that the existence of a [verbally expressed] norm proves . . . is that there are people who want it to exist."[16] It does not prove that they want to, or will, comply with it. Compliance of behavior with stated norms, or consistency between operative values and conceived values, must be discovered empirically, rather than assumed *a priori.*

The full statement of Kluckhohn's definition, however, asserts such consistency. Values, he said, are conceptions of the desirable *which influence selection* from available modes, means, and ends of action. We can avoid the "hopeless and useless circularity"[17] that arises when we try to explain behavior by merely "reading into" it the very values by which we purport to explain it, if we make a sharper distinction than Kluckhohn and others have made between definition and hypothesis. To this end, it is useful to amend Kluckhohn's definition of value to read: *A value is a conception of the desirable which is implied by a set of preferential responses to symbolic desiderata.* (Unless modified by some adjective, the term "value" is hereinafter used in accord with this definition.) In keeping with modern social psychology, it may be further assumed that these conceptions of the desirable are socially acquired. We learn them in the socialization process. Many of the cultural precepts which we internalize as values are customarily stated as absolutes. The above definition suggests, therefore, that we should study "conceived values" which are *taken by the valuer* to be "object values." The members of most societies, it seems safe to say, tend to reify the values of their respective cultures.[18]

Relation of Values to Choices

The part of Kluckhohn's definition which was deleted now becomes an empirically contingent hypothesis. It may be stated as follows.

Hypothesis 1: Socially acquired conceptions of the desirable (values) influence human choices among nonsymbolic desiderata.

The rationale for this hypothesis is this: If the human personality is

[16] Adler, "The Value Concept in Sociology," p. 278.
[17] See Adler's criticism of such circular analysis, *ibid.* Cf. the equally trenchant criticism of the same type of circularity by Robert M. MacIver, *Social Causation,* Boston: Ginn and Company, 1942, p. 181.
[18] See William L. Kolb, "The Changing Prominence of Values in Modern Sociological Theory," in Howard Becker and Alvin Boskoff (eds.), *Modern Sociological Theory.* New York: The Dryden Press, Inc., 1957, p. 100.

viewed as a single, coherent system, we must suppose that what goes on in one part of that system tends to affect the behavior of other parts, so that "conceived values" may be expected to have some influence upon "operative values" (and perhaps vice versa). For purposes of conceptual clarity the sociologist can distinguish between symbolic and nonsymbolic desiderata, but it must not be supposed that people in general habitually act in accord with such a distinction. Their patterns of preference among desiderata are unlikely to reflect clear boundaries between symbolic and nonsymbolic items. Americans who wished to invade Castro's Cuba may have felt the urge to smash a regime that symbolized America's lack of omnipotence, but their desires were expressed in terms of the alleged threat to American security posed by a Communist regime so close to United States territory.

Those who insist that the essential differentiating characteristic of human behavior is that it is teleological, goal-directed, purposive, or value-oriented, thereby imply that Hypothesis 1 is a fundamental sociological axiom rather than a proposition to be tested empirically. In trying to be naturalistic, then, all that I have done is to embrace some operational definitions of key concepts and to express some tentativity about a proposition the vitalists take to be axiomatic.

It may be stretching a point to assume this much overlap in their universes of discourse, but the philosopher who insists that human behavior is essentially purposive is saying to the naturalist, in effect, if you ascertain a man's values by analyzing the pattern of preferences he expresses among symbolic desiderata, then you can predict his choices among nonsymbolic desiderata—including alternative courses of action. Is this so? Do values predict actions?

In a recent study of organizational behavior, I had an opportunity to shed some light on this question. This study began with the simple hypothesis that members of a voluntary association are likely to participate in its activities in proportion to their agreement with the values of the leaders of that organization.[19] Thus, if it were possible to measure the degree of agreement of individual members with the values of an organization's leaders, and if the extent to which the members participated in the activities of that organization could also be measured, by this hypothesis we would expect these two series of measures to be significantly and positively correlated.

In order to measure these variables, we assumed that organizations generally articulate reasons for being and typically strive to attain a multi-

[19] A version of this hypothesis appearing in the literature on organizational behavior is as follows: ". . . The intensity of the desire to be active in a group is a function of the extent of congruence between individual and group norms." J. G. March, "Group Norms and the Active Minority," *American Sociological Review*, 19 (December, 1954), p. 738 (footnote 15). See also, Chris Argyris, "Fusion of the Individual with the Organization," *American Sociological Review*, 19 (June, 1954), pp. 267–272.

plicity of goals. Further, it was assumed that among the several goals pursued by a given organization there will typically be a more or less clear order of priority, with some goals more highly valued than others. The order of priority assigned by an organization (or by an individual) to the several goals pursued by it would, according to the definitions given above, reflect the *values* of the organization (or of an individual).

To measure the degree to which a member of an organization agrees with the organizational leaders' values, we can observe the extent to which he and the leaders assign *similar orders of priority* to a list of goals. A list of goals quoted from the literature of the organization could be assigned a rank order by some group of officials empowered to speak for the organization, or they could be given relative numerical ratings, and this rank order or set of numerical ratings could be compared with the rank order or numerical ratings assigned the same goals by any individual member. The higher the correlation coefficient between the two sets of rankings or ratings, the greater the value agreement between member and leaders. The lower the correlation coefficient, the less the member and leaders agree on values.

Operationally stated, the hypothesis now reads: The extent to which each member participates in the activities of an organization will vary directly with the size of the correlation coefficient between the order of priority he assigns to a set of organizational goals and the order of priority assigned those goals by the organization's leaders. Thus the predictor variable is a correlation coefficient, computed for each individual, showing the degree to which that individual concurs with the values of the organization's leaders. The hypothesis expects this series of individual correlation coefficients to be correlated with another variable, a series of individual scores on a scale of organizational participation.

This hypothesis was tested on the membership of a local chapter of a nationwide voluntary association, consisting of persons who, for the most part, were college graduates, whose median age was about fifty-five, and whose median family income was about $25,000 annually. To avoid any embarrassment to the organization, whose members responded confidentially to the questionnaire, we shall make no reference to the specific identity of the organization. The pseudonym "Organization X" will be used.

Responses to 18 goals stated in the organization's literature were actually obtained from three objectively distinguishable groups—the leaders of Organization X, self-acknowledged members of the organization's chapter in one city, and nonmembers whose names had somehow been included on the chapter's mailing list. From each set of responses it was, of course, possible to calculate a set of scale scores showing the worth attached to each goal relative to the other goals by the respondents in that group. Each set of scale scores was indicative of the values of a given group of respondents, in the sense that they showed that group's *collective* assignment of priority among the goals (collective preference among desiderata). A comparison between the three sets of scale scores would then amount to a comparison between three systems of collectively held values—the values of Organization X leaders, the values of Organization X members, and the values of nonmembers.

It turned out that the relative importance to Organization X leaders of the 18 goals was not significantly more predictive of their relative importance to members than to responding nonmembers. The correlations between the three sets of scale scores are shown in Table 2. They are

Table 2   Correlations between three sets of scale scores based on ratings of relative importance of 18 goals to Organization X or to respondents personally

	Importance to chapter members	Importance to non- members
Importance to Organization X, as rated by a panel of its leaders	.90	.81
Importance to chapter members		.89

all significantly greater than zero at the 1 percent level, but none of the differences between correlations is significant even at the 5 percent level. Moreover, the 18 *differences* between members' and nonmembers' scale scores were not significantly correlated (either positively or negatively) with leaders' scale scores.

Thus it can be said that in this local chapter, members and nonmembers were not significantly differentiated from each other in the extent of their acceptance of the values of Organization X as measured by agreement with a panel of leaders of that organization in regard to ordering the relative importance of 18 stated goals. Collectively, then, the three groups of respondents did not differ significantly in their values, though they obviously had quite different relationships to the organization.

Individually, too, behavior was not highly predictable from values. For self-acknowledged members of the chapter, the product-moment correlation coefficient between their activity scores and their concurrence scores turned out to be .26, which was significantly different from zero at the 1 percent level. This gives *some* support to the contention that members' organizational behavior was a function of acceptance of organizational leaders' values, but it is well to note that the correlation was quite small, even though significantly different from zero. Less than 7 percent of the variance in members' activity has been "explained" by concurrence with organizational leaders' values (since $r^2 < .07$). Those sociologists and others who hold that human behavior is value-determined should be challenged by this finding to carry out further research. The direction and significance of the correlation supports their contention, but the magnitude of the correlation is so small that the support is too weak for them properly to rest on it.

To ensure that this finding was not just due to the particular method of measurement employed, we undertook another study in which the method of measurement was modified. A smaller list of more inclusive goals was composed, and printed in a questionnaire that was mailed out to a nationwide random sample of 1,030 persons named on the Organization X mailing list. Once again, the list turned out to include a number of nonmembers. Each respondent was asked to *rank* eight objectives according to their relative importance to him. Since the ratings in the local chapter study had all tended to cluster toward one end of the rating continuum, this ranking procedure was tried as a means of compelling respondents to make finer discriminations among the goals.

Some of the nonmembers in the sample had formerly been members. On the assumption that one important factor in the alienation of ex-members is ideological disagreement, we would expect this to be reflected in their ranking of a list of hypothetical objectives of the organization. If the order assigned to a set of desiderata is a function of one's values, persons with different values would be expected to order a given set of desiderata differently. Specifically, the correlation between the mean ranks assigned to the eight items by members and the mean ranks assigned by nonmembers should either be near zero or it should be negative—to indicate ideological disagreement.

The two sets of mean ranks turned out to have a significant *positive* correlation; the correlation coefficient was .85. In other words, the collective response of nonmembers agreed rather closely with the collective response of members. This finding again suggests that *non*ideological factors were largely responsible for some persons in the sample being members and others being nonmembers.

In addition, concurrence of each individual member with Organization X values was measured by determining the degree of agreement between his ranking of the eight goals and the collective ranking of the eight goals by all members, i.e., the rank order of the mean ranks. This index of concurrence was not significantly associated with any of the following activity variables: (1) frequency of attempts to proselytize nonmembers; (2) frequency of attendance at local Organization X meetings; (3) frequency of reading its official journal; (4) attendance versus nonattendance at any national convention of the organization. Together these four activity items constituted a Guttman scale with 90.2 percent reproducibility. Correlation of the whole scale with the concurrence scores was not significantly different from zero. It was clear, then, that concurrence of members with values of Organization X was not predictive of members' activity in the organization. Activity seemed to depend on factors other than value concurrence, as measured.

Still another set of data, from the same questionnaire study, cast further doubt on the notion that organizational behavior is essentially goal-directed. Respondents were asked to rate *several* organizations (including Organization X) on a seven-point numerical scale, indicating "the extent to which each organization is, in your opinion, 'on the right track'—that is, working toward goals with which you happen to agree." Each of the organizations listed drew its membership largely from the same ethnic minority that included the members of Organization X, and many of the members of Organization X were also members of one or more of the other organizations.

For responding members of Organization X, only about 11 percent of the activity variance could be explained by variance in endorsement of goals of Organization X. On the next page of the questionnaire, the various organizations were listed again, and respondents were asked to check "yes" or "no" to indicate whether or not they either belonged to or made financial contributions directly to each of them. Biserial correlation coefficients were computed, measuring the degree to which respondents' support of each of the organizations in turn depended on endorsement of its perceived goals. Professed degree of agreement with organizational goals accounted (on the average, over the several organizations) for only about a third of the variance in reported support, and this would again suggest that nonideological factors were of considerable importance in this respect, although somewhat less so for the other organizations than for Organization X. One is reminded by these findings of the doctrines of Pareto regarding the "nonlogical" character of human action.[20]

Organization X was a rather controversial voluntary association. It is impossible to describe in detail the difficulties besetting it without thereby disclosing its identity, but it can be said that many of the ethnic peers of its members regarded membership in it as a violation of the mores of the larger ethnic community. Data from interviews with various articulate members of Organization X suggest the following three reasons for some members remaining inactive even while concurring with the organizational leaders' values: (1) a social stigma attaching to membership in the organization, and a fear of economic reprisal; (2) disagreements within the organization regarding the policies of its leadership intended to implement the goals, and disputes over the personalities of certain prominent persons in the leadership; (3) paucity of close primary-group ties among members with resulting lack of positive social reinforcement of membership.

There are other objective indications that this particular organization

[20] See Vilfredo Pareto, *The Mind and Society*. New York: Harcourt, Brace & World, Inc., 1935, vol. 1, chaps. 2 and 3. On such nonlogical aspects of social movements, see C. Wendell King, *Social Movements in the United States*. New York: Random House, Inc., 1956, pp. 115–116.

was atypical in regard to the hypothesis of purposiveness of behavior. It was peculiar in such a way as perhaps to lend confirmation to that hypothesis to a weaker degree than might occur with other organizations. When members were asked to rate the extent to which they felt this and a dozen other organizations were "on the right track," the extent to which they felt a certain other organization was on the *wrong* track turned out to be a better predictor of their scores on the four-item Guttman scale of activity in Organization X than was the extent to which they thought Organization X was on the *right* track. As a protest organization, then, its members apparently were more motivated by having something to protest *against* than by feeling that they had an effective organization to protest *with*.

Similar research conducted on other organizations of a different type, and not beset with the same sorts of difficulties, might not only yield a *significant* correlation between value concurrence and organizational activity, but the absolute *size* of the correlation coefficient might be expected to be somewhat larger.[21] However, in a study of levels of participation in church activities in two Protestant parishes of different denomination (and conspicuously different theology), Karber obtained results very similar to the results of the Organization X study. He used procedures very much like those reported here, and found that in both a fundamentalist and a theologically liberal parish the concurrence of parishioners with the values of their respective denomination was not highly predictive of their degree of participation in church activities.[22]

In Organization X, members who were in minimal agreement or in actual disagreement with the leaders' values were persons who typically participated only to the extent of making yearly financial contributions. On the other hand, all highly active members were in high agreement with the leaders' values. Not all members who were in high agreement were highly active, however. In short, concurrence with the values of the organization's leaders appeared to be a necessary but not a sufficient condition for intense activity in the organization. This pattern would make it seem reasonable to suppose that for other voluntary associations not having the same peculiarities as this one, organizational activity might be somewhat more predictable from value concurrence.

The findings indicate, then, that values do predict actions, as we are

[21] Another factor that probably lowered the correlation was the insistence by the leaders of Organization X that the instrument not include any negative goals—any goals antithetical to the actual aims of Organization X. They feared questionnaire recipients might misinterpret inclusion of any such fictitious goals and take them for expressions of the organization's position. Had the range of goals not been thus truncated, the instrument might have been a somewhat more sensitive device for measuring the priority-determining values of leaders and members of Organization X.
[22] David Karber, "A Comparative Analysis of Two Church Congregations: Sacred versus Secular Orientation," unpublished M.A. thesis. Seattle: University of Washington, 1961.

told by those who insist on this as an essential uniqueness of human behavior. But their insistence seems exaggerated in the light of the small magnitude of the correlations obtained. *The predictive power of values seems easily attenuated.* If the naturalistic sociologist will concede that values are somehow (and somewhat) involved in a full explanation of human actions, he may find fertile ground for naturalistic inquiries into the attenuating factors.[23]

Hypothesis 1, which asserts that values influence human choices among nonsymbolic desiderata, appears to be empirically true, but by itself it may often be empirically trivial. In naturalistic sociology it needs to be supplemented, both by corollaries making it more specific in its reference and by further hypotheses regarding the various factors that attenuate the dependence of actions on values. Working toward effectively supplementing Hypothesis 1 would be truer to the tenets of naturalism than merely condemning it (in the manner of an extreme positivist) for its insufficiency or for its use of illata.

Two researchable corollaries of Hypothesis 1 may be stated as follows.

Hypothesis 1a: Significant correlations may be found, at any given time, between shared values and personal desires.

Hypothesis 1b: Within an isolated social system, such correlations tend to increase through time. That is, there is a strain toward alignment of desiring with socially acquired values.[24] Such alignment is one of the main accomplishments of the normal socialization process.

Factors Attenuating the Predictiveness of Values

1   Indications of Attenuating Factors

As MacIver pointed out, human motivations have to be interpreted in relation to the objective situation in which behavior occurs. If values are one determinant of behavior, they are clearly not the sole determinant. Some members of Organization X may have wished to be more active than they were, but felt they dared not. Others who concurred with leaders' values may simply have been too busy (in their business, family, or in

---

[23] This is similar to Max Weber's suggestion that "it is convenient to treat all irrational, affectually determined elements of behavior as factors of deviation from a conceptually pure type of rational action. . . . By comparison with this it is possible to understand the ways in which actual action is influenced by irrational factors of all sorts, such as affects and errors, in that they account for deviation from the line of conduct which would be expected on the hypothesis that the action were purely rational." Max Weber, *The Theory of Social and Economic Organization.* New York: The Free Press of Glencoe, 1947, p. 92.

[24] See Allen L. Edwards, *The Social Desirability Variable in Personality Assessment and Research.* New York: The Dryden Press, Inc., 1957, chap. 3.

other organizations) to attend meetings, read the journal, etc. Correlations between values and behavior ought to be expected to be small because of the part played by other factors. For example, current efforts to curtail the rate of population growth have had to take into account many other fertility-influencing variables besides values. Attitudes favoring small families often exist without resulting in small families. Fertility reduction depends not just on instilling such attitudes but on making their implementation possible and probable. If the means of implementing values are not available, not understood, or not appropriate to the situation, the action that occurs will not always be in accord with the existing values. Moreover, values favoring low fertility may be offset by other coexisting values favoring high fertility—i.e., people may be ambivalent.[25]

In Jamaica, it was found that both males and females preponderantly agreed on an ideal family size of three children or fewer. Most of those questioned had at least heard of one or more methods of contraception, too. But the males, at least, were disinclined to put these methods to use, apparently because of the prevalent pattern of frequent desertion. This pattern insulates the males from at least the direct economic burdens of high fertility.[26] Thus, their values in regard to family size were not very predictive of their procreative behavior.

In Japan, on the other hand, one of the striking developments since the Second World War has been the reduction of fertility, and this has been accompanied by legislation favorable to fertility limitation. Since legislation can be construed as an expression of the values of those empowered to enact it, then to the extent that a legislature is democratically constituted, legislation could be taken as an expression of public values. In Japan, by this reasoning, there appears to have been a postwar change of fertility values accompanied by a change in procreative behavior. Those who insist on values as the fundamental variable in sociology, allegedly setting it apart from natural science, might wish to cite the Japanese experience as an indication of the relevance of values in explaining actions. But it is not clear that fertility reduction was *accomplished* by the legislation, apart from other factors. Even before the war, Japan had gone further than any other Oriental nation toward industrialization and urbanization. These are changes that ordinarily tend to result in lowered fertility, but this effect was perhaps delayed in Japan by an officially pronatalist policy prior to the war. The decline expected by the theory of the demographic transition had already begun, however, and was facilitated rather than instigated by the postwar legislation.[27]

[25] See J. Mayone Stycos, "Obstacles to Programs of Population Control: Facts and Fancies," *Marriage and Family Living*, 25 (February, 1963), pp. 5–13.
[26] Judith Blake, *Family Structure in Jamaica*. New York: The Free Press of Glencoe, 1961, *passim*.
[27] John Y. Takeshita, "Population Control in Japan: A Miracle or Secular Trend," *Marriage and Family Living*, 25 (February, 1963), pp. 51–52.

It is as important in naturalistic sociology, then, to take into account whatever factors mediate the relationship between values and behavior as it is to study values as such. Not only the values of people, but the characteristics of desiderata and many other variables influencing their connection must be studied. If Jones and Smith have internalized different values toward alcoholic beverages, Jones may order scotch and soda to quench his thirst while Smith orders a chocolate soda. The difference in their behavior reflects not only the difference in values but also their knowledge of the difference in alcoholic content of the two beverages.

2 Knowledge

More than the "objective" characteristics of the desideratum would be relevant to the present theory, however. At least as important would be the characteristics *perceived* by the valuer. The teetotaler might readily consume a "spiked" chocolate soda if he were ignorant of its extra ingredient. It should be noted also in this connection that the same behavior, in different cases, may have to be accounted for in terms of different values. That is, one person may be a teetotaler because of moral conviction that alcohol is evil; another may abstain because of a digestive problem or for financial reasons. In both instances overt nonsymbolic preferential behavior is a function of conceived values. And in both instances this behavior is also a function of the perceived characteristics of the desideratum. This discussion leads to the formulation of the following hypothesis to account for some of the attenuation of the power of values to determine behavior (or of the power of value data to predict actions).

Hypothesis 2: The influence of values upon human choices among nonsymbolic desiderata is conditioned by knowledge of the characteristics of the desiderata.

In many (perhaps most) instances, the salient knowledge will have been socially acquired, and hence will be subject to cultural and subcultural refraction. Therefore the sociological observer who wishes to predict the subject's actions from the subject's values must know how the subject perceives given desiderata, rather than simply impute to the subject whatever objective knowledge the observer himself may have about those desiderata.

3 The Concept of Value Perspective

Even though a valuer may have full knowledge of the "actual" characteristics of various desiderata, his perception of them still would depend on certain other considerations. If Jones and Smith happen to be thirsty, a drink (alcoholic or otherwise) available in New York will be of no immediate worth to them if they happen to be in Seattle. In their perspective, this desideratum is *perceived* as infinitesimal even though in its intrinsic characteristics it might be identical with a drink located nearer where they are. The effort they would expend to obtain it (in preference to an "equal" desideratum at closer range) may be expected to be correspondingly infinitesimal. Their "motivation" to strive for it would be approximately zero.[28]

Something like a value-perspective concept seems to underlie the behavior described by Hull's "goal gradient hypothesis." This hypothesis asserts that "there exists an excitatory gradient extending with positive acceleration according to the logarithmic law in an upward direction from the beginning of a maze to the reward box."[29] The intensity of effort to attain the goal, and the appropriateness of actions in its pursuit, tend to increase with decreases in distance from it. In other words, the *apparent* worth of an object is a function of its spatial proximity.

Dimensions other than physical space also seem to give rise to value perspectives. Ask any PTA member for what goals he or she is striving, and the answer probably will include "better schools." But, other things being equal, it will very likely be easier to enlist that member's participation in a crusade for the betterment of the particular school in which his own children are enrolled than for a school attended principally by some minority group from which he remains aloof. The goal is perceived as less valuable when the relevant *social distance* is increased.

Similarly, time may be important. To a small child, the promise that he may go to the movies tonight is almost invariably more desirable than the promise that he may go next week. If his parents take him to a theater to see a certain Walt Disney film, say, that has been playing there, only to find that a different feature (unsuitable for children) has just taken its place, the child may be exceedingly difficult to placate with the promise that as soon as the Disney film is booked into some other theater in the city he will be taken to it. A child may value a piece of candy *now* so strongly that the promise of several pieces after dinner will hardly appease him. "The very young person will have time perspectives of limited range, while the successive age groups will show more extensive ranges. . . ."[30] Such perspectives, whatever their range, appear to be characteristic of human perception, adult as well as juvenile. Immediacy of interest tends to blind us in many instances, as Merton has noted, to the more remote

---

[28] For a similar use of the term "motivation," see L. L. Thurstone, "Experimental Methods in Food Tasting," *The Psychometric Laboratory*, University of Chicago, 52 (June, 1950), p. 4.
[29] C. L. Hull, "The Goal Gradient Hypothesis and Maze Learning," *Psychological Review*, 39 (January, 1932), pp. 42–43.
[30] L. K. Frank, "Time Perspectives," *Journal of Social Philosophy*, 4 (July, 1939), p. 297.

consequences of an action which is consciously intended to secure only some proximate goal.[31] Part of what we generally mean by maturity is the ability to defer gratification, but delayed goals are never fully equal at the moment to immediate goals.

In general, then, for several dimensions, the *apparent* worth (attractiveness) of an object may be a function of its proximity to the valuer. Hartmann has drawn the analogy with physical gravitation: ". . . The attraction of a goal is (directly?) proportional to its 'value' and inversely proportional to (the square of?) the 'distance' between the organism and the objective."[32] Laird, too, has suggested a physical analogy: ". . . Desire has to do with accelerations, not with simple velocities,"[33] which is a simple affirmation of the inertial axiom of naturalism. Parsons's language was less clear, but he apparently intended to convey a similar idea when he defined "concrete ends" as physical states of affairs that are desired, and "ends as a factor in action" as the *departure* of such a state of affairs from the state anticipated by the valuer in case he does not act.[34] Or, expressed in hedonistic terminology by Laird, ". . . Desire is not moved by pleasure as such, but by greater pleasure or lesser pain. In other words, desire is always *preference*—a transition to greater satisfaction, not the search for satisfaction taken simply and absolutely."[35] The economist's concept of *marginal* utility obviously has implications similar to those of the concepts cited.

Since, in physical mechanics, "that which" produces an acceleration is a force, by analogy again we may speak of desire as a force, and employ as a model for values the concept of a force field. In the book in which his ambivalence between animism and naturalism was apparent, namely, *Social Causation*, MacIver opposed physicalistic explanations but nevertheless stated that a scheme of values could be likened to a field of force.[36] The gravitational analogy cited above is one case of such a force-field conceptualization of valuing. By means of this analogy, then, we arrive at the following hypothesis.

Hypothesis 3: The desiring, or motivation, resulting from a given value will vary inversely with a power of the "distance" (in an *n*–dimensional

[31] Robert K. Merton, "The Unanticipated Consequences of Purposive Social Action," *American Sociological Review*, 1 (December, 1936), pp. 901–902.

[32] George W. Hartmann, "Immediate and Remote Goals as Political Motives," *Journal of Abnormal and Social Psychology*, 33 (January, 1938), p. 87. Hartmann's inclusion of the parenthetical queries suggests that he was *tempted* to commit a merely slavish imitation of physical mechanics. Their enclosure in parentheses, however, seems to indicate his intuitive resistance to that temptation. The wisdom of such resistance will become apparent in chap. 8.

[33] John Laird, *The Idea of Value*. London: Cambridge University Press, 1929, p. 138.

[34] Talcott Parsons, "The Place of Ultimate Values in Sociological Theory," *The International Journal of Ethics*, 45 (April, 1935), p. 285.

[35] Laird, *op. cit.*, p. 138.

[36] MacIver, *Social Causation*, p. 373.

psychological coordinate system, or value space) between the valuer and the desideratum.

This hypothesis asserts that at least part of the residual variance in desiring (after some variance has been accounted for by diversity of values) can be accounted for by the phenomenon of value perspective. Valuing is seen then as a function of: (1) socially acquired values (force fields surrounding the valuer in value space); (2) socially acquired definitions of the characteristics of various desiderata; and (3) distances in some *n*-dimensional value space between valuers and desiderata. The dimensions of value space remain to be specified.

An approach like this, based on physical analogies, will arouse many objections, of course. Most of sociology's defects, and the weaknesses of its sister social sciences, have been attributed by Sorokin, for example, to "a clumsy imitation of the physical sciences."[37] It is not entirely clear whether he meant mainly to object to the fact that the physical sciences were being imitated or to the clumsiness of the imitation. Quite probably it was not the clumsiness that provoked him, for his own writing has many signs of animistic predilection in it. He has argued that devotees of "'natural science sociology' are usually deficient in their knowledge of physical science," however.[38] He would doubtless find distasteful the above attempt to frame a hypothesis of value perspective by analogy with principles of physical gravitation.

Such objections would be well founded if the naturalistic sociologist made the mistake of asserting that desire *must* vary inversely with distance simply *because* gravitational attraction is an inverse function of distance between physical bodies. No genuinely naturalistic sociologist would make such an assertion. Analogy may be legitimately and sometimes profitably used for heuristic purposes, but it is not a method of proof. To be naturalistic, one must recognize this. The validity of Hypothesis 3 will therefore be assessed empirically in Chapter 8. The hypothesis is developed in the present chapter with the aid of the analogy, but it remains hypothetical until confirmed with data.

It should be noted, incidentally, that if a sociological proposition is not proven by its similarity to a physical science principle, *neither does physicalistic analogy render a sociological hypothesis false.* Opponents of naturalism sometimes forget this. Attempts are made to reject hypotheses by construing their physical ancestry as *prima facie* evidence of their sociological illegitimacy. A proposition's validity depends on its correspondence with sociological data, and does not depend on either isomorphism with or *difference from* the propositions of another discipline.

[37] Pitirim A. Sorokin, *Fads and Foibles in Modern Sociology and Related Sciences.* Chicago: Henry Regnery Company, 1956, p. 174.
[38] *Ibid.*

4 Intermittent Desiring

In at least one respect *magnetic* fields might provide a better analogue than gravitational fields for socially acquired values, since magnetism can be induced in certain previously nonmagnetic objects. By using an *electro-magnetic* model for valuing behavior, we may consider another important difference between magnetism and gravitation and thereby gain further insight into the processes of human valuing. The difference to be considered rests in the fact that, whereas gravitational fields are constant, in the case of electromagnets the force field may be "turned on and off," thus simulating intermittent desiring or nonconstant motivation.

Desiring is intermittent, but it does not go on and off simply at random. Its varying intensity is systematic. Maslow has pointed out that desires cease to function as soon as they are gratified.[39] It is as if our electromagnet were wired so that when it came into direct contact with an object to which it had been attracted its field would be automatically turned off. It is empirically evident that gratification reduces motivation at least temporarily. Unlike the electromagnet, however, the human valuer does not become simply deenergized when a desire is gratified. Instead, a new desire comes into play. Here the physical analogy is not adequate to represent the facts of human desiring. We would have to imagine that when the electromagnet comes in contact with the object to which it had been drawn, not only is its force field turned off, but another (qualitatively different) force field is automatically turned on and begins attracting it toward a different class of objects.

For the human valuer, Maslow envisaged a hierarchy of "needs" in which the "lower" ones dominate if unsatisfied. The lowest unsatisfied level of needs at any given moment is dominant or "prepotent," according to Maslow, who referred to a "hierarchy of prepotency."[40] The levels in it are, from highest to lowest: (6) desires to know and to understand, (5) need for self-actualization, (4) esteem needs, (3) love needs, (2) safety needs, and (1) physiological needs. The meaning Maslow attributed to each of the above phrases need not detain us. The general idea is indicated by one extreme example, however: A hungry person may be obsessed with food, but only a relatively well-fed person is likely to become obsessed with working out a theory of valuing. I do not necessarily hold that Maslow's delineation of specific levels in it is correct, but I regard the broad notion of a prepotency hierarchy as sound. I think it can account for variations in behavior among persons with similar values; they behave differently when different levels in their value hierarchy happen to be activated by the satiation of the next lower level.

[39] A. H. Maslow, "A Theory of Human Motivation," *Psychological Review,* 50 (July, 1943), p. 393.
[40] *Ibid.,* p. 394.

To sum up this value theory so far, a socialized human being may be conceived as if:

1 He were the center of several socially induced fields of force related to each other in a hierarchy of prepotency, with each field when activated tending to attract him toward (or in the case of negative desiderata, repel him from) a specific class of desiderata.

2 The magnitude of this attraction in each case is a function of the proximity of the desideratum to the valuer in an n-dimensional value space.

3 Within a given person the several force fields tend to inhibit one another so that as the strength of one increases the strength of the others decreases.

4 For each kind of field and for each person there exists a more or less clearly defined class of desiderata by which the force of that field can be activated, whereas it cannot be activated by objects outside this class.

5 For each person, definition of the classes of desiderata activating each of his force fields is largely a function of enculturation and social interaction.

The preceding paragraph summarizes a naturalistic theory of valuing. It is not naturalistic just because it involves certain physical analogies; this is incidental. It is naturalistic because it describes valuing in researchable terms. Values, as operationally defined for this theory, and as related by it to other measurable variables, are no longer mere entelechies (allegedly powerful but always inscrutable and mystical). They become measurable. They precede their consequences. They account for accelerations of behavior, not for constancy. They are subject to modification in action, and they invoke no unmoved movers. And their relation to behavior involves enough variables and enough relationships among variables so that in principle the theory should be able to embrace a rather highly assorted array of human actions. Thus the variety and complexity of human behavior ceases to suffice as an excuse for animistic doctrines. The operation of the attenuating variables can account for the appearance of caprice (or "freedom") in human preferring and should thus take the wind out of the vitalist's sails.

In its broadest outlines, as stated thus far, the theory suggests only in general and abstract terms the effects to be expected from value fields. In order to specify predictions of valuative behavior it would be necessary to know the mathematical structure of value fields and to measure, among other things, the "distances" between valuers and desiderata. On the basis of what has been said so far, however, a further hypothesis can be stated.

Hypothesis 4: For a given set of values and given distance between valuer and desideratum, desiring will vary with the activation of different levels in some prepotency hierarchy.

In operational terms, this hypothesis states that the intensity of a person's desire for a given object will vary systematically from time to time, and that this intensity at any particular time will be a function of the continuously perceived similarity of the object to other objects strongly desired at that time. Similar desiderata will tend to be chosen in common or rejected in common. In partial confirmation of this hypothesis, reference can be made to the familiar finding of some of the earliest research on mass communication, where readers of a novel proved to be more likely than nonreaders of that novel to attend its motion-picture version. For another example, consider again the demographic transition in Japan. There it was found that when induced abortion was legalized, it was more often used by those persons who had already been using contraceptives than by those who had not. In 1961, only 9 percent of the nonusers of contraception had had at least one induced abortion, as against 54 percent of the users of contraception.[41] Two alternative techniques of fertility limitation were thus practiced in common or avoided in common.

5   Dimensions of Value Space

In developing the concept of value perspective, above, on which Hypothesis 3 was based, I gave examples which suggest, plausibly, that value space has at least the following dimensions: physical distance, social distance,[42] and remoteness of the desideratum in time.[43] Value space, then, is probably multidimensional. Moreover, it seems likely that more than just these most obvious dimensions are required to depict value fields adequately.

Another plausible dimension, that of *probability,* may be traced back to the thinking of Jeremy Bentham.[44] This dimension may be expressed as follows: The more probable a valuer considers his attainment of a given desideratum to be, up to a point, the more strongly attracted he will be to that desideratum. Probability need not be regarded as an attribute of the desideratum, nor is it altogether dependent on the characteristics of the valuer. It may be regarded as an aspect of the valuer's *relation* to the desideratum. It is thus appropriately considered a dimension of value space. Quite possibly the intensity of striving to attain a goal will be *curvilinearly* related to perceived probability—with less striving for the impossible and less striving for the automatic than for the goal of medium likelihood.

[41] Takeshita, *op. cit.,* p. 47.
[42] See George W. Hartmann, "Pacifism and Its Opponents in the Light of Value Theory," *Journal of Abnormal and Social Psychology,* 36 (April, 1941), p. 164.
[43] See Kurt Lewin, *Field Theory in Social Science.* New York: Harper & Row, Publishers, Incorporated, 1951, p. 34; Hartmann, "Immediate and Remote Goals . . .";
Frank, *op. cit.*
[44] See Laird, *op. cit.,* p. 34; Hartmann, "Pacifism and Its Opponents . . . ," p. 168.

Somewhat similar conceptually to the probability dimension is the dimension of *irrevocability*, suggested by Hartmann.[45] It has to do with the *im*probability of recurrent access to a goal. To the extent that the valuer perceives a particular opportunity for obtaining a certain desideratum to be his *only* opportunity, that desideratum's attractiveness for him at that time would be enhanced. The dimension of irrevocability, then, refers to the tendency of the valuer to perceive a given object on a "get it now or never" or "opportunity knocks but once" basis.

One further dimension will complete this tentative list of the coordinates of value space. In my experience, and on the basis of general knowledge of contemporary American culture, it seems that people are more attracted to an object if they are in a position to believe that they have chosen it freely, uncoerced either by edicts or by such circumstances as the physical absence of alternative choices. The symbiotic interdependence that causes a number of automobile dealers to be contiguously located, or a number of department stores to be near one another in a city's central business district rather than insulated from each other's competition by geographic separation, results from customers' desire to "choose" even a standard branded item after some shopping around. Faris has noted, too, that people perform imposed tasks more grudgingly than self-chosen tasks, and show less completion tendency when the task is not self-chosen.[46] The actual characteristics of the desideratum may not be what determines whether it has been imposed as a goal or has been freely chosen. Military service, for example, may involve identical tasks and identical living conditions for the volunteer and the conscript. So this variable also may be regarded as an aspect of the *relation* of valuer to desideratum, and hence a dimension of value space. I call it the dimension of "free selectability."

The list of hypothetical dimensions now includes the following: (1) spatial distance, (2) social distance, (3) remoteness in time, (4) probability, (5) irrevocability, and (6) free selectability. The procedures necessary for determining the actual dimensionality of value space are not specified here. However, by assuming merely that value space is multidimensional, with dimensionality of the order of six or more, a conceptual basis is available for formulating a further hypothesis to account for attenuation of the relation of values to behavior.

Value space must be regarded as a sociocultural product. This is what Stouffer presumably had in mind when he suggested substituting intervening opportunities for physical distance in the study of migration differentials. His basic insight was correct, then, even if his operational index of value space was inadequate and misleading. Value space may appear to have somewhat different subsets of dimensions in different cultures

---

[45] Hartmann, *ibid.*, pp. 164–165.
[46] Robert E. L. Faris, *Social Psychology*. New York: The Ronald Press Company, 1952, p. 350.

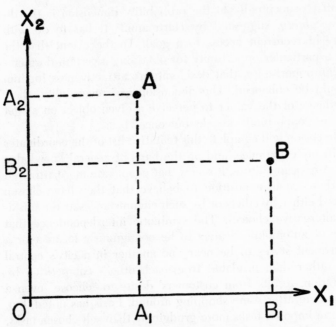

Figure 1. Schematic representation of different orders of
preference due to one-dimension projections of desiderata
located in two-dimension value space

or in different subcultures. If preferences among desiderata are a function
not only of people's values, but also of the relative locations of the desiderata in value space, then even with invariant values the structure of
preferences could vary if the *effective dimensionality* of value space varies
from one person or group to another.

For explanatory purposes, imagine for the moment that value space
"really" consists of two dimensions, X_1 and X_2. In this two-dimensional
value space the desiderata A and B are located as shown in the accompanying figure, with the valuer located at the origin. Now suppose that
the persons in one group have been enculturated so that they tend to
perceive desiderata in terms of the one-dimensional space X_1, while persons in another group tend to overlook that dimension and perceive the
same desiderata in terms of a different one-dimensional space X_2. Thus,
in Figure 1, the one-dimensional "projections" of these desiderata will
have a different order of apparent proximity, and hence will evoke a different order of preference for these two groups. A_1 will seem closer than
B_1 for one group, but B_2 will seem closer than A_2 for the other group—although the *values* of the two groups might be identical. This reasoning
results in our fifth hypothesis.

Hypothesis 5: Even among persons or groups with full consensus on values, the order of preference among a set of desiderata may vary as a result of the absence of one or more dimensions from the perceived value space of each person or group, with different dimensions missing for different groups or persons.

To illustrate what is meant by Hypothesis 5, consider a two-dimensional value space in which one or the other dimension might quite commonly be neglected. Let one dimension represent physical distance, and let the other represent various degrees of remoteness in time. Assume that two valuers hold identical conceptions of what is desirable, but suppose that Mr. Brown is somewhat less "mature" than Mr. Green, so that Mr. Brown's value perspective in regard to the time dimension shows a steeper gradient than that of Mr. Green. In effect, then, value space would be more nearly one-dimensional with emphasis on time for Mr. Brown, whereas for Mr. Green, it would at least relatively be more nearly a one-dimensional framework on physical distance. Now suppose a touring art collection is to be exhibited some 200 miles away in City A in the near future. Some time later than that it is to appear in City B, which is 50 miles closer to where Mr. Brown and Mr. Green live. Both valuers want very strongly to see the exhibit. By Hypothesis 5 we would expect Mr. Brown to go to City A to see the exhibit (his earliest opportunity) and Mr. Green might be expected to defer gratification a little longer and go the lesser distance to City B to see the exhibit.

Such behavior as this is actually a common phenomenon. Some people pay the higher price to see first-run Hollywood films promptly at downtown theaters, whereas others wait longer and see them eventually at lower prices in neighborhood theaters. The difference in behavior could have led to inferring different values, but it may be more useful instead to infer somewhat differently structured value spaces. Whichever inference is more fruitful in the long run, allowing us to organize more data under one theory and to predict more accurately in more instances, behavior differences will have been accounted for naturalistically. Not only values, as I have defined them, but value space and its varying dimensionality are legitimate and researchable illata. They are not mere entelechies.

6 Subsidiation and Congruency

If we imagine that valuers are in motion in value space, moving toward positively attractive desiderata and away from negative ones, a *relation* among dimensions is suggested. Perry has asserted that something tends to be perceived as more valuable the more "inclusive" it appears to be.[47]

[47] Ralph Barton Perry, *General Theory of Value*. Cambridge, Mass.: Harvard University Press, 1930, pp. 615ff.

In terms of the model presented here, inclusiveness can be resolved into two relational concepts, "subsidiation" and "congruency." Pointing to the obvious fact that a goal may be pursued in order that it in turn can be used as a means for attaining some more ultimate goal, Cattell has suggested the subsidiation of one desideratum to another.[48] In value space, then, desiderata may vary in the degree to which they appear to lie directly *along the path* from the valuer to other desiderata. In similar fashion, they may vary in their proximity to a vector extending outward from the valuer directly away from such other goals as he is currently pursuing. Two desiderata which "pull" a valuer in "opposite directions" are incongruent. Thus a particular object may be characterized as more or less *congruent* with other desiderata.[49] This reasoning leads to a sixth hypothesis.

Hypothesis 6: The apparent worth of a desideratum to a valuer will be enhanced to the extent that its location in his value space makes it congruent with other positive desiderata or subsidiated to them.

Thus, any desideratum may be expected to evoke more intensive striving for it to the extent that it is a means to more ultimate ends, or at least seems to be a "stepping-stone" or "halfway station" en route to more remote goals. But it must be remembered, in the light of Hypothesis 5, that this means-end relationship will be subject to variations in perception of the dimensionality of value space. Whether a given desideratum appears to lie en route to a desired end will depend not only on whether it is in fact instrumental to the attainment of that end, but also on the value space dimensions that are salient for the given valuer. Different experiences, or different socialization, can cause different valuers to define their respective value spaces differently.

In some religious circles, for example, "good works" are perceived as a means to salvation, and people are taught to be their brothers' keepers or to act as Good Samaritans, etc., so as to obtain their reward in Heaven. For other religious groups, however, this means-end relationship does not exist. The "elect" are believed to be predestined by the Grace of God for salvation, and others are predestined for damnation. Good works are advocated as a means of glorifying God, not as a means of salvation. The subsidiation of morally commendable acts to more ultimate goals is dependent, then, on socially instilled perceptions. For both religious groups, salvation is considered desirable, and the glorification of God is considered desirable. Both groups have the same values in common, but their value spaces are differently structured.

Or to take a more mundane illustration, I used to have retired relatives living in Michigan who spent their winters in Florida. They always went

[48] Raymond E. Cattell, *An Introduction to Personality Study*. London: Hutchinson & Co. (Publishers), Ltd., 1950, pp. 47ff.
[49] Hartmann, "Pacifism and Its Opponents . . . ," pp. 164–165.

to Florida "by way of" the Chicago area, where they had formerly resided and where they still had acquaintances and relatives. In terms of physical space, Chicago was not exactly en route to Florida from their Michigan village, but in terms of their social space it was. In their letters they even used the expression "leaving for Florida" to refer to their departure from Chicago, not their departure from their home in Michigan.

In this value theory, then, six basic hypotheses (plus two corollary hypotheses) have been presented. All of them are related by the concept of value space and by a magnetic model to a general theory of valuing. Because the variables it involves are, in principle, observable and measurable, this theory can be called naturalistic. It treats value as a *force*.

Value is not a physical force, and the theory is not physicalistic just because it does use such terms as "force." Value is a social-psychological force, influencing human and social entities only, but influencing them in the same way that physical forces influence physical bodies—accelerating them in the direction of the force and in proportion to its strength. The theory is thus naturalistic without being reductionist. It does not "reduce" human behavior to interrelations between physical variables. It does assume that the relevant social variables are as truly empirical as the variables of physical science and that genuine knowledge of their interrelations is no more *a priori* than is physical knowledge.

This theory should enable social scientists to order many important data concerning preferential behavior. It also suggests two promising avenues of future research: (1) empirical attempts to differentiate the several mutually inhibitory force fields in a prepotency hierarchy; (2) investigation of the mathematical structure of value space. A modest beginning of the latter quest will be presented in Chapter 8.

Summary

Opponents of naturalism have claimed that sociology cannot get along without the value concept, but they have also claimed that values cannot be studied scientifically. Extreme positivists have reinforced the latter claim by asserting that science should do without illata and study only concreta. Both views are obstacles to effective inquiry and must be rejected if naturalistic sociology is to proceed. Illata should be chosen wisely, not categorically excluded, and not adopted on *a priori* grounds.

Those who advocate including the concept of values in sociological theory are obligated to show empirically that it can be scientifically useful; otherwise they invite positivist rejection of the concept as mere sociopsychological phlogiston, and they make themselves appear to be interested in the occult. It turns out, however, that human behavior is less directly and conspicuously value-determined than animists suppose. It is also evident that values and their relation to behavior can be studied naturalistically. Naturalistic study of values encounters resistance from persons who are unwilling to consider any challenge to their notion of a single, transcultural, objectively valid system of values.

Important distinctions can be made between "operative values" reflected in nonsymbolic preferential behavior, "conceived values" reflected in preferences among symbolic desiderata, and "object values" alleged to be real and absolute. It is only the latter that remain unverifiable for naturalism. Unlike animistic thinkers, the naturalistic sociologist takes as hypothetical rather than axiomatic the expected correspondence between conceived and operative values. Finding statistically significant but quantitatively unimpressive confirmation of the hypothesis that values influence action, the naturalistic sociologist can go on to formulate and test a series of hypotheses accounting for the weakness of this link.

Given that (1) values influence behavior, this influence is expected by naturalistic value theory to be mediated by such factors as: (2) valuers' varying knowledge of the characteristics of desiderata, (3) valuers' varying remoteness from desiderata in a multidimensional value space, (4) activation at different times of different levels in a prepotency hierarchy of values, (5) varying dimensionality of value space from culture to culture and from person to person, (6) varying congruence or subsidiation of one desideratum in relation to others. Probably as a result of such variables, the predictive power of values in relation to behavior is easily attenuated. Thus, two or more persons with different values may easily be found to behave alike, while two or more persons with similar values may easily be found to behave differently. It is little wonder, therefore, that values have seemed to be inscrutable and mystical phenomena.

The naturalistic investigation of factors that mediate the link between values and actions should deprive vitalism of the plausibility it has had, avoiding at the same time the positivist error of improperly foreclosing consideration of useful inferential constructs. Considered as force fields, values can be objectively studied within the naturalistic framework. The fact that forces and force fields are concepts ordinarily associated with physics does not invalidate their use in sociology any more than it suffices to prove the hypotheses presented in this chapter.

Chapter Six

INSTITUTIONALIZATION AND MEASUREMENT OF SUBLIME VALUES

Spiritual Values and Scientific Study

"I will lift up mine eyes," wrote the Psalmist, "unto the hills. From whence cometh my help? My help cometh from the Lord who made heaven and earth." In the millennia that have elapsed since those words were set down, naturalistic inquiry has greatly increased our knowledge of celestial and terrestrial phenomena and of how the objects of heaven and earth were created. We know vastly more today than then about the hills, but little or nothing new has been learned about the help we obtain by reverently looking upon them with uplifted eyes. In this chapter, a step will be taken in that direction, in spite of the common contention that such topics are beyond the purview of science.

One fact must be acknowledged at the outset. All that we know now of the processes by which the hills of our planet were formed, of the immense time it took, the vast differences between the scene upon which we gaze today and the landscapes of primordial times, augments rather than diminishes the inspirational qualities of the high places. The advancement of such sciences as geology, archaeology, paleontology, ecology, botany, zoology, etc., has enhanced our perception of the world we live in. Hills don't mean much if we only see them as land that is hard to cultivate, as objects that are there for the sun to set behind, as obstacles to be gotten around, or as a supposedly eternal backdrop for our social world of flux. We gain maturity, we lengthen our time perspectives, when we see the hills as products of the *forces* of diastrophism, volcanism, and erosion, and when we recognize that these processes are at work now as always. Intermediate between the vast reaches of geologic time in which the hills themselves come and go and the brief intervals in which human events take place are the periods of ecological succession in which the flora and fauna inhabiting the hills and giving them their character as biotic communities undergo change.[1]

Reasonably accurate knowledge of such biotic communities has been widely popularized in recent years by a series of films produced by Walt Disney, called "True Life Adventures." In color, and using remarkable live-action film footage of animals and plants in their natural habitats, these have been, for the most part, marvelous works of art. Apart from this quality, however, two minor traits will be cited here not by way of criticizing these motion pictures, but in order to illustrate a point at issue in the present context. One of these traits is the rather conspicuous anthropomorphism in the films' narratives, which seems to imply a still prevalent feeling that life is not truly adventurous unless seen in terms of such superficial concepts. The other trait I want to mention is the artistically clever device which introduces each of the films. Cartoon animators cause the image of a watercolor brush to dart quickly around the screen, dripping color which flows conveniently into the form of the scene in which the live-action adventure is set. In their own graphic and appealing language, the Disney artists have been portraying creation in about the way it was portrayed in the book of Genesis, where ancient Hebrew writers supposed that the brush was supernaturally wielded only a few generations before their own time. Are not mountains that we know were thrust up and eroded into their present contours over millions of years nobler than any that might have been casually brushed into the landscape? Are not the forests on their flanks at least as magnificent by virtue of prolonged evolution as they would have been as products of a simple command to grow and to clothe the mountain?

In ignorance of the forces that built them, one can yet be inspired by such mountains as the Tetons in Wyoming. But to stand amid the sagebrush of the flat floor of Jackson Hole and to look westward toward what one has learned is a superb specimen of block faulting and glacial erosion is to see these peaks as all the more awesome. The picturesque lakes

[1] A number of readable presentations of ecological, geological, and other scientific knowledge that can amplify the benefits of lifting up one's eyes unto the hills are available. They include: Lorus J. Milne and Margery Milne, *The Balance of Nature.* New York: Alfred A. Knopf, Inc., 1960; John A. Shimer, *This Sculptured Earth.* New York: Columbia University Press, 1959; James L. Dyson, *The World of Ice.* New York: Alfred A. Knopf, Inc., 1962. As examples of works revealing the inspirational utility of scientific knowledge in connection with specific places, see Joseph Wood Krutch, *Grand Canyon: Today and All Its Yesterdays.* New York: William Sloane Associates, 1958; and Howel Williams, *Crater Lake: The Story of Its Origin,* Berkeley, Calif.: University of California Press, 1961.

at their feet take on additional beauty after a visit to the Jenny Lake Visitor Center where National Park Service people have constructed a diorama which vividly shows how the lake basins were formed by the terminal moraines deposited by glaciers that once were engaged in destruction of the mountains but have long since melted away.

One can live in Colorado, as I did as a boy, and be impressed with high mountain lakes so that one remarks to tourists from the urban East that Colorado is a state where you go *up* to find water. But it is more thrilling to recognize as an adult that these blue lakes of clear cold water are situated where they are because of the actions of mountain glaciers tens of thousands of years ago which carved the cirques the lakes now occupy. Where one formerly saw merely a lake, one now sees a lake in a rocky cirque, and one visualizes vast quantities of snow in ages past compacting into ice and forming the tools of creation.

One can marvel at the deep blue of Crater Lake in Oregon, and fill one's lungs with the fresh mountain air atop its rim, and be helped by the experience. That help is far surpassed, however, when one envisions the projection of the caldera's rim up to the vanished summit of once mighty Mount Mazama, and especially when one realizes there were Stone Age human beings in the vicinity who had watched for years as the smoke and ash spewed forth from the mountain and blighted the leeward landscape for a hundred miles. Many millions of tons of the mountain's interior were strewn across the countryside as cinders. One can empathize with those bewildered Indians who must have trembled in fear as the earth under their feet trembled from the eventual collapse of the great hollow volcano. The empathic experience augments the help to be derived from lifting up one's eyes to these particular hills. To think on these things and *then* look out across the blue water toward the cinder cone called Wizard Island (representing a later series of eruptions within the caldera) is to experience something of great value. To see the forest beginning to establish itself on that recently barren cone of volcanic ash is to be transported back to earlier days of creation when the forest was getting started on the flanks of Mount Mazama itself.

MacIver has looked back over an eighty-year life span and remarked that there are "high moments of experience" during which we are fully possessed by the life spirit "as though all unknowingly we had reached a mountain top and seen below us the wonder of the earth, as it never appears to our ordinary sight. And when we have descended, we say in effect: It was good for us to have been there. And the memory bequeaths something to many quieter hours, conveying the sense that our time is no longer being lived through but being lived."[2]

Knowledge itself is like a high mountain; it affords a perspective not

[2] Robert M. MacIver, *The Challenge of the Passing Years: My Encounter with Time.* New York: Trident Press, Inc., 1962, p. 126.

available from lower places. Knowing more, we see more, just as climbing higher, we see farther. *This should be no less true of sociological knowledge than of geological knowledge.* The metaphor is apt, and MacIver has pursued it. "We must spend many hours in the valley and on the rising slopes," he wrote, "before we ascend to a peak, but having been there we have a vision that stays with us."[3] Knowledge is not easily produced, and its accumulation in any field may take a long time and much effort—often with an intricate division of labor. If a part of the exhilaration we get from lifting up our eyes unto the hills is the anticipation of the panorama to be seen from their summits, perhaps likewise to know the basis upon which substantial knowledge can be acquired is to anticipate some of the advantages of possessing that knowledge.

The help that cometh from the hills apparently derives at least partly from quiet contemplation, as well as from anticipatory exhilaration. In tracing the history of a marvelous human institution which embodies this value, John Ise has noted that "there is something satisfying to the soul—to *some* souls—in the quietness and serenity of the wilderness, in being away from the hurrying crowds and the roar and clangor of ubiquitous machines, away from business and commerce, away from all the works of man, away from the 'prostitution of civilization.' "[4] Such testimony sounds more poetic than scientific, but it is the aim of this chapter to show that genuinely naturalistic sociology need not neglect the values which inspire the poet, and does not defile them by studying them.

After seeing the waste committed in logging operations in Maine, Henry David Thoreau exclaimed in his diary a century ago: "It is the poet . . . who makes truest use of the pine. Every creature is better alive than dead, men and moose, and pine trees, and he who understands it aright will rather preserve its life than destroy it."[5] Thoreau suggested as early as 1858 that we ought to have "for inspiration and our own true recreation" a number of "national preserves, in which the bear and the panther, and some even of the hunter race may still exist, and not be civilized off the face of the earth. . . ."[6]

The National Parks

It was not directly as a result of Thoreau's opinion that we obtained it, but today we have such an institution, and it has been emulated in varying

[3] *Ibid.*, p. 131.
[4] John Ise, *Our National Park Policy: A Critical History.* Baltimore: The Johns Hopkins Press, 1961, p. 652.
[5] Quoted in Stewart L. Udall, *The Quiet Crisis.* New York: Holt, Rinehart and Winston, Inc., 1963, p. 51.
[6] *Ibid.*

ways by many other nations. In the United States there are 32 national parks, most of which were created to serve the needs cited by Thoreau and to ensure that people would always have opportunities to make the true and poetic use of the pine, the flowing water, the towering block of granite. Millions of modern, civilized citizens visit the national parks each year, and in many cases they seek some approximation of a preurban way of life. A major project of the National Park Service in recent years has been the enlargement and refinement of campgrounds in nearly all the national parks and many of the national monuments. In each campground, individual campsites are laid out clearly enough and in close enough harmony with indigenous features so visitors will fit themselves into the arrangement with a minimum of conscious direction or sense of coercion. An attempt has been made to space the campsites in such a way that quietness and serenity are not lost in a quasi-urban crowd. Adequate sanitary facilities, rustic fireplaces, and roads and trails to channel the vehicular and pedestrian traffic are provided so that the extensive human invasion of the wilderness will not utterly demolish its characteristics and its values for the human invader.

In many of these skillfully organized campgrounds there is a nightly ritual during the tourist season. The campers congregate at dusk in an amphitheater where they sit on wooden (or sometimes stone) benches under the stars or beneath the stately, murmuring trees. In most instances their attention is centered on a screen on which they will be shown photographic slides by a man with the seasonal role of ranger-naturalist. He will try to infect them with his own enthusiasm for the area and the institution. He will attempt to convey enough information to them to sensitize them to features of the park from which they can draw greater pleasure and inspiration through being equipped with knowledge and understanding. But to one side of the screen there is usually a circle of stones in which a bonfire is built prior to the illustrated lecture. It is an important part of the ritual. After leading the crowd in some lighthearted singing, the ranger-naturalist will preface his talk with some remarks on the need for park preservation, for staying on the trails and not trampling the meadows, for respecting the wild character of the seemingly tame animals. Then he will allude to the symbolic significance of the campfire.

It was around an evening campfire in 1870 that a party of explorers of the Yellowstone region turned from festive activities to serious discussion of what ought to be done with that land. The tale is a simple one, but it has a nobility that survives repeated tellings. Many park visitors have heard it from numerous lips because they have attended many of these campfire lectures. The Yellowstone explorers, it is said, were at first contemplating the profits that could be made by staking claims to the land around Yellowstone Lake, the Grand Canyon of the Yellowstone River, the geyser basins, etc., and exploiting these natural wonders as

tourist attractions and in other ways. But this mercenary theme evoked
a countersuggestion that the area should be preserved unspoiled and somehow dedicated to the nation. Consensus quickly formed around this proposal, and the explorers pursued the idea after departing from the Yellowstone region. A movement was launched, seeking protection of these wonders from use on less than the highest plane. Two years later, Congress,
whose members have not generally been noted for assigning priority to
poetic values, was persuaded nevertheless to enact a law establishing Yellowstone as the first national park.

There had been two previous instances in which Federal land was set
aside from the usual course of homesteading or commercial exploitation,
but they hardly constituted precedents for the Yellowstone Act.[7] A hot-
springs area in Arkansas had been made a Federal reserve as early as
1832, not for artistic reasons but on account of the supposedly medicinal
effects of the waters. In 1864, the Yosemite Valley, in California, had been
ceded by the Federal government to the state, to be administered as a
state park. The act of Congress required California to hold the land per-
manently inalienable and to administer it for public use, recreation,
and resort. Later, of course, after the national park concept had come
into being, it was arranged for California to cede the valley back to the
Federal government for inclusion in the surrounding Yosemite National
Park.

The gradual crystallization of the national park concept, and especially
the development of the national park system as an institution, was a
crescive process rather then a matter of deliberate design. It would be
misleading to describe it in wholly voluntaristic or even in functional
terms. Yet out of this crescive evolution of an institution remarkable values
have emerged. What is significant for this book is that this institution
and the behavior it stimulates among the people can be studied naturalistically. Though the institution in its present form embodies sublime values,
they are not occult qualities and their effect on human behavior is not
the inscrutable influence of mere entelechies. Moreover, because national
parks have fixed spatial locations and yield their benefits to people holding
certain conceptions of the desirable which cause them to journey to them,
the parks happen to afford an unusual opportunity to test some of the
hypotheses presented in Chapter 5. Their spatial fixity resolves the abstract notions of value space into the more readily observable dimensions
of geographic space. In the present chapter I will take advantage of this
fact to begin the empirical evaluation of Hypothesis 6 as it was stated
in the preceding chapter—"The apparent worth of a desideratum to a

[7] The following account of the gradual emergence of the national park concept is
based chiefly upon Ise, *op. cit.*, and C. Frank Brockman, *Recreational Use of Wild
Lands.* New York: McGraw-Hill Book Company, 1959, chap. 5.

valuer will be enhanced to the extent that its location in his value space makes it congruent with other positive desiderata or subsidiated to them." Other hypotheses will be examined later.

Evolution of Park Values

The unplanned, crescive character of the development of the national park concept and institution can be readily seen in a brief review of the history of the national parks. For example, Congress at first had no notion that national parks required funds for administration or development. The first several parks were established without appropriations even for a superintendent's salary, and when the first appropriations finally were made, salaries for minimal personnel was about the only item they did cover. In the case of Yellowstone, for a number of years after it had been legally created, the park had no protection from vandalism, from poaching of game, from private enterprise exploitation of its resources or construction of facilities. It was repeatedly subjected to threats (or what would now be regarded as threats in the light of the more fully matured national park concept). Attempts were made again and again to acquire rights to cross it with a railroad; one entrepreneur actually was granted a lease to build an elevator down the side of Yellowstone Falls. And it was not until 1894, twenty-two years after the park's ostensible "setting aside," that Congress passed legislation to protect its birds and animals.

In 1906, Congress passed into law The Act for the Preservation of Antiquities, commonly referred to as the Antiquities Act, or the Lacey Act. It authorized the President to set aside landmarks, historic sites, structures, archaeological features, etc., situated on government-owned land, and designate them by proclamation as national monuments. As such they were protected from destruction, unauthorized excavation, alteration, or other injury, and penalties for violation were provided in the act. By this legislation, many significant areas that are too small or have insufficient variety of scenery to merit national park status have been protected. Moreover, another important result of this act was that some areas which subsequently did become national parks by specific congressional authorization were temporarily protected as presidentially proclaimed national monuments. Until they could be considered by the members of Congress, such areas could now be given interim protection by the President.

Several more national parks were established in the decades after the setting aside of Yellowstone, but each was separately administered, and in each case little or nothing was done at first about staffing, budgeting, guarding, or developing facilities in the park. There simply was no national park *system*. The national park concept had not yet crystallized fully, and certainly was not yet widely disseminated. It could at best be said that there was only an incipient institution.

From 1911 to 1916, however, the Department of the Interior began to pull together the administration of the various parks then in existence, and a number of aspects of park operation and protection began to be coordinated under an assistant to the Secretary, and subsequently a Superintendent of National Parks. In 1912, Congress was urged by President Taft to establish a Bureau of National Parks. Bills were introduced for this purpose in the 62d, 63rd, and 64th Congresses, and finally such legislation was enacted and was signed by President Wilson in 1916.

The National Parks Act of 1916 established the National Park Service and stated its purpose: ". . . to conserve the scenery and the natural and historic objects and the wild life therein, and to provide for the enjoyment of the same in such manner and by such means as will leave them unimpaired for the enjoyment of future generations." In 1918, a letter from the Secretary of the Interior, Franklin K. Lane, to the first Director of the National Park Service, Stephen Mather, referred to the national parks as "dedicated" areas and instructed the Director that they "must be maintained in absolutely unimpaired form for the use of future generations as well as those of our own time. . . ." The Secretary insisted that "the national interest must dictate all decisions affecting public or private enterprise in the parks."

In 1932, an official statement of national park policy was prepared by Louis C. Cramton, former congressman and then special attorney for the Secretary of the Interior. It noted that full enjoyment of the parks by the people would require education as a means to adequate interpretation, appreciation, and inspiration. Exotic forms of amusement should be discouraged, so that recreation within the parks would relate to the "inherent values" of the parks and would tend toward the broadest intellectual and spiritual meaning of recreation. The national parks were said to be "essentially noncommercial in character" and were "established for the permanent preservation of areas and objects of national interest" and "are intended to exist forever."

The conception of the desirable which had been expressed in nascent form around the 1870 campfire had become much more palpable by 1916, 1918, and 1932. The continuing efforts of the National Park Service to disseminate such values have been supplemented by nongovernmental activities of voluntary organizations. One of these, the National Parks Association, at its first meeting in 1919, announced its purpose: "To defend the National Parks and Monuments fearlessly against assaults of private interests and aggressive commercialism." Whereas the first national park had been congressionally defined in 1872 as a "pleasuring ground," Robert

Sterling Yard of the National Parks Association wrote in 1923 that the parks were more than this. They were a national museum, he said, whose purpose was "to preserve forever . . . certain areas of extraordinary scenic magnificence in a condition of primitive nature." There were other segments of the public domain which also afforded outdoor recreational opportunities (in the ordinary sense), so it was not in this respect that the national parks were unique. "The function which alone distinguishes the national parks system from the national forest," Yard insisted, "is the museum function made possible only by the parks' complete conservation."[8]

In these outdoor museums, the visitor would view (and be inspired by) the process of creation going its own way, neither guided nor misguided by man. He would lift up his eyes unto the hills, and would be helped by doing so. The parks would indeed be pleasuring grounds, but the distinctive pleasure afforded by them would derive from intimate contemplation of extensive specimens of nature as nearly immune from human modification as a human institution could make them. This conception of the national parks' desirability has gained wide currency, yet the word "museum" hardly conveys it. Better terms might be "shrine" or "sanctuary," since the items displayed become endowed with a quality of sacredness by many of their beholders. In such sanctuaries, human "improvement" becomes tantamount to desecration.

In increasing numbers, the people have been flocking to these outdoor museums, and just their presence is in itself sufficient to modify the character of areas whose national park status was supposed to protect them from modification. In response to this dilemma, and in anticipation of the fiftieth anniversary of the establishment of the National Park Service, a ten-year development program called "Mission 66" was inaugurated, scheduled for completion in 1966. As park visitation has rapidly increased, the national parks have begun to require additional facilities which will channel visitor use and minimize the extent to which visitors' activities and the mere presence of crowds will impair park values. It is no easy task, however, to prevent the facilities themselves from detracting. Mission 66 was intended to "provide for the protection and preservation of the wilderness areas within the National Park System and encourage their appreciation in ways that will leave them unimpaired." By making the parks "more meaningful" some of the developments included in Mission 66 have been designed to elicit visitor cooperation and thereby facilitate park protection. The very name, "*Mission 66*," suggests the almost religious devotion of many Park Service men to the protective interpretation of the areas under their stewardship.

[8] Robert Sterling Yard, "Economic Aspects of Our National Parks Policy," *Scientific Monthly*, 16 (April, 1923), pp. 380–388.

Reverent Expressions of Value

If organized effort has been required to instill such values in a substantial portion of the general population, there have been from time to time an assortment of men and groups, with keener than average sensitivity to the inspirational qualities of their environment. Thoreau has been mentioned. John Muir was another such person. For him, each time he ventured into the wilderness he beheld the processes of creation and felt himself fulfilled. He wished this experience for others. He wrote that in the wilderness "life seems neither long nor short, and we take no more heed to save time or make haste than do the trees and stars. This is true freedom, a good and practical sort of immortality."[9]

Of the many organizations which have expressed and defended conceptions of this sort, the Alpine Club of Canada is a clear example. Half a century ago it was described as undertaking to defend "our mountain solitudes against . . . all the vandalisms of this luxurious, utilitarian age." It sought to keep alpine country in Canada "free from the grind of commerce" and to protect from spoliation these retreats from "the fever and fret" of daily life.[10]

More recently, the United States Secretary of the Interior, Stewart Udall, has cited the need of every citizen in modern times to enjoy "the spiritual exhilaration of the wilderness" which requires the nation to protect such places from "commercialism . . . , factories, subdivisions, billboards, power plants, dams," etc. He has called ours an "increasingly commercial civilization" which nevertheless has need for "natural sanctuaries."[11] He cited an 1876 article by Muir in which forests were called "God's First Temples," and a later piece in which Muir sought to prevent construction of the Hetch Hetchy dam in a then magnificent valley in Yosemite. The quality of sacredness has never been more fervently ascribed to wilderness than when Muir wrote: "These temple destroyers, devotees of ravaging commercialism, seem to have a perfect contempt for Nature, and, instead of lifting their eyes to the God of the Mountains, lift them to the Almighty Dollar. Dam Hetch Hetchy! As well dam for watertanks the people's cathedrals and churches, for no holier temple has ever been consecrated by the heart of man."[12] But Muir lost that fight; in spite of his eloquence the dam was built, and the valley destroyed. It had not yet been consecrated in the hearts of enough men to protect it from the wish to evade the greater monetary expense that would have been incurred in providing a city water source for San Francisco on lands outside Yosemite.

[9] Quoted in Udall, *op. cit.*, p. 112.
[10] Elizabeth Parker, "The Alpine Club of Canada," *Canadian Alpine Journal*, 1 (1907), p. 5.
[11] Udall, *op. cit.*, p. 125.
[12] Quoted in *ibid.*, p. 121.

The same attitude of consecration was manifest in Freeman Tilden's reaction to a proposal to build a nonsectarian church near the rim of the Grand Canyon. "The Grand Canyon *itself*, in its integrity and its perfection, is a religious institution," Tilden wrote. "A familiarity with Grand Canyon can be what William James called a 'religious experience.' "[13]

Some men develop reverence toward such places even when the areas have not been formally sanctified as national parks. Mountaineering has been said to be distinguished from all other sports by a "strange mysticism" which has been widely expressed in mountain literature. A quasi-religious fervor has been ascribed to many of the devotees of mountaineering, even those with little sympathy or with actual hostility toward institutional religion.[14] I am almost reluctant to repeat George Leigh-Mallory's famous aphorism about why men climb mountains. It is so apt that one is saddened to note how hackneyed it can seem from frequent use. And yet at least one sociologist—Stouffer—has felt that men might be attracted to such destinations not just "because they are there" but in proportion as intervening opportunities are, so to speak, *not* there. Are eyes one lifts up to nearby heights thereby blinded—or are they thus alerted—to the glories of more distant peaks?

The Hypothesis of Intervening Opportunities

When Stouffer published his theory of intervening opportunities, he fitted his equation to data on residential relocation, and then went on to suggest various other sorts of distance gradients he thought the theory might "illuminate." These included the pattern of residential propinquity in mate selection, spatial distributions of crime rates, and the use of leisure time in vacation travel.[15] Elsewhere I have tried out the intervening opportunities equation with mate selection data and found it wanting.[16] Here I will analyze vacation travel data from national parks visitors in such a way as to clarify and evaluate some assumptions that are implicit in Stouffer's theory, which directly contradict my Hypothesis 6 (on subsidiated goals).

[13] Freeman Tilden, "Interpreting the Grand Canyon," *National Parks Magazine*, 36 (April, 1962), p. 7.
[14] Arnold Lunn, *A Century of Mountaineering.* London: George Allen & Unwin, Ltd., 1957, pp. 45–46.
[15] Samuel A. Stouffer, "Intervening Opportunities: A Theory Relating Mobility and Distance," *American Sociological Review*, 5 (December, 1940), p. 867.
[16] William R. Catton, Jr., and R. J. Smirich, "A Comparison of Mathematical Models for the Effect of Residential Propinquity on Mate Selection," *American Sociological Review*, 29 (August, 1964), pp. 522–529.

1 Stouffer's Evasion of Distance

In order to make clear the implications of the data, I find it useful to refer to an historical controversy in sociological thought, and thus to see what it was that Stouffer's formulation was intended to accomplish. Sociology was not until recently securely established as an academic discipline, and it used to have to be defended against the charges that its subject matter could not be studied scientifically, or else that its subject matter and methods were not distinguishable from such other sciences as psychology or biology. Durkheim's well-known insistence that "social facts are to be treated as things" provided a tide-turning rebuttal to both these charges. The "thingness" of social facts referred to the inadequacy of *a priori* reasoning and to the sociologist's obligation to rely on empirical data.[17] Some facts, however, were distinctively social, and this gave sociology a measure of independence from other disciplines. It was this latter notion that took on something of the character of a shibboleth.[18] Durkheim came to be remembered by later sociologists less for his naturalism than for his adamant opposition to "reductionism," since he had explicitly disavowed an intention "to reduce the higher to the lower forms of being." He had *not* insisted that social facts are material things "but that they are things by the same right as material things, although they differ from them in type."[19]

This was the spirit in which Stouffer offered his theory of intervening opportunities to account for distance gradients in migration. To explain the social fact of distance differentials in rates of migration by reference to another *social* fact, as Durkheim had advocated,[20] Stouffer wished to transform physical distance into the social variable, intervening opportunities.

Stouffer had noted that "movement of people in space is a basic subject of sociological inquiry,"[21] but he was not content to treat space as space. He proposed "a conceptual framework for attacking the problem of distance." Toward this end he offered a theory which "assumes that there is no necessary relationship between mobility and distance. Instead it introduces the concept of *intervening opportunities*."[22] Distance gradients are observed, this theory asserts, because of "an auxiliary relationship,

---

[17] See Emile Durkheim, *The Rules of the Sociological Method* (trs. Sarah A. Solovay and John H. Mueller; ed. George E. G. Catlin). New York: The Free Press of Glencoe, 1950, p. xlv.

[18] See the criticism of this reaction in Alex Inkeles, "Personality and Social Structure," chap. 11 in Robert K. Merton, Leonard Broom, and Leonard S. Cottrell, Jr. (eds.), *Sociology Today*. New York: Basic Books, Inc., Publishers, 1959, pp. 249–250.

[19] Durkheim, *op. cit.*, p. xlv.

[20] *Ibid.*, pp. 110–111.

[21] Stouffer, *op. cit.*, p. 845.

[22] *Ibid.*, p. 846.

which expresses the cumulated (intervening) opportunities as a function of distance."[23]

The number of opportunities more accessible than a given opportunity is a social variable. Physical distance happens sometimes to be a convenient index of it, but by relegating physical distance to the status of a mere index Stouffer had supposedly purified sociological theory a little bit. To go behind the physical index, however, Stouffer had to make a psychological assumption about how people generally respond to this social variable of intervening opportunities. His hypothesis was that the number of persons going a given distance would be proportional to the ratio between opportunities at that distance and intervening opportunities. This only followed if a nearer opportunity was *assumed* to operate psychologically as an obstacle to traveling to a more remote opportunity. It is precisely this assumption that is called into question by national park travel data. National park visitation rates vary inversely with distance between a park and visitors' home state, but the pattern is not exactly in accord with the Stouffer formula. Intervening national parks sometimes facilitate rather than inhibit travel to more remote parks.

2 Research Procedures

In the summer of 1963, I sent mail-back questionnaires with stamped return envelopes to 514 persons from outside the state of Washington who had visited Mount Rainier National Park during July and August, 1962, and had signed one of the visitor registers there. Usable mailing lists can no longer be compiled from these visitor registers in the national parks, because a column for the visitor's street address is no longer included. But in 1962, at one of the visitor centers in Mount Rainier National Park, namely, at the Ohanapecosh campground, the old forms which included a place for street address were still being used.

For reasons developed in a previous phase of the study, I limited the sample to persons from 23 states—comprising all states west of the Mississippi River except Arkansas and Louisiana, excluded as part of the "Eastern culture area" of park travel, and excepting also the state of Washington, excluded because visits to Mount Rainier by its residents did not involve out-of-state travel; four additional states east of the Mississippi were included in this "Western culture area"—Wisconsin, Illinois, Michigan, and Indiana. Questionnaires were sent only to visitors from this 23-state area. Among the addresses from the visitor register, 11 proved to be incorrect or insufficient for mail delivery, but 503 questionnaires apparently reached their addressees. Of these, 328 (65.2 percent) were

[23] *Ibid.,* p. 847.

answered in the first wave. A postcard reminder brought in 91 more (18.1 percent) in the second wave. An additional 61 returns (or 12.1 percent) were obtained in a third wave after duplicate questionnaires had been sent to the holdouts. Total response, then, was 480 questionnaires out of 503, or 95.4 percent. I am inclined to attribute this unusually high rate of return to the following considerations: (1) the fact that the topic of the questionnaire (their own visits to and sentiments about national parks) was strongly interesting to the members of the sample; (2) the fact that it was completely innocuous to them—no hidden dangers in answering were implied by any promise of anonymity; (3) the fact that the sample members were a select group—persons who had traveled to at least Mount Rainier National Park in 1962 and had taken the time to sign a visitor register there.

The questionnaire contained a list of the other United States national parks, in alphabetical order. A box in front of each park name was to be checked if that park had been visited on the same trip that had brought the respondent to Mount Rainier in 1962. A box after each park name was to be checked if the respondent had *ever* visited that park. Each respondent who had ever visited two or more parks was asked to indicate his favorite and to state reasons for his choice. The "ever visited" data and the "favorite park" data will not be considered here.

3 Findings

Since the state of Washington is in one corner of the continental United States, virtually all the other Western national parks constituted "intervening opportunities" for many persons in our sample. For others, Mount Rainier was an intervening opportunity located nearer their homes than various other national parks. Now if Stouffer were correct in assuming that intervening opportunities tend to deter travel to more remote destinations, a sample of Mount Rainier visitors should be found to consist mainly of persons who had "missed" any intervening opportunities, or had been deterred by Mount Rainier from going on to more distant parks. That is, they would have lower visitation rates at other national parks than was the case for the general public.

In contrast to this expectation, 273 out of 480 responding Mount Rainier visitors (or 56.9 percent) reported having visited at least one other national park on the same trip. Many had visited several parks, coming or going. For comparison, the *total* number of visits in 1962 at all other national parks was only 37.2 percent of the population of our 23-state sample area. Evidently visiting Mount Rainier enhanced rather than reduced the probability of visiting other parks on the same trip.

Stouffer had argued that among those departing from a given place the number of people reaching a given destination would decline as its distance from their starting point increased, because greater distance would imply more abundant intervening opportunities which could curtail their journey. We can look at this hypothetical mechanism from the perspective of the destination, too. Then Stouffer's postulate would lead to the expectation that among those actually arriving at Mount Rainier, the proportion visiting on the same trip other national parks closer to their homes would vary inversely with the distance from their home state to Mount Rainier. That is, by Stouffer's assumption, one's likelihood of arriving at Mount Rainier would have to depend, if not on the physical absence of intervening parks, then at least on one's having eluded what intervening parks there were. But instead, we find virtually the opposite pattern, as shown in Table 3. The percentage visiting another national park on the

Table 3   Probability of Mt. Rainier visitors in 1962 sample visiting any other national park at all, by rank-order distance of visitor's home state from Mt. Rainier

Tier of states	Percent visiting other parks	N
First tier, states adjacent to Washington	24.7	(158)
Second tier, states contiguous to first-tier states	63.2	(87)
Third tier, states contiguous to second-tier states	88.0	(75)
Fourth tier, states contiguous to third-tier states	68.4	(95)
Fifth and sixth tiers	86.2	(65)

same trip tended to increase as distance from home state to Mount Rainier increased.

Besides Mount Rainier, the state of Washington contains the Olympic National Park. It is located to the west of Puget Sound, on the Olympic Peninsula, and thus for nearly all out-of-state visitors, it lies farther from their homes than does Mount Rainier. The latter is then in an obvious sense an intervening opportunity. Visiting Mount Rainier should, according to Stouffer's assumption, reduce the probability of visiting Olympic National Park. Among the sample of Mount Rainier visitors, however, 26.9 percent reported also visiting Olympic on the same trip. For comparison, the total number of Olympic National Park visits in 1962 was only 2.5 percent of the population of this 23-state sample area.[24]

My previous research had shown that national park visitation rates do indeed vary as an inverse function of distance between a park and the

[24] By calculation from data given in *Statistical Abstracts of the United States,* 1963. It should be noted that this 2.5 percent figure is a "generous" estimate. Visits by Washingtonians were included in the numerator, as were visits by persons from the "Eastern culture area." The denominator, however, was limited to the population of the 23 states in this study. Similarly, the 37.2 percent comparison figure is a "generous" estimate of the rate of visitation at other national parks by nonvisitors of Mount Rainier.

traveler's home state. The above findings indicate, however, that this distance gradient cannot be explained by the intervening opportunities mechanism as Stouffer conceived it. As Table 4 shows, the probability of visiting a national park apparently depends on its proximity to another national park as well as on its proximity to one's home. In general, the proportion of Mount Rainier visitors going to each other park was higher if the other park was close to Mount Rainier and decreased as distance from Mount Rainier increased. No such result would have been expected from Stouffer's implied assumption that travel destinations are mutually exclusive alternatives. In the Stouffer hypothesis the reason that the drawing power of destination X varies with its proximity to the traveler's starting point, it is assumed, is that such proximity generally reduces the num-

Table 4 Probability of Mt. Rainier visitors in 1962 sample visiting other particular national parks on same trip*

Parks (in order of proximity to Mt. Rainier)	Distance (100s of miles)	Percent visiting (N = 480)
Olympic	1.3	26.9
Crater Lake	3.0	18.3
Glacier	3.7	16.9
Lassen Volcanic	4.7	5.0
Yellowstone	5.6	20.6
Grand Teton	5.8	16.2
Yosemite	6.7	7.3
Kings Canyon	7.4	2.3
Sequoia	7.7	5.6
Bryce Canyon	8.2	5.2
Zion	8.2	5.2
Wind Cave	9.2	0.8
Grand Canyon	9.2	5.0
Rocky Mountain	9.3	5.8
Mesa Verde	9.8	2.5
Carlsbad Caverns	13.8	0.6
Isle Royale	15.3	0.0
Platt	15.5	0.0
Big Bend	16.0	0.2
Hot Springs	17.2	0.2
Mammoth Cave	19.1	0.2
Great Smoky Mountains	21.2	0.2
Shenandoah	22.4	0.0
Acadia	25.3	0.0
Everglades	26.8	0.6
Mt. McKinley		0.6
Haleakala		0.0
Hawaii Volcanoes		0.0
Virgin Islands		0.0

* The 32d national park, Canyonlands, in Utah, was established after completion of this questionnaire study. The 31st, Petrified Forest, was still a national monument in 1962.

ber of intervening opportunities that might compete with X. Similarly, then, the Stouffer model would imply that the proximity of X to other destinations of like character ought to *reduce* its drawing power by putting it in competition with alternative opportunities. The data contradict this implication of Stouffer's model.

It might have been supposed, perhaps, that the gradient shown in Table 4 is an artifact of the spatial distribution of the respondents' residences. Since the Mount Rainier sample included higher proportions of visitors from states close to the state of Washington, and lower proportions from states farther away, it is important to control for distance from home to Mount Rainier in order to ascertain the independent effects of distance from Mount Rainier to another park. This is done in Table 5. Again it is apparent that Mount Rainier visitors from far away were more, rather

Table 5   Percent of Mt. Rainier visitors in 1962 sample who also visited on the same trip other national parks

| | Visitor's state of residence | | | | |
	States adjacent to Washington	Second tier of states	Third tier of states	Fourth tier of states	Fifth and sixth tiers
Olympic	13.4	35.6	37.3	23.2	41.5
Crater Lake	5.1	36.8	21.3	14.7	27.7
Glacier	3.2	10.3	33.3	22.1	32.3
Lassen Volcanic	1.3	14.9	5.3	1.1	6.2
Yellowstone	3.2	4.6	34.7	34.7	47.7
Grand Teton	1.3	4.6	29.3	26.3	38.5
Yosemite	1.3	8.0	14.7	3.2	18.5
Kings Canyon	0.0	2.3	2.7	1.1	9.2
Sequoia	0.6	8.0	8.0	4.2	13.8
Bryce Canyon	0.0	3.4	13.3	3.2	13.8
Zion	0.0	2.3	14.7	3.2	13.8
Wind Cave	0.0	0.0	0.0	4.2	0.0
Grand Canyon	0.0	1.1	17.3	1.1	13.8
Rocky Mountain	0.0	0.0	9.3	9.5	18.5
Mesa Verde	0.0	0.0	2.7	6.3	6.2
Carlsbad Caverns	0.0	1.1	0.0	0.0	3.1
Isle Royale	0.0	0.0	0.0	0.0	0.0
Platt	0.0	0.0	0.0	0.0	0.0
Big Bend	0.0	0.0	0.0	0.0	1.5
Hot Springs	0.0	0.0	0.0	0.0	1.5
Mammoth Cave	0.0	1.1	0.0	0.0	0.0
Great Smoky Mountains	0.0	1.1	0.0	0.0	0.0
Shenandoah	0.0	0.0	0.0	0.0	0.0
Acadia	0.0	0.0	0.0	0.0	0.0
Everglades	0.6	1.1	0.0	1.1	0.0
Mt. McKinley	0.0	1.1	2.7	0.0	0.0
Haleakala	0.0	0.0	0.0	0.0	0.0
Hawaii Volcanoes	0.0	0.0	0.0	0.0	0.0
Virgin Islands	0.0	0.0	0.0	0.0	0.0

than less, likely to include visits to other national parks in the same trip. But now it is also apparent that for a given tier of states (or, roughly, for a given distance from home) the probability of a particular park's inclusion in the Mount Rainier visitor's itinerary varied directly with the nearness of that park to Mount Rainier.

So far I have treated each national park as "an opportunity," as if all the parks were equal in recreational value except for the matter of relative location. But this is evidently not the case. In a matrix of visitation rates at a number of parks by persons from a number of states, it is possible to partial out the effects of location and calculate relative "recreational opportunity coefficients" or "attractiveness scores" for the different parks. The procedure for obtaining such weights will be explained next. The apparent exceptions to the generalizations offered above regarding Tables 4 and 5 can be largely accounted for by variations in these park weights. Yellowstone, for example, far outweighs Lassen Volcanic.

Measuring National Park Attractiveness

1 Opportunity Coefficients

Stouffer assumed that it is not distance as such which diminishes the attractiveness of a destination. Instead, alternative destinations closer at hand (and hence more accessible) deter travel to the more remote place, and the more remote it is, the more such alternatives nearer by there will be and hence the greater the deterrent to the longer journey. As Stouffer put it, the number of people who will travel a given distance will depend on the ratio of opportunities at that distance to intervening opportunities.

In the case of national park travel, this could be expressed in the form of the following equation:

$$\frac{R_{ij}I_{ij}}{O_j} = c \tag{1}$$

where R_{ij} is the visitation rate from state i at park j, I_{ij} is the number of opportunities at lesser distances than park j is from state i, O_j is the number of opportunities at park j, and c is a constant. If each of the national parks were equal, so that each could be considered a unit "opportunity," this formula would simplify to

$$R_{ij}I_{ij} = c \tag{2}$$

where I_{ij} would simply denote the *number of parks* nearer than park j is to state i. I wanted to try out this simplified version of the formula on a complete matrix of visitation rates for all states and all parks. Unfortunately, the files in the various national parks I visited were not complete, and neither were the files in National Park Service headquarters in Washington, D.C. By 1952 the volume of traffic had grown to the point where National Park Service personnel were no longer able to take the time to count all cars or persons entering the parks and after that year such tabulations ceased to be a service-wide requirement. Many older tabulations were not preserved in the files after that time. The largest matrix of visitation figures for a single year which I could put together was for 1940. Complete and comparable state-by-state tabulations of automobiles entering 12 of the parks were available for that year. I converted these frequency tabulations to rates by dividing them by corresponding state auto registration figures and multiplying by 100,000. These rates are given in Table 6, wherein the rows represent states, the columns represent parks, and each R_{ij} entry is the number of autos from state i (per 100,000 registered in that state) entering park j.

Equation 2 accounted for only 57.2 percent of the variance among these visitation rates. The more elaborate formula (Equation 1) requires a complicated computational procedure to solve iteratively for an "opportunity coefficient" for each park, and these can only be calculated for those parks for which state-by-state visitation rates happened to be available. A high-speed electronic computer was used to obtain the opportunity coefficients for 12 parks, by the following procedure.

First, a three-dimensional matrix with 24 rows, 12 columns, and 12 layers, containing entries of zeroes and ones, was read into the machine. Its rows represented the 24 states in the "Western culture area," its columns represented the 12 national parks for which visitation data were available for 1940, and its 12 layers also represented these parks. In a given cell, represented generally as a_{ijk}, there was a one if park k was nearer than park j to state i—or, in other words, if park k afforded an intervening opportunity. When park k was farther than park j from state i, a zero was entered. Zeroes were entered in the diagonal cells, for no park was considered to intervene between itself and a given state. When two parks happened to be equidistant from a given state, each was considered intervening in respect to the other, and ones were entered in both cells. (For the units of distance used and the method of measuring it, see Chapter 8.)

Next, the layers of this three-dimensional matrix were added together, forming a two-dimensional matrix whose entries were simply the number of parks closer than park j to state i. Now if the parks were all of equal attractiveness, so that each could in fact be assigned unit value, then the entries of this two-dimensional matrix would represent the number of intervening opportunities between park j and state i (except that only 12 of the parks then in existence were represented in it, owing to limitations of available data).

Table 6 Matrix of visitation rates, 1940 (Number of automobiles entering park per 100,000 state auto registration)

	Crater Lake	Grand Teton	Great Smoky Mtns.	Kings Canyon	Lassen Volcanic	Mesa Verde	Mt. Rainier	Rocky Mountain	Sequoia	Shenandoah	Yellowstone	Yosemite
Arizona	195.1	162.4	71.5	172.1	56.5	173.9	95.3	452.8	280.7	83.8	607.3	565.8
California	962.9	168.1	38.1	..	..	40.8	274.2	181.7	..	50.1	669.1	..
Colorado	63.0	456.4	50.0	50.7	6.1	..	64.7	..	84.8	71.1	1323.7	170.9
Idaho	473.0	1889.9	33.2	33.2	23.2	30.1	355.0	152.8	53.2	29.3	4749.9	158.2
Illinois	33.1	147.2	1443.0	26.0	5.4	31.0	58.9	1103.3	56.6	296.4	653.6	139.3
Indiana	17.7	57.2	1691.7	24.2	2.8	13.9	33.9	309.7	41.3	310.5	307.3	83.7
Iowa	31.7	95.8	122.2	24.3	4.6	23.1	44.1	1283.4	41.5	81.6	634.8	80.9
Kansas	49.8	123.9	74.1	39.4	6.9	93.4	53.9	2490.7	73.3	80.8	548.9	131.2
Michigan	24.2	62.4	808.0	19.3	2.8	13.3	36.0	209.4	35.8	336.9	333.6	84.7
Minnesota	31.6	79.8	58.2	16.2	3.9	11.8	72.8	175.1	28.6	65.3	663.7	66.8
Missouri	27.1	106.4	396.0	24.0	8.2	40.8	29.7	1210.3	53.2	156.4	456.9	118.4
Montana	167.8	703.9	48.9	57.3	14.7	18.2	294.3	185.9	39.8	33.6	9290.0	108.3
Nebraska	51.2	243.4	47.2	27.0	7.2	42.9	59.5	3597.8	46.6	75.1	937.5	96.6
Nevada	695.4	359.0	101.8	172.4	766.1	45.2	197.9	472.1	178.1	66.0	1410.7	1393.7
New Mexico	50.1	112.7	69.9	68.9	18.8	390.4	27.1	492.7	135.7	39.7	408.2	239.0
North Dakota	59.6	79.5	30.8	12.3	2.7	4.8	103.5	113.1	20.6	29.5	1132.9	45.2
Oklahoma	30.0	126.8	158.3	50.2	6.8	64.5	28.5	742.3	111.5	89.8	331.6	131.3
Oregon	..	126.6	29.8	34.1	174.9	11.7	1201.0	78.6	47.9	34.4	939.8	249.8
South Dakota	43.4	123.0	22.0	15.9	3.1	16.5	70.4	280.3	33.0	39.2	958.6	47.1
Texas	17.7	58.4	139.9	29.3	4.4	43.2	20.3	546.9	63.6	128.2	218.3	122.6
Utah	97.7	2337.6	26.3	39.1	37.4	237.1	200.5	356.9	56.9	37.4	5659.1	246.4
Washington	1094.3	138.3	83.7	49.8	60.3	17.3	..	84.1	52.1	39.8	1313.6	214.6
Wisconsin	21.7	76.5	238.1	16.9	3.5	13.0	46.3	203.4	30.9	117.9	489.0	68.0
Wyoming	94.4	...	647.1	53.9	15.0	92.9	83.9	3157.7	85.4	58.4	...	145.3

The third step involved multiplying each entry in this two-dimensional matrix of intervening parks by the corresponding entry in the matrix of visitation rates, according to Equation 2. *If* all parks were equal, and *if* the 12 parks for which data were available had been all the parks in existence, and *if* Stouffer's theory were correct, then the resulting products should all have been equal. They were not, though their variance (expressed in units of their mean) was 57.2 percent less than the variance of the visitation rates (expressed in units of the mean visitation rate).

Consider now the *j*th column of this matrix of products. According to Equation 1, which could be rewritten as $R_{ij}I_{ij} = cO_j$, the various entries in the *j*th column of this matrix of products may be regarded as several independent estimates of the opportunity value of park *j*. The mean of such a series of independent estimates may, of course, be taken as a first approximation "best estimate." This is what was done as the fourth step: the columns of the matrix of products were summed, and column means were computed. These were normed so that they would add up to 12, since in the oversimplified unit version of the Stouffer model, total park attractiveness for 12 parks was 12 units. The 12 normed means, then, constituted first-approximation opportunity coefficients.

To obtain second approximations, the first-approximation coefficients were simply substituted into the original 24 by 12 by 12 matrix. That is, wherever park *k* was nearer than park *j* to state *i*, the first-approximation opportunity coefficient for park *k* was now substituted for the unity that had been in cell a_{ijk}. Again the layers of this revised three-dimensional matrix were added together, to form a 24 by 12 two-dimensional matrix whose entries were second-approximation estimates of the number of opportunities intervening between state *i* and park *j*. Again these sums were multiplied by the corresponding visitation rates. From the resulting matrix of products, column means were again taken, and normed so that they totaled 12. All of this was step five, and yielded second-approximation "best estimates" of the park opportunity coefficients.

As step six, these second-approximation coefficients were substituted back into the 24 by 12 by 12 matrix, and the process was repeated to yield third-approximation coefficients. The process was continued through 15 iterations. Each of the coefficients in the fifteenth approximation differed from its counterpart in the fourteenth iteration by less than 0.001, so that the process was clearly convergent, and the resulting coefficients could be regarded as empirically derived measures of the relative attractiveness of the 12 parks. These measures are given in Table 7.

Unfortunately, the value of each park that is obtained in this manner is a function of the set of other parks with which it is compared, so that even for these 12 parks, their respective opportunity coefficients might have had different magnitudes had there been visitation data available for other parks besides these 12. The iterative solution has to involve the pretense that the parks represented in the matrix of intervening opportunities are all the parks that exist. And no opportunity coefficients at all, accurate or otherwise, could be calculated for the other existing parks whose visitation data had not been preserved. These difficulties beset the Stouffer model, but not certain other models with which I will compare it in this chapter and in Chapter 8. For the available data, however, the iterative procedure did provide an apparently unique solution; when the computations were begun with park acreages rather than unity in those cells of the three-dimensional matrix where park k constituted an intervening opportunity between park j and state i, the process converged on a set of coefficients that were identical to the third decimal place with those obtained when we started from unity.

Table 7   Stouffer opportunity coefficients for twelve national parks

Crater Lake	0.789
Grand Teton	1.539
Great Smoky Mountains	0.677
Kings Canyon	0.434
Lassen Volcanic	0.289
Mesa Verde	0.213
Mt. Rainier	0.830
Rocky Mountain	1.573
Sequoia	0.642
Shenandoah	0.480
Yellowstone	3.506
Yosemite	1.027

For the 12 parks from which 1940 visitation data were preserved, the Stouffer opportunity coefficients and Equation 1 accounted for 73.9 percent of the variance in Western states' visitation rates.

With all its faults, the Stouffer model does yield numerical opportunity coefficients that may be taken as measures of some aspect of the value of national parks. These coefficients could not have been obtained by simple common sense or by just going and looking at the parks or talking to the people in them. Yet, like many other sociological generalizations, Stouffer's formula has been castigated as "little more than a polysyllabic expression of a commonplace observation."[25] It deserves criticism for other reasons, as indicated earlier in this chapter and in the preceding chapter, but this particular accusation is quite unwarranted. The same critic, who mistakenly supposed the Stouffer formula was the epitome of naturalistic sociology (to which he was staunchly opposed), attributed "circular reasoning" to the migration studies that were devised to test it.[26] If he understood the above iterative procedure, he might regard it as circular, too.

[25] A. H. Hobbs, *Social Problems and Scientism.* Harrisburg, Pa.: The Stackpole Company, 1953, p. 106.
[26] *Ibid.,* p. 107.

At any rate, it must be acknowledged that the opportunity coefficients given in Table 7 are measures of what Morris termed *operative* values, and it remains to be seen whether *conceived* values can be independently measured for these parks, and whether the two sets of measures would be empirically correlated with each other.

The opportunity coefficients obtained with the Stouffer model purport to array the national parks along a single continuum of value, and the model assumes that the attraction exerted by a given quantity of opportunities at a given location depends on their relative accessibility in comparison with other opportunities at other locations. Various travel destinations are treated by the model as mutually exclusive alternatives. I have cited questionnaire data indicating that intervening parks may serve as stepping-stones to more distant parks, rather than as barriers. This amounts to broad confirmation of my Hypothesis 6 (about subsidiated and congruent goals) as stated in Chapter 5. As with any other reasonably precise formulation, the Stouffer model's greatest theoretical importance may lie in the problems posed by the discrepancies between its expectations and the data. Bright and Thomas, for example, applied the formula to interstate migration and found that all but six states (the exceptions all being Southern) sent more migrants to California than the model predicted when applied to state-of-residence and state-of-origin data from the 1930 census. They ventured the opinion that "an important part of the migration to California has been . . . motivated more by climate and legend than by superior job opportunities. Insofar as this is true we are dealing with noncompetitive opportunities in the intervening states and in California." From the census data it was not possible for them to determine the extent to which interstate migrants had come directly to California or had used intervening opportunities as way stations.[27]

But Bright and Thomas overgeneralized their recognition that an intervening opportunity could serve as a stepping-stone rather than as a barrier. They concluded that Kentucky, West Virginia, North Carolina, Pennsylvania, and Virginia were not really intervening opportunities between Indiana as a source of migrants and Minnesota as a prospective destination, because these other states were in the opposite direction (more or less) from Indiana than was Minnesota.[28] They were correct, of course, in noting that an Indiana out-migrant would be unlikely to go to Minnesota *by way of* West Virginia. The latter state is simply not en route, in the ordinary conception of geographic space. (It might be en route, as noted in Chapter 5, in the subjective value space of some migrants.) But for migration that was not a multistage process, then as mutually competing prospective destinations, all states closer than Minnesota to

[27] Margaret Bright and Dorothy S. Thomas, "Interstate Migration and Intervening Opportunities," *American Sociological Review*, 6 (December, 1941), pp. 780–781.
[28] *Ibid.*, p. 782.

Indiana would be intervening opportunities because their direction from Indiana could be disregarded.

Because the Stouffer formula assumes that intervening opportunities only compete with and do not pave the way to more distant opportunities, the formula is more applicable to situations in which "intervening" opportunities and the more distant opportunities lie in opposite directions from the source. It neglects the relationship between goals referred to as "subsidiation" in my Hypothesis 6 in the preceding chapter, and therefore is most likely to be confirmed in instances where there is no such subsidiation. In the case of national parks, Crater Lake and Great Smoky Mountains happen to be almost exactly equidistant from South Dakota, and have approximately comparable opportunity coefficients (see Table 7). Yellowstone and Grand Teton are very much nearer than either of them to South Dakota, and hence constitute intervening opportunites for South Dakotans contemplating national park vacations. These intervening opportunities might be expected to deter travel by South Dakotans to either Crater Lake or Great Smoky Mountains, according to Stouffer's hypothesis, but my Hypothesis 6 would only expect them to deter travel to Great Smoky and would expect them to augment travel to Crater Lake. From Table 6 it can be seen that South Dakota's Crater Lake visitation rate is almost twice its Great Smoky visitation rate. It should thus be apparent that the opportunity coefficients that were calculated by applying Stouffer's formula to park visitation rates and distances, without regard to direction, must contain some error.

2   Population and Inverse Distance

An alternative model is needed, in which distance is treated as distance rather than being sublimated into intervening opportunities out of deference to antinaturalistic dogma. One possible alternative that has been explored is George K. Zipf's P_1P_2/D formula for intercity migration, which Joseph Cavanaugh applied to various batches of travel data, including some data for some national parks.[29] Zipf's formula says that the amount of interaction between any pair of human aggregates will tend to be proportional to the product of their populations divided by the distance between them. Its applicability to national park visitation is questionable on grounds that national parks are hardly "human aggregates." Some sociologists have considered this a "gravitational" formula insofar as P for population is analogous to M for mass. As I will show later, this is a bad analogy. The national park studies clarify its fallacy. Cavanaugh embraced the analogy in his work, however, and the faults of the analogy have been persistently overlooked by his mentor, Stuart C. Dodd.

[29] Joseph A. Cavanaugh, "Formulation, Analysis and Testing the Interactance Hypothesis," unpublished doctoral dissertation. Seattle: University of Washington, 1950.

As recently as 1961, Dodd wrote that "interaction decreases as a function of the intervening distance. This inverse distance factor appears in the same form and for the same reason in the social law of interactance or demographic gravitation and in Newton's law of gravity."[30] He cited in support his 1950 paper on "the interactance hypothesis" which was a generalization of Zipf's formula.[31] Also, in 1955 he had published a paper on dimensional analysis in which he referred to the hypothesis of interactance as a "candidate law of demographic gravitation" supposedly tested by data presented in that paper.[32] The data included the national park travel figures which Cavanaugh, his student, had analyzed.

According to Dodd, the formula for demographic gravitation or human interactance is designed to predict at a particular time and place the number of interacts of a specified type between two or more groups of people. The formula involves as a unit "an act of one person with another person across unit distance in unit time." The formula, as written by Dodd, is

$$I_{AB} = kI_A P_A I_B P_B T/L \tag{3}$$

where I_{AB} is the expected number of interacts between group A and group B, I_A and I_B are group properties that are analogous, Dodd says, to specific molecular mass, and P_A and P_B are analogous, he says, to the number of "molecules" in each group respectively. T and L, of course, stand for time and distance.[33] As I have argued before, I would insist again that its expression in physicalistic metaphor does not suffice to make this formula wrong for sociology, any more than it suffices to make it correct. But in this instance it does appear that the taste for physicalistic terminology has impeded comprehension of conceptual issues and has impaired accurate analysis of empirical data.

Table 8   Some findings reported by Dodd in support of the interactance formula

Unit Interact, I	r	P_A	P_B	I_A or I_B weights	
Auto entering	.88	Yosemite National Park	48 states	1	1
Auto entering	.75	Yellowstone National Park	48 states	1	1
Auto entering	.62	Glacier National Park	48 states	1	1
Auto entering	.86	Mt. Rainier National Park	48 states	1	0.8

Table 8 is a portion of a larger assembly of findings from Cavanaugh's thesis which were reported in Dodd's article. I have selected for discussion here only the portion dealing with national park visitation. Following his

[30] Stuart C. Dodd and Peter G. Garabedian, "The Logistic Law of Interaction When People Pair Off 'At Will,'" *The Journal of Social Psychology*, 53 (1961), p. 147.
[31] Stuart C. Dodd, "The Interactance Hypothesis: A Gravity Model Fitting Physical Masses and Human Groups," *American Sociological Review*, 15 (April, 1950), pp. 245–256.
[32] Stuart C. Dodd, "Dimensional Analysis in Social Physics," in Baljit Singh (ed.), *The Frontiers of Social Science.* New York: St Martin's Press, Inc., 1955, p. 203.
[33] *Ibid.*, pp. 212–213.

definition of I_A and I_B as analogues of specific molecular mass, Dodd *seems* to have been saying that Cavanaugh found four national parks—Yosemite, Yellowstone, Glacier, and Mount Rainier—to be equal in weight.[34] Their equality is doubtful if one knows them well, though Dodd and Cavanaugh were evidently not sufficiently familiar with them. The appreciable correlations reported between expected state-by-state visitation frequencies and observed frequencies (not rates) were construed by Dodd as confirmation of the interactance (or the Zipf P_1P_2/D)formula. Unlike MacIver, who said that a correlation was only the first step in the quest for explanation, Dodd has often seemed to imply that a large product-moment correlation coefficient speaks for itself. At any rate, the apparent implication of equal attractiveness attributed to these four national parks was not pursued or questioned in Dodd's own discussion of the data and the model.

Further insights can be obtained if this aspect of the study is looked into more carefully. In Zipf's formula, if P_1 is taken to represent the "population" of a national park, and P_2 the population of a given state, the equation could be rewritten as

$$V_2/P_2 = bP_1/D \tag{4}$$

where V_2 is the number of visitors to the park from that state, and b is some constant of proportionality. Or, generalizing, and using the same notation employed in connection with the Stouffer model,

$$R_{ij} = bP_j/D_{ij} \tag{5}$$

which, for more direct comparison with Equation 1, can be expressed as

$$\frac{R_{ij}D_{ij}}{P_j} = b \tag{6}$$

The most obvious flaw in this formula is the concept of "park population." National parks don't have populations in the sense that cities do. Taking annual totals of visits at each of the parks (as shown in Table 9) as indices of the average population present at any given time in each park, however, and applying Equation 6 to the 1940 matrix of visitation rates, we can account for 68.7 percent of the variance. Thus, Zipf's formula is slightly inferior to the Stouffer formula and is not as handsomely "confirmed" as Dodd had supposed.

But even if the Zipf formula had been more effective, it wouldn't have made sense conceptually. Purporting to be gravitational, it implies that the "mass" exerting an attracting force consists of a human population present at the destination of travel. This is hardly true of a national park. Many of us, in fact, go to the national parks *in spite of* the other people

[34] *Ibid.*, p. 215.

there. Though there may be some exceptions, certainly it is not *generally* the case that the people already there are what constitutes a national park's attractiveness. If it were used in assessing the relative attractiveness of various national parks, the Zipf model would be dealing with operative values rather than with conceived values, as clearly as in the case of the Stouffer model. But it would boil down to the assertion that a park which is visited by twice as many people per year as another is twice as valuable as the other. It makes sense to suppose that the volume of park use is

Table 9   Number of visits in 1940 at twelve national parks (in thousands)

Crater Lake	252
Grand Teton	103
Great Smoky Mountains	861
Kings Canyon	202
Lassen Volcanic	105
Mesa Verde	36
Mt. Rainier	457
Rocky Mountain	628
Sequoia	282
Shenandoah	951
Yellowstone	526
Yosemite	507

SOURCE: Marion Clawson, *Statistics on Outdoor Recreation*. Washington, D.C.: Resources for the Future, Inc., April, 1958, p. 109.

some function of park value, but it is hardly likely to be a *linear* function unless all parks are equally accessible to all people. This is obviously not the case. Yet this is what is assumed in applying the Zipf formula to national park visitation data.

3   Verstehende

Dodd's physicalism might have been saved from sterility by an infusion of *Verstehende*. By itself, of course, the *Verstehende* approach is not naturalistic any more than is doctrinaire positivism or naïve social physics. But wed to each other, these opposite persuasions could bring forth naturalistic progeny, as I will show in the next few pages. By *Verstehende* sociology, I mean, as did Theodore Abel in an incisive article, the kind of thing common to Cooley's interest in "empathic knowledge," Znaniecki's concept of a "humanistic coefficient," Sorokin's preference for a "logico-meaningful" method over a so-called "causal-functional" approach to cultural phenomena, and perhaps especially MacIver's method of "imaginative reconstruction."[35] When they obtained high correlations between expected and observed visitor frequencies at national parks with the interactance model, Dodd and Cavanaugh should have gone on to ask themselves, "Were the tabulated visitors really attracted to the parks," as the model purports to say, "by the number of people usually present there?" Adequate empathic appreciation (or *understanding*) of visitor motivations, or of national park values, would have challenged any such notion.

Efforts to attain such understanding would not have to be confined to introspection—a notably hazardous pursuit. Nor need they consist of the somewhat mystical process of "empathizing." Assuredly it would be possible to employ the technique of *participant observation*; by permitting themselves to visit a number of the national parks and fully assume the tourist role, Dodd and Cavanaugh might have come to question whether it was the presence of hordes of people in the parks which constituted the attraction. Or, short of this pleasant research step, some consultation of the relevant literature (including, perhaps, a bit of testimony by poetic souls) might have been helpful.

As James Truslow Adams once noted, it does not follow that because 100 cars on a given stretch of road can give pleasure to the people in them, ten times as many people can enjoy themselves in 1,000 cars on that same stretch of road. Nor does it follow, he said, that because a dozen people can enjoy a beautiful place thousands at the same time can do so. Beyond some point the increasing number find nothing left to enjoy. If too many people try to enjoy the same desideratum they can destroy its value.[36] In a recent article raising the question of what may be wrong with our national parks, an appreciative writer answered, "Nothing much, if you can evade tourist traps and get away from the crowds," and spoke of the continual conflict between increasing human use of the parks and preservation of their values.[37] His views hardly accord with the implications of the interactance hypothesis or Zipf's formula. The Secretary of the Interior, Stewart Udall, has spoken of human erosion of park values, and noted the recurrent effort of the National Park Service to resolve what he called its "use-but-don't-spoil dilemma."[38]

In an article I wrote for the *National Parks Magazine* pointing to the need for those who love the national parks to take the population explosion personally and act to halt it, I said, "National parks are created for people. But people—as their numbers increase—are a threat to national

[35] Theodore Abel, "The Operation Called *Verstehen*," *American Journal of Sociology*, 54 (November, 1948), pp. 211–212.
[36] James Truslow Adams, "Diminishing Returns in Modern Life," *Harper's Magazine*, 160 (April, 1930), p. 536.
[37] Michael Frome, "What's Wrong with Our National Parks," *National Wildlife*, 2 (June–July, 1964), p. 4.
[38] Udall, *op. cit.*, p. 124.

parks."[39] Because of such statements some of my nonsociological friends
have wondered aloud how a sociologist can be so "antipeople." My response is that in seeking to prevent human beings from inundating and
destroying one of their finest institutions and thereby depriving themselves
and their posterity of its aesthetic and spiritual benefits I am hardly being
a misanthrope.

At Mount Rainier National Park, the 90-mile Wonderland Trail which
circles the mountain, passes at one place alongside a magnificent example
of glacial polish, where masses of ice once abraded the Mountain's rocky
flanks into rounded contours with smooth and occasionally glossy surfaces,
and scored them with striations that reveal the glacier's direction of flow.
Here the tools of creation were at work for thousands of years, and they
produced something from which the knowledgeable visitor can gain a
sense of time, and as John Muir so well knew, the feeling of being an
eyewitness to the formation of the world. But a few short years ago, a
road was built that passes only 100 yards or so from this spot, and within
weeks of its opening to public travel, new marks had been inscribed in
the rocks by people who apparently supposed their own initials as worthy
of immortality as the natural features the road was meant to reveal to their
eyes.

Very early in the automobile age, objections were already being raised
to the indiscriminate construction of roads into wilderness areas. One ob-
servant writer noted in 1906 that it was not really roads but people that
the wilderness devotees wished to exclude. They seemed to be adherents
of a paradox, saying: "'There should be wilderness areas preserved for
the use of the great American public,' and in the same breath, 'there can't
be wilderness areas if more than a few of the people enjoy them.'"[40] And
a century ago, George Perkins Marsh, a Vermonter, while serving as
United States Minister to Italy wrote a book in which he stressed the
integrity of nature's web of life, and said, "Man is everywhere a disturbing
agent," adding that "wherever he plants his foot, the harmonies of nature
are turned to discords."[41]

Secretary Udall, with overall responsibility for the national park system,
appeared out of sympathy with the implications of Zipf's and Dodd's formulas when he noted the change between 1940 and 1960. The 1960 population of 180 million Americans inherited an overcrowded system of national parks from a 1940 population of 50 million fewer persons. In 1940
the parks had seemed spacious; little area was added to them over the
twenty-year span, but visitation increased markedly.[42] "It is obvious," he
wrote, "that the best qualities in man must atrophy in a standing-room-

[39] William R. Catton, Jr., "Letting George Do It Won't Do It," *National Parks Magazine*, 38 (March, 1964), p. 4.
[40] Howard Flint, quoted in Ise, *op. cit.*, pp. 653–654.
[41] Quoted in Udall, *op. cit.*, p. 77.
[42] *Ibid.*, pp. 176–177.

only environment."[43] He complained of the "bureaucratic trance" gripping those engaged in planning for the future use of American resources, who assume the inevitable doubling of United States population by the end of the century and either suppose nothing can be done about it or else unthinkingly equate growth with progress.[44]

More intensive discussion of the question of "reducing" sociological issues to terms of other sciences will be undertaken in Chapter 9, but here it should be pointed out that this exercise in *Verstehende* does not simply reduce sociology to psychology. One of the reasons Karl Popper cited for the impossibility of such reduction is the concern of the social sciences with the unintended consequences of human activities. As an example he pointed out that "although some people may claim that a liking for mountains and solitude may be explained psychologically, the fact that if many people like the mountains, they cannot enjoy solitude, is not a psychological fact; but this kind of problem is at the very root of social theory."[45]

Nagel was certainly right, however, in insisting that whatever heuristic importance it may have, *Verstehende* is not knowledge.[46] If the testimony cited in the preceding paragraphs calls into question the assumptions imbedded in Dodd's and Zipf's formulas, it does not of itself provide a superior hypothesis. If it suggests a direction of thought by which a superior model may be formulated, it does not suffice to verify that model. Verification must once again be empirical, and preferably quantitative and precise.

4 Successive-intervals Scaling

A more incisive attempt to measure national park attractiveness in terms of conceived values and to ascertain what these values comprise will now be described. Questionnaires were sent to two categories of people having far better than average familiarity with the parks. One sample consisted of 90 persons affiliated with the National Park Service (the superintendent, chief ranger, and chief park naturalist, at each of 30 park units— Sequoia-Kings Canyon being jointly administered, the 31 existing parks formed 30 administrative units). The other sample consisted of leaders named on the letterheads or on officer rosters of various voluntary associations concerned with national parks, wilderness, wildlife preservation, etc.

The questionnaires were one-page rating forms, listing the 31 national

[43] *Ibid.*, p. 186.
[44] *Ibid.*, p. 185.
[45] Karl R. Popper, *The Poverty of Historicism.* Boston: Beacon Press, 1957, p. 158.
[46] Ernest Nagel, *The Structure of Science.* New York: Harcourt, Brace & World, Inc., 1961, p. 484.

parks in alphabetical order, with a series of numbers printed after each park name. The recipient was asked to check which parks he'd ever been to, and to circle a number from 1 to 9 after each such park in order to indicate his judgment of its relative attractiveness. Then he was asked to state on the back of the form, if he wished, his own standards of park attractiveness. Through two follow-up mailings (a reminder postcard, and a duplicate questionnaire), responses were obtained from all but seven of the 90 National Park Service personnel. At least one person at each park returned a questionnaire. The rate of returns was also gratifying, though less spectacular, from the voluntary association leaders sample.

The questionnaire was simple in format but this did not imply necessarily that it was easy to answer. Thoughtful comparisons between the parks were expected to require extensive soul-searching. The cover letter accompanying the questionnaire acknowledged that comparisons on a single continuum between things that differ in a great variety of ways are not always easy, but noted that most of us manage to do this every day. "If we can do it with books, with symphonies, with paintings, or with personalities, it should be possible to do it with National Parks." The high rate of returns thus seems to reflect a commendable willingness among the people to whom the questionnaire was sent to tackle difficult assignments. The difficulty is further underscored by the conviction of some who know the national parks best that they are organically interrelated. "Like chapters in a book," a forestry professor and former park naturalist has written, "various units of the National Park System portray, in dramatic, inspirational fashion, various segments of a complete story."[47] To put it in the terminology of a Sorokin, there were convictions that the parks could not be quantitatively compared and rated, but could only be related to each other in "logico-meaningful" terms.

Not all the questionnaires that were returned were actually filled out as requested. Some members of both samples indicated which parks they had been to, but insisted that it was impossible to give comparative ratings of their relative attractiveness.[48] Some of these partial refusals did go on to indicate what park attractiveness consisted of for them. Their comments are worth quoting. One wrote, "I have been in 30 of the 31 listed parks. I would not attempt to single out by comparison any one being most attractive. Each has its individuality as to attractiveness. . . . If I were to single out any one, of course I would be charged as being biased, for it would be [the park where I work]." Another respondent said, "To

---

[47] Brockman, *op. cit.*, p. 136.

[48] A similar insistence that comparisons could not be made at all, or would be meaningless if attempted, was voiced by a number of clergymen who were asked to choose between a series of "infinite" desiderata. The choices they did make, however, were patterned, and the items proved quite scalable. See William R. Catton, Jr., "Exploring Techniques for Measuring Human Values," *American Sociological Review*, 19 (February, 1954), pp. 49–55.

rate one more attractive than the other is like asking a person which is more valuable, your eyesight or your hearing. Collectively the national parks help to form a composite representation of the 'crown jewels' of our nation. Each in its own way contributes to the whole." Another expressed the difficulty of the rating task by saying, "I find it most difficult to comply with your request. It's a little like asking a mother which one of her children she likes best."

One detailed comment merits quotation in full:

I have been inside of all thirty-one of our National Parks with the sole exception of that in the Virgin Islands which I hope sooner or later to visit. Many of them I have visited repeatedly. It is utterly impossible to comply with your request to rate them comparatively in "relative attractiveness" and in my opinion such a rating would have no useful significance whatever. As well compare a cyclone with an earthquake.

Moreover, in my view, publication of the results of such a superficial rating as you propose might do great harm in misleading the uninformed public into thinking some parks of great scientific and cultural importance to be relatively unimportant—which would be a sad distortion of the facts, and might furnish an excuse for neglecting needed appropriations for areas thus discriminated against.

In my opinion research and effort would be much more usefully employed in emphasizing the value of the National Parks generally and the need for adding outstanding areas, such as the North Cascades, before they are commercially exploited and lost.

A number of respondents suggested that meaningful comparisons might be made within subsets of parks that had similar characteristics—e.g., comparing Carlsbad Caverns, Mammoth Cave, and Wind Cave, or comparing Mount McKinley, Mount Rainier, and Glacier. They felt, however, that it was meaningless to compare a park from one category with a park from another category that was different in kind. Several of these respondents, nevertheless, gave as a general criterion of park attractiveness the "naturalness" of the scene, or alluded in some way to wilderness. Allusions to this sort of criterion are not surprising in view of the sorts of people included in the samples, and it is not because they were at all unexpected that I mention them. What is significant is that they transcend the conviction that the various parks are incommensurable. Of similar significance is the fact that out of 25 questionnaires returned with the comment that no meaningful comparisons could be made, numerical ratings were nevertheless indicated on 14 of them.

On another 90 questionnaires, numerical ratings were given, but no verbal indication of the attractiveness criteria was offered. Another 51 respondents rated the parks and included among their stated criteria some more or less emphatic reference to preservation of the area in its primeval condition. Only 2 questionnaires listed quality of man-made facilities as a prime factor in evaluating park attractiveness, though 2 others suggested that the important criterion was the *balance* between natural features and man-made facilities. A variety of other criteria, usually including some reference to scenic aspects, wildlife, geological features, etc., were listed on 27 other questionnaires. Finally, 2 questionnaires gave ratings and then commented on the back not about the criterion of attractiveness but on the assumed improbability of rating the parks in identical order another time. By implication, these respondents were contending that the criteria of park attractiveness were nebulous and merely intuitive.

A few of the statements of criteria deserve quotation. One respondent who stressed "preservation" maintained that "such indescribable beauty brings out the best in us." This implies that we visit national parks for what they do to us. What we do to them, on the other hand, diminishes them, as another respondent indicated by saying, "Parks are generally attractive to me in proportion as the natural scene is not obscured by developments for the mass accommodation of visitors." One of the voluntary association respondents, referring to a particular park she felt had been overused, said she would never wish to see it again "or recommend [it] to others seeking the ultimate in soul-satisfaction, because it is so infested with human beings, their parking lots and cafeterias, stage shows in the evenings," etc. Another woman wrote the following statement, quoted in full:

In a five-month tour of the parks checked, I came to realize that all of them, *if* they had been left in their natural condition, would deserve a rating of nine. However, since the parks bear the scars of human intrusion, I have rated them as to:

1 naturalness of scene
2 wilderness areas as opposed to commercial developments
3 management—commercial vs. natural
4 naturalism of features—were they overdone, such as tame bears and fenced pools, in Yellowstone, or were they left in a natural condition for viewers to enjoy in their original state?
5 ratio of hiking, horseback riding, walking vs. auto sightseeing, motel-hopping, and fishing.

In sum, my rating of a park depends on its *natural* condition: the more natural the park, the higher the rating.

Again I make no pretense that this kind of statement is surprising when it comes from a person in the categories to which the questionnaire was sent. However, knowing that these were the kinds of criteria the respondents had in mind makes interpretable the scale values that have been calculated from their numerical ratings.

Only a few of the respondents had visited all or nearly all of the parks, though most had visited at least half a dozen or more. Only 14 were able to rate Virgin Islands National Park, whereas 154 rated Yellowstone.

Other parks were rated by varying numbers of respondents ranging between these two extremes.

The numbers to be circled on the rating form were arbitrary, of course, and could not be taken at face value as cardinal quantities. A person who gave a certain park a rating of 8, for example, was not necessarily calling it twice as attractive as another park he rated at 4, or eight-ninths as attractive as one he assigned the top rating of 9. And those respondents who suspected that they might not be able to repeat their ratings identi-

Table 10   Scale values obtained by the method of successive intervals measuring attractiveness of 31 national parks

	From ratings by National Park Service personnel	From ratings by leaders of voluntary associations	Mean
Acadia	2.588	1.872	2.230
Big Bend	2.129	1.872	2.000
Bryce Canyon	2.615	2.256	2.436
Carlsbad Caverns	2.129	1.585	1.857
Crater Lake	2.457	2.196	2.326
Everglades	2.588	1.703	2.146
Glacier	3.773	2.836	3.304
Grand Canyon	3.163	2.902	3.032
Grand Teton	3.432	2.752	3.092
Great Smoky Mtns.	2.830	2.003	2.416
Haleakala	2.749	1.913	2.331
Hawaii Volcanoes	2.830	1.862	2.346
Hot Springs	0.340	0.447	0.394
Isle Royale	2.535	2.168	2.352
Kings Canyon	2.878	2.463	2.670
Lassen Volcanic	2.569	2.030	2.300
Mammoth Cave	1.440	1.208	1.324
Mesa Verde	2.238	2.071	2.154
Mt. McKinley	2.950	3.466	3.208
Mt. Rainier	2.970	2.200	2.585
Olympic	3.071	2.680	2.876
Petrified Forest	1.442	1.268	1.355
Platt	0.470	0.173	0.322
Rocky Mountain	2.887	2.169	2.528
Sequoia	2.960	2.706	2.833
Shenandoah	1.967	1.872	1.920
Virgin Islands	2.588	1.872	2.230
Wind Cave	1.390	1.169	1.280
Yellowstone	3.589	2.704	3.146
Yosemite	3.341	3.022	3.182
Zion	2.814	2.313	2.564

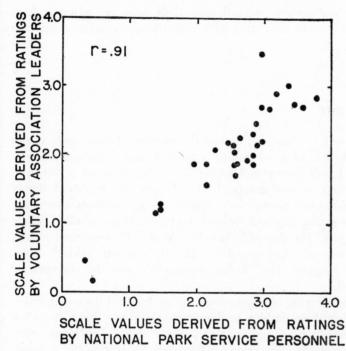

Figure 2. Reliability of attractiveness scale values obtained
by the method of successive intervals applied to
31 national parks

cally a second time were, of course, correct. No individual's ratings of
the parks should be regarded as definitive. But there is a straightforward
method for ascertaining from *frequency distributions* of the ratings what
the average subjective width of each numerical interval was for the various respondents. By the "method of successive intervals," these interval
widths were inferred in terms of the normal curve as a model, and then
the median scale value of each park was calculated.[49] Two separate sets
of scale values were obtained, one from each respondent sample. These
are given in Table 10. (To avoid misunderstanding, it should be borne
in mind that the numbers in the table do not refer to the original series
of integers from 1 to 9 that appeared after the park names on the questionnaires. Instead the numbers in the table take as their unit the average
standard deviation of the frequency distributions of judgments.)

In Figure 2, the scale values computed from the voluntary association
leaders' ratings are plotted against the scale values calculated from the
ratings by Park Service personnel. It is evident visually that the two sets

[49] A step-by-step explanation of the method of successive intervals is given in Allen
L. Edwards, *Techniques of Attitude Scale Construction.* New York: Appleton-Century-Crofts, Inc., 1957, chap. 5.

of scale values are linearly related, and their intercorrelation is high ($r = .91$). It can be said, then, that park attractiveness can be scaled with high reliability.

Nothing to Fear

In Chapter 8, I will analyze and discuss the relation of these scale values of park attractiveness to a naturalistic model of park visitation patterns. First, however, I will survey in Chapter 7 the development of the conceptual foundations of such a model. For the present, it should simply be noted that unless we assume the questionnaire respondents were quite blind to their own thoughts and feelings, and unwittingly testified falsely to the conception of the desirable which guided their numerical ratings of the parks, this study has forged a real link between "poetic" values and naturalistic inquiry. The "logico-meaningful" and the quantitative have been united.

Moreover, the gathering of questionnaire responses and the computation of scale values has done nothing to depreciate the parks themselves. Nor did any responses to the questionnaire indicate that I had in any way lessened the intensity of admiration for the parks by getting the respondents to assign comparative ratings to them. No member of either sample bewailed his own ratings by saying he thought less of the parks now that he had put numbers on them.

It has been suggested by an art critic that we "can learn to interrogate a picture in such a way as to intensify and prolong the pleasure" we get from it.[50] By the well-chosen term "interrogate" he means that viewing great art is a process of *interaction* between viewer and object, not a one-way process of passive perception. What MacIver called "dynamic assessment" takes place. Similarly, one can learn to interrogate a mountain or a forest. And when these have been preserved in a national park, I see no reason why our appreciation of it cannot be enhanced by all that we learn of the *institution*, and the evolution of attitudes toward it. To sense the greatness of the institution while visiting one of the parks in the Eastern part of the United States, especially, it is not enough to have a well-developed sense of color and form. It is not enough even to know some geology and some botany. It helps also to know of the devotion of thousands of average citizens, hundreds of congressmen and state legislators, and a few wealthy philanthropists, who together redeemed these areas that were no longer in the public domain but had already gone into private ownership by the time of the advent of the national park

[50] Kenneth Clark, *Looking at Pictures*. New York: Holt, Rinehart and Winston, Inc., 1960, p. 15.

idea. Now that national park status has been given to these places of beauty, it seems hardly reasonable to assume that public attitudes toward them will forever be so frail as to be shattered by sociological examination.

After I had sent out my questionnaires to obtain park attractiveness ratings, and had done the calculations which converted the distributions of ratings into scale values, I again visited the oldest of the national parks—Yellowstone. In it there is a small and unprepossessing visitor center, near the junction of the Firehole and Gibbon Rivers. Its exhibits emphasize the human history of the area, whereas the exhibits at the other visitor centers elsewhere in the park stress the geology, the biology, etc. At the back of this rustic little building there is a picture window, framing a view of the meadow. After studying some of the exhibits, my eye wandered out toward the trees beside the confluence of the two rivers near the foot of what is now called National Park Mountain. Realizing I was seeing the very spot where mercenery thoughts were submerged under a noble vision at that 1870 campfire, I felt my spine tingle. A few moments later, in a plain glass case in this little museum, I saw a facsimile copy of The Yellowstone Act. I read these quietly momentous words:

Be it enacted by the Senate and House of Representatives of the United States of America in Congress assembled, That the tract of land in the Territories of Montana and Wyoming lying near the headwaters of the Yellowstone River, and described as follows . . . is hereby reserved and withdrawn from settlement, occupancy, or sale under the laws of the United States, and dedicated . . . . "

I swallowed, and squared my shoulders. As I looked around me, I saw no evidence that those tourists who knew nothing of opportunity coefficients, inverse distance functions, or successive-intervals scale values were any more deeply moved.

There are men, however, who imagine that naturalistic sociology threatens true values by subjecting them to study. Krutch's book on the Grand Canyon amply testifies to the compatibility between scientific knowledge of geology and paleontology, on the one hand, and reverence for that great chasm and appreciation for its national park status, on the other. But he also wrote another book, protesting study of social phenomena by the methods and in the spirit of natural science.[51] In his review of the book, Nagel rightly rejected the notion that scientific discoveries impoverish the content of nature.[52] Elsewhere Nagel pointed out that it is not naturalism, as often supposed, but a dualistic antinaturalism that imperils human values. By treating as irrelevant any verifiable knowledge

---

[51] Joseph Wood Krutch, *The Measure of Man*. Indianapolis: The Bobbs-Merrill Company, Inc.
[52] Ernest Nagel, *Logic without Metaphysics*, New York: The Free Press of Glencoe, 1956, p. 426.

of the causes and consequences of men's value commitments, such attitudes deprive human choice of effectiveness, open the way to irresponsible pursuit of intuitive yearnings, and separate the scientific control of nature from humane understanding.[53]

In spite of it all, there are men who insist that our ability to reduce such phenomena, for example, as weather to measurements of temperature, atmospheric pressure, humidity, and readings of a wind gauge, must remain forever alien from the euphoria we feel when certain weather conditions prevail.[54] But the science of meteorology has not destroyed that euphoria; it could be argued that it has even enlarged the variety of occasions on which it can be experienced. Whereas men formerly cowered in the face of a thunderstorm they attributed to divine wrath, some men have been enabled by increased knowledge to marvel at the electrical and acoustical display they witness when certain natural forces are in operation. And the truistic assertion that meteorology cannot explain euphoria ought no more to obstruct naturalistic inquiry into values and attitudes than the equally misleading contention that sociology becomes reductionist if it acknowledges a connection between meteorological events and the incidence of euphoric attitudes in human beings. We should no more insist that all causes of euphoria are social than that euphoria has no causes among antecedent conditions or is unmeasurable.

If we acquire the ability to manipulate weather, we will not thereby refute meteorological principles, either. By the same token, our ability to modify social organization does not render "real" social science impossible, as some argue. Our ability to measure human values and to predict human choices, it should be added, need not preclude the evolution of those values and the alteration of those choices. Antideterministic opponents of naturalism argue that we cannot as human beings make choices if human behavior and human attitudes can be studied naturalistically. Such contentions confuse legitimate determinism with misconceived fatalism. It is erroneous to maintain that valid theoretical knowledge and effective human control are antithetical. What we have learned of chemistry, for example, has certainly not been an obstacle to metallurgical engineering, nor has our ability to refine crude ores into useful metals refuted the laws of chemistry by showing chemical phenomena to be unlawful.[55]

There is no need to fear the impact of naturalistic sociology on the values we cherish. Why not confidently expect that there will emerge from accumulated sociological knowledge new values not now dreamed of? To those who fear that it might result in disillusionment, I suggest that their anxiety betrays a commitment to certain illusions in lieu of durable values. Through naturalistic sociology it ought to be possible to pro-

---

[53] *Ibid.*, p. 38.
[54] For example, see Hobbs, *op. cit.*, p. 15.
[55] Cf. Nagel, *The Structure of Science*, pp. 461–462.

vide a firmer foundation for the pursuits to which we devote ourselves most earnestly.

Summary

The acquistion of knowledge is like the ascent of a mountain. Much effort and organization may be involved in the quest, and the result is an altered perspective and perhaps a keener appreciation for what one sees. Deep appreciation can lead to poetic expression, but this fact does not preclude scientific study, nor does scientific study destroy sublime values.

In the United States one institution that has evolved as an embodiment of such values is the national park system. Its clearly crescive and non-deliberate development makes voluntaristic or even functionalistic description of it inappropriate. But both the accumulated literature on the parks and the testimony of questionnaire respondents provide data from which the conceptions of the desirable which motivate park visitation can be inferred. The fact that the parks have fixed spatial locations and that visitors must travel to them in quest of their spiritual enrichment affords a convenient context for beginning the empirical study of some of the hypotheses included in the theory of value offered in Chapter 5. Abstract value space is resolved in this instance into the more easily observable framework, geographic space.

The hypothesis of intervening opportunities, which Stouffer offered as an explanation of distance differentials in migration, was ostensibly applicable to national park travel. It turned out, however, that park travel was patterned in such a way that the Stouffer equation—which neglects the phenomena of subsidiation and congruency among goals—did not fit. Travel from one's home state to a distant national park is often facilitated rather than inhibited by the existence of intervening parks. A visit to one park seems to enhance rather than reduce the probability of visiting others. The Stouffer formula can be used, with an iterative procedure, to solve for "opportunity coefficients" that might be regarded as measures of the relative value of the various parks, but these coefficients must contain some error for two reasons. One reason is that intervening parks are not, as the model assumes, in a strictly competitive relationship with more remote parks. The other reason is that the model requires the pretense that the subset of parks for which visitation data happened to be available was equivalent to the set of all existing parks.

An alternative visitation model, not beset with these particular difficulties, is the Zipf P_1P_2/D formula, or Dodd's interactance hypothesis. Not only does this model turn out to be empirically inferior to the Stouffer equation, however, but it commits an egregious conceptual error. It purports to be gravitational, but it equates the attracting mass of a national park with the "population" of that park. A careful excursion into *Verstehende* sociology makes it clear that people do not in general visit the parks because of the presence therein of other people, but in spite of the crowds. By itself, of course, the *Verstehende* approach is no more naturalistic than an exclusively physicalistic approach, but a proper blend of the two can be fruitful.

By means of a simple questionnaire, a sample of National Park Service members and a sample of leaders of certain conservationist organizations gave numerical ratings of relative attractiveness of the various national parks they knew at firsthand. From these distributions of ratings, scale values were computed by the method of successive intervals. High reliability characterized the scale values obtained in this manner, and the conception of the desirable which many respondents testified had guided their ratings was centered around preservation of these dedicated areas in as nearly their natural state as possible. The national parks were valued as sanctuaries in which human intrusion was to be kept as inconspicuous as it could be. This was the diametric opposite of the notion of "mass" in the Zipf model. The relation of the successive-intervals scale values to a naturalistic model for park travel patterns will be explored further in Chapter 8.

The measurement of park values had been alleged to be impossible, and a good many people have supposed that scientific examination of sublime values like these would somehow tarnish or imperil them. Geological and biological knowledge relevant to park features has generally enhanced their value, yet sociological knowledge is often feared. None of the questionnaire respondents in the present study gave any indication that their appreciation of the national parks was diminished by participation in the study, however, and my own sense of awe in regard to both the scenic and the human institutional elements in the national park system is unimpaired. I am firmly convinced that naturalistic sociology is no threat to human values. At least one writer has argued that "science is most significant as one of the greatest spiritual adventures that man has yet known. . . ."[56] Stouthearted men should be eager to embark on that adventure.

[56] Popper, *op. cit.,* p. 56.

Chapter Seven

SOCIOLOGICAL AXIOMS OF MOTION

The Use and Misuse of Metaphor

Magnetic and gravitational analogies were cited in an earlier chapter as aids in the development and elucidation of a naturalistic theory of valuing. Conceptions of the desirable, with which that theory is concerned, have now been shown to be reliably measurable. It remains to see whether such measured values are in fact predictive of human behavior. Chapter 8 will take up that question. But first I think it is important to inquire in the present chapter into the propriety and possible pitfalls in the use of physical metaphors such as magnetism or gravitation.

I have attempted to use analogy as a guidepost in the open-minded quest for a theory whose acceptance or rejection must ultimately depend not on the plausibility of the analogy but on empirical test. In contrast, one might sometimes be tempted to avail oneself of analogy *in lieu of* explanation. The philosophical manipulation of metaphor as a substitute for the rigorous use of scientific language has been said by Reichenbach to arise from the fact that the philosopher often tries to answer questions before the means for formulating and testing a scientific answer are available. Regrettably, however, there have also been people who have persisted in using such "picture language" after scientific means of solving the problems they raised did exist; in such instances analogy may do more harm than good.[1]

[1] Hans Reichenbach, *The Rise of Scientific Philosophy.* Berkeley, Calif.: University of California Press, 1951, p. 25.

The term "rationalistic" is sometimes used in the classification of philosophical thought to refer to reliance on reason without concern for observation. It is contrasted in this way with "empiricist." According to Reichenbach, such a nonempiricist as the mathematician might be more likely than others to backslide into rationalism because he has experienced great success in the use of logical deduction in his own subject matter. What makes this success possible, and what he may tend to neglect in responding to the fact of success, is that mathematics is a purely conceptual discipline not involving any direct reference to the empirical world. Because mathematics is nonobservational and is yet useful to the empirical sciences, the mathematically minded person might be tempted by a theory of knowledge in which insight is deemed a substitute for sense perception. From there it is only a short step to mysticism.[2] If mysticism tempts the true mathematician (who usually resists the temptation, be it noted), the mathematically naïve admirer of mathematics is presumably more susceptible yet.

Such are the pitfalls. We need to be reminded again and again that in the development of scientific knowledge, analogy can be used for heuristic purposes only, and is not a means of proof. Explanation is achieved only when verifiable generalizations are related to specific observations. It is not achieved simply by applying an appealing metaphor to a set of observations.[3] Translation of truisms into mathematical notation does not make them sociologically important, and the mathematical formulation of hypotheses does not eliminate the necessity of comparing them with data. With such reminders before him, however, the naturalistic sociologist ought not to have to abstain altogether from the use of physical analogy or mathematical notation. He must avoid misusing them, but he does not have to avoid using them properly.

Proper use of analogy may depend partly on the motivation of the user. If he is genuinely seeking explanation he may be less inclined to mistake metaphor for proof than if his goal is prestige. Spencer is an example of a sociologist who misused analogy, and there is some reason to suppose that his misuse stemmed from excessive concern for scientific status rather than for producing genuine knowledge. Stark has pointed out that Spencer was born into an era of advancing individualism, and when Spencer's own ideological commitments to individualism and *laissez faire* are noted it is indeed paradoxical that he should have so outspokenly preached what Stark called "organicism." Stark attributed the paradox to the fact that the kind of science most fashionable in Spencer's day was biology. It was the prestige of biology that Spencer coveted more than truth, according to Stark.[4]

[2] *Ibid.*, pp. 32–33.
[3] Cf. William S. Beck, *Modern Science and the Nature of Life*. Garden City, N.Y.: Anchor Books, Doubleday & Company, Inc., 1961, pp. 183–184.
[4] Werner Stark, *The Fundamental Forms of Social Thought*. New York: Fordham University Press, 1963, pp. 104–105.

I would add that in my opinion at least some of the importation of physical concepts and models by sociologists into their own discipline has been motivated by envy of the physicist's prestige—but comparable prestige is certainly not often attained by the sociologist through borrowing the prestigeful science's concepts—and it is *not always* the goal sought. Other critics of "social physics" have written as if they supposed that prestige seeking was the whole story and that the use of physical analogies is always and inherently without empirical merit.

For Stark it seemed that the most reasonable and expectable response of social thought to the Great Depression of the 1930s would have been to emphasize holistic concepts and get away from what he termed "mechanicism." But this was not what happened, and so Stark sought an explanation for what was, to him, the unexpected. He found it in the fact that physics had become the prestige science in the twentieth century. Just as Spencer had coveted the biologist's prestige a century ago, Pareto and his disciples in more recent times have liked the physicist's mantle.[5] Stark cited Pareto's *The Mind and Society* as the "most massive and impressive" formulation of positivistic mechanicism, and accused Pareto of pursuing conformity between social science principles and physical laws rather than conformity of social science to social facts.[6]

Another outspoken critic of social physics has been Sorokin, who wrote of a long series of attempts to create a theory of social mechanics or social geometry. Such attempts, he said, occurred even in ancient times in China, India, Greece, and Rome. From the sixteenth century through the eighteenth, many systematic efforts to describe and explain sociocultural events in terms of Newtonian mechanics were made by Europeans. All of these Sorokin criticized on grounds that they mistakenly used the concept of *physical* space.[7] It is not physical motion that the sociologist has in mind in speaking of "social movements," and accordingly, Sorokin said, sociology requires its own independent and distinctive conception of space and time.[8] A mathematically sophisticated admirer of Sorokin, Nicholas Rashevsky, has also indicated that a "too literal" imitation of physics must be abortive. The mathematical methods of physics may be legitimately and usefully imitated, he said, but not the exact form. As an independent subject matter, sociology should expect to find its phenomena described by equations that will often be different in form from those of Newtonian mechanics.[9]

Worse than too literal imitation, in the opinion of E. T. Bell, are attempts to transform a theory that is not yet mathematical into one that

[5] *Ibid.*, p. 198.
[6] *Ibid.*, pp. 125–126.
[7] Pitirim A. Sorokin, *Sociocultural Causality, Space, Time*. Durham, N.C.: The Duke University Press, 1943, pp. 103–104.
[8] *Ibid.*, p. 35.
[9] Nicholas Rashevsky, *Mathematical Theory of Human Relations*. Bloomington, Ind.: Principia Press, 1947, pp. v–vi.

is, by mere citation of sophisticated mathematical disciplines and undiscriminating adoption of mathematical symbols. He regarded such work as little more than a "feeble mathematical pun."[10] Specifically, Bell's criticism was directed at the "S-theory" of Dodd, whose work was vigorously rebuked by others besides Bell on different but related grounds. Ethel Shanas ventured the opinion that Dodd's work would remain empirically sterile, was tautologous, and was based on misconceptions of the use of mathematical and operational methods.[11] Sorokin described Dodd's *Dimensions of Society* as pushing mechanistic methods "to obvious absurdity and nonsense."[12] In Chapter 6, I showed how cautious reliance on the *Verstehende* approach might have corrected some of the errors in Dodd's social physics, but I will also show (later in the present chapter) that in some respects his errors have been less serious than those committed by a number of other imitators of Newtonian mechanics.

The Debatable Relevance of Physics

The imitations have often been clumsy and misconceived. It is not surprising that some students of the history of sociological thought, such as Stark, have concluded that the formulas of physical mechanics have nothing to offer sociology. In Stark's opinion, such formulas have no applicability to society and will always be a nuisance or a source of error when sociologists try to use them.[13] As I pointed out in Chapter 2 and Chapter 3, the empirical validity of a formula in physics (or any other nonsociological discipline) is no guarantee of its validity in relation to *social* facts. But it must also be remembered that it does not follow that because a formula fits physical facts it *cannot* fit social facts. Nor does it follow that none of the concepts ultimately found useful in sociology will have physical analogues.

One concept of sociology, still used without rigorous definition for the most part, sounds physical and could have a direct counterpart in physics if sociologists so defined it. It is the concept of "social forces," which Albion Small long ago pointed out "was never challenged so long as it was merely an everyday commonplace. When it passed into technical forms of expression," he said, "doubts began to be urged."[14] It ought to be added that the doubts were usually less concerned with the distortions

[10] E. T. Bell, Review of Dodd's *Dimensions of Society, American Sociological Review,* 7 (October, 1942), p. 709.
[11] Ethel Shanas, "A Critique of Dodd's *Dimensions of Society," American Journal of Sociology,* 48 (September, 1942), pp. 227, 230.
[12] Sorokin, *op. cit.,* p. 49.
[13] Stark, *op. cit.,* p. 168.
[14] Albion W. Small, *General Sociology.* Chicago: The University of Chicago Press, 1905, p. 533.

of the original denotations of the word "force" in physics that were committed when sociologists used the word than with the physicalistic connotations it did retain. If sociologists were to define the term carefully so that it remained clearly analogous to the meaning of force in physical mechanics, then the following series of questions posed by Small would summarize an important program of sociological inquiry:

Of what sort are the forces that join men's destinies? What are the conditions, the modes, the laws, of their action? How may we distinguish between the constants and the variables among these forces? How may we report the equilibrium of these forces in a given situation, and how may we foresee resultants of forces? How may we detect, and discriminate, and measure, and if possible control, the particular combinations of forces in our own society?[15]

I know of no reference to Small as a "social physicist," but many of the studies carried out by those to whom that label is conventionally applied could be subsumed under the above program. However erroneous the conclusions Pareto drew, or the lists of elements he constructed, his distinction between "residues" and "derivations" was certainly an attempt to "distinguish between the constants and the variables" among social forces. A good deal of the work of Zipf and Dodd, though misguided through neglect of *Verstehende*, nevertheless sought to report "the equilibrium of forces in a given situation." If it contains empirical errors, such work deserves criticism on empirical grounds, but it should not be criticized merely for using concepts which originated in physics.

The hidden assumption in such criticisms is that a concept can only be useful to a sociologist if it was invented by a sociologist. When this assumption is stated explicitly its absurdity is readily apparent. If sociologists continued to abide by it, the progress of other sciences could choke further progress of sociology. That is to say, if there *are* social phenomena which sufficiently resemble any of the phenomena dealt with in other sciences so that a common concept might aptly designate both, any time the other science happens to develop the appropriate conceptualization first, the work of sociology must consequently be impeded. In my judgment, this hidden assumption has worked enough mischief and sociologists should at last abandon it.

There is a long-standing division among social scientists regarding the appropriateness of emulating in social research the procedures of natural science. Some even hold that social science ought not to seek explanatory theories if these have to employ abstract distinctions that are not common to the vocabulary of everyday life, or if they require validation by rigorously observed and classified evidence rather than mere "common-sense" experience.[16] In answer it needs to be said that though cautious use of

[15] *Ibid.*, p. 105.
[16] Ernest Nagel, *The Structure of Science*. New York: Harcourt, Brace & World, Inc., 1961, pp. 448–449.

Verstehende can prevent or correct some of the errors of social physics, uncontrolled rationalism or sociology-by-insight can also make serious errors, some of which might be prevented or corrected by cautious indulgence in a social physics approach.

It is easy to dismiss physics as irrelevant to sociology if the sociologist knows no physics. It may be even easier when the social physics at issue has been formulated by a physicist who seems to know no sociology. The defense of its own territorial boundaries always seems virtuous to the ingroup. But intellectual parochialism inhibits inquiry and thwarts the construction and discovery of new knowledge. It is antithetical to naturalistic sociology. The naturalistic sociologist should have a sympathetic ear for C. P. Snow's account of the cocktail parties he has attended in the company of "literary intellectuals," highly educated, who conversed incredulously about the "illiteracy" of scientists because the latter didn't know the latest novels or had not recently read any works of Shakespeare. He said he got a chilly response when he asked his literary friends to describe the second law of thermodynamics, and he believed the result would have been about the same if he had asked the even simpler question: What is meant by mass, or acceleration? The latter, he pointed out, was roughly the scientific counterpart of "Can you read?"[17]

The naturalistic sociologist ought to be able to pass this literacy test. He expects, of course, to select his concepts on the basis of their empirical utility and not their ancestry. But naturalism is more than empiricism, and if a sociologist is so unmindful of the development of modern natural science that he does not know the meaning of "mass" and "acceleration," and what crucial conceptual innovations these were, he is not likely to understand the other three elements of naturalism which I outlined in Chapter 1. Natural science acquired its basic conceptual foundations when Newton formulated his axioms of motion. They employ concepts that are abstract and not common to the vocabulary of everyday life, but for the record I will state them here, implying my conviction that sociologists can benefit from contemplating them.

Newton's Axioms of Motion

1 The Propositions

Newton originally published his *Principia* in Latin, of course, and his axioms of motion are usually stated in textbooks in a more modern form of English than that of his own time. There should be no problem in

[17] C. P. Snow, *The Two Cultures and the Scientific Revolution.* New York: Cambridge University Press, 1959, p. 16.

understanding his meaning in the following sentences, however. They are from Cajori's revision of Motte's translation.[18]

Axiom I: "Every body continues in its state of rest, or of uniform motion in a right line, unless it is compelled to change that state by forces impressed upon it."

Axiom II: "The change of motion is proportional to the motive force impressed; and is made in the direction of the right line in which that force is impressed."

Axiom III: "To every action there is always opposed an equal reaction: or, the mutual actions of two bodies upon each other are always equal, and directed to contrary parts."

In the next section of this chapter I want to consider the various attempts that have been made to formulate equivalent axioms for sociology. Such attempts have encountered much opposition. It is important, in evaluating both the attempts and the opposition to be clear about (1) what contrary assumptions would be ruled out of sociology if a truly comparable set of axioms were taken as a point of departure, and (2) what role these axioms of Newton's actually played in physical science, and thus what role their counterparts might be expected to play in social science.

2   Their Costs

Furfey, one of the opponents of the kind of sociology that would employ Newtonian axioms, has said that it is admittedly possible but not profitable to develop sociology purely as a natural science. The reason it would not be profitable, in his view, is that there are methods that would be inapplicable elsewhere but are useful in studying phenomena that involve human behavior. These methods would be ruled out of sociology if it began with the postulates of natural science. To substantiate his argument, Furfey invoked the concept of "free will" as a case in point. Natural science sociology could not, in his view, acknowledge the voluntaristic element in human action. "The most characteristic human activities, those principally studied in sociology, are free acts, and *the fact of freedom differentiates them essentially from all occurrences in the subhuman world.* . . ."[19]

I must confess that I am uncertain of Furfey's meaning. If he were merely protesting against flagrant fatalism, I would completely agree with

[18] Florian Cajori (ed.), *Sir Isaac Newton's Mathematical Principles of Natural Philosophy and His System of the World.* Berkeley, Calif.: University of California Press, 1962, p. 13.

[19] Paul Hanly Furfey, *The Scope and Method of Sociology.* New York: Harper & Row, Publishers, Incorporated, 1953, p. 117. (My italics.)

him. Our acts as human beings are certainly "free" in the sense that their direction is subject to change if the circumstances to which we respond change. I would be as strongly opposed as Furfey to the supposition that our actions are so much a matter of fixed destiny that nothing that happens to us between now and next year has any bearing on our next year's behavior. Such a supposition would be as thoroughly contrary to naturalism as it is to the tenets of Furfey's philosophy. But it hardly seems reasonable to suppose that his statement was merely intended as a rejection of fatalism; it was offered as a rejoinder to "natural science sociology." Therefore, if it is possible to join issues between theological and naturalistic points of view, it seems more probable that Furfey meant by the term "free acts" to assert that human behavior is somehow exempt from any such principles as the Newtonian axioms.

His assertion that human behavior is essentially differentiated from all events in the subhuman world by "the fact of freedom" seems to be intended as a denial of the first axiom. It expresses the conviction that as time passes human behavior can be nonuniform from one instant to another due to causes other than those which could meaningfully be termed "forces impressed upon it." In short, Furfey would have us not take uniformity of rate and direction of action for granted, change being problematic; change in human behavior may be expected, he implied, as a *spontaneous* event, and uniformity of action would therefore be problematic. If this is indeed what Furfey meant, he was right in contrasting it with naturalism. It is not self-evident, though, that he was right in inferring from his antinaturalistic axiom that naturalistic sociology would be unprofitable. That remains an empirical question, on which Chapter 8 should throw some light. It cannot be settled by merely insisting on *a priori* grounds that "my axiom is better than your axiom." When the antinaturalists are asked to specify *what* causes, other than "impressed forces," can interrupt the uniformity of behavior, they seem unable to do more than ritualistically invoke the shibboleth "free will." By dogmatically calling it a "fact" they imagine they have given an empirical answer.[20]

Sometimes it is the second Newtonian axiom, rather than the first, that is repudiated. The "freedom" of human action is occasionally explicated by noting that the magnitude of the response may often be vastly larger than the magnitude of the stimulus. If it is assumed that stimulus and response are the nearest sociological (or psychological) analogues of force and acceleration, it is then felt that Axiom II has been shown to be inapplicable in human affairs. If a person shouts "Fire!" in a crowded theater, the pandemonium in the aisles and at the exits is likely to exceed greatly the kinetic energy of the stimulus. In its efforts to escape, the

[20] For example, see Hans Driesch, *The History and Theory of Vitalism* (tr. C. K. Ogden). New York: St. Martin's Press, Inc., 1914, pp. 207, 216.

crowd may—among other responses—emit noises louder by many decibels than the original warning. Or, it is pointed out, the impact on an individual's life history of two softly spoken words, "I do," cannot be explained as a function of the amplitude of motion of the eardrums of those present. In such instances, the antinaturalist purports to be showing that for sociology the "change of motion" is not "proportional to the motive force impressed." Hence social action supposedly has the property of freedom. But when I step on the gas pedal in my 3,000-pound automobile, the car is impelled forward with far greater force than is exerted by my toes. The effect of my foot pressure on the throttle simply *controls* the rate of energy transformation in the cylinders, and the amount of torque applied to the rear wheels. To be consistent, the antinaturalist would have to impute "free will" to my automobile because its response so far exceeds the magnitude of the stimulus. Or when I need to stop my car, it is presumably obvious that I can accomplish more by applying a certain amount of foot pressure in a forward direction on the brake pedal than by standing in the road and applying the same amount of pressure in a backward direction against the front bumper. But this only specifies the mode of operation of the braking mechanism and in no way refutes Newton's second axiom. It hardly demonstrates that the behavior of motor vehicles is differentiated from other mechanical phenomena by "the fact of freedom."

Perhaps Furfey meant to deny the third axiom, of equal and opposite reaction to every action. The antinaturalistic assumption is widely held, I think, that persons or groups do not necessarily incur changes in their own behavior in the process of changing the behavior of others. Such a conviction should not be held by sociologists, however. Newton was saying, in his third axiom, that every action ought to be viewed as one aspect of an interaction. Sociology purports to be the science of *inter*action among human beings and groups. If any difficulty is experienced in perceiving sociological relevance in the axioms stated by Newton, this difficulty ought to be least in the case of Axiom III— if we adhere to our own definitions of what our discipline is about.

3 Their Role

The central concept in this set of axioms is the concept of "force." If we are going to retain in the sociological vocabulary such a term as "social forces," it seems to me that we at least ought to consider whether we are using it in close, or only very rough, analogy to the physical concept. In physics, where the word "force" has acquired a rigorously standardized meaning, it is defined in accord with Newtonian axioms, and the earlier Aristotelian views have been abandoned. If we have chosen to use the

word in sociology but have altered its meaning appreciably in comparison
with physics, we should give explicit consideration to the reasons for, and
appropriateness of, the alteration. In particular, if we have reverted to
the Aristotelian sense of the word, we should not do so thoughtlessly.
It might be useful to explore the consequences of either abandoning the
word or defining it so that all the difference between a physical force
and a social force is adequately denoted by the respective adjectives. I
think Small was correct when he wrote in 1905 that if we did not discern
social forces and their effects then there would be only two alternatives:
"On the one hand, social science would at most be a subdivision of [physi-
cal] science; on the other hand, the remaining alternative would be the
impossibility of social science altogether."[21]

The big conceptual breakthrough in Newton's axioms was the concept
of inertia. Without it, physical mechanics could not have been put on
a rigorous mathematical basis. The principle of inertia asserted that bodies
in motion unimpeded would cover equal distances in equal times. It thus
yielded a definition of the congruence of time intervals in terms of congruence of spatial intervals.[22] It is not possible to take one time interval
and lay it alongside its successor to see if they are of the same length.
If time were to be treated as a dimension, measurable in such a way
that the various arithmetical operations could legitimately be performed
on numbers denoting time spans, it had to be associated with a manipulable index such as distance. Newton's first axiom provided such an association. If sociology must reckon with time as a variable, it requires a
counterpart of Newton's first axiom (or, if conceivable, some functional
alternative thereto, at least). This necessity cannot be evaded just by insisting that "social time" is different from "physical time." It cannot be different *in this respect* and still merit the label "time."

Hermann von Helmholtz is said to have remarked that "to understand
a phenomenon means nothing else than to reduce it to the Newtonian
laws."[23] Others, not identified with careers in physical science, have felt
the same way. The men whom Popper has termed "historicists" have been
greatly impressed by long-range astronomical prediction based on Newtonian theory, and they have insisted that sociological forecasting of major
future historic developments should be possible in a similar fashion.[24]
Aware that celestial mechanics came of age with the study of motions
as determined by the interplay of forces, they have sought to explain history (past and future) in terms of what they called "social movements"

[21] Small, *op. cit.*, p. 534.
[22] A. d'Abro, *The Evolution of Scientific Thought from Newton to Einstein.* New York:
Boni & Liveright, 1927, p. 75.
[23] Quoted in Norwood Russell Hanson, *Patterns of Discovery: An Inquiry into the
Conceptual Foundations of Science.* New York: Cambridge University Press, 1958,
p. 91.
[24] Karl R. Popper, *The Poverty of Historicism.* Boston: Beacon Press, 1957, p. 36.

which they attributed to "social forces."[25] But they did not define "force" as the physicist does. Moreover, they mistook Newton's axioms for *conclusions*. Axioms are not conclusions but conceptual premises for the derivation of theorems which can be accepted as conclusions only after empirical verification. It is an error to imagine that sociology must seek ultimately to arrive at conclusions that will be isomorphic with Newton's axioms of motion. To employ similar propositions as a point of departure, however, is altogether a different matter.

The confusion of axioms with conclusions is but one of the uncertainties that have characterized the attitudes of thinkers in various fields in regard to the Newtonian principles. Nagel has pointed out that Newton's axioms of motion have been variously interpreted as (1) *a priori* truths, (2) necessary presuppositions of experimental science, but incapable of logical demonstration or empirical refutation, (3) empirical generalizations induced from observation, (4) conjectures with high probability but insufficiently confirmed for belief with certainty, (5) definitions or conventions, without empirical content, and (6) guiding principles for acquisition of knowledge, but not knowledge in themselves.[26] My own view is that their major effect was to provide rigorous definitions of a few concepts, such as force and mass, which have been indispensable to natural science, but I hold that they were not *merely* definitions or conventions. They have empirical content, in the sense that the concepts they defined have measurable physical referents. If analogous axioms are formulated for sociology, in the long run they must earn their adoption by performing the same task—defining concepts which will turn out to have measurable empirical referents that are germane to sociology.

Another way of looking at such axioms, as Popper has shown with certain other physical laws, is to reexpress them as negated existential propositions. They would then take the following form:

Axiom I: You cannot have a change in the velocity of a moving body without having some force impressed upon it.

Axiom II: You cannot have a change of motion that is disproportional to or not in the direction of the impressed force. (The apparent exceptions to this, such as the acceleration of a ton and a half of car in response to a few ounces of foot pressure on the gas pedal, cease to be exceptions when *all* the operative forces are taken into account—e.g., the pressure of expanding combustion gases on the tops of the pistons, etc. The softly spoken "I do" is not the force that changes the course of an individual's life; it is only the force that turns a sort of social valve that directs a larger constellation of forces.)

Axiom III: You cannot accelerate one body in one direction without comparably accelerating another (or others) in the opposite direction.

[25] *Ibid.*, p. 39.
[26] Nagel, *op. cit.*, p. 174.

Popper himself has suggested possible sociological laws which came close to being equivalents of two of these axioms: "You cannot introduce a political reform without strengthening the opposing forces, to a degree roughly in ratio to the scope of the reform." This is a sociological instance of the third axiom, and in my judgment the following statement amounts to a sociological instance of Axiom I, the inertial axiom: "There are always interests connected with the status quo."[27] These propositions are too specific in content to serve as fundamental axioms for a social mechanics, but they serve to illustrate the plausibility of generalizing Newton's axioms to a wider domain than physical mechanics. One might even get away with asserting them without being stigmatized as a "social physicist."

It has been argued that issues are confused by supposing that social forces act like physical forces—in accord with the Newtonian axioms. Cohen has claimed that the term "social force" is only a metaphor, unless social phenomena are taken to be merely physical. Therefore it is essential, he feels, that the real difference between a social force and a physical force be emphasized.[28] The force of attraction that unites two stars in a binary system is certainly not the same kind of force of attraction that unites a man and a woman in a monogamous marriage. It is quite possible, however, that in both cases there is a proportionality between force and acceleration, and that in both cases action and reaction are equal and opposite. That the action is of a different kind in the matrimonial case than in the stellar case does not *require* that Newton's axioms apply only to one and not to the other. Confusion on this point arises, as I see it, not because social forces are thought to *act like* physical forces but because a few overly enthusiastic social theorists have actually *equated* social forces with physical forces. Others who were more careful have yet had careless readers.

Much usage of the term "force" in the sociological literature is vague and imprecise. It should not always be inferred that the referents to which the term happens to be applied behave according to principles that are isomorphic with physical laws. But this does not mean the term has to be used so crudely. I agree with Cohen that the whole notion of law as the physical scientists intend it may not be applicable in sociology unless we can *measure* social forces in terms of standardizable units. But I do not agree with his implication that there is no hope of achieving this.[29] Nor do I quite see how he could seem to give up so easily and almost urge suppression of the term "social force" after suggesting that

[27] Popper, *op. cit.*, pp. 61–62.
[28] Morris R. Cohen, "Reason in Social Science," in Herbert Feigl and May Brodbeck (eds.), *Readings in the Philosophy of Science*. New York: Appleton-Century-Crofts, Inc., Copyright, 1953 (From Morris R. Cohen, *Reason and Nature*. New York: Harcourt, Brace & World, Inc., 1931), p. 670.
[29] *Ibid.*, pp. 669–670.

we would have a useful methodological principle if we were to assume, following Newton's first axiom, that "all social phenomena persist unless something is brought into play to change them."[30] He even extended this a step further with a "law of social heredity—all social institutions will be transmitted by parents to children, or people will believe and act as did their fathers before them except in so far as certain factors produce changes in our social arrangements and in our ideas and sentiments."[31]

The fundamental insight in Newton's axioms, as I have said, was the concept of inertia, relating force to acceleration rather than to velocity. Taken together, the three axioms explicated this concept by operationally defining measurable inertial *mass*. The concept was an important departure from Aristotelian thoughtways, and the ability to measure inertial mass facilitated the measurement of forces. Quantification of both these concepts made theorems in physical mechanics fully empirical. Sociology is already fairly strongly committed to empiricism, and if it is to increase its naturalism by adopting the inertial axiom, to remain empircist it must also work out a way of measuring the social analogue of mass.

Nagel has said we must regard the Newtonian axioms as theoretical postulates and not as experimental laws, for this reason: they take the form of second-order differential equations, and only have empirical meaning when rules of correspondence between their concepts and observable phenomena are supplied.[32] If so, then there is no reason to suppose that such rules of correspondence for social phenomena could not also be supplied (unless we *try* it and never get anything but trivial results). Can there not be measurable rates of social action, and rates of change in such rates of action? If so, what basis have we for refusing to regard changing social rates as social accelerations, to be attributed to social forces, and entailing equal and opposite social reactions?

According to Nagel, what was distinctive about the Newtonian axioms was their selection of uniform velocity as the state of a body requiring no explanation. This selection could not be justified on *a priori* grounds, though attempts were made by successors of Newton to provide such justification. Of equal *a priori* merit would have been the alternative assumptions that either uniform location or uniform acceleration (such as is involved in orbital motion) required no explanation in terms of the operation of forces. Aristotle, in fact, took these latter assumptions in regard to terrestrial and celestial phenomena respectively.[33] An important step in the development of modern science was the abandonment of Aristotle's assumptions. In advocating their abandonment in sociology, I have no

---

[30] *Ibid.*, p. 669.
[31] *Ibid.*
[32] Nagel, *op. cit.*, pp. 161–162.
[33] *Ibid.*, p. 177.

a priori justification, and even the observation that it paid to give them up in physical science does not prove that they ought to be abandoned elsewhere. But what sociology needs very much to do is to distinguish relevant factors from those which are irrelevant to the explanation of social phenomena. That is the beginning of knowledge.[34] If the variables we have tended to study on the basis of Aristotelian assumptions have not been very fruitful, it is reasonable to suggest that a different fundamental assumption might sensitize us to more effective variables. If we were to embrace Newtonian axioms in sociology, we would be led to seek correlates of the magnitudes of *changes* in rates of social behavior rather than correlates of the magnitudes of the rates themselves.[35]

Nagel has referred to the Newtonian axioms as the "ultimate premises" of the explanations of phenomena in classical mechanics.[36] He suggested still another way of writing them:[37]

Axiom I: If $F = 0$, then $dv/dt = 0$.

Axiom II: $m \dfrac{dv}{dt} = kF$, or in units that make $k = 1$, then $F = ma$.

Axiom III: Between two bodies, A and B, $F_{AB} = -F_{BA}$.

In this form, I will consider the three axioms in reverse order in assessing their roles as foundations of natural science. If mass is an essential scientific concept, it has to be measured. Axiom III indicates a way of measuring it. It is a combination of a definition and an empirical hypothesis. It defines the mass of one body (taking as a unit the mass of another body with which it interacts) as the negative inverse ratio of its acceleration and the concomitant acceleration of the other. Because the equation omits all other variables, such as position, velocity, temperature, color, odor, bulk, etc., it asserts the hypothesis that the ratio of the two masses is independent of these.[38]

In conjunction with this third axiom, Axiom II affords a means of measuring the other important concept, force. It is sometimes construed as a definition of force, and sometimes as a mere methodological rule telling the physicist what to look for in analyzing the motions of bodies. Nagel has contended that the rule is not always indispensable.[39] But the equation tells us that if we know the mass of an object, and can measure its acceleration (by measurements of time and distance, and relevant calculations), the force to which we attribute that acceleration is proportional to the product of the two known factors. Or if the force is known, and the acceleration, then the mass can be calculated; it is their ratio.

[34] Cf. Reichenbach, *op. cit.*, p. 5; and Beck, *op. cit.*, p. 218.
[35] Cf. Nagel, *op. cit.*, p. 200.
[36] *Ibid.*, pp. 157–158.
[37] *Ibid.*, p. 159.
[38] *Ibid.*, p. 196.
[39] *Ibid.*, pp. 185–192.

Axiom I might be regarded as a mere convention, since it has no *a priori* justification. It only seems to define the term "force" as a name for that which changes a body's velocity rather than that which changes a body's position. But I noted earlier that Axiom I can also be taken as an operational definition of the uniformity of flow of time. It makes time measurable. If time were not measurable, accelerations could not be measured, and then neither force nor mass could be measured. Nagel has pointed out that once we adopt Axiom I for a particular physical system, periodicities in that system become usable as a clock by which it can then be found empirically that events in a large class of other physical systems conform to this proposition.[40] It is only a definition or a convention, then, in the case of the first system for which it is assumed; for subsequent systems that can be observed in relation to the first system, it becomes an empirical hypothesis, amply confirmed in the physical world.

Of course, it makes a difference what spatial frame of reference we adopt for the study of motions. In different frames of reference, the magnitudes of the accelerations of various bodies would be different and would thus have to be attributed to different amounts of force.[41] Viewed from the observatory of the rotating earth, all celestial bodies seem to have a diurnal motion in circular paths. Until men became aware of the rotation of the earth, the motions of the heavenly bodies could hardly be explained in terms of so simple a set of forces as were discovered to apply after the diurnal motion was stripped away. This was because motions were imputed to the stars and planets which they did not in fact undergo. The advance to a frame of reference that did not rotate once in each twenty-four hours greatly simplified the celestial motions requiring explanation. Were we living in a universe in which all the stars actually did circle the earth daily regardless of their varying distances from it, the Newtonian axioms could *not* be true. With their orbits having vastly different radii, the various stars would be subject to vastly different accelerations if each made its transit daily, and it would require an impossibly complex theory to account for the differences. No wonder the ancients supposed stellar motions were the result of divine will and not explicable in the same terms as terrestrial mechanical events. But Copernicus, Kepler, Galileo, and Newton discarded that universe by discarding the earthbound spatial frame of reference. In its place was conceived a universe in which the Newtonian axioms did apply—an "inertial" frame of reference.[42]

What has all this to do with sociology? Just this: so long as it dealt with the most obvious frame of reference, physics had to contend with a universe as hopelessly complicated as social behavior still seems, and

[40] *Ibid.*, p. 183.
[41] *Ibid.*, p. 205.
[42] *Ibid.*, pp. 211–212.

physicists were fortunate to find that by shifting their frame of reference from the rotating earth to the less obvious one of Newton's imaginary "absolute space" (for which the so-called "fixed stars" provided approximate coordinates) their problems were simplified. By analogy, the lack of an accepted "inertial frame of reference" in sociology just might be what makes social behavior seem capricious and complex. The achievement by sociologists of the insight of cultural relativity is the analogue of only one side of the Newtonian revolution. It taught us not to use our native culture or subculture as an evaluational frame of reference in observing behavior in other societies or groups. But this was as if Newton had merely declared the spinning earth *not* to be the most satisfactory frame without discovering a more adequate frame in his fictitious "absolute space." I am not advocating that sociological inquiry revert to the ethnocentrism that prevailed in the social thought of past ages. I am urging that our emancipation from this most obvious but grievously misleading frame of reference is only half the battle; we should be seeking the sociological equivalent of an inertial frame.

Can it be expected that sociology will find such a frame of reference? Again, analogy offers some hope. To avail himself of an inertial frame of reference, Newton did not have to transport himself off the earth, except by imagination. He didn't have to journey out among the "fixed" stars. Nor did he need to place himself at the center of the planetary orbits in order to comprehend universal gravitation. He only had to know where that center was—in the sun—in order to attribute to the sun the forces producing the centripetal accelerations of the planets and causing them to depart from motion in a "right line." And Kepler before him had laboriously shown that the elliptical orbits of all the planets had one of their foci in the sun. Because of the sun's gravity, no free body in its vicinity would actually move with uniform velocity in a straight line as depicted by Axiom I. But without the inertial axiom Newton's predecessors had been unable to explain the vast array of phenomena Newton succeeded in explaining. If Newton could work with an inertial frame that in reality could only be approximated, and could do so without even being able to *touch* the approximation, the problem for sociology ought not to be insoluble.[43] The inertial frame we seek can hardly be more impalpable than Newton's. Invention of the concept of an inertial frame required prodigious creative imagination. But now, even though neither Newton nor any of his successors has ever actually stood on such a platform, the concept of inertia is so firmly imbedded in our intellectual heritage that it is difficult for modern man to interpret his observations of the heavens in any other way.[44] Similarly, our posterity may someday find

[43] Cf. Popper, *op. cit.*, p. 101.
[44] Nagel, *op. cit.*, p. 213.

it difficult *not* to regard social change rather than social persistence as problematic.

Sociological Imitations

Without having worked through an exploration of the historic and philosophical significance of Newton's axioms, a number of social theorists have formulated sociological imitations of them. Some of these imitators have been enthusiastic in their aspiration to do for sociology what they supposed Newton had done for physical science, while others have shown some reluctance in their imitation. Imperfectly correlated with this enthusiastic-reluctant dichotomy, there has been another twofold division among the imitators. Some have conceived sociology in basically mechanistic terms, whereas others have conceived it in basically organic terms, making Newton's ideas seem more peripheral. These two dichotomies, I think, as well as personal idiosyncrasies, have resulted in considerable variety among the imitations. Almost none have really been close to sound sociological equivalents of Newton's three fundamental axioms. There has been no clear trend of improvement, either.

I cite these imitations here not just in order to point out their faults but more in order to clarify still further what my own view is as to the real significance for naturalism of the Newtonian prototypes. Perhaps, too, by noting just how each imitator has missed the mark, I may be able to shed further light on "forces" that have continued to pull sociology off the right theoretical path (if I may be permitted such a metaphor at this juncture).

There have doubtless been other notable imitators besides the seven I propose to discuss, but these will suffice for my purposes. I will take them up in as nearly chronological order as possible, just because nothing much would be gained by dealing with them in any other sequence. The seven men are: Auguste Comte, Henry C. Carey, Herbert Spencer, Lester F. Ward, Stuart C. Dodd, Robert M. MacIver, and Talcott Parsons (in collaboration with Robert F. Bales). Apart from the fact that Comte's work in his later years degenerated into the abortive effort to found a new "Religion of Humanity," all these men except Carey have been assigned by their contemporaries or their successors some measure of academic legitimacy—in some cases a considerable amount of it. Carey was partly self-educated, and his publication of multivolume treatises on sociological topics was facilitated by participation in a pamphleteering career and publishing business with his father. None of these seven imitations of Newton should be brushed aside as the work of a mere crank. Not even Carey was that. Each imitation was taken seriously by its author and some of his serious-minded contemporaries. It is not my intention to hold any of them up to ridicule. That has been done elsewhere and has accomplished nothing. But I will criticize.

1 Comte

In his own eyes, Comte was not so much an imitator of Newton as a generalizer. He took the position that "each of the three laws on which rational Mechanics is founded is, in fact, only a mechanical manifestation of a general law, applicable to all possible phenomena."[45] This much was a sound insight, and should be preserved and used. But Comte was not entirely clear about the meaning of the three principles, and they were not exactly the same three I have been discussing.

For Comte, the first axiom was what he said was "inaptly called" the law of inertia, and he attributed its discovery to Kepler, not Newton. He stated it in this way: ". . . All motion is rectilinear and uniform; that is, any body impelled by a single force will move in a right line, and with an invariable velocity."[46] This formulation really misses the point of Newton's first axiom, for it does not make acceleration problematic; it still sounds as if motion itself has to be continuously impelled. Yet Comte did not misunderstand the first axiom quite so badly as his statement of it would suggest, for he also alluded to it as "the law of mechanical persistence." Generalizing it, he said it was "merely a particular case of the tendency of all natural phenomena to persevere in their state unless disturbed. . . ."[47] Biologically, he found the principle manifested in habit, and sociologically it was exemplified by "the obstinate tendency of every political system to perpetuate itself."[48]

There was confusion in Comte's writing, incidentally, about the numbering of the axioms. Early in his course of lectures on positive philosophy he attributed to Newton what he termed the *second* law—"equality of action and reaction"—which Comte stated in this form: ". . . Whenever one body is moved by another, the reaction is such that the second loses precisely as much motion, in proportion to its masses, as the first gains."[49] But much later he made reference to "the third law of motion,—Newton's law of the equivalence of action and reaction. . . ."[50] Since he spoke of one body being "moved" (rather than accelerated) by another, it was

[45] Auguste Comte, *The Positive Philosophy* (tr. Harriet Martineau). New York: Calvin Blanchard, 1856, p. 820.
[46] *Ibid.*, p. 111.
[47] *Ibid.*, p. 819.
[48] *Ibid.*
[49] *Ibid.*, p. 111.
[50] *Ibid.*, p. 820.

again apparent that it was not clear to Comte that *change* of motion was the problem to be explained. And his social equivalent to this second-third axiom consisted of the mutual dependence of all social phenomena, and their "close and prevalent interconnection."[51] That Newton's Axiom III opened the way to *measurement* of masses was entirely missed by Comte. He did not proceed from his sociological version of it to a technique for measuring social mass.

What Comte called the third axiom was not one of Newton's three axioms at all but "the principle of the independence or co-existence of motions." It states that "any motion common to all the bodies of any system whatever does not affect the particular motions of these bodies with regard to each other; which motions proceed as if the system were motionless." This principle he attributed to Galileo.[52] It does show a rough comprehension of the nature and importance of an inertial frame of reference, but it is clearly not one of the Newtonian axioms. "Upon this alone," said Comte, "can be based the important law of the proportion of forces to velocities."[53] He had, then, tried to go behind Newton, so to speak, but again he had missed the key idea, for the important proportionality Newton spoke of was between forces and accelerations, not velocities. That proportionality is precisely what he meant by "mass." Later, Comte renumbered this coexistence principle as the second axiom, and called it "Galileo's law of the reconciliation of any common motion with various particular motions. . . ."[54] It is interesting to note that in extending this principle to sociology Comte, having missed the real point, nearly anticipated an idea that was subsequently to attract considerable sociological attention—cultural lag. Comte had written: "In sociology, we find [Galileo's law] again; any disturbance in the interior of any political system being due to the unequal progressive action on the different parts which, if participating in the movement in any equal degree, would be unaffected by a much more rapid progression."[55] Ogburn's statement three generations later was far more lucid.

Comte never did recognize the fundamental physical concept of mass, and never generalized it so that a sociological version of it could be incorporated into his theories. His concern in social statics for a "principle of equilibrium"[56] was as close as he came to a correct appreciation of Newton's second axiom, but for Comte it was a distraction that led him off into an excessive (and essentially sterile) concern for dichotomizing the propositions of all sciences into departments of statics and dynamics. The development of sociology in its early years was impeded, it would seem,

[51] *Ibid.*
[52] *Ibid.*, pp. 111–112.
[53] *Ibid.*, p. 113.
[54] *Ibid.*, p. 819.
[55] *Ibid.*, pp. 819–820.
[56] *Ibid.*, pp. 115–116.

not so much by Comte's fascination with the natural sciences as by his misunderstanding of their fundamental axioms. His sociology (or "social physics," as he originally dubbed it) might have been improved had he understood physics better. Certainly he ceased to be naturalistic when he wrote that the three axioms were "the experimental basis of the science of Mechanics" from which "the mind may proceed to the logical construction of the science, without further reference to the external world."[57]

2 Carey

The index at the end of the third volume of Carey's *Principles of Social Science* lists such terms as: "Acceleration of the societary motion," "Force, a result of the consumption of matter," "Gravitation, molecular. Subjection of man to the great law of," "Momentum of society grows with increase of the societary circulation," and "Motion." The fact that such items are included while there are no entries for such terms as "energy," "inertia," "mass," or "velocity," strongly suggests that Carey utterly missed the significance of Newton's axioms, and produced a badly garbled social physics.

There were some very rough approximations of Newton's first axiom in Carey's magnum opus. "All force results from motion,"[58] for example, sounds like an image of it in a mirror—reversed. Newton would not have said, however, that all *motion* results from force; what he did say was that all *acceleration* is the result of force. Carey came closer to the mark when he said, "A body moved by a single force proceeds always in the same direction until stopped by some counteracting one."[59]

I could find no direct analogy in Carey's work to Newton's second axiom on the proportionality of force and acceleration. The nearest approximation was Carey's assertion that progress in the human conquest of nature is proportional to "the substitution of continued for intermitted motion."[60] In nature itself, he said, "power exists in the ratio of the continuity of motion. . . ."[61] Referring to "the accelerated motion that is witnessed in a body falling towards the earth," Carey said similar observations could be made in regard to society. "In the outset, there is little motion and little power of progress; but as its members are more and more enabled to associate, the power of further advance is found to grow with constantly increasing rapidity."[62] These passages hardly suggest that Carey under-

[57] *Ibid.,* p. 113.
[58] Henry Charles Carey, *Principles of Social Science*. Philadelphia: J. B. Lippincott Company, 1858, vol. 1, p. 200.
[59] *Ibid.*
[60] *Ibid.,* p. 201.
[61] *Ibid.,* p. 202.
[62] *Ibid.,* p. 204.

stood Axiom II as an operational definition of force in terms of measured mass and measured acceleration.

He badly misunderstood Axiom III. Rather than seeing it as the denial of unmoved movers, or construing it as an operational definition of relative mass, he confused it with the empirical fact of the equality of centrifugal and centripetal forces affecting planetary motions. He wrote: "To the equal action of opposing forces it is due, that the celestial world is enabled to exhibit such wonderful harmony and such unceasing motion—and to the same principle, here carried out to a greater extent than elsewhere in the world, it is due that the history of the Union has presented no case of civil war. . . ." (Carey's book was published in 1858.) Assuming the role of prophet, he continued: "Destroy the State governments and centralize power in the hands of the general government, and the result would be found in a steady diminution of the power of voluntary association for the purposes of peace, and increase in the tendency towards involuntary association for the purposes of war. Destroy the central government, and conflicts among the States would become inevitable."[63] In the index, at the end of volume 3, this passage is cited under "Action and reaction essential to the existence of harmony," so it is clear that Carey supposed this was the meaning of Axiom III.

Like Comte, Carey completely missed seeing Axiom III as an operational definition of mass, and read into it the moral implications of harmony. Even among nations, he thought, the tendency toward harmony and peace was a function of their independence.[64]

As among individuals, the power of association grows with the development of individuality, and as this latter grows with the growth of the habit of combination, so does the tendency towards peaceful action among communities grow with the growth of local centres, and with that of self-dependence—subordination to the laws of right and justice, among nations, growing with the growth of the power of self-direction and protection.—Here, as everywhere throughout nature, action and reaction are equal and contrary—harmony being the result of the perfect balance of these opposing forces.

So, as in the case of Comte, it was not the fact that some physics had gotten mixed into it that spoiled Carey's sociology. His social physics suffered from his miserably scrambled perception of physics itself.

3 Spencer

Before commencing to write *Principles of Sociology*, Spencer wrote a book of "first principles" to serve as a conceptual foundation for his treatises on biology, psychology, and sociology. In it he stated approximate versions

[63] *Ibid.*, p. 46.
[64] *Ibid.*, vol. 3, p. 464.

of two of Newton's axioms, but their only ultimate connection with his sociology seems to have been through his "derivation" of his general law of evolution from them and from a couple of other premises.

Something like an epistemological version of Axiom I is implied in Spencer's statement that reality means "persistence in consciousness." We separate the real from the unreal, he said, solely by the test of persistence.[65] A more specific approach to Axiom I was evident later, when he said, "Movement set up in any direction is itself a cause of further movement in that direction, since it is the embodiment of a surplus force in that direction." He said this principle was "expressed in the law of inertia."[66] His use of the phrase "surplus force," however, makes it quite uncertain whether he had really grasped the significance of Newton's first axiom. Movement in a given direction would indeed be "set up" (presumably meaning "accelerated") by a "surplus force" (*net* force, presumably) in that direction, but the point of Newton's axiom was that it did not take any continuation of that force to produce continuation of the motion. Spencer's version did not clearly say that, nor did it clearly proclaim the Aristotelian alternative either.

Spencer did seem to have grasped the idea, and was trying to generalize it, when he wrote that "every physical and psychical change is generated by certain antecedent forces. . . ." When he went on to approximate Axiom II, though, he omitted the concept of mass, so essential in the meaning of Newton's version of it. He said, ". . . From given amounts of such forces neither more nor less of such physical and psychical changes can result."[67] This does not make it clear that in a given case the acceleration produced depends on the ratio of force and mass, and that mass *means* the ratio of forces and corresponding accelerations—with that ratio being constant for a given body. Spencer's statement of the axiom is insufficient, for it is possible for a large force to produce a small acceleration and a small force to produce a large acceleration (contradicting Spencer) if the large force is applied to a body of large mass and the small force is applied to a body of very small mass. Regardless of this insufficiency, however, there is a hint in Spencer's work that his statement of the axiom *was used* by him as at least a nebulous guide to his thinking. He employed a loose procedure called "comparative method," which examines a phenomenon in varied instances and circumstances in an effort to discriminate between nonessential factors on the one hand and what is essential on the other. It is roughly what J. S. Mill called the method of "concomitant variations," and it shows at least a vague sense that the effect ought to be proportional to the cause.[68]

[65] Herbert Spencer, *First Principles*, 4th ed. New York: P. F. Collier & Son Corporation, 1902, p. 165.
[66] *Ibid.*, p. 231.
[67] *Ibid.*, p. 227.
[68] Cf. John Madge, *The Origins of Scientific Sociology*. New York: The Free Press of Glencoe, 1962, pp. 535–538.

So far as I can discover, Spencer was oblivious of the significance of the concept of mass. His conception of "forces" was unrigorous from the standpoint of physics, and constituted his chief conceptual importation from that discipline. What he did with it was merely to conclude that forces can be classified into the categories of attraction and repulsion, and that motion was always in the direction of greatest attraction and least resistance (or was in the direction of the resultant of all forces acting). He expressly said that this was true not only of the motions of physical bodies, but equally so of organic processes, psychic actions, and changes in the structure and activity of societies.[69] Without the additional concept of mass, and an operational definition rendering it—and hence also forces—measurable, this tautological proposition had to remain sociologically sterile.

Spencer's chief fault may have been his overworking of the organic analogy and his overly pedantic spelling out of the ideological implications of his doctrines. But as far as his injection of physics into sociology is concerned, his error seems to have consisted of not doing enough with it, rather than doing too much.

4 Ward

When he wrote his *Applied Sociology*, published in 1906, Ward looked back over his previous sociological publications and noted that he had consistently argued that sociology was a true science, a domain of natural forces in which phenomena fully conform to the Newtonian principles.[70] He had begun this insistence in 1883 with his *Dynamic Sociology*, in which he said it was not merely a convenient analogy but a literal truth that desires are forces. Because they are, the theorems of physics could be extended to apply to biological phenomena, he said. To Ward, the chief criterion of a true natural force is conformity to "the mechanical axioms of physics as established by Newton, and popularly known as the laws of motion." He said it could be shown that these axioms do apply to desires, and that desires, or "conative forces," were most like the forces of gravitation and magnetism, among all mechanical forces. He compared the object of desire with the magnet, and the organism attracted to it represented the substance upon which the magnet acted. "It is not pretended that in this there is identity, but only that the nature of the force is identical in as far as are the characteristics of any two forms of force."[71] In other words, desire was as much like magnetism as magnetism is like gravity; similar equations would describe all such phenomena. Again in

[69] Spencer, *op. cit.*, pp. 228–254.
[70] Lester F. Ward, *Applied Sociology*. Boston: Ginn and Company, 1906, pp. 331–332.
[71] Lester F. Ward, *Dynamic Sociology*. New York: D. Appleton & Co., Inc., 1883, vol. 2, p. 95.

1897, in *Outlines of Sociology*, Ward repeated the statement that social forces consist of human desires and are true natural forces which conform to the axioms of Newton.[72]

In *Dynamic Sociology*, Ward had said that the first axiom was that motion "takes place in a straight line."[73] He did not mention uniform speed. He cited such observations as the flight of insects in a "bee line" toward their goals as evidence of "the fidelity with which the bee conforms to Newton's first law."[74] Thus, even though he correctly referred to Newton's propositions as axioms, in extending them to organic behavior Ward seemed to treat at least the first axiom as an empirical hypothesis substantiated by data. He seemed to forget that its significance consisted in declaring acceleration rather than persistence problematic.

In a similarly empirical vein, Ward went on to say that animals move on uneven stretches of terrain in as nearly straight lines toward their goals as impinging forces allow. He cited this observation as indicating the biological (and hence sociological) applicability of Axiom II, which he did not state fully, though he referred to it as "the second mechanical maxim as to the amount and direction of changed motion. . . ."[75] He made no explicit mention of the proportionality of force and acceleration; thus he presented no definition of mass.

In *Pure Sociology*, 1903, Ward did succinctly state this proportionality principle, but did nothing more with it after stating it. He did not acknowledge that it had anything to do with rendering fundamental concepts measurable, and he did not go on to try to measure social forces. He wrote, "I have probably made more of the social forces than any other writer in sociology, and I may not have as fully recognized the distinction between force and energy in my early works as I should have done, but I have consistently used the expression, and in a paper entitled 'The Social Forces,' published in 1896, I fully set forth the distinction."[76] He repeated the distinction here, in the form of equations, and the equation for force correctly asserted it proportional to the product of mass and *change* of velocity.

Ward had correctly stated an abbreviation of Newton's Axiom III when he wrote in *Dynamic Sociology* that "action and reaction are equal."[77] He went on to say that psychic phenomena conform to this principle, and that this was their most important attribute. "It is manifested in the fact that the results accomplished are equal to and no greater than the energy expended. There is no disproportion between the cause and the

[72] Lester F. Ward, *Outlines of Sociology*. New York: The Macmillan Company, 1897, p. 166.
[73] Ward, *Dynamic Sociology*, vol. 2, p. 95.
[74] *Ibid.*
[75] *Ibid.*, p. 96.
[76] Lester F. Ward, *Pure Sociology*. New York: The Macmillan Company, 1903, p. 166.
[77] Ward, *Dynamic Sociology*, vol. 2, p. 96.

effect."[78] From the quotation it is unclear whether Ward was really thinking in terms of Axiom III or of Axiom II. On the next page, he shifted his position and said, "The essential difference between purely physical and even the lowest form of psychic phenomenon consists in the power the latter possess *through organization* of producing effects . . . of greater value than, the causes themselves; and . . . this is really the fundamental distinction between genetic and teleological phenomena."[79] His concern, then, seemed to be actually with Axiom II, and he correctly discerned the manner in which its application can be modified—"through organization."

Ward didn't really go on to make use of Axiom III as such, but at least he avoided the error of Comte and Carey in construing it as a doctrine of peace and harmony. In his *comprehension* of Newton, Ward seems to have been much clearer than any of the previous three men, but somehow he didn't quite make real *use* of the axioms of motion. It was as if he was content to say that social forces are really forces, and didn't particularly care to go on from that orientation to measure them and study the social accelerations they produced.

For him, the hallmark of a science was that it must deal with forces.[80] With respect to the division of sociology into social statics and social dynamics, Ward argued that these terms were not "remote analogies" but must have exactly the meaning they have for mechanics and astronomy.[81] One might see in this an indication that Ward was only interested in elevating the status of sociology by linking it to more prestigious sciences, like the student whose aspiration is to "be a doctor" rather than to practice medicine. But another interpretation is at least as plausible. After all, Ward had creditable publications in an already legitimated science. He should have had no personal need to assert the scientific status of sociology. It might make more sense, then, to suppose that Ward was warning that such terms ought only to be imported into sociology if they are going to be used with precision and in accord with the meanings they had in the science from which the sociologist borrowed them. Ward also brought many botanical terms into his sociological writing, apparently because for him they were meaningful and helped illuminate sociological issues. They have mostly not been retained in the sociological vocabulary, however, presumably because they were not so helpful to others without Ward's scientific background.

He insisted that "social mechanics" was a better designation than "social physics," because the concern was with social forces, not with material bodies. But he did not use the phrase "social mechanics" to refer to the

[78] *Ibid.*
[79] *Ibid.*, p. 97.
[80] Ward, *Outlines of Sociology*, p. 143.
[81] *Ibid.*, pp. 168–169.

whole of sociology. By it he meant only "a subscience of the science of sociology. It is that branch of sociology which deals with the action of social forces."[82]

5 Dodd

A notational system which Dodd has called "dimensional analysis" preceded his formulation of sociological versions of the Newtonian axioms. In physical science, the sequence went the other way. The axioms of mechanics came first, and provided operational definitions of certain concepts whose interrelations were subsequently systematized in an equation-assessing and theory-extending procedure known as "dimensional analysis." For Dodd, the basic social dimensions include time (T), length (L), people (P), desire (D), and the complement class which he defined as "indices of anything else" (I). The province of social physics was defined in Dodd's thinking by the three dimensions T, L, and P, just as, he said, T, L, and M define physical mechanics. "When the number of people, P, is substituted for mass, M, in the formulas of mechanics we get such concepts as demographic momentum, force, energy, gravitation, etc. . . ."[83] Dodd's dimensional analysis resembles the like-named procedure in physics in that he has employed his notation chiefly in writing formulas for social situations S, which take the form of products of powers of the basic dimensions.

In the previous chapter, I pointed out what a serious error it was to assume so easily that P is analogous to M. But it was a plausible analogy, and it is only fair to attribute the fault to the plausibility. In sociology there were already numerous references to mass communication (a term not likely now to be abandoned), mass movements, mass behavior, mass action, and even mass psychology. In all these phrases the word "mass" simply connoted large populations—without even implicit reference to the property of inertia. It said nothing of the *persistence* of any of the traits or practices of such populations, but only referred to their bigness. Dodd simply adopted a quasi-mathematical notation which included the symbol, P, that rendered this common usage more manipulable. His acquiescence in this conventional usage might even be said to have had bona fide physical precedent, too. Newton began his *Principia* with a series of nominal definitions of terms which preceded his axioms. This obscured the important fact that his three axioms actually functioned as operational definitions. His opening words were, "Definition I: The quantity of matter is the measure of the same, arising from its density and

[82] Ward, *Pure Sociology*, pp. 147, 150.
[83] Stuart C. Dodd, "Dimensional Analysis in Social Physics," in Baljit Singh (ed.), *The Frontiers of Social Science*. New York: St. Martin's Press, Inc., 1955, p. 206.

bulk conjointly."[84] This definition was really a vestige of prenaturalistic conceptualization that lingered in Newton's terminology. In all his theorems, "mass" denoted the magnitude of the inertial property of a body, but verbally it was still linked to "quantity of matter." Newton did less of what in Chapter 4 was termed "sleepwalking" than Kepler did, but here was one instance. It was a mistake for Dodd to make quantity of people the social analogue of mass, but it was certainly plausible for him to suppose it was the sociological counterpart of the quantity of matter.

In his *Dimensions of Society*, Dodd stated sociological versions of the Newtonian axioms that were a good deal closer to the prototype than some of the others I have already discussed. For Axiom I he wrote: "Whatever changes the status of a population, or its process . . . , in rate or direction is called a societal force."[85] Like Newton's axiom, this one simply declares that the word "force" is to be used to designate that which changes the rate or direction of motion, rather than that which sustains motion.

For Axiom II he wrote, "The societal force is proportional to the rate of change of the rate of societal change, and takes place along the line defined by the index measuring the change."[86] The repetition of the word "change" in this sentence makes it confusing; it would have been a cleaner parallel to Newton, I think, if it had said, "The societal force is proportional to the rate of change of the rate of occurrence of some societal process . . . ." At any rate the idea of proportionality is clearly expressed. But Dodd was not free to construe this axiom as an operational definition of force in terms of measured social mass, or social mass in terms of measured force, because he had already equated social mass with population. He could not *use* the axiom in the way Newton's axiom was used, even though it was verbally isomorphic.

Dodd's version of Axiom III was simply, "Forces and their total resistances are equal and opposite,"[87] which has a different sound than Newton's version, but can be interpreted somewhat similarly to it. It was certainly closer to the target than Comte or Carey. It would be difficult, however, to use it in opening the way to measuring masses relative to each other when these have already been defined in mere census terms.

Did Dodd formulate these propositions to serve as tools for getting on with further inquiry, as Newton's axioms were, or as mere tokens of the scientific status of sociology? He had prematurely foreclosed the chief avenue of their use by his identification of population as social mass. But there is an important indication that he nevertheless seriously wished them to be a point of departure for sociological investigations, rather than ulti-

[84] Cajori, *op. cit.*, p. 1.
[85] Stuart C. Dodd, *Dimensions of Society*. New York: The Macmillan Company, 1942, p. 744.
[86,87] *Ibid.*

mate conclusions in themselves. Using his dimensional notation,[88] he made it clear that he meant to *generalize* the analogy with the formulas of physical mechanics, because he defined a social force dimensionally as $F = T^{-2}L^0P^1D^0I^1$. The zero exponents have the effect of dropping out of the formula the base letter to which they are attached, so this could be written more briefly as $F = T^{-2}PI$. What is significant is that it was *not* $F = T^{-2}PL$. In other words, Dodd was going to be concerned with accelerations along *any* relevant social scale, not just along a scale of physical distance.

This permitted a more succinct reformulation of the first two axioms: "1. A societal force is whatever changes an index of some population. 2. The force is proportional to the celeration of the index and acts along the vector defined by the index."[89] It was change, or "celeration" (i.e., either acceleration or deceleration), that was to be problematic. Dodd referred to his own statements as a "paraphrase" of Newton's axioms, and said they were intended to provide an operational definition of "force," or a "frame of reference by which a force may be quantitatively determined," and were not to be taken as "a law of nature or of society. . . ."[90] In this respect, Dodd was much closer than Newton's other sociological imitators to an accurate comprehension of the prototype he was trying to imitate.

In a review of Dodd's work, Parsons said that by its logic research would have to consist of trying "to determine every possible observable characteristic" of the particles studied, whether molecules or human beings. In contrast, physical mechanics made headway, Parsons said, by "the rigorous *selection* of those variables which are significant to the system," including mass, spatial location, velocity and direction of motion.[91] On this point, Parsons's criticism of Dodd was sound. But surely there is middle ground between studying changes in all conceivable variables, on the one hand, and confining our attention to motion in physical space, on the other. Parsons could hardly have seriously intended that sociology study no other kind of change than geographic migration, yet that was what he seemed to imply in criticizing Dodd for substituting "change" for "motion."[92] The particular weakness in Dodd's system which Parsons emphasized was far less serious than Dodd's prenaturalistic assumption that population size—as the social "quantity of matter"—was the proper analogue of mass. In Chapter 3, I showed how the distinction between inertia and homeostasis has been blurred in Parsons's own writing. He may

[88] Dodd, "Dimensional Analysis in Social Physics," p. 211.
[89] Dodd, *Dimensions of Society*, pp. 743–744.
[90] *Ibid.*
[91] Talcott Parsons, Review of Dodd's *Dimensions of Society*, *American Sociological Review*, 7 (October, 1942), p. 711.
[92] *Ibid.*, pp. 711–712.

have been as unclear regarding the concept of mass in natural science as Dodd was.

6 MacIver

Chronology is not quite a perfect guide for the ordering of cases. MacIver was born sooner, and entered sociology sooner, than Dodd, and might therefore have been taken up ahead of him here. But he held back longer before imitating Newton, and his *Social Causation* was published in the same year as Dodd's *Dimensions of Society* (with the appearance of the latter having been somewhat delayed by the onset of the Second World War).

In Chapter 4, I showed how MacIver was gradually transformed from a wholehearted opponent of naturalism to reluctant and imperfect acceptance of one of its subtle but fundamental tenets, the inertial axiom. By way of very brief recapitulation here, it will suffice to note that in 1937 he wrote the following passage which left it somewhat unsettled as to whether "force" designates the cause of motion or the cause of acceleration: "Where we discover direction in change we know that there are persistent forces cumulatively at work."[93] In the context it was not clear whether "change" referred to social processes or to social evolution, revolution, and reform. Only five years later, this had been cleared up, and MacIver was able to say that "every social system tends to maintain itself, to persevere in its present state, until compelled by some force to alter that state."[94] This was a close parallel to Newton's Axiom I, and MacIver recognized it as such. It was the indispensable basis for causal inquiry.[95] But MacIver kept reexpressing this axiom in language still fraught with animistic connotations, and when he referred to inertia, he put quotation marks around the word as if he did not consider its use in sociology quite legitimate.

For Axiom II, MacIver stated no direct analogy, but there seemed to be an implicit acceptance of *some* sort of proportionality principle when he said. "We employ statistical analysis and other methods common to all the sciences in order to learn whether and to what extent and in what areas and over what length of time the phenomenon under consideration is associated with certain other phenomena."[96] His statement was too weak an approximation of Axiom II to serve that axiom's function of operationally defining force in terms of measured mass, or vice versa. Moreover,

[93] Robert M. MacIver, *Society: A Textbook of Sociology*. New York: Holt, Rinehart and Winston, Inc., 1937, p. 499.
[94] Robert M. MacIver, *Social Causation*. Boston: Ginn and Company, 1942, p. 173.
[95] *Ibid.*, p. 176.
[96] *Ibid.*, p. 390.

MacIver showed that he was less concerned with proportionality as such than with "understandable" connections between variables. He gave the following example: At the time of the Depression of the 1930s the marriage rate, which had already had a mild downward trend, showed a relatively sharp additional decline. With business recovery it went up again a trifle higher than before the drop. MacIver wrote:[97]

Here we have a strong presumption that the depression adversely affected the marriage rate. If we find, as in fact we do, that other depressions have been accompanied by a fall in the number of marriages we have strong grounds for inferring a causal connection, *since there is also an understandable relationship between the prospect of attaining, maintaining, or enhancing an income and the mode of behavior we call "getting married."*

If the fluctuations in marriage rate were not proportional to the fluctuations in prosperity, MacIver did not make it clear whether the "understandability" of the relationship between financial prospects and getting married would be of less importance, or would be less substantial, or would remain the overriding consideration.

As to Axiom III, MacIver had some misgivings, but eventually subscribed fully to at least the outright rejection of unmoved movers. First he argued that it would be hopeless to establish cause-effect relationships if every event had to be attributed to the whole situation from which it emerged. This would amount to saying, he felt, that "the whole is the cause of the whole, a statement as unhelpful as its correlative that the whole is the effect of the whole."[98] And yet Newton, in developing his gravitational theory, had asserted that all bodies in the universe do interact with all others—and are mutually attracted in proportion to the products of their masses divided by the square of the intervening distance. All celestial movements, then, are caused by all celestial movements, but this does not make physical mechanics hopeless. What keeps this from rendering the gravitational formula useless is that most of the distances are so large that all but a very few interactions with relatively near neighbors can be neglected in accounting for a given body's movements. Some pages later, MacIver began to clarify this for sociology. He said:[99]

Possibly, if we were to include sufficiently remote links in the temporal sequence, there is no phenomenon or event that does not depend on the whole history of the universe. But the infinite regress of causes is no reason why we should not seek the connection between an immediate phenomenon and its immediate antecedents. It is a curious logic that would allow us nothing because we cannot have everything.

Finally, toward the end of his book, MacIver warmed up to the third axiom enough to say: "Something that itself moves must be the explana-

[97] *Ibid.*, pp. 353–355.
[98] *Ibid.*, p. 41.
[99] *Ibid.*, p. 66.

tion of a movement."[100] This might be termed a "near miss." To have said "Something that itself accelerates must be the explanation of an acceleration" would have been still better. But even that would have left out the important assertion of inverse proportionality between relative masses and relative accelerations of the two somethings. For MacIver, Axiom III simply was not understood as the conceptual device by which mass became measurable.

In MacIver's case, what attention he paid to the axioms of physical mechanics certainly left his sociology unimpaired. If his use of mechanical concepts was too impoverished to do sociology much good, it was not because of their associations with physics but because of his reluctance. Once more the failures of the imitation did not prove that physics ought not to be imitated, but only that it doesn't pay to imitate it badly.

7 Parsons

In discussing convergences in recent sociological work, Timasheff cited Lundberg's paper on the natural science trend, and then said that Parsons and Bales had worked out four laws of social action, of which, three were "practically identical with those of classical mechanics," an accomplishment he said was "clearly consistent" with that trend.[101] But a careful inspection of Parsons's and Bales's "laws" will show that they are not "practically identical" with Newton's axioms, as their authors supposed (with Timasheff's apparent concurrence). The belief in such identity indicates that the content and scientific role of Newton's axioms continue to be misunderstood.

Parsons and Bales gave some indication that they did mean to regard their propositions as axioms rather than as substantive conclusions. They said, along this line, that to state the "laws" of a system meant to state a few fundamental generalizations regarding the nature of its "equilibrating processes" from which could be deduced hypotheses about the responses of the system to a "disturbance."[102] But other comments they made appraising the importance of their propositions seemed to indicate a very different perspective, as will be seen below.

As a preliminary to further discussion, I will reproduce Parsons's and Bales's own "succinct statements of the four generalized conditions of equilibrium. . . ." In their essay, more detailed versions had preceded this summary version. The labels of the first three statements will easily sug-

[100] *Ibid.*, p. 335.
[101] Nicholas S. Timasheff, *Sociological Theory: Its Nature and Growth*, rev. ed. New York: Random House Inc., 1957, p. 308.
[102] Talcott Parsons and Robert F. Bales. "The Dimensions of Action Space," chap. 3 in Talcott Parsons, Robert F. Bales, and Edward A. Shils (eds.), *Working Papers in the Theory of Action*. New York: The Free Press of Glencoe, 1953, p. 99.

gest which Newtonian axiom they supposedly mirror. Later I will quote
Parsons's and Bales's own assertions regarding these ostensible parallels.[103]

1   *The Principle of Inertia:* A given process of action will continue unchanged
in rate and direction unless impeded or deflected by opposing motivational
forces.
2   *The Principle of Action and Reaction:* If, in a system of action, there is
a change in the *direction* of a process, it will tend to be balanced by *a com-
plimentary change which is equal in motivational force and opposite in
direction.*
3   *The Principle of Effort:* Any change in the rate of an action process is
directly proportional to the *magnitude* of the motivational force applied or
withdrawn.
4   *The Principle of System-integration:* Any *pattern* element (*mode of organization* of components) within a *system* of action will tend to be confirmed
in its place within the system or to be eliminated from the system (extinguished) as a function of its contribution to the integrative balance of the
system.

Most of this sounds on the surface as if Parsons and Bales had taken
persistence of action for granted, and had decided to regard *change* (acceleration) as problematic. Unlike MacIver, for example, they spoke of
inertia without even putting quotes around the word. But having said
that their first proposition was "obviously closely similar to the law of
inertia in classical mechanics," they went on to call it "another way of
stating one aspect of the fundamental postulate that we are dealing with
equilibrating systems."[104] Thus they stumbled over the confusion of
homeostasis with inertia about which I commented in Chapter 3. Newton,
in stating Axiom I, was hardly imputing homeostatic capacities to the
universe of material bodies.

Parsons and Bales had noted that continuance of certain levels of performance is a prerequisite for social equilibrium, an ongoing process.
They had spoken of an "active" phase of the equilibrium process which
could be termed "acceleration of the rate of action," and a "passive" phase
in which a rate is slowed down. "In either case a disturbance of equilibrium results which in turn necessitates a process of readjustment throughout the system."[105] Here was the concept of acceleration apparently being
given a central position in Parsons's and Bales's conceptual scheme. Their
intent in using it, though, seemed not to be to say that the force concept
must be invoked to explain a change of rate (rather than to explain a
continuing rate of a given magnitude), but to say instead that changes
of rates of action typically elicit forces to suppress them. And elsewhere
in the same volume, Parsons had clearly seemed to regard the persistence

[103] *Ibid.,* pp. 102–103.
[104] *Ibid.,* p. 100.
[105] *Ibid.,* p. 78.

of action rates as more problematic than their change when he stressed culture as a device that promotes stability and spoke of the plasticity and sensitivity of human organisms as a source of "extreme potential instability."[106]

Some years later, Parsons defined a goal as "a *directional change* that tends to reduce the discrepancy between the needs of the system, with regard to input-output interchange, and the conditions in the environing systems that bear upon the 'fulfillment' of such needs."[107] He seemed to be speaking of a social analogue of acceleration, yet he did not use the term. Thus he was not continuing to pursue the analogy he and Bales had outlined. This raises some questions. Had the analogy turned out to be sterile? Or had Parsons not had his heart in it in the first place? Or had it never really been intended as a conceptual basis on which to build further inquiry, but only as a metaphor by which sociology could borrow some prestige from a more mature science? Or had Parsons supposed the "principle of inertia" was a conclusion rather than an axiom? These questions are underscored by the fact, too, that in discussing the problem of multiple goals of a social system Parsons did not even allude to the principle of composition of forces, which would have been natural for him to do if the force and acceleration concepts had still been on his mind.

At this later date, however, Parsons was still using the term "inertia." With it in mind as a general concept, he said, "We may say that endogenous change occurs only when the lower-order mechanisms of control fail to contain the factors of strain."[108] Evidently by "inertia" he meant homeostasis. It was still not change but persistence that seemed problematic to him, for he said that "the crucial focus of the problem of change lies in the stability of the value system."[109] Parsons, at least, was persistent in not assuming persistence, for in his own paper on the superego he had written eight years before that culture was the core of the mechanisms for stabilizing a system of interaction.[110] It should be clear from all this that Parsons's so-called "principle of inertia" was *not* (as Parsons himself understood it) "practically identical" with Newton's Axiom I. As he understood it, it was really quite a different idea.

With respect to the second proposition, too, there are clues that it was not really intended to mean for sociology what Newton's second axiom had meant for physics. Parsons and Bales mentioned that it was "close

[106] Talcott Parsons, "The Superego and the Theory of Social Systems," chap. 1 in Parsons, Bales, and Shils (eds.), *op. cit.*, pp. 16–17.
[107] Talcott Parsons, "An Outline of the Social System," in Talcott Parsons, Edward Shils, Kaspar D. Naegele, and Jesse R. Pitts (eds.), *Theories of Society*. New York: The Free Press of Glencoe, 1961, p. 39. (My italics.)
[108] *Ibid.*, p. 72.
[109] *Ibid.*
[110] Parsons, "The Superego and the Theory of Social Systems," p. 18.

to common sense" that changes in rates of action were dependent on effort.[111] When effort increased or decreased in relation to the established rate of an action process, this was a "disturbance of equilibrium," they said.[112] Then, to quantify this, they wanted "to state in hypothetical form that the change in the rate of action process is directly proportional to the *magnitude* of the motivational force added to or withdrawn from the unit in question." The context made it rather clear that by the phrase "in hypothetical form" Parsons and Bales intended this principle of proportionality to be an empirical generalization, not an axiom. They said that in its qualitative form it was pretty well known "what the generalization means empirically," and that "testing of the quantitative statement" would have to wait until there had been developed adequate measures of action process rates.[113] Clearly, they did not expect the proposition itself to serve as an operational definition of social force in terms of measured social mass, or social mass in terms of measured social force, and acceleration.

Oddly, Parsons did later seem to have a concept such as social mass in mind when he wrote that the impact of change-producing forces would depend on something besides the magnitude of the disturbance. In a very stable system, he said, a relatively large disturbance might not result in major change, while considerable change might be wrought by a smaller disturbance if the system were less stable.[114] This came fairly close to suggesting that acceleration would be proportional to the ratio of force to mass. But this time Parsons was not so insistent as before that his assertion had an obvious resemblance to Newton's Axiom II. He had in fact strengthened the resemblance, but he seemed less sure of it or less concerned about it.

Parsons and Bales were clear off the target in their statement of a generalization they thought was "directly parallel" to Axiom III. In their brief summary version they simply referred to "a complementary change" associated with a given change; but in the original and longer statement they had said, ". . . Once a disturbance had been introduced into an equilibrated system there will tend to be a reaction to this disturbance which tends to restore the system to equilibrium."[115] They seem to have imagined that what Newton meant by "reaction" was the same thing a psychologist means in speaking of an organism's reaction (i.e., response) to a stimulus. Newton had no such notion in mind. When a rolling billiard ball collides with a stationary one, it loses as much momentum as the other gains. It is its loss of momentum that is called the "reaction" which is equal and opposite to the "action" of imparting momentum to the previously

[111] Parsons and Bales, "The Dimensions of Action Space," p. 100.
[112] *Ibid.*, p. 101.
[113] *Ibid.*
[114] Parsons, "An Outline of the Social System," p. 73.
[115] Parsons and Bales, "The Dimensions of Action Space," p. 100.

stationary ball. It does not "restore" a threatened equilibrium; it is simply the other aspect of an *inter*action between two bodies. There is something ironic in the way this concept of interaction has so often eluded sociologists.

Quite obviously, having earlier confused a system's homeostatic capacity with inertia, Parsons and Bales were now confusing the homeostatic process with the principle which denies unmoved movers (i.e., unaccelerated accelerators). And again they seemed to mean this as an empirical generalization rather than an axiom, for they said it could be suggested "hypothetically" that the reaction would be in the opposite direction from the disturbance and would be "in some sense" equal in motivational force.[116] The phrase "in some sense" seems to indicate that this principle was *not* expected to serve as an operational definition of relative mass, as did Newton's Axiom III; the import of Newton's axiom had been to *specify* the sense in which action and reaction were equal.

What Parsons and Bales did was to misconstrue Newton's third axiom as if it were a description of the operation of a servomechanism. That was not what it was at all. It simply says that the acceleration of one body by another entails an equal and opposite acceleration of the other body, where *equality is defined by* $m_1a_1 = -m_2a_2$. Or this could be written: $m_1/m_2 = -a_2/a_1$, which simply means that if time and distance can be measured, so that accelerations can be expressed in cardinal numbers, then relative mass can be measured as the reciprocal of relative acceleration in the interaction of two bodies. Parsons and Bales were either oblivious of this, or else they supposed the ratio $-a_2/a_1$ was analogous to deviance and the ratio m_1/m_2 was analogous to the feedback principle in a servomechanism. Any such supposition would be a gross error in conceptualization.

To make matters worse, a few pages later they went out of their way to deny that empirical systems necessarily behaved like servomechanisms. They said they had concentrated on equilibration processes in "carefully defined, indeed in a strict sense in hypothetical, systems of action." They had not meant to imply, they insisted, "any inherent presumption that empirical systems must remain in equilibrium, or return to any given state when the equilibrium has been disturbed."[117] It is usually wise, of course, for the sociologist to express considerable tentativity in stating his generalizations, and Parsons and Bales were doubtless striving to partake of that wisdom. But this was a case of *misplaced* tentativity. It simply meant they were not remaining consistent with their own conceptions. First they misconstrued the Newtonian axioms and then they deliberately rejected the assumptions that would have been required to make the misconstrued form of the axioms applicable to sociological subject matter. It was also

[116] *Ibid.*
[117] *Ibid.*, pp. 107–108.

an instance of misplaced tentativity when they said the reaction would "tend to be" equal to the disturbance. Axioms don't state tendencies; they state rigorous relationships between concepts. Newton would have failed if he'd tried to work with the notion that action and reaction "tend to be" equal or "tend to be" opposite. Mass could not have been measured with the precision the physicist required if relative mass only *tended* to be inversely related to relative acceleration.

Parsons and Bales also tried to make something of the fact that Newton had stated only three axioms, while their system involved four. The metaphor, laws of "motion," was in their view meaningful because what they wanted to investigate was changes of position in "action space." There were, they said, four dimensions to this space: the goal-achievement or instrumental dimension (G), the expressive dimension (E), the adaptive dimension (A), the integrative dimension (I). Roles and need dispositions could be located in this space. That is, a role or a need disposition could be more instrumental or less instrumental, or it might be more or less expressive, or more or less adaptive, or more or less integrative. Moreover, it could "move" along any of these axes, singly or in combination. Direction of change would be the "resultant" of motions in relation to the four coordinates simultaneously. The motions in any stable system of action (person, group, culture) would tend to occur at constant rates unless accelerated by a disturbance.[118] Having created this model, they then professed to see "general significance in the fact that with a system using a four-dimensional space, we have found four fundamental generalizations which are essential to defining the conditions of equilibrium of a system described in terms of that space." The reason it seems probable that this has significance, they said, "is that classical mechanics had three fundamental laws of motion, and operated in terms of a three-dimensional space."[119]

Such an assertion would be sheer pseudo-scientific numerology if Parsons and Bales had not attempted to explain it by implying that their first three action-space dimensions were analogous to the three dimensions of physical space and that their fourth generalization was intrinsically linked to their fourth action-space dimension in some more important sense than just that both were fourth in their respective lists.[120] For my part, I see no correspondence between their dimensions G, E, and A, on the one hand, and length, breadth, and depth, on the other hand. The latter three are, of course, mutually interchangeable by rotating the coordinates in any direction about an arbitrary origin. But I gather that Parsons and Bales believed there was a fundamental difference between

[118] *Ibid.*, pp. 88–90.
[119] *Ibid.*, p. 102.
[120] *Ibid.* For further indication of how far Parsons's conceptions differed from Newton's, see Parsons, "The Organization of Personality as a System of Action," in Talcott Parsons and Robert F. Bales (eds.), *Family, Socialization and Interaction Process.* New York: The Free Press of Glencoe, 1955, esp. pp. 178–186.

the instrumental, the expressive, and the adaptive dimensions of action, and I doubt that they intended that these coordinates could be arbitrarily interchanged.

Parsons had been very critical of Dodd's social physics for failing to specify a finite list of the most relevant variables for sociologists to study. Parsons had correctly noted that specification of relevant variables was a major accomplishment of Newtonian mechanics. Apparently his own efforts to specify the dimensions of action space were meant to provide an analogous service to sociology. If so, it should simply be noted that Newton's accomplishment did not consist in telling us what the three dimensions of interstellar space should be called, nor even in telling us that there were three dimensions. His accomplishment consisted of showing how profitable it would be for science to study the *accelerations* of bodies with the property of inertial and gravitational *mass*, and how we might measure both mass and force.

But apparently Parsons and Bales themselves felt that their bold interpretation of the 4:3 ratio required further justification, for they added, "Furthermore it also seems evident that the necessity for both the fourth dimension and the fourth law derives from the fact that we are here dealing with boundary-maintaining systems."[121] In my judgment, that is what they should have said in the first place, but ironically it was only a few pages later that they weakened this rationale by insisting that they did not want to assert that empirical systems do in fact maintain their boundaries.

It might also have been illuminating for them to have acknowledged that their fourth proposition amounted to a restatement of Darwin's principle of natural selection. The reason that the action systems we can observe do behave like servomechanisms is that had they or their ancestors not done so they would not have survived and could not now be observed. Whether, therefore, sociology needs a set of axioms blended from the work of *both* Newton and Darwin should be judged on a more substantial basis than the degree of success or failure achieved by Parsons and Bales in attempting such a blend. Insofar as they missed the real meaning of Newton's work, the sociology that could be built upon their imitation of it would be no test of the possible value of a sociology that correctly adhered to the third and fourth elements of naturalism as listed in Chapter 1 and as expressed originally in Newton's axioms.

Obstacles in Terminology

In spite of the fact that Newton's axioms have been so repeatedly imitated in the sociological literature, and by men who run the gamut of emi-

[121] Parsons and Bales, "The Dimensions of Action Space," p. 102.

nence—the nonacademic, the self-taught, the founding fathers, two past presidents of the American Sociological Society—there remains a belief that borrowing concepts from physics is the mark of a slightly mad or at least unrealistic sociologist. I reject this view, as I reject the milder conclusion of Popper that it is chimerical to hope that we may someday find society's "laws of motion." He says there is no sense in which societal motion is sufficiently similar to the motion of physical bodies for such laws to be found.[122] He says we ought to be clear that social movements are only metaphorically related to physical movements, and it is a very misleading metaphor at that.[123]

It is true that the term "social movement" has taken on a meaning that is not really analogous to the motion of a material body. It refers to an organized campaign by a subgroup in a society to alter the structure or mores of that society. Sometimes the term even refers to an identifiable voluntary association engaged in such a campaign. We use the expression "civil rights movement," for example, to refer to the various organizations participating in the campaign to extend equality of opportunity among diverse population categories—rather than to the rate of occurrence of such extension. But this only means that some other phrase is required as a label for such rates of occurrence of social phenomena which *can* be regarded as analogous to the motion of bodies in space. Parsons and Bales were right in attempting to define an action space in which sociocultural entities could be located and in which they could be depicted as undergoing motion. Dodd was right in suggesting that the sociologist's attention should not be confined to motion in physical space only, even if he fell short of offering any concrete alternatives when he merely substituted I for L in his formulas.

But Popper was correct in pointing out that when physics speaks of the movement of a body it does not imply any internal change in the structure of that body, and refers only to a shift in the body's position relative to other bodies. Since the sociologist does refer to structural change within the system, Popper said, he tends to assume that "a movement of society is to be explained by *forces* while the physicist assumes that only *changes* of movement . . . have to be so explained."[124] Popper's statement refers partly to the vestiges of animism in sociology, and the need to outgrow them, but partly it signifies the need for a mere terminological reform. It suggests that a great deal of the debate over whether social change is "immanent," or must instead be attributed always to causes external to the system that changes, arose from the unfortunate semantic development that gave the word "movement" a quite different sort of meaning in sociology and in physics.

Even superficial language habits are hard to change, but among scholars

[122] Popper, *op. cit.*, p. 115.
[123] *Ibid.*, pp. 113–114.
[124] *Ibid.*

committed to the goal of effective communication terminological preferences ought not to be as resistant to change as among the general population. Deep-rooted assumptions and concepts which serve as the basis of
our very perceptions may be much harder to alter than our word preferences. If they eventually do change, however, then a way of conceiving
social phenomena which until now has seemed unsatisfactory largely because of its unfamiliarity may come to be regarded as obvious.[125]

I have suggested, though, that some sociologists are ambivalent in their
attachments to the traditional animistic concepts. For a long time there
has been at least a latent receptivity to naturalism. This receptivity is
not restricted in its occurrence to those expressions which are avowedly
intended to ape Newton. It is visible in the occasional straightforward
use of the concepts defined by the Newtonian axioms. William Graham
Sumner, for example, long ago noted that "every religion is a resisting
inertia" and that as conditions changed and the mores changed, religion
was confronted by "moving forces." He identified "philosophy"—by which
he appeared to mean both verified knowledge and a general world view
one absorbs through participation in the social process—as a "force of revision and revolution."[126] His choice of words may have seemed even to
him to be metaphorical, but the entire essay in which he used these expressions was strongly naturalistic. And Sumner did not have to say where
he got the concepts of inertia and force in order to prove they were useful
in saying what he wanted to say. Ellsworth Faris, under the heading "The
inertia of culture," said that "culture tends to produce itself indefinitely."[127]
If this sounds almost Euclidean in language and Newtonian in meaning,
the interesting thing is that Faris had no compulsion to point that out.
He let the statement convey its meaning without any fanfare. And again,
when he stressed the need for recognizing the impact of sharply contrasting cultural influences in understanding the personality and changing customs of a people such as the forest Bantu of the Belgian Congo, he said,
"When West meets East we must draw a parallelogram of forces."[128] He
simply said it, and went on, without pausing to prove the aptness of the
expression by mentioning the science he had borrowed it from.

Axioms of Naturalistic Sociology

Once and for all sociology needs to expunge the false stigma that attaches
to concepts that are called metaphorical. If a force is that which produces

[125] Cf. Nagel, *op. cit.*, p. 115; and Reichenbach, *op. cit.*, p. 155.
[126] William Graham Sumner, "Religion and the Mores," in Albert G. Keller and Maurice
R. Davie (eds.), *Selected Essays of William Graham Sumner.* New Haven, Conn.:
Yale University Press, 1924, p. 343.
[127] Ellsworth Faris, *The Nature of Human Nature.* New York: McGraw-Hill Book
Company, 1937, p. 3.
[128] *Ibid.*, p. 280.

an acceleration, then a physical force is that which accelerates material bodies in physical space, and a social force is whatever accelerates social processes. It makes sense to use the term "force" in both contexts because both physical forces and social forces are special cases of the general concept. It makes sense to attach the adjectives to differentiate them because the two kinds of forces accelerate different entities in different kinds of dimensions. It may make sense not to bother always using the adjective "physical" when we mean a physical force, because physics got there first and has a prior claim on the word "force." That does not mean that when the adjective "social" *is* employed the phrase needs to be regarded as an illegitimate "aping" of physics, or a mere figure of speech.

We ought not to be content to use such terms as "social acceleration," "social force," "sociocultural mass," etc., as merely "sensitizing" concepts. If we are going to use them at all, we should strive to define them operationally so that they become measurable. And our choice of such labels for these concepts can only be fully justified if the operational definitions provide measurable concepts that are truly analogous to the corresponding concepts in physics. Otherwise we should, as many writers have advocated, adopt a less physicalistic vocabulary.

The study of social change, I think ought to concern itself with accelerations of social rates, and with the analysis of social forces associated with such accelerations. I think it should do this because I think this will pay off in predictive laws. This approach would not be reductionist, either. I will go into that issue more fully in Chapter 9. For now, note that only if we sought to explain social accelerations by invoking physical forces, etc., would we be guilty of reductionism. An explanation of social accelerations in terms of social forces has no such fault.

To define these concepts in an operational way, I offer the following axioms of social motion. I offer them without apology, for I think they avoid the kinds of errors I have pointed out in the various paraphrases of Newton previously reviewed. They are asserted here as axioms, not as hypotheses. They cannot be directly tested, but their vindication will depend on the empirical confirmation of other propositions employing the concepts these axioms define and assert to be fundamental. For sociology to become naturalistic, such axioms would have to be adopted whether there had ever been precedent for them in physics or not. (To paraphrase Voltaire, if Newtonian mechanics had not existed, naturalistic sociologists would have had to invent it.) In fact, of course, there was such a precedent, but its existence only means that the burden of proof ought to rest a little more heavily on those who oppose such axioms than on those who subscribe to them. Otherwise the precedent of a highly successful science of physics has no direct relevance for sociology. Sociological adoption of the concepts defined by these axioms is desirable if they work for sociology, not just because their counterparts worked for physics.

Sociological Axiom I: Every social pattern continues to manifest itself in constantly recurring social action at an unaltered rate unless some social force modifies the rate or pattern of such action.

Sociological Axiom II: For a given sociocultural entity, the magnitude of an acceleration which it exhibits will be directly proportional to the magnitude of the net social force acting upon it.

Sociological Axiom III: Every social action is part of an interaction; an observed acceleration of a social rate involves comparable acceleration of some other social rate or rates opposed to it.

The first of these axioms simply postulates for sociology a uniform flow of time and defines a social force as that which is inferred from accelerations rather than that which is inferred from stable rates of social action. Of course in the derivation of theorems this axiom must be coupled with due recognition that stable rates may in some instances reflect offsetting accelerations (*net* force = 0). Offsetting accelerations may result from homeostatic processes or from the coincidence of equal but opposing external forces. This first axiom lays the conceptual foundation for beginning to discern an inertial frame of reference for sociology. It regards patterned social action as given, requiring no explanation, and defines *change* in the patterns and rates of social action as problematic. As noted in Chapter 3, this axiom is implicit in a sound theory of social and cultural evolution. For natural selection to operate, it must be assumed that viable elements persist and are reproduced unchanged.

The second axiom defines the sociocultural mass of "a given entity" as the ratio between the social force applied and the social acceleration attained. Or if the mass were already known (relative to the mass of another interacting entity), this axiom would define the magnitude of the force as the product of that mass and the attained acceleration. It makes either concept measurable in terms of the other and measured acceleration.

The third axiom denies that there can be unaccelerated accelerators (or in the old scholastic parlance, unmoved movers). But it does more. It says that when two sociocultural entities interact, the ratio of the acceleration of the first to the acceleration of the second provides a measure of the mass of the second relative to the mass of the first. Alone, this axiom would be tautological, and so would the second axiom by itself. But the third serves to break the tautology of the second—given the availability of cardinal measures of social rates and their rates of change. And though it is an axiom rather than a hypothesis, this proposition ought to have at least as much heuristic value as the assumptions of functionalism. It alerts the sociologist to the intrinsic concomitance of pattern-maintenance and pattern modification. It says, in effect, "When pattern-maintenance (homeostasis) is observed, look for pattern modification in the same system."

These sociological axioms constitute precise statements of the last two of the tenets of naturalism that were listed in Chapter 1. They are also the "ultimate premises" for the theory of valuing presented in Chapter 5 and for the application of that theory to the study of national park visitation rates which was begun in Chapter 6 and will be continued in Chapter 8. Together with the commitment to observation as the ultimate test of truth and the abandonment of final causes as explanations, then, these axioms define *naturalistic* sociology.

Summary

Analogy has sometimes been used as a substitute for scientific explanation. Its proper use in a naturalistic discipline is confined to serving as a guide in the formulation of propositions whose ultimate acceptance or rejection must depend on empirical tests. With this in mind, we can resolve much of the debate over the propriety or impropriety of sociological imitation of physics. Crude sociological hypotheses do not become more profound by expression in physicalistic terminology or in quasi-mathematical notation. The construction of sociological propositions with concepts borrowed from physics does not obviate the necessity of empirical testing. But sociological ideas are not necessarily invalidated just by expression in physicalistic form, either.

The naturalistic sociologist ought to be able to pass the scientific equivalent of a literacy test; he ought to be accurately conversant with such fundamental concepts as mass, force, and acceleration. Lack of familiarity with the role these concepts have played in the development of science is a serious obstacle to comprehension of all the tenets of naturalism as a mode of inquiry.

Newton's three axioms have been widely imitated in sociological literature, but in one way or another each imitation has failed to reflect some essential aspect of what the prototype set of axioms actually did for natural science. Axiom I, the inertial axiom, defined the uniform flow of time and accepted motion as a phenomenon requiring no explanation as such. It made change of motion, or acceleration, problematic. A number of sociological imitators have fallen short of recognizing or matching this meaning in their attempts to phrase what they thought was the sociological counterpart of this axiom.

Axiom II, the principle of proportionality between force and acceleration, served as an operational definition making force measurable in terms of acceleration and measured mass. In effect it defined mass as the constant ratio between forces and accelerations for a given body. Previously, mass had been primitively conceived as the quantity of matter. No such conceptual refinement has been accomplished by the various sociological paraphrases of this axiom up to now. One of them even failed precisely because social mass had been prematurely equated with quantity of people.

Axiom III, the principle of equal and opposite reaction, has been grossly distorted in its imitations. The prototype axiom operationally defined relative mass as inversely proportional to relative acceleration, and thus made mass measurable. Sociologists have tended to read into this axiom extraneous notions of euphoric harmony or of servomechanistic social control.

The failure of these imitations can be attributed to the inaccuracy of the paraphrase in each case. Their failure does not indicate that physics is an inappropriate model to follow. They have not proven that sociology must inevitably be misled by borrowing concepts from physics—if it accurately understands the concepts it borrows.

Adoption of an accurately expressed set of sociological axioms conceptually equivalent to Newton's would entail certain philosophical costs. Inasmuch as the "free will" concept seems to be intended to deny the applicability of such axioms in the realm of human and interhuman behavior, naturalism would cost us the abandonment of some cherished notions. Adoption of such axioms would also require a commitment to more precise quantitative expression and reasoning than has seemed necessary with the cruder language of animistic sociology.

But there would be advantages, too. Sociological problems that now can be only vaguely defined should become more amenable to solution. The axioms would have immediate heuristic value, too, in alerting the sociologist to look for concomitant pattern modifications when he observes instances of active pattern-maintenance or homeostasis. This is a line of study that has usually been neglected, but it could become at least as important as the inquiry now prompted by more animistic heuristic models such as functionalism.

Sociological axioms can be stated which do directly parallel the axioms of Newton. The charge that they are metaphorical can be dismissed as irrelevant. The sociological concepts they define and the counterpart physical concepts should simply be viewed as special cases of more abstract concepts applicable generally to all fields of naturalistic inquiry. The utility of these concepts in sociology must be empirically demonstrated.

Chapter Eight
PREDICTION AND EXPLANATION
OF VISITATION RATES

The Challenge to Causal Inquiry

There is a standard form in which all scientific laws either are stated or can at least be translated. Radcliffe-Brown expressed this form as "Any instance of X is also an instance of Y." As an example he noted that the familiar regularity that water expands when it freezes can be restated as "every instance of water freezing is an instance of expansion." Even statistical laws (as found in sociology) can be put into a special version of this standard form, asserting that in a sufficiently large number of instances of X, a predictable *proportion* of them will also be instances of Y.[1]

In Chapter 6 it was apparent that national park visitation rates were some kind of inverse function of distance. If that function can be specified, we would have a lawlike statement in the above form which would assert that in a sufficiently large population of state i, located D_{ij} distance from park j, a predictable fraction (R_{ij}) of that population will be visitors at park j in a given year. Specification of the exact form of the equation $R_{ij} = f(D_{ij})$ would "explain" the magnitude of R_{ij}, where "explanation" consists of subsuming a specific instance under a general rule.

Apparent trends, or cycles, or patterns that can be discerned in such a body of statistical data challenge the sociologist to search for causes.

[1] A. R. Radcliffe-Brown, *A Natural Science of Society*. New York: The Free Press of Glencoe, 1957, p. 6.

238

In seeking causes, he assumes that changing rates or indices can be attributed to some discoverable aspect of group life, or to its dynamic processes, by which the trends, cycles, or patterns are caused.[2] MacIver cited Durkheim's study of suicide rates as exemplary.[3]

It might seem that the magnitude of R_{ij} does not require explanation, in the light of Sociological Axiom I as stated in Chapter 7. That axiom asserted that every social pattern (e.g., vacation travel) continues to manifest itself in constantly recurring social action at an unaltered rate (in this case, R_{ij}) unless some social force modifies the rate or pattern of such action. Careful thought will quickly indicate, however, that there is an ever-present factor in the situation which could be expected to lower the magnitude of R_{ij} unless counteracted continuously or recurrently by an accelerative force. Since R_{ij} is the proportion of state i residents visiting park j in a given time interval, it is a measure of the fraction of persons dwelling in state i who traveled the distance D_{ij} to reach park j. It costs money and time and effort to travel. Therefore D_{ij} is an index of a kind of resistance that would tend to lower the magnitude of R_{ij} unless balanced by a travel-fostering force.

The expansion of naturalism received great impetus from a crucial insight of Sir Isaac Newton. That insight consisted not only in defining acceleration rather than motion as problematic, but also in recognizing that the orbital motions of the planets were compounded of an inertial element and an element of centripetal acceleration. With this insight one could ask what sort of force caused the acceleration, whereas previously such men as Kepler and all his predecessors had felt that they must ask what "force" caused the planets to move at all. The problem had seemed to be to account for the forward progress of a planet along its path; Newton redefined the problem and sought an explanation for the centripetal acceleration of planets. His formulation of the law of universal gravitation provided that explanation.

Moreover, though it was continuous, orbital motion was clearly not an instance of goal-directed, homeostatic behavior. One does not have to conceive the solar system as an organism, or a giant servomechanism, in order to understand the maintenance of a near equality between centripetal and centrifugal forces. I say "near equality" because there are actually only two points in a planet's orbit where these counteracting forces are exactly equal. Since a planet's orbit is an ellipse rather than a circle, the planet climbs away from perihelion toward aphelion because in that half of its orbit the (inertial) centrifugal force exceeds the centripetal force of gravity. The planet descends to perihelion again because having slowed down in the ascent it once again responds to an excess of gravity over centrifugal force. The recurring balance of forces *has the effect* of keeping the planet

[2] Robert M. MacIver, *Social Causation*. Boston: Ginn and Company, 1942, pp. 137–138.
[3] *Ibid.*, pp. 138–143.

in orbit with a stable period of revolution. It would be incorrect (and animistic) to say that the forces are balanced *in order to* produce this effect.

There is a somewhat similar periodicity in park visitation. For most parks, the main tourist season is (obviously) in the summer. Occupational commitments and travel hazards due to weather are but two considerations that enlarge the resistive effect of D_{ij} during the winter. If *annual* visitation rates remain relatively stable, this indicates that on the average there is a long-run balance between the centripetal force exerted by each park and the resistance to travel which distance entails.

The search for an explanation of the magnitudes of R_{ij} is in keeping with the inertial axiom, then, when the presence of factors tending to depress those magnitudes is acknowledged so that the search is directed toward finding and analyzing the kind of counteracting factor or factors that might just offset them. A model involving offsetting forces is not necessarily a model of a homeostatic (directively organized) system. It would be misleading to refer to it by Parsons's term, "pattern-maintenance." And it does not imply merely a blind search among an infinite number of possible factors to counteract the effects of D_{ij}. If the magnitude of the decelerating force is known, then the magnitude of an accelerating force that must be involved if R_{ij} is stable is thereby given. The search is narrowed to forces of given magnitude.

The implicit involvement of offsetting accelerations in a matrix of R_{ij} can also be grasped if the park visitation problem is compared to problems in psychophysics. In that area, the data take the form of "response matrices"—showing the responses of persons to stimuli. A response matrix can take either of two forms, however. An "individual matrix" has a column for each stimulus and a row for each individual, and the cell entries are response data. An "occasion matrix" presents data from repeated stimulation of the same individual. It has a column for each stimulus and a row for each occasion on which the various stimuli were administered. Most psychophysical theory is stated in terms of occasion matrices, but much psychophysical experimentation has to resort to the construction and analysis of individual matrices. The latter are taken to be approximately equivalent to the former, and thereby the experiments and theories are construed as relevant to each other.[4]

For national parks, our response matrix of state visitation rates (Table 6 in Chapter 6) could similarly be described as indicative of what an occasion matrix would look like. It shows that the probability of a person visiting a given park depends on the location of the state in which he resides, and we can *infer* that this probability in his case would change if he moved to another state. Thus in explaining variations among simul-

[4] See J. P. Guilford, *Psychometric Methods,* 2d ed. New York: McGraw-Hill Book Company, 1954, p. 27.

taneous R_{ij} for spatially distinct populations we would implicitly be explaining "accelerations." It was this kind of interpretation that lay at the foundation of Durkheim's study of suicide rates which MacIver so admired. MacIver pointed out that Durkheim's strategy was to relate problematic differences in suicide rates to the differences in social cohesion apparently characterizing the various situations in which suicide occurred. Durkheim's perception of the nature of causal inquiry was, according to MacIver, unusually clear.[5]

The Inverse Distance Pattern

Distance must be measured if it is to be used in explaining visitation rate variations. But the distance between a state and a national park is at best an ambiguous quantity. States and parks are not points; they have areal extent. Most of the parks are small enough in area, relative to most states, to be reasonably treated as point locations. And presumably some point within a state's area could be objectively designated and used to "represent" the location of the state relative to the various parks. Even then, however, definitional problems would remain. By what route should distance be measured from a given state to a given park? Since most park visitation is by automobile, highway mileage would seem to be an appropriate type of distance measure. Often, though, there are two or more equally plausible routes between a given state and a given park. Moreover, from year to year new construction, road repair operations, etc., may temporarily close particular routes or increase the driving time entailed in traveling over them. Precise data on all these specifics would be exceedingly hard to assemble and take into account. Therefore, in the present study a simplifying assumption was made. I assumed that generally the travel routes actually followed would be rather highly correlated (for the several parks and several states) with simple air-line distances between centers.

On the basis of this assumption, I measured the distances shown in Table 11 in the following manner. An ordinary conic projection map of the continental United States was laid out flat on a drawing board. On it were shown the boundaries of all the national parks and all the states. A cardboard strip was calibrated in units of 100 scale miles, and a pin was pushed through its zero point. With the pin inserted in the center of a national park, the strip was rotated back and forth over the map so that I could visually estimate the point on the strip that just about bisected the area of a given state. I thus obtained the approximate median distance of points in state i from the center of park j.

[5] MacIver, *op. cit.*, p. 143.

Table 11 Distances from 24 states to 12 national parks (in 100s of miles)

	Crater Lake	Grand Teton	Great Smoky Mtns.	Kings Canyon	Lassen Volcanic	Mesa Verde	Mt. Rainier	Rocky Mountain	Sequoia	Shenandoah	Yellowstone	Yosemite
Arizona	8.4	7.0	16.1	4.3	7.0	3.1	10.5	5.5	4.3	18.8	7.5	5.2
California	4.6	7.1	20.1	...	...	6.3	7.3	7.9	...	22.2	7.2	...
Colorado	9.2	4.5	12.4	7.2	8.4	...	10.1	...	7.3	14.7	5.0	7.7
Idaho	4.1	2.3	17.8	5.8	4.7	6.0	3.9	5.5	6.1	19.2	2.1	5.7
Illinois	17.1	11.3	4.4	16.0	16.9	10.5	16.9	8.8	16.1	5.9	11.4	16.4
Indiana	18.5	12.8	3.5	17.4	18.3	12.0	18.2	10.2	17.5	4.3	12.9	17.8
Iowa	14.6	8.9	7.0	13.8	14.4	8.5	14.2	6.4	13.9	8.2	8.9	14.1
Kansas	12.9	7.5	8.4	11.2	12.3	5.5	13.3	4.3	11.1	10.7	7.8	11.7
Michigan	18.4	12.7	6.1	18.2	18.4	13.0	17.7	10.8	18.3	5.2	12.6	18.4
Minnesota	13.8	8.2	9.3	14.0	14.0	9.7	12.9	7.2	14.1	9.3	8.1	14.1
Missouri	15.8	10.2	5.5	14.1	15.3	8.8	15.9	7.2	14.2	7.6	10.3	14.7
Montana	6.8	2.8	15.9	8.4	7.2	7.1	5.8	5.3	8.9	17.0	2.2	8.2
Nebraska	11.5	5.9	9.8	10.5	11.2	5.5	11.5	3.2	10.8	11.3	6.0	10.9
Nevada	3.9	4.6	18.2	2.2	2.9	4.8	5.9	6.0	2.3	20.3	5.1	2.2
New Mexico	10.7	7.3	12.8	7.2	9.5	2.5	12.1	4.4	7.3	15.5	7.8	7.9
North Dakota	11.1	5.8	12.1	11.8	11.3	8.3	10.0	5.8	12.1	12.7	5.4	11.9
Oklahoma	14.1	9.1	7.9	11.8	13.2	6.1	14.8	5.5	11.8	10.7	9.3	12.2
Oregon	1.0	5.1	20.4	5.4	2.8	8.0	2.6	8.1	5.6	22.1	5.1	4.8
South Dakota	11.0	5.2	10.8	10.9	11.1	6.8	10.5	4.1	11.1	12.0	5.2	11.1
Texas	15.0	10.8	9.5	11.9	14.0	6.8	16.1	7.3	11.9	12.7	11.3	12.8
Utah	6.0	3.3	15.6	4.2	5.3	2.4	7.6	3.3	4.3	17.8	3.9	4.6
Washington	3.4	5.4	20.7	7.7	5.1	9.5	...	9.1	8.0	22.0	5.1	7.0
Wisconsin	16.1	10.4	7.2	15.9	16.2	10.9	15.4	8.8	16.0	7.3	10.3	16.1
Wyoming	7.4	...	13.9	7.2	7.2	4.2	7.4	2.3	7.3	15.5	...	7.3

Inspection of Table 11 in comparison with Table 6 will show that there is some sort of inverse relationship between R_{ij} and D_{ij}. In Chapter 6 the possible applicability of both the Stouffer intervening opportunities formula and the "demographic gravitation" formula of Zipf or Dodd was explored. Either formula could be expected to "explain" *some* of the visitation rate variance just because visitation rates are *somehow* inversely dependent on distance. But both formulas were found deficient, empirically and also conceptually.

For purely heuristic purposes, reference can again be made to the work of Kepler which so importantly paved the way for the naturalistic breakthrough achieved by Newton. Before Kepler, nobody had asked why Saturn, with an orbit twice as long as that of Jupiter, should take $2\frac{1}{2}$ times as long to go around it. But this proved to be a very fertile question. To answer it, Kepler surmised that there must be a force which emanates from the sun and impels the planets around their orbital paths. The force must diminish with distance, and hence the outer planets move more slowly than the inner ones.[6] Newton, as everyone knows, went on to show that the planetary motions could indeed be accounted for on the assumption of a universal gravitational force that waned with distance. The point is that if the orbital periods had varied with the first power of the distances of the planets from the sun, rather than with the $\frac{3}{2}$ power, their motions would not have implied a gravitational explanation. By the old Aristotelian assumptions, however, there was no reason to expect the distance exponent to be a constant for all planets, and especially there was no reason to expect that if it were constant it would not be an integer.

I don't think it is intolerably physicalistic to follow Kepler's example to the extent of posing the following question. In the case of national park visitation, does a state that is twice as far as another state from a given park tend to have about half the visitation rate, or will the rate be less than half? The question can be generalized. Do visitation rates vary inversely with the first power of the distance, or do they fall off more sharply than that?

Figure 3 provides a partial answer to this question. When R_{ij} is plotted against D_{ij} on logarithmic coordinates (with log cycles of R equal in length to log cycles of D), the dots would be expected to fall approximately along a line with a downward slope of 45 degrees if the rate of visitation varied inversely with the first power of the distance. In Figure 3 it is apparent that at least in the case of 1940 travel to Mount Rainier and Shenandoah National Parks the slope was steeper than this. (Lines with 45-degree slope have been drawn above the dots to aid visual comparison.)

In the case of Mount Rainier, a Western national park, the scatter is

[6] Arthur Koestler, *The Watershed.* Garden City, N.Y.: Anchor Books, Doubleday & Company, Inc., 1960, p. 55.

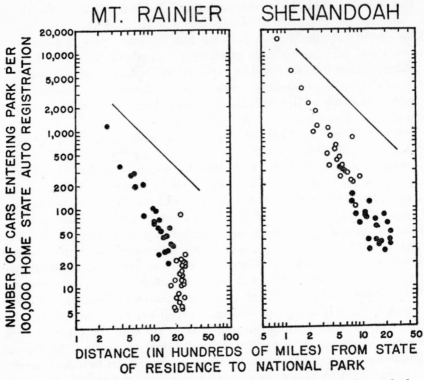

Figure 3. Automobile visitation rates at Mount Rainier and Shenandoah National Parks in 1940 as a function of distance

not linear, either. In Chapter 6, I referred to division of the country into an Eastern and a Western culture area with respect to national parks. Some justification for this division is evident in Figure 3. Black dots have been used to represent the states in the Western culture area, and white dots represent the Eastern states. Eastern state visitation at a Western park shows a steeper slope than Western state visitation at that park. For the Eastern park, however, there is little difference in the slopes exhibited by Eastern or Western state visitation. It seems reasonable to infer that the same mechanism determines the response of all states to an Eastern national park, and the response of Western states to a Western national park. But some different mechanism apparently determines Easterners' responses to a Western park.

For the present, therefore, I will lay aside the question of why Easterners respond differently to Western parks. To simplify the exploration of other issues, I will consider visitation data from only the states in the Western culture area, as I did in Chapter 6. For this more limited array of data, the scatter appears to be approximately linear for either park.

The relationship $R_{ij} = f(D_{ij})$ can therefore be stated more explicitly in the following form:

$$R_{ij} = \frac{b}{D_{ij}^d} \tag{1}$$

where b is a constant of proportionality, and d is some unspecified exponent. For both Mount Rainier and Shenandoah, however, it is also apparent from Figure 3 that $d > 1.0$, since the slope is steeper than 45 degrees downward.

The Dual Effects of Distance

Most residents of the state of Washington live close enough to Mount Rainier National Park to visit it within the span of a weekend, and the state's most populous counties are close enough to the park that their residents can easily make brief visits to it and return home the same day. On the assumption that there are important differences between vacation travel, on the one hand, and weekend or nonovernight travel, on the other, no visitation rate at a given park has been computed or plotted for residents of the state within which that park is located. Nearly all out-of-state visitation to most national parks represents vacation trips, however, and it is a reasonable assumption that over the range of distances represented in the data, travel costs tend to be approximately linearly dependent on distance. If so, the decline in visitation rates as distances increase should yield $d = 1$, if distance affects R_{ij} only by retarding travel through increased cost. But *if a park's attraction actually wanes* as such, besides being *counteracted* by increased travel cost, then d should be larger. The fact that $d > 1.0$ for Mount Rainier and Shenandoah can therefore be tentatively construed as supporting Hypothesis 3 in the theory of valuing that was presented in Chapter 5. That hypothesis expected the desiring which results from a given value to vary inversely with the value-space distance between valuer and desideratum. Where the desideratum is a visit to a national park, the physical distance separating the prospective visitor's residence from the park is certainly a principal dimension of the relevant value space. It is the dimension that has to vary from state to state just because their relative locations on the map are not identical. If they share a common culture, then there would presumably be little or no systematic differences between states on other value-space dimensions. The steeper slope for the Eastern states in the left half of Figure 3 thus suggests the effect for them of some additional dimension of value space besides physical distance. It must be a dimension correlated with physical distance if it has the effect of raising the exponent on D_{ij}.

Kepler's observation that orbital times vary with a power of planet-to-sun distances that is greater than 1.0 led to the inference that orbital motions depend on a force whose magnitude varies inversely with distance from its solar source. In the same manner, the discovery that national park visitation rates vary inversely with a power of state-to-park distances that exceeds 1.0 can be taken to imply that park attraction wanes as the distance of one's residence from a park increases. I have not said that park attraction must depend on park proximity *because* gravitational attraction varies with proximity to a massive body. It was that kind of "proof" by analogy which early sociologists were often guilty of pursuing and which a later generation has wisely sought to outgrow. What I have done is to use the physical model heuristically to call attention to the *possibility* that the distance exponent might be greater than 1.0, and to suggest what that might mean. Then I have turned to data and shown empirically that a larger exponent does in fact apply. I have interpreted this finding to mean that people who live farther away from a national park actually have less desire to visit it than those living near it. Visitation rates decrease more rapidly than distance increases because of the combined effects of reduced desire and increased travel cost. The theoretical significance of such an inference is not impaired by the fact that a physical analogy helped bring it to light.

Note the difference between this heuristic use of a gravitational model and the allegedly gravitational formula imported into sociology by Zipf and Dodd, which implied that R_{ij} would tend to be inversely proportional to the first power of D_{ij}. Not only did their model mistakenly equate population with mass, as was pointed out in Chapter 6, but it made no allowance for the dual effects of distance. Distance apparently both reduces desire for visiting a remote destination and inhibits travel to that destination by increasing travel costs. Zipf's and Dodd's formula fell far short of explaining all the variance in a matrix of R_{ij} not just because it derived a sociological hypothesis from physics but partly because it garbled the physics on which that hypothesis was based.

The Value Field

1 Size of the Exponent

From the fact that R_{ij} and D_{ij} seem to be linearly related on logarithmic coordinates it is apparent that *proportional* changes in rate of park visitation depend on *proportional* changes in distance. The exponent on distance simply specifies the relation between the two proportions.[7] From

[7] Guilford, *op. cit.*, pp. 71–72.

the slope of the double-log scattergram, it is evident that $d > 1.0$, but it remains to be shown how much it exceeds unity, and why it does so by just that much. The excess, $n = d - 1.0$, is to be interpreted as a measure of the rate at which desire to visit a park wanes as park remoteness increases. It is reasonable to suppose that n will either be an integer or some simple fraction such as $\frac{1}{2}$, $\frac{3}{4}$, or $\frac{1}{3}$, etc. Such an expectation is reasonable just because a more elaborate theory would be required to account for a value of, say, $n = 2.7143 = 19/7$. The value of $d - 1.0$ will depend on the mechanism by which desire to visit a park is diminished by remoteness from it, and it is appropriate to begin by expecting that mechanism to be simple—introducing complications if necessary later on.

2 Force-field Models

Once again, heuristic use may be made of a physical model. Since "desire to visit" means "attraction toward" a given park, its spatial variation *might* resemble such physical phenomena as gravitational, electric, or magnetic *fields*. This was suggested in Chapter 5. It is not necessary to argue that desiring *is* magnetism or gravity, but one can at least form a testable hypothesis of the manner in which desiring varies with distance from the desideratum by looking at the way in which magnetic, electrical, or gravitational attractions vary with distance from a magnet, a charged body, or a massive body. Once formed, of course, the hypothesis must be empirically tested; its validity depends on data, not on the facile use of analogy to formulate it.

Electric fields are mathematically similar to gravitational fields even though electrical interactions are quite distinct from gravitational interactions. Therefore there is no justification for insisting that value fields, because they pertain to a different kind of phenomena, could not mathematically resemble gravitational fields. It happens that Coulomb's law is exactly isomorphic with Newton's law of gravity.[8] Coulomb's law says that between two bodies with charges Q and q, the force of repulsion is given by

$$F = K \frac{Qq}{D^2} \tag{2}$$

and this is clearly analogous to Newton's law of gravity, which is

$$F = G \frac{Mm}{D^2} \tag{3}$$

Of course the law of gravity relates forces to masses, and the masses can be measured inertially (and thus independently of any assumption that

[8] Cf. J. J. G. McCue, *The World of Atoms*, 2d ed. New York: The Ronald Press Company, 1963, pp. 280–281.

the law is valid) whereas Coulomb's law provides a definition of relative charge.[9] But this is not actually a fundamental difference because once the relative magnitudes of a series of charges have been defined by Coulomb's law, various combinations of charges can be added together, and the forces between various pairs of sums can then be measured to provide an empirical test of the law. And while it is a force of repulsion, rather than attraction, that is given by Coulomb's law, when Q and q have opposite signs then we get a negative repulsion—or an attraction.

In the case of gravity, the law can also be stated

$$F = \gamma m \tag{4}$$

where gamma is the gravitational field strength at a given location, and m is the mass of a body acted upon at that location. The value of gamma is independent of the body acted upon, and depends only on the masses and locations of other bodies. In interstellar space it could be determined by the field of a single body if all others were sufficiently remote.[10] From Equation 3, it is obvious that with all other bodies sufficiently remote, then

$$\gamma = \frac{GM}{D^2} \tag{5}$$

Electric field strength is given by[11]

$$E = \frac{KQ}{D^2} \tag{6}$$

which has exactly the same form.

3 Adapting the Formula

Before simply postulating a similar formula for value-field strength, we would be wise to consider the reason for the exponent of 2 on distance in Equations 5 and 6. A magnetic field can be graphically represented in a form that is widely familiar by sprinkling iron filings on a sheet of white paper resting on one end of a bar magnet. They form into lines that radiate in all directions from the perimeter of the magnetic pole. Though there is no comparably easy way of producing their graphic image, electrical and gravitational fields can similarly be represented by lines of force. Field strength, then, is represented by the relative density of the lines of force in a given region. Nearer the source they are more

---

[9] *Ibid.*, p. 282.
[10] *Ibid.*, pp. 88–89.
[11] Cf. *ibid.*, pp. 283–284; and R. E. Peierls, *The Laws of Nature.* London: George Allen & Unwin, Ltd., 1955, pp. 41–42.

dense, and farther away from it they are more spread out. In the case of an isolated point charge, the lines of force would radiate in all directions in three-dimensional space and would be straight. Their density at a given distance from the source would thus vary inversely with the *square* of the distance (since the number of lines is constant, but the area of the spherical surface they penetrate at a given distance from the origin depends on the square of that radius).[12] The exponent on distance is 2 in Coulomb's and Newton's laws, then, because they deal with interactions in three-dimensional physical space.

Travel to national parks takes place in what amounts to a two-dimensional space. The parks and their visitors are located on a surface—which is, for practical purposes, flat. Accordingly, the only "lines of force" we need to consider in estimating field strength as a function of distance are the lines we imagine to radiate from each park in all directions on an approximately flat surface. (It seems unlikely that the curvature of the earth would have to be taken into account as long as we confine our attention to travel over no larger a sector of its surface than is encompassed within the continental United States.)

In the present problem, then, the relevant value space is approximated by a mere two dimensions of physical space, and the density of lines of force intersecting a circle (rather than a sphere) at a given distance from the origin will vary inversely with the first power of its radius (rather than with the square of the radius). This applies only to the Western culture area, of course, among whose states there is presumed to be no variation in any dimensions of value space other than physical proximity to the parks. For states in the Eastern culture area, on the other hand, the effective dimensionality of value space is apparently greater than that of a surface.

In noting this difference between the structure of value fields motivating vacation travel and the structure of gravitational, electric, and magnetic fields, I hope to show that my heuristic use of such models is no "slavish imitation" of physics. Some of the forays into social physics in the past have not been altogether innocent of such conceptual servitude. Such an approach would simply have taken it for granted that field strength always diminishes with the *square* of distance, whatever the universe of discourse.

The strength of the value field by which a given national park is seen as a desirable place to visit should vary inversely with the first power of the distance between a given location and the park in question. For different parks, the field strength at a given distance ought to be expected to vary directly with some quantity characteristic of the park and analogous to M or Q in Equations 5 and 6. Without implying any *identity* between a park's characteristic attractiveness and the mass of a material body, I shall use M_j to denote the quantity which for park j is *analogous*

[12] Peierls, *op. cit.*, pp. 46–47.

to the mass of a body generating a gravitational field. The value-field strength at a given location could then be given by

$$v_{ij} = \frac{aM_j}{D_{ij}} \tag{7}$$

where a is some constant of proportionality.

By analogy with Equation 4, then, the force tending to accelerate R_{ij} would be

$$F_{ij} = v_{ij}m_i \tag{8}$$

where m_i is a property of state i measuring its degree of susceptibility to the attraction of park j. Such a property ought to be considered an aspect of culture and might be supposed to have something to do with the degree of institutionalization of the national park idea and of recreational habits in relation thereto. Within an approximately homogeneous culture area, however, m_i should be approximately constant for all states, and can be ignored, so that Equation 8 simplifies to

$$F_{ij} = v_{ij} \tag{9}$$

Thus the force tending to accelerate park visitation rates is expected to be proportional to the ratio of "park mass" and intervening distance. But again, discretion requires that differences as well as similarities between physical interactions, such as gravity, and sociocultural interactions, such as park visitation, be carefully considered.

4 Mental Forces and Social Forces

The value field generated by M_j only "exists" *in the minds* of the people whose residences are scattered among the various states and whose habits of leaving home annually for a vacation trip make them potential park visitors. Strictly speaking, the force F_{ij} cannot propel them as physical bodies toward park j. If they go to park j, it will generally be by automobile, and it will be the kinetic energy released by burning gasoline that will actually propel them. It will be the expenditure of money for such gasoline, for food and lodging, and for the other expenses of travel that will constitute the *social* force which interacts with the resistive effects of distance to yield R_{ij}. I propose to call that social force f_{ij}, and to regard it as a response to F_{ij}. The next step in predicting the magnitude of R_{ij}, then, is to specify the form of the function relating f_{ij} to F_{ij}. The solution is not hard to find.

Long ago, Ward suggested that the psychological law most likely to be important to sociology—among those known in his day—was "the well-known Weber-Fechner law that sensations represent the logarithms of their stimuli."[13] It ought to be applicable in the present instance where a relation is sought between a force f_{ij}, which can move some fraction of the residents of state i across the land between their homes and park j, and a clearly nonphysical force F_{ij}, which arises from a *conception* of the desirable—a value. We are confronted with the relation of mind and matter, the very sort of problem Fechner was trying to solve. Fechner's solution was based on the supposition that an arithmetic series of mental intensities might be linked to a geometric series of physical stimulus energies.[14]

Fechner's idea might have been empirically meaningless and therefore theoretically sterile if he had not made an assumption that rendered mental intensities measurable. He assumed the mental equality of all "just noticeable differences" between stimuli.[15] Such an assumption was as justified as Newton's equating of the successive time intervals in which equal-distance intervals are successively traversed by a moving body subject to no net force (Axiom I). By means of Fechner's assumption, mental intensities (or a behavioral result of them) could be measured and compared with physical stimulus intensities. For varied kinds of phenomena, and for limited ranges of the variables, responses were found to vary in proportion to the logarithm of the stimulus. Fechner argued that the logarithmic relationship actually occurred within the mental realm. Excitation of receptors was assumed to be linearly proportional to the stimulus intensity, but sensation (mental response) was proportional to the logarithm of the excitation. His most cogent argument for this was to note the difference between sleep and waking and between attention and inattention, with these differences indicating that the intercept of his logarithmic equation was the limen of consciousness rather than the limen of excitation.[16]

I have found experimental support, too, for Fechner's assumption that it is in the mental link between excitation and response, rather than in the physicochemical link between stimulus and excitation, that the logarithmic relation occurs. I presented some 70 phrases to a large number of college student subjects for sorting into successive intervals on a numerical continuum. The phrases denoted various degrees of antiquity. On the basis of the collective judgments, 10 phrases located at approximately equal subjective intervals on the antiquity scale were selected for use in a questionnaire. The questionnaire listed 20 familiar events of American history, and about 50 college students were asked to select 1 of the 10 phrases to indicate how remote in time from the present each event

[13] Lester F. Ward, *Pure Sociology*. New York: The Macmillan Company, 1903, p. 160.
[14] Edwin G. Boring, *A History of Experimental Psychology*, 2d ed. New York: Appleton-Century-Crofts, Inc., 1950, p. 280.
[15] *Ibid.*, p. 290.
[16] *Ibid.*, p. 292.

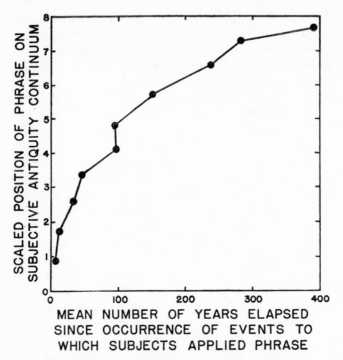

Figure 4.   Relation of subjective time to calendar time

seemed. There is a clearly curvilinear relationship between the subjective degrees of antiquity represented by the phrases and the mean calendar dates of the events associated with them. In Figure 4 it can be seen that the further back one's attention goes from the present, the longer the calendar intervals associated with constant subjective intervals. Since most of the dates in question were prior to the birth of the subjects who made the judgments and the associations, their awareness of objective calendar time was not a matter of sensory excitation by physical stimuli, but was a matter of symbolically mediated cognition. Figure 4 therefore represents the relation between a pair of cognitive processes. Its curvilinearity indicates the correctness of Fechner's supposition that it is within the mental realm that the logarithmic relation arises.

DeFleur and Larsen have shown that Fechner's law can be applied to communities as well as to individual subjects. When eight towns were stimulated by airborne leaflets, the percentage of inhabitants who learned the message approximated an arithmetic series while the stimulus intensities (ratios of leaflets dropped per capita) formed a geometric series.[17] Similarly, then, geometric variations in the stimulation provided by na-

[17] Melvin L. DeFleur and Otto N. Larsen, *The Flow of Information.* New York: Harper & Row, Publishers, Incorporated, 1958, chaps. 5 and 6.

tional parks might be expected to result in arithmetically varying responses by state populations.

Fechner's thinking on the relation of mind and matter, however, concerned a material stimulus and a mental response. In the case of F_{ij} and f_{ij} we are reversing this order, being concerned with a culturally conditioned mental stimulus and a social response that involves the physical movement of human organisms and their paraphernalia. But this reversal of the order is unimportant, as I will now show. If the transformation from a geometric series to an arithmetic series occurs *within* the mental realm, then we could just as well expect either an arithmetic series of physical events resulting from a geometric series of mental stimuli, or the more familiar arithmetic series of mental responses resulting from a geometric series of physical stimuli. For elucidating this, I shall refer to mental phenomena as "internal" and social or physical phenomena as "external" events. Fechner interpreted his law to mean that

$$E_1^n = I_2^n = I_3 \tag{10}$$

where the subscripts denote the sequential order of the events, and the equation tells us that the third event (which is internal) is proportional to some power of either the second event (which is also internal) or of the first event (which is external)—with the first and second events being linearly proportional to each other.

On the basis of Fechner's assumption that the curvilinearity occurs *within* the mental (or internal) realm, the sequence of events could be extended to include a fourth event, external and linearly dependent on the internal third event.

$$E_1^n = I_2^n = I_3 = E_4 \tag{11}$$

Experimentally, of course, psychophysics always deals with the relation of E_4 to E_1, and it is only inferred that I_3 (of which E_4 is taken to be an index) varies arithmetically as E_1 varies geometrically. It is the arithmetic variation of E_4 and the geometric variation of E_1 that is observed. Equation 11 simply asserts that the transition from geometric to arithmetic progression occurs between steps 2 and 3, rather than between 1 and 2 or between 3 and 4. If we accept this assumption of Fechner's, then in the case of a value—or conception of the desirable, a mental event—we *begin* at step 2 in the sequence. Thus we have

$$I_2^n = I_3 = E_4 \tag{12}$$

which can be simplified by omitting the middle term that is linearly related to the last term, and by changing the subscripts for greater generality, to

$$E_r = I_s^n \tag{13}$$

which says that an external response will be observed to vary arithmetically in relation to geometric variations in an internal stimulus. Or to relate a social force to a mental force,

$$f_{ij} = F_{ij}^n \tag{14}$$

This equation tells us that the magnitude of the force that accelerates physical people and their vacation paraphernalia toward a national park varies arithmetically with geometric variations in the subjective strength of a park's attraction. The human mind is like a valve which is turned by F_{ij} and which regulates the release of f_{ij}.

Throughout the above argument, I have omitted any proportionality constants and any constants representing intercepts. This was done for simplicity. Their inclusion would only have cluttered the equations without materially affecting the argument and conclusion.

From Equations 7, 9, and 14, we can write

$$f_{ij} = \left(\frac{aM_j}{D_{ij}}\right)^n \tag{15}$$

But we also know that, for R_{ij} to be approximately stable for a given state i and park j, then f_{ij} and D_{ij} must have exactly offsetting effects. Hence,

$$f_{ij} = R_{ij}D_{ij} \tag{16}$$

Consequently

$$R_{ij} = \frac{(aM_j/D_{ij})^n}{D_{ij}} \tag{17}$$

Now if we let $(aM_j)^n = b$, and $1 + n = d$, we would have

$$R_{ij} = \frac{b}{D_{ij}^d}$$

which was Equation 1 and which we already saw held for the data presented in Figure 3. Additional data conforming to this model will be presented later.

The Kepler Model

Equation 1, it will be recalled, was suggested by analogy with Kepler's third law.[18] Now we see that it can be derived from Equations 15 and 16. Newton combined his gravitational formula for centripetal force and

[18] For a statement of Kepler's third law, see V. M. Blanco and S. W. McCuskey, *Basic Physics of the Solar System*. Reading, Mass.: Addison-Wesley Publishing Company, Inc., 1961., p. 36.

the formula for centrifugal force as a function of radius of revolution, and thereby reproduced Kepler's third law. That result gave overwhelming support to Newton's inference that planetary motions which conform to Kepler's law are gravitationally and inertially determined. Equations 15 and 16 in the present argument are not direct counterparts of the centripetal and centrifugal force formulas which Newton combined, but there is an obvious general similarity in the reasoning. Newton had to show how a planet's constant tendency to fly off into space was just offset by its constant tendency to fall inward toward the sun. For national park travel, the problem was to show how the accelerative effects of a park's attraction just offset the travel-deterring effects of intervening distance, resulting in predictable R_{ij} magnitudes.

Since the above reasoning makes due recognition of the distinction between mental and physical events, perhaps I will be pardoned if I pursue the physical analogy one step further at this point. In Kepler's third law, the exponent on distance was $\frac{3}{2}$. Without implying that I regard park visitation as a case of "orbital motion," but purely on the basis of a need for *some* hypothetical magnitude of d, I shall try the value $\frac{3}{2}$. This makes $d - 1.0 = 0.5$, and is in keeping with what I said earlier about the reasonableness of expecting the excess over unity to be either a small integer or some simple ratio between small integers. It was actually from the use of Kepler's third law as a model that I came to the hunch that $d = \frac{3}{2}$ and that therefore $n = \frac{1}{2}$, but *the validity of the hunch does not have to depend on the plausibility of the analogy.* It can be empirically tested, and in more than one way.

Taking $d = \frac{3}{2}$, then from Equations 1 and 17, we get

$$(aM_j)^{\frac{1}{2}} = D_{ij}^{\frac{3}{2}} R_{ij} \qquad (18)$$

which means that if we take the square roots of the distances given in Table 11, multiply each square root by the corresponding distance so as to get a table of cubed square roots $(D_{ij}^{\frac{3}{2}})$, and multiply the entries in that table by the visitation rates in Table 6 (R_{ij}), all the entries in the *j*th column of the resulting matrix of products would constitute independent estimates of $(aM_j)^{\frac{1}{2}}$ for the *j*th park. That is to say, the products in a given column should be approximately constant, while the column means should be proportional to the square roots of the respective park "masses." If all entries in the *j*th column of the matrix of $D_{ij}^{\frac{3}{2}} R_{ij}$ are then divided by $(aM_j)^{\frac{1}{2}}$—i.e., by the column mean—and this is done for all columns, the entire set of quotients should approximate a constant.

In the form of an equation that can be easily compared with the models explored in Chapter 6, the present model can be written:

$$\frac{R_{ij} D_{ij}^{\frac{3}{2}}}{M_j^{\frac{1}{2}}} = k \qquad (19)$$

This differs from the equation for the Stouffer model given in Chapter 6 in this respect: it substitutes the square root of the ratio of cubed distances divided by park masses for the ratio of intervening opportunities divided by opportunities at a given park. In the same manner, it differs from the equation given in Chapter 6 for the Dodd-Zipf model, in which the variance-reducing ratio was taken to be distances divided by "park populations." As before, the model can be empirically evaluated by the following procedure. The various values of k can be normed so that their mean is equal to the mean of the visitation rates. Then the variance of the normed k can be compared with the variance of R_{ij}. The smaller this residual variance, the greater the proportion of the original variance that has been removed by application of the model, and the better the model can be said to fit the data.

It turns out that for the 1940 data given in Table 6, Equation 19 accounts for 91.8 percent of the variance. This exceeds the 73.9 percent explained by the Stouffer formula (in the sophisticated version employing the iteratively obtained opportunity coefficients). It even more conspicuously exceeds the 68.7 percent variance reduction achieved by the allegedly gravitational formula of Zipf and Dodd.

To ensure that this degree of empirical confirmation of Equation 19 was not peculiar to the 1940 batch of data, I wanted to assemble another table of visitation rates for a different year. For the year 1949, it happened, state-by-state tabulations were available for a total of 13 parks. I had not used that year's data originally because not all of the 13 parks had tabulated the same kind of information. At 5 parks, people had been counted, while at 2 others, cars were counted. Fortunately the other 6 parks had made both kinds of tabulations, counting people *and* counting cars. If tabulations of visitors were divided by state populations, and tabulations of cars were divided by state auto registrations, it might be supposed that the resulting sets of visitation rates would be sufficiently comparable to be subjected to a common analysis in a combined table of R_{ij}. I thought it important to check this supposition, however. I found that the automobile visitation rates at Crater Lake for 23 Western states averaged 8 percent higher than person visitation rates at that same park, but the product-moment correlation coefficient was .994 between the two sets of rates. For Glacier, automobile rates averaged 2 percent higher than person rates, with a correlation of .995 between the two sets. For Mesa Verde, automobile rates averaged 6 percent higher, with .992 correlation between them and the person rates. For Mount Rainier, automobile rates averaged 13 percent *less* than person rates, but even so there was a correlation of .998 between them. For Rocky Mountain, automobile rates averaged 5 percent less than person rates, with .996 correlation between the two sets. For Shenandoah, automobile rates averaged 17 percent higher than person rates, with the correlation dropping to .988. In view of these relationships it seemed reasonable to go ahead and pool the two kinds of rates in one R_{ij} matrix, recognizing simply that there might be some small amount of error in the resulting estimates of M_j.

In Table 12, visitation rates computed from tabulations of people are given for the following national parks: Bryce Canyon, Crater Lake, Glacier, Grand Canyon, Hot Springs, Kings Canyon and Sequoia (combined), Mammoth Cave, Mesa Verde, Mount Rainier, Rocky Mountain, and Shenandoah. Automobile visitation rates are given for Lassen Volcanic and Yosemite, and are assumed to reflect fairly accurately what the person visitation rates for those two parks would have been, had they been available. In Table 13, distances are given for those parks not included earlier in Table 11.

The result for these 1949 data was that the model given in Equation 19 accounted for 92.6 percent of the visitation rate variance. The empirical support for the model previously provided by the 1940 data was evidently not peculiar to that particular year's visitation pattern.

The Meaning of the Model

1 Parks Attract

The significance of Kepler's third law was that it implied that the sun provides the force which keeps the planets in orbit. Cohen has pointed out that the fact that the planets' speeds were so precisely dependent on their respective distances from the sun could not be explained in any other way.[19] I used the Kepler law to suggest reasoning which led to an empirically effective explanation of variations in national park visitation rates in terms of distance. It is therefore tempting to draw the parallel conclusion, that Equation 19 implies that people are *drawn* to the national parks by a force that depends on characteristics of the parks—rather than being merely impelled outward from their places of residence either by objectionable features of their environments or by normative pressures requiring people to "go away" for a vacation. Caution is required, however, since Equation 19 depends on Equations 7 and 9 in which F_{ij} was asserted to vary inversely with the *first* power of D_{ij}, rather than with the second power of distance that diminishes the force of physical gravity.

Newton showed that for any orbiting body, if the periodic time of its revolution was any power of the radius of its orbit, R^s, than its velocity would be inversely proportional to R^{s-1} and the centripetal force required to keep it in orbit would be inversely proportional to R^{2s-1}. The perfect

[19] On the significance of Kepler's third law, see I. Bernard Cohen, *The Birth of a New Physics*. Garden City, N.Y.: Anchor Books, Doubleday & Company, Inc., 1960, p. 144.

Table 12 National park visitation rates, 1949 (number of persons entering park per 100,000 state population, or cars per 100,000 state registration)

	Bryce Canyon (people)	Crater Lake (people)	Glacier (people)	Grand Canyon (people)	Hot Springs (people)	Kings Canyon and Sequoia (people)	Mammoth Cave (people)	Mesa Verde (people)	Mt. Rainier (people)	Rocky Mountain (people)	Shenandoah (people)	Lassen Volcanic (cars)	Yosemite (cars)
Arizona	738.2	183.9	136.8	1128.3	68.3	83.3	34.0	214.1	115.4	684.9	61.2	12.1	668.2
California	596.6	1167.4	240.2	···	42.6	···	23.6	89.0	354.5	374.0	54.6	···	···
Colorado	353.9	96.8	187.0	871.6	84.2	96.8	28.6	···	111.5	···	60.7	21.2	226.7
Idaho	595.8	580.5	1060.0	527.2	17.7	78.1	23.2	64.4	320.4	259.3	38.4	37.9	251.5
Illinois	102.6	43.6	123.0	416.6	687.5	58.1	276.4	43.6	86.5	1512.2	197.1	9.4	178.5
Indiana	74.6	37.1	60.2	406.4	138.4	53.7	572.3	29.0	58.6	620.5	320.9	4.8	130.4
Iowa	127.7	67.7	164.0	450.2	176.6	63.1	84.7	62.4	136.1	3017.0	118.0	9.4	128.9
Kansas	101.9	89.7	107.6	635.7	183.2	88.7	78.0	165.4	132.4	4654.8	107.0	14.7	173.4
Michigan	88.4	33.8	88.5	311.4	110.1	44.3	257.3	27.4	66.4	352.0	310.1	5.4	105.3
Minnesota	78.0	58.7	339.9	283.9	142.4	41.2	27.8	22.6	185.2	426.2	55.9	5.4	90.6
Missouri	64.2	34.8	62.2	417.1	373.3	8.0	72.8	50.7	60.5	1655.0	109.7	.6	147.4
Montana	220.4	182.6	···	326.9	48.0	53.8	22.5	34.4	312.3	179.8	24.4	53.4	131.6
Nebraska	147.8	96.2	159.4	429.8	126.4	64.8	45.2	87.0	143.8	6838.3	77.9	12.4	141.0
Nevada	1333.8	752.2	286.0	1807.0	66.9	321.0	17.2	109.6	182.2	579.6	52.9	898.1	1690.5
New Mexico	182.8	72.9	70.2	1400.5	61.3	113.5	26.6	609.3	59.8	706.2	48.8	29.4	340.5
North Dakota	47.4	60.5	750.1	231.6	219.8	28.0	19.8	13.9	234.3	209.5	23.3	2.2	63.0
Oklahoma	49.0	45.8	54.4	573.9	578.8	99.1	61.1	101.5	51.4	1172.2	79.1	12.0	171.0
Oregon	185.1	···	602.4	431.1	16.4	97.2	13.6	43.1	1392.6	198.7	42.2	266.6	346.5
South Dakota	63.9	84.2	243.7	260.4	136.1	40.2	19.5	31.2	135.3	666.7	42.0	4.4	83.5
Texas	72.8	36.4	40.8	499.3	289.5	65.7	52.4	96.1	45.5	1072.5	130.5	8.7	140.9
Utah	···	165.1	523.2	2101.2	15.6	74.1	12.5	420.9	189.4	627.0	36.4	60.5	357.2
Washington	241.6	1293.5	1058.2	388.4	15.0	69.1	20.0	35.1	···	143.8	44.4	117.2	236.4
Wisconsin	78.5	41.5	153.5	250.7	156.5	42.0	117.8	26.6	90.3	476.2	96.5	6.6	111.3
Wyoming	379.8	170.0	604.0	557.0	67.5	92.8	39.7	127.4	119.1	4679.8	67.1	33.3	225.4

Table 13   Distances from 24 states to seven national parks (in 100s of miles)

	Bryce Canyon	Glacier	Grand Canyon	Hot Springs	Kings Canyon– Sequoia	Mammoth Cave	Lassen Volcanic
Arizona	2.8	10.4	...	10.8	4.4	14.3	7.0
California	4.1	8.9	4.5	14.9	...	18.2	...
Colorado	3.8	8.3	4.2	7.7	7.3	10.4	8.4
Idaho	4.8	3.2	5.8	13.7	6.0	15.6	4.7
Illinois	12.5	13.5	12.8	4.5	16.1	2.5	16.9
Indiana	13.9	15.0	14.2	5.3	17.4	2.0	18.3
Iowa	10.3	11.0	10.9	5.3	13.9	5.0	14.4
Kansas	7.6	10.7	7.8	4.0	11.2	6.6	12.3
Michigan	14.8	14.1	15.3	8.3	18.2	5.0	18.4
Minnesota	10.9	9.5	11.7	8.2	14.2	7.4	14.0
Missouri	10.9	13.0	10.9	2.9	14.2	3.4	15.3
Montana	6.9	...	8.0	12.4	8.9	14.0	7.2
Nebraska	7.2	8.6	7.7	6.2	10.8	7.8	11.2
Nevada	3.0	6.9	3.5	13.3	2.1	16.3	2.9
New Mexico	4.4	10.9	4.0	7.3	7.2	11.1	9.5
North Dakota	9.2	6.3	10.1	9.8	12.0	10.1	11.3
Oklahoma	8.2	12.3	8.2	2.8	11.9	6.2	13.2
Oregon	6.5	4.6	7.3	16.1	5.7	18.5	2.8
South Dakota	7.8	7.2	8.6	8.0	11.1	8.9	11.1
Texas	8.9	14.3	8.4	4.5	11.7	8.2	14.0
Utah	...	6.8	2.4	11.0	4.2	13.8	5.3
Washington	8.1	3.1	9.2	16.9	8.0	18.7	5.1
Wisconsin	12.4	11.8	13.0	7.3	16.0	5.5	16.2
Wyoming	4.6	5.3	5.6	9.9	7.4	11.8	7.2

matching of such a centripetal force by a gravitational force obeying the inverse square law was predicted, then, in the case where orbital periods varied with $R^{\frac{1}{2}}$ in accordance with Kepler's law.[20] Since F_{ij} does *not* conform to the inverse square law, it is not possible simply to extend Newton's reasoning about the motions of material bodies to cover the patterns in park visitation data.

There may nevertheless be merit once again in making purely heuristic use of the physical model. If it cannot simply be argued *mathematically* that Equation 19 implies that the national parks are the sources of the travel-inducing forces shaping patterns of park visitation rates, it is nevertheless reasonable to *suppose* that they are. The supposition can then be

[20] Florian Cajori (ed.), *Sir Isaac Newton's Mathematical Principles of Natural Philosophy and His System of the World*. Berkeley, Calif.: University of California Press, 1962, p. 46.

checked by comparing instances in which it is most reasonable with other instances in which it is less reasonable and seeing whether the applicability of Equation 19 varies accordingly. It so happens that separate tabulations have been preserved for a number of travel years for the five separate entrances to Yellowstone National Park. These data can be analyzed in such a way as to shed light on this issue.

Not all persons who visit Yellowstone would regard it as the exclusive or even the principal destination of their trip. The Yellowstone visit may be part of a multidestination itinerary, and may in some instances be rather incidental to the process of getting to or returning from an ulterior destination. If a comparison could be made between visitation rate patterns for visitors mainly interested in seeing Yellowstone versus those visiting it quite incidentally on a trip to some ulterior place, then Equation 19 should be more applicable in the former case than in the latter. Visitation rates for incidental visitors should be more dependent on distances from their homes to their ulterior destinations than on distances to Yellowstone. When the ulterior destinations are quite far from Yellowstone, then Equation 19 should not be expected to fit visitation rates and distances from home state to the park.

For each state in our Western culture area, some of the entrances to Yellowstone are on the near side of the park and others are on what is the far side in respect to that state. Persons entering the park on the side nearer their homes may or may not be going on to ulterior destinations before returning home. But persons entering by the "back door" have quite probably already been to some ulterior destination. If it was a long way from the park, and especially if it was unlike the park, then the inclusion of such visitors in the back-door visitation rates should make them *not fit* the pattern described by Equation 19. By sorting the states into two categories in respect to each entrance so as to distinguish states for which it is a front door from those for which it is a back door, we can make a distinction between tabulations of apparently outward-bound travelers versus apparently homeward-bound travelers. This amounts to a crude distinction between a batch of travelers containing some unknown proportion of incidental visitors and a batch presumably containing a higher proportion of incidental visitors.

It does not follow, however, that Equation 19 should apply to front-door tabulations and not to back-door tabulations. The problem is not that simple. There are differences between the five entrances in regard to what kinds of ulterior destinations they imply in the itineraries imputed to homeward-bound entrants. For example, most persons entering Yellowstone from the South might be presumed to have visited nearby Grand-Teton National Park. Its nearness, and the fact that this possible ulterior destination is also a national park, suggest that for the south entrance to Yellowstone, there might be little difference between the visitation rate patterns for the front-door states and the back-door states. If anything, tourists from those states for which this is a back door and who seem therefore to have gone out of their way to see Grand Teton "en route" to Yellowstone might be supposed to include slightly *fewer* visitors for whom the two parks jointly were only an incidental destination on their way to do business or visit relatives in some remote city.

The east entrance would be quite a different case. Persons from states to the west of Yellowstone are unlikely to be entering the park from the east unless they are returning from some nonpark destination which in most cases will have been relatively remote from this park. If Equation 19 has the meaning I have attributed to it in deriving it, then it should *not* fit visitation rates for homeward-bound travelers using the east entrance.

The northeast entrance would be an intermediate case. More persons for whom Yellowstone was an incidental destination would be included among homeward-bound than among outward-bound visitors using this entrance, but the difference should be less conspicuous than for the east entrance. The scenery along the route outside the northeast entrance (through the Beartooth Mountains) is more spectacular than the drive through the Big Horn Mountains along the route to or from the east entrance. It even resembles the high tundra along the Trail Ridge Road in Rocky Mountain National Park. Thus a higher proportion of the entrants coming in by the northeast back door might only have been to a quite nearby ulterior destination (whose scenic character is nearly of national park quality, at that). Furthermore, people coming in from the northeast would be less likely than those coming in through the east entrance to have been to any of the major Midwestern cities as ulterior destinations.

The north entrance would resemble the south entrance. Urban destinations to the north of Yellowstone are almost nonexistent. Visitors for whom the north entrance is a back door to Yellowstone might be supposed in many instances to have gone first to Glacier National Park.

The west entrance is accessible from due west only by minor roads. The main roads which lead to this entrance come down from the north and northwest or up from the south. Hence some of the homeward-bound people from the south and east who had first visited Glacier might enter Yellowstone by the west entrance as a back door. Or people from the Midwest making a vacation loop might enter Yellowstone's west entrance if they had first been to any of the numerous national parks in Utah, Arizona, California, Oregon, or Washington. Prior visits to these parks would generally augment D_{ij} by hundreds of miles, but these increments would be only minor fractions of their total mileage for visitors from most of the more populous communities in the Midwest, far to the east of Yellowstone. Visitors from states west of Yellowstone, however, have not obviously been subjected to any screening process implied in having visited other parks prior to entering Yellowstone by the west gate, for that is simply the gate nearest their homes. It is easily possible that for many of them, Yellowstone is but a way station en route to ulterior destinations further east. Such ulterior destinations would make proportionally greater differences in D_{ij} for them than visits to other parks west of Yellowstone would make in the D_{ij} for homeward-bound visitors from states east of Yellowstone. In general, then, Equation 19 ought to fit west entrance homeward-bound visitation rates better than it would fit outward-bound patterns for that gate. But the difference would be considerably less than the reverse difference for the east entrance.

In Table 14, the five entrances are listed, along with the states for which each is a front door and for which each is a back door. For each batch of data, in each of six years, the percentage of variance reduction achieved by Equation 19 is given. In general, the pattern of these percentages is in accord with the expectations specified in the preceding discussion. In short, the model best fits those batches of data to which it could most reasonably be applied by assuming national parks to be the source of F_{ij}, and it either achieves less variance reduction or actually enlarges the variance in instances where that assumption cannot be made. Empirical support is thus given to the inference that the travel patterns described by Equation 19 are shaped by forces of *attraction* to the national parks.

2 Approach to Equilibrium

I have argued that there are institutionalized values which so define the characteristics of national parks that the latter exert an attractive force on persons holding those values. I have also said that intervening distances impede travel to the national parks. Visitation rates at the various parks can therefore be considered an expression of some balance between these opposing factors. These rates will be stable, that is, when the travel-inducing park values and the travel-reducing effects of distance are in equilibrium. Equation 19 can be construed as describing the equilibrium condition. When there is an excess of either the travel-inducing or the travel-reducing factor, however, Equation 19 should be expected to fit visitation rates less well than when these factors are in balance.

Since the national park system is a relatively young institution, it is likely that park visitation rates have only recently approached equilibrium magnitudes. For a particular park, taken as an example, it can be readily shown that more recent data fit Equation 19 better than earlier data. Only 52.6 percent of the variance among Western States' visitation rates at Crater Lake National Park in 1930 was accounted for by Equation 19.

Table 14   Comparison of variance reduction percentages for Equation 19 applied to outward-bound vs. homeward-bound visitors entering Yellowstone

	South entrance	East entrance	Northeast entrance	North entrance	West entrance
States for which the entrance is a front door	Arizona California Colorado Idaho Illinois Indiana Iowa Kansas Missouri Nebraska Nevada New Mexico Oklahoma Oregon Texas Utah	Colorado Illinois Indiana Iowa Kansas Michigan Minnesota Missouri Montana Nebraska New Mexico North Dakota Oklahoma South Dakota Texas Wisconsin	Illinois Indiana Iowa Kansas Michigan Minnesota Missouri Montana Nebraska North Dakota South Dakota Wisconsin	Michigan Minnesota Montana North Dakota Oregon South Dakota Washington Wisconsin	Arizona California Idaho Montana Nevada Oregon Utah Washington
Percent variance reduction in					
1935	83.5	71.9	70.1	78.6	20.6
1937	83.2	50.4	86.0	77.0	30.4
1938	83.8	46.2	87.0	74.8	21.5
1939	84.6	38.8	86.1	73.1	29.7
1940	81.3	19.9	84.9	72.8	25.8
1948	83.5	58.5	83.6	83.6	27.2

By 1940, the model accounted for 74.1 percent of the variance. In 1950, the model accounted for 87.4 percent of the variance. Crater Lake happened to be one of the few parks continuing to make state-by-state tabulations after 1952. For 1955, the model explained 88.3 percent of the variance.

These findings suggest a trend toward an equilibrium condition, but it remains to show *how* the visitation rates are modified with the passage of time in the direction of closer fit to Equation 19. In this connection, note that the distances separating potential visitors from potential park destinations already would have been having their travel-deterring effects before the parks were legislatively created. Park values, however, would hardly have had much effect on inducing travel to a given area before that area had been designated a national park. (A few souls, mostly living nearby, might be expected to know the natural features of the area and to use

Table 14 (continued)   Comparison of variance reduction percentages for Equation 19 applied to outward-bound vs. homeward-bound visitors entering Yellowstone

	South entrance	East entrance	Northeast entrance	North entrance	West entrance
States for which the entrance is a back door	Michigan Minnesota Montana North Dakota South Dakota Washington Wisconsin	Arizona California Idaho Nevada Oregon Utah Washington	Arizona California Colorado Idaho Nevada New Mexico Oklahoma Oregon Texas Utah Washington	Arizona California Colorado Idaho Illinois Indiana Iowa Kansas Missouri Nebraska Nevada New Mexico Oklahoma Texas Utah	Colorado Illinois Indiana Iowa Kansas Michigan Minnesota Missouri Nebraska New Mexico North Dakota Oklahoma South Dakota Texas Wisconsin
Percent variance reduction in					
1935	84.0	−230.9*	48.5	86.1	84.6
1937	84.9	−122.3*	30.1	90.5	86.3
1938	90.4	−112.9*	49.4	91.1	86.1
1939	91.9	− 89.0*	39.0	90.7	72.8
1940	85.3	− 80.1*	36.2	92.0	82.0
1948	79.0	− 68.3*	55.1	95.6	79.8

* Indicates Equation 19 enlarged variance rather than reduced it.

it in much the way legions of visitors would eventually use it after it was given park status.) An area may be designated a national park on a specific date, but it is unlikely that its legal status or its natural features would become simultaneously known to all potential visitors at that time. The process of institutionalization is not instantaneous. It is reasonable to suppose that the probability that a person knows an area has been designated a national park and is endowed with park values will at first be higher if he lives nearby than if he lives far away. As institutionalization proceeds, however, at any given distance from the park the probability of a person's according it park status will presumably approach some upper limit.

This reasoning suggests that when a park has first been legally established we should expect R_{ij} to vary inversely with some power of D_{ij} even greater than $\frac{3}{2}$. Visitation rates will be less as distance is greater be-

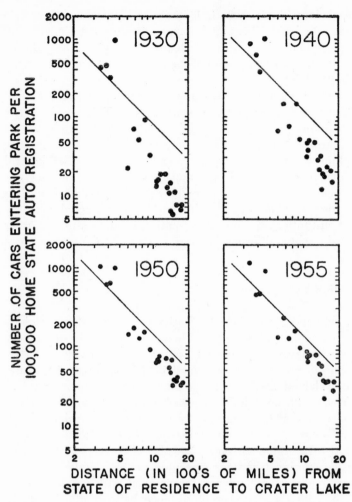

Figure 5. Changes in the relation between visitation rates and distance

cause of *three* considerations during this institutionalizing phase of a park's history: travel cost as a deterrent to visitation, value perspective by which distance weakens attraction, and the proximity-dependent probability of attributing park values to a recently established park. As time passes, and institutional values diffuse through the population, the third consideration washes out, and the steepness of the spatial gradient will decrease, tending to stabilize at $\frac{3}{2}$ in accordance with Equation 19. In the case of Crater Lake, again, this appears to be what has happened, and this would account for the improved capacity of Equation 19 to account for visitation rate variance. In Figure 5, I have stretched out the distance scale so that each logarithmic cycle is $1\frac{1}{2}$ times as long as each log cycle on the visitation rate scale. This makes it easy to represent Equation 19 with a line drawn at 45 degrees (with a draftsman's triangle). I have drawn such lines in such a way that the mean of the expected R_{ij} would be equal to the mean observed R_{ij}.

From inspection of Figure 5, one can readily see that the visitation rates have tended to increase with the passage of time. This may be partly due to improved automobiles and improved highways making travel easier (but leaving the relation at a given time between travel cost and distance presumably still linear). It may, as well, be partly due to increased general interest in national parks. But it is also apparent that visitation rates for the more remote states have tended to increase proportionately more than for the states closer to Crater Lake. This pattern is in accord with the expectation that institutionalization of the national park status of Crater Lake has involved a spatial diffusion process.

3   The Case against Voluntarism

In Chapter 1, reference was made to Stark's contention that sociology needed emancipation from naturalistic thoughtways which supposedly compel us to see social phenomena not as they "really are" but as they would have to be in order to be explained in the same way as natural phenomena are explained. Stark seemed to be advocating a more animistic approach.[21] Writers with an animistic outlook seem to assume that there is some method that is not naturalistic by which it is possible to know how things "really are," and thereby to know that naturalistic methods are misleading. If their argument is not altogether circular, then it is surely challenged by the empirical findings presented in this chapter. It seems clear that there "really is" a tendency for national park visitation rates to vary inversely with the $\frac{3}{2}$ power of distance between the homes of potential visitors and the parks that are their potential destinations. Pointing out the similarity between this pattern and Kepler's law is not creating a "fiction" as long as care is taken to show that a reasonable sociological theory of valuing can explain the pattern just as a reasonable physical theory of gravitation explained Kepler's law. Value fields, like gravitational fields, are illata. Each is legitimately invoked to account for a specified array of concreta and abstracta. Neither can account for what the other accounts for, of course. An *unwarranted* fiction would indeed have been created if the physical theory of gravitation had been used to "explain" the park visitation pattern—a social phenomenon.

Natural science no longer invokes values to explain celestial motions

[21] Werner Stark, *The Fundamental Forms of Social Thought*. New York: Fordham University Press, 1963, p. 256.

as did philosophers of a former age. I contend that it is animism rather than naturalism which asserts a fiction and distorts reality when it refuses to recognize sociological reality. The Aristotelian view of the heavens supposed that celestial bodies revolved in circular orbits (supposedly about the earth as a common center) just because their celestial character entailed circular motion. That view did not require any regular relationship between orbital periods and orbital radii, and provided no explanation for the empirical regularity so neatly summarized in Kepler's third law. Similarly, the sociological theorist who starts from a voluntaristic premise has no way of expecting any regular relationship between park visitation rates and distances, and provides no explanation for the regularity observed. Observation thus challenges voluntarism.

If national park visits result from acts of a free will—where "free" implies denial of the sociological axioms of motion stated in the previous chapter—then there would be no reason to expect persons residing at greater distances from a park to will less strongly to visit it than those living near it.

A thoroughgoing animism ought even to deny that the *implementation* of a desire for a visit to a given park would depend in any way on one's physical distance from that park, because any such dependence connects a physical variable with action by living creatures. I can hardly imagine a modern sociologist adhering to animistic principles as dogmatically as that, however. If we suppose that all sociologists would recognize the ability of distance from one's goal to impede implementation of one's desire to attain that goal, then it might be that a *somewhat* animistic sociologist (as truly as a thoroughly naturalistic one) would see that R_{ij} would vary inversely with D_{ij}. But when R_{ij} varies inversely *with the* $\frac{3}{2}$ *power* of D_{ij}, it becomes necessary to account for the additional fact expressed by the exponent. I have given an explanation which apportions part of the exponent to the travel-resisting effects of distance and part to the phenomenon of value perspective as I described it in Chapter 5. I submit that the value-perspective principle is as incompatible with full voluntarism as Newton's inverse square law of gravity was with Aristotelian cosmology.

If any reader who is animistically inclined has not by now abandoned the reading of this book, he may wonder at this point if I am suggesting that travel to national parks constitutes "involuntary" action. Unfortunately, the seeds of metaphysics have always been nourished by the imprecisions of language. To deny the assumptions of voluntar*ism* is not to assert that all action is "involuntary." I have suggested that empirical regularities in park visitation rates contradict the assumptions of free will. That is, these regularities contradict the assumed inapplicability of the inertial axiom, the axiom of proportionality of force and acceleration, and the axiom of equal and opposite action and reaction. I say such axioms do apply to human behavior. When I make the contingent statement that *unless* some social force modifies it, social action recurs in a constant pattern, I am not declaring that there are no social forces. To say human willing is not "free" is not to say humans do not will. They will in predictable ways. Visits to national parks are voluntary in the sense that virtually all persons who enter a national park wished to do so; but such visits are clearly not "voluntary" if that word is taken to mean that the visitor's desire to come was in principle unpredictable. Park visitation is voluntary also in the sense that it is generally nonobligatory, a fact whose importance I shall discuss later.

The burden of proof should be upon the defenders of animism in sociology. Animistic assumptions should be abandoned unless they can generate a better explanation than can be derived from naturalistic assumptions to account for such phenomena as the trend toward an exponent of $\frac{3}{2}$ in the relation of distance to visitation rates. Within a fully voluntaristic framework there would be no reason to expect the spatial diffusion of an area's national park status to cover a span of decades. It might just as well be conceived as instantaneous. And there would be no reason in voluntaristic premises to expect that at a given date in that diffusion period the spatial gradient among visitation rates would be steeper than it would be after institutionalization of park values was complete. Animism is certainly not vindicated merely by claiming that Equation 19 obscures "reality."

The Dimensions of Park Attractiveness

1 Measurement and Factor Analysis

Kepler's third law applied to the motion of satellites around planets, as well as to the orbiting of planets around the sun. The product of a satellite's orbital period and the $\frac{3}{2}$ power of its mean distance from the parent planet would be constant for all satellites of the same planet. The magnitude of the constant would vary from one planet to another as a function of planetary mass. Kepler's third law thus made it possible to calculate the masses of the various planets, relative to each other and to the sun, from data on their satellites' movements, and data on their own movements around the sun.[22] In a similar way, if Equation 19 provides a reasonably accurate description of the pattern of variation among national park visitation rates, then it can also yield measures of relative park attractiveness, or mass. That is, Equation 19 can be rewritten as

$$M_j^{\frac{1}{2}} = \frac{R_{ij} D_{ij}^{\frac{3}{2}}}{k} \tag{20}$$

[22] See Blanco and McCuskey, *op. cit.*, p. 38.

It will be instructive now to compare measures obtained from the 1940 data for 12 parks by the various approaches. In Chapter 6, opportunity coefficients were calculated in accord with the Stouffer model, and normed so that their mean value was unity. I have called them "Stouffer coefficients." For comparison, we can set k in Equation 20 just large enough to make the mean $M_j^{\frac{1}{2}}$ equal unity also. I shall call these normed values "Kepler coefficients." The "park population" figures (total 1940 visits per park) which purport to be measures of park attractiveness (in the model of Zipf and Dodd) can also be normed to a mean of unity for direct comparison. The successive-intervals scale values, however, cannot be normed, since they are not calibrated from an absolute zero point. In other respects they are, of course, cardinal numbers and can be manipulated accordingly. They can be added and subtracted (with some restrictions), but they cannot be multiplied and divided. In short, they do not yet constitute a "ratio scale." Establishing an absolute zero would involve addition or subtraction of some unknown constant. But adding or subtracting a constant does not alter the correlation of a variable with another variable. So the lack of an absolute zero does not preclude calculating correlations between these scale values and the other measures, even though the operation of multiplication is involved in obtaining product-moment correlations.

Table 15   Comparison of four measures of national park attractiveness

	"Park popula-tion"*	Stouffer coefficient*	Kepler coefficient*	Mean successive-intervals scale value
Crater Lake	.616	.789	.636	2.326
Grand Teton	.252	1.539	.797	3.092
Great Smoky Mtns.	2.104	.677	1.313	2.416
Kings Canyon	.494	.434	.254	2.670
Lassen Volcanic	.257	.289	.117	2.300
Mesa Verde	.088	.213	.156	2.154
Mount Rainier	1.117	.830	.664	2.585
Rocky Mountain	1.535	1.573	2.108	2.528
Sequoia	.689	.642	.453	2.833
Shenandoah	2.324	.480	.786	1.920
Yellowstone	1.286	3.506	3.693	3.146
Yosemite	1.239	1.027	1.023	3.182

* Normed so the mean of each column is 1.000.

In Table 15 these four ways of measuring park attractiveness are compared. It is evident from inspection that they tend to be positively associated with one another. An analysis of the pattern of intercorrelations should further illuminate issues developed in this and previous chapters. The product-moment correlations are given in Table 16.

I have tried to show how different are the rationales for the Kepler model, the Stouffer model, and the Dodd and Zipf model, respectively. Yet each in its own way "explains" a substantial portion of the variance among visitation rates, and each model employs as an explanatory variable some purported measure of park attractiveness. It is not surprising, therefore, that these measures tend to be positively intercorrelated. The Kepler coefficients obtained from Equation 20, and the opportunity coefficients obtained from the Stouffer model, are also positively correlated with the successive-intervals scale values. But there is a small *negative* correlation between the scale values and "park populations" or total visits. This negative sign casts some doubt on the otherwise plausible notion that the four variables represented in Table 14 are really alternative measures of a single underlying factor. Moreover, when this notion is explicitly tested by attempting to calculate Spearman "general factor" loadings from Table 16,

Table 16   Correlations among four measures of national park attractiveness

	"Park popula- tion"	Stouffer coefficient	Kepler coefficient	Mean successive- intervals scale value
"Park population"		.178	.450	− .182
Stouffer coefficient	.178		.931	.629
Kepler coefficient	.450	.931		.434
Mean successive-intervals *scale value*	− .182	.629	.434	

two of the variables come out with loadings in excess of 1.0, which is a mathematical absurdity. It is therefore evident that more than one dimension is involved in the data of Table 15.

As an alternative to the general factor analysis, which is empirically unworkable in this case, Hotelling's method of "principal components" analysis[23] reveals meaningful relationships among the four measures of park attractiveness. Table 17 contains the loadings of the four variables on each of the four principal axes. All four variables have positive loadings on the first factor. That factor accounts for 60.4 percent of the variance in Table 15. I propose to call it the "recreational desirability factor." The two variables with highest loadings on Factor I are the measures of park attractiveness based on the Kepler and the Stouffer models. By squaring the factor loadings we can see that Factor I also accounts for nearly half of the variance in the successive-intervals scale values, but less than one-eighth of the variance in "park population." In short, the coefficients obtained from either the Kepler or the Stouffer models constitute practically pure measures of Factor I, and this factor is a major dimension of park

[22] See Godfrey H. Thomson, *The Factorial Analysis of Human Ability*. Boston: Houghton Mifflin Company, 1939, chap. 5.

Table 17　Principal axis factor matrix

	Factor I loadings	Factor II loadings	Factor III loadings	Factor IV loadings
"Park population"	.338	.889	.310	.029
Stouffer coefficient	.968	− .100	− .205	.102
Kepler coefficient	.952	.215	− .196	− .097
Mean successive-intervals scale value	.677	− .607	.418	− .015

ratings by judges, but is not a major determiner of a park's total visits. The "park populations" are very far from being pure measures of Factor I. It is clear from the model developed in the present chapter why this should be so. Park tabulations of total visits should depend, I have argued, on park attractiveness *and* on proximity of parks to sources of visitors (i.e., populated areas). Park location would have nothing to do with Factor I, except by sheer coincidence. It is not an attribute of the desideratum, but a relation in value space between desideratum and valuer.

The successive-intervals scale values are appreciably loaded with the first factor, but they are almost equally loaded with Factor II. Factor II is only negligibly associated with the Kepler and Stouffer coefficients. It is *negatively* correlated with the successive-intervals scale values almost as much as the first factor was positively correlated with them. And Factor II has a high positive correlation with "park populations." Thus, if we want to ascertain the position of a national park on the dimension represented by Factor II, we could say that parks which are relatively crowded and have low scale values define one end of this continuum, and that parks which are sparsely populated with visitors and have high scale values define the other end. Accordingly, I think this could appropriately be termed the "wilderness-invasion factor," since many of the scale judges testified that wilderness qualities (and absence of crowds and crowd-serving facilities) were a principal criterion in their judgments. This factor accounts for 30.3 percent of the variance in the data of Table 15.

Factor III, which only accounts for 8.8 percent of the variance, has negative loadings on the first two variables, but of small enough magnitude to be considered negligible. It has positive loadings both on the scale values and on total visits. Any interpretation of this factor must be considered tentative because less than one-tenth of the variance is involved. Perhaps, though, it could be called the "popularity factor"—by which I mean to imply that unlike the first two factors this one suggests a slight tendency for scaled attractiveness to depend on how many people visit a national park, *independently* of its recreational opportunities or of any property analogous to gravitational mass. Such an interpretation focuses on the difference between the patterns of loadings for Factor III versus Factors I and II. It might be inferred that in Factor III is seen the impact of one's peer group being partially included among visitors to a given park. This inference depends on the following considerations. First, each judge made successive-intervals scale judgments of only those parks he had personally visited. The dependence of scale values on total visits cannot then be due to any tendency for travelers (including scale judges) to hold in higher regard those parks they have visited than those they have not visited. Second, the judges tended to downgrade the parks for overcrowding (as in Factor II). But the crowds one perceives simply as crowds and finds objectionable would usually consist solely of strangers; when friends are found among them, they often cease to be mere crowds. The greater the total visitation, the greater the chances of inclusion of one's acquaintances. Thus we can infer that the underlying *positive* association between scale values and park population that is represented in Factor III was possibly the result of a tendency to upgrade those parks the judges had visited in the company of friends (whose status as acquaintances would have exonerated their participation in park crowding!). The scale judges would probably have had subsequent reminiscent conversations with them about the mutual pleasures of their park visits, and this would tend to reinforce the favorable side of any ambivalent evaluations.

It seems to me that this is as close as we come to an indication that park visitation is *normatively* induced. Factors I and II can both be viewed as measures of park attributes. In Factor III, however, we have a suggestion that the way park attributes are perceived depends slightly on the attitudes of other persons with whom one interacts—provided the above interpretation of that factor is sound. (If a lot of my friends have visited park X, the argument goes, my interaction with them increases my tendency to perceive it as an especially attractive park.) Factor III suggests that underneath their tendency to dislike overcrowded parks, the scale judges had a latent tendency to perceive parks that *are* visited by many people as parks that *should be* visited. What is interesting is that this normative orientation seems to be so latent in regard to the evaluation and visitation of parks that it shows up only in the factor which ranks third in importance—after two others have accounted for over nine-tenths of the variance!

Factor IV involves only 0.5 percent of the variance in Table 15, and it would be quite useless to attempt any interpretation of this factor.

By squaring the entries in the fourth row of Table 17, we can see that the variance among the successive-intervals scale values for the 12 national parks whose visitation rates have been studied can be apportioned as follows: approximately 46 percent is due to Factor I, the recreational desirability component; approximately 37 percent is due to Factor II, the wilderness-invasion component; the remaining 17 percent is due to Factor III, the popularity component.

As noted earlier, the scale values computed by the method of successive intervals from frequency distributions of ordinal judgments can be treated as cardinal numbers—except that they refer to an arbitrary (rather than an intrinsic or natural) zero point. That is to say, we know how much greater the attractiveness of one park is than that of another park, but not the absolute attractiveness of either. It would be legitimate to compute ratios between two differences in the attractiveness of two pairs of parks (park Z exceeds park Y by twice the difference in attractiveness between parks W and X), but it would be meaningless and misleading to compute ratios between two park scale values.

This defect is not unique to the measurement of values, and is not a crippling defect. Other quantitative measures which people use in everyday life fall short of constituting "ratio scales" in the full sense. For example, if the temperature were 40 degrees on Monday and it warmed up to 50 degrees on Tuesday and continued warming until it reached 60 degrees on Wednesday, we could legitimately say that it had warmed up twice as much from Monday to Wednesday as from Monday to Tuesday. But we could not legitimately say that it was "50 percent warmer" on Wednesday than it had been on Monday, since the 60 degrees and the 40 degrees were both measured from the same arbitrary zero point. Zero on the Fahrenheit scale is not absolute zero, but this fact only limits, it does not destroy, the utility of thermometers calibrated in that scale.

For certain purposes, of course, measurement on a true ratio scale (with an absolute zero) is indispensable. If our successive-intervals scale values could be converted into a linearly related set of numbers with a natural zero point, then they could be used in the following formula to predict relative visitation rates for different states at various national parks:

$$R_{ij} = \frac{kA_j}{D_{ij}^{\frac{3}{2}}} \tag{21}$$

Equation 21 is simply an adaptation of the Kepler model, Equation 19. It substitutes A_j, the attractiveness scale value of park j, for $M_j^{\frac{1}{2}}$. The Kepler coefficient is obtainable, of course, only for existent parks for which visitation tabulations have been made. In principle, however, A_j could be obtained for areas whose features could be judged in comparison with various national parks by a panel of knowledgeable judges, whether or not those areas had yet attained park status. Hence, predictions of future visitation rates for *proposed* new national parks could be made. Such predictions could be useful in planning for the development of park facilities, staffing, providing for protection of park features, etc. They could be of indirect use to states and communities in the proposed park's vicinity, or along travel routes leading to it, in preparing for increased volumes of tourism. Just incidentally, too, this kind of foreknowledge could have some bearing on the fate of park-creating legislation.

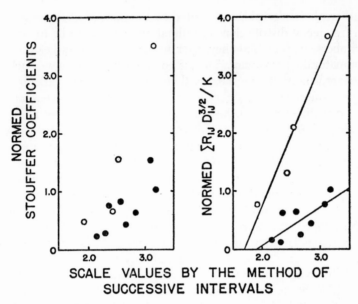

SCALE VALUES BY THE METHOD OF SUCCESSIVE INTERVALS

Figure 6. Relation of two measures of park attraction (derived from travel data) to a psychometric measure of park attractiveness

2 Classifying National Parks

Since Table 15 includes both Kepler coefficients and successive-intervals scale values for 12 parks, an attempt at establishing an absolute zero on the A_j scale might be made by looking at the regression of the scale values on $M_j^{\frac{1}{2}}$—the latter being already a ratio scale, with an absolute zero, since it was defined by Equation 20. From Table 16, however, it can be seen that the park attractiveness scale values are more highly correlated with the Stouffer coefficients than with these Kepler coefficients. Why not then try to establish the absolute zero for A_j by its regression on the Stouffer opportunity coefficients? The high intercorrelation between the Stouffer coefficients and the Kepler coefficients might suggest that either would yield substantially the same results anyway. But careful examination of Figure 6 reveals an important difference.

In the left-hand scattergram in Figure 6, the 12 Stouffer coefficients are plotted against the corresponding successive-intervals scale values. The scatter departs from linearity somewhat and is not quite homoscedastic. This suggests a confounding of variables, and implies that the higher magnitude of their product-moment correlation with the scale values may not be an advantage for the Stouffer coefficients (in comparison with the Kepler coefficients). From the factor analysis, we know the scale values really do "confound" two or three variables—the recreational desirability factor, the wilderness-invasion factor, and perhaps also a popularity factor. The Stouffer coefficients seem to reflect less clearly than the Kepler coefficients, in Figure 6, the multidimensionality of park attractiveness which the factor analysis revealed. In the right-hand scattergram in Figure 6, the 12 Kepler coefficients are plotted against the scale values. Now some meaning seems to emerge from the heteroscedastic shape of the scatter. I have plotted 4 of the parks as white dots, and the other 8 as black dots, in order to emphasize a partitioning of the data which seems to me to be in keeping with what has been said previously about the dimensions of park attractiveness. Regarding the 12 dots as two bivariate arrays rather than one, it can be seen that these two arrays are more clearly separable in the right-hand scattergram than in the left-hand one. Two regression lines have been fitted by the least-squares method to these two arrays. Each can provide an estimate of an absolute zero on the A_j scale, but at a cost resulting from the fact the two regressions will not coincide. The price is the necessity of providing a rationale for discriminating two qualitatively distinct categories of national parks.

The four white dots in each of the scattergrams in Figure 6 represent Yellowstone, Rocky Mountain, Great Smoky Mountains, and Shenandoah National Parks. I will refer to these as "Series A," and the other eight as "Series B." As justification for distinguishing one series from the other, I suggest that the parks in Series A receive great numbers of visitors for reasons not essentially dependent on their designation as national parks except insofar as that status has resulted in their increased accessibility via construction of highways to and through them. For the Series B parks, I think this is less true; their visitation is proportionately more purely national park visitation per se. The Series A parks are either more famous (in some stereotyped way) or closer to main travel routes, or closer to large population sources. Consider, for example, the many tourists who allude to their Colorado vacation destination as Estes Park (the *town* filled with souvenir shops) rather than the adjacent Rocky Mountain National Park. The occurrence of the word "park" in both names fosters confusion, of course, and confusion may also arise (to a lesser extent) from the fact that the mailing address of the park administration is Estes Park, by virtue of the location of the headquarters building in the town. Many visitors drive across the national park on the famous Trail Ridge Road without stopping over. Perhaps they paused in Estes Park to refuel and to buy picture postcards, and the national park was not a destination at all but the merest incident en route between such urban centers as Chicago or St. Louis and the pleasure spots of glamorous California. Or consider the tourists from all the states who include the Skyline Drive in Virginia in the itinerary of their visits to Washington, D.C. Many of them are unaware, or unappreciative, of the fact that this famous road is within a national park (named Shenandoah). Some are doubtless oblivious of the very concept, "national park." The uniformed park service ranger in the checking station at the park entrance may have been perceived as a mere collector of revenue for a toll road.

At this stage, my grouping of parks into these two series is a matter of judgment. The distinction between Series A and Series B is empirically meaningful, however, in that further research could be undertaken to test the hypothesis that a higher proportion of visitors to Series B parks have a clearer perception of "the national park idea." Factor I probably makes the major contribution to visitation rate patterns for Series B parks, while Series A park visitation involves a considerable contribution from Factor II as well.

For the four parks designated as Series A, the regression of Kepler coefficients on scale values turns out to have a slope of 2.44 and an intercept of −4.13. For the eight parks designated as Series B, the slope is 0.65 and the intercept is −1.21. Using these slope and intercept figures, we can project two "absolute" scale values or hypothetical Kepler coefficients for each park. These are given in Table 18. With two projected coefficients for each park, a justifiable choice of one of them must be made if recourse to Equation 21 is desired for prediction of visitation rates. In Table 18, I have segregated the parks I judge to belong to Series A from those I judge to belong to Series B. In Series B are included several parks which would present special problems in the application of Equation 21. They would present special difficulties because they lie outside the 48 contiguous states or are otherwise inaccessible to ordinary automobile travel. But in each of these cases—Mount McKinley, Isle Royale, Hawaii Volcanoes, Haleakala, and Virgin Islands—Series B membership seems conceptually more realistic than Series A membership. The appropriateness of each park's assignment could be empirically tested, though I have not obtained the required data for doing so at this writing. The test would consist of questionnaire or interview assessment of the comparative awareness of the national park concept by the average visitor at each park, with high awareness expected for visitors to Series B parks and low awareness among visitors to Series A parks.

3   The Problem of Negative Coefficients

In Table 18, by both regression equations, five national parks received projected coefficients with minus signs. Evidently, if the partition of Series B from Series A is legitimate, yet another set of parks can be distinguished. I will call them "Series C." The five parks in this third series are: Petrified Forest (which was until recently a national monument instead of a national park), Mammoth Cave, Wind Cave, Hot Springs, and Platt. In general, what distinguishes these from the parks in the first

Table 18   Projected Kepler coefficients based on successive-intervals scale values

		Series A projection	Series B projection
Series A parks	Yellowstone	3.545*	.841
	Grand Canyon	3.267*	.767
	Rocky Mountain	2.037*	.438
	Great Smoky Mtns	1.764*	.365
	Shenandoah	.554*	.042
	Carlsbad Caverns	.400*	.001
Series B parks	Glacier	3.931	.944*
	Mt. McKinley	3.697	.882*
	Yosemite	3.633	.865*
	Grand Teton	3.413	.806*
	Olympic	2.886	.665*
	Sequoia	2.782	.637*
	Kings Canyon	2.384	.531*
	Mt. Rainier	2.176	.475*
	Zion	2.125	.462*
	Bryce Canyon	1.813	.378*
	Isle Royale	1.608	.324*
	Hawaii Volcanoes	1.593	.320*
	Haleakala	1.557	.310*
	Crater Lake	1.544	.307*
	Lassen Volcanic	1.481	.290*
	Acadia	1.310	.244*
	Virgin Islands	1.310	.244*
	Mesa Verde	1.125	.194*
	Everglades	1.105	.189*
	Big Bend	.749	.094*
Series C parks	Petrified Forest	− .825	− .327
	Mammoth Cave	− .900	− .347
	Wind Cave	−1.008	− .376
	Hot Springs	−3.170	− .953
	Platt	−3.345	−1.000

* Denotes the projected Kepler coefficient judged to be more probable.

two series is that they are small in size or small in variety of features. If we follow the statistical regression through, however, and assign negative projected Kepler coefficients to these parks, then Equation 21 would result in the anomalous prediction of negative visitation rates. To avoid this anomaly, I suggest that these five parks simply be regarded as falling below the limen or threshold of scalable park attractiveness.

There is ample precedent for this assumption in other psychometric studies. In illustrating the method of scaling by paired comparisons, for example, Guilford cited judgment data on nine vegetables. On the positive side of an estimated indifference point, the most-liked vegetable was corn, followed in order by peas, string beans, spinach, carrots, asparagus, beets, and cabbage. Turnips, however, received a negative scale value.[24] But this fact did not have to imply "negative sales" of turnips (analogous to the negative visitation rates Equation 21 would predict for the Series C parks). Around the negative scale value of that vegetable, as around the scale values of the vegetables on the positive side of the indifference point, there was a discriminal dispersion. The minority of subjects whose tastes put them in the extreme (positive) tail of that discriminal dispersion would occasionally express their positive liking for turnips by buying some. The others would merely refrain from buying any; obviously they would not express their dislike by consuming them and demanding to be paid for it (negative price), nor would they ordinarily take any action to prevent turnip consumption by others. A positive quantity of turnip sales, then, could be associated with a negative scale value for that vegetable. In the same manner, those tourists with a positive liking for the Series C parks will presumably visit them even though possibly outnumbered by others whose judgments average in to give these parks negative scale values. The negative judgments may cause those who hold them to abstain from visiting Series C parks, but need not lead them to obstruct visits by others.

Psychophysical measurement relates subjective sensation to either an observed or a presumed objective metric. There is always a liminal magnitude of the stimulus on the objective metric—a magnitude below which its positive departure from zero is noticed less than half the time. It is common practice to simplify calculations by adopting the liminal stimulus as the unit on the objective metric. When this is done, Fechner's law, $S = k \log R$ (where R is the psychologist's conventional symbol for stimulus magnitude and is not to be confused with our notation for park visitation rates) takes the form shown in Figure 7. All stimuli with magnitudes less than the threshold magnitude (but nevertheless greater than zero) on the objective metric, will have negative scale values on the subjective metric.[25]

What needs to be borne in mind, then, is that the successive-intervals scale values array the national parks along a subjective metric of attractiveness. If we can relate these scale values linearly to the Kepler coefficients, it is because the latter are also measures of park attraction as *reflected in the responses* of travelers. The reason for designating them as $M_j^{\frac{1}{2}}$ is not just to conform to the analogy of Kepler's third law, but to take the more directly relevant Fechner law into account. It is the fractional exponent that does this. It implies that the calculated Kepler coefficients are logarithmically related to actual park characteristics. As a presumed park attribute that is analogous to gravitational mass varies geometrically, measured park attractiveness varies arithmetically. The applicability of the Fechner law serves as a reminder that there is nothing

[24] Guilford, *op. cit.*, pp. 159–174.
[25] Figure 7, which makes this clear, is adapted from Boring, *op. cit.*, p. 290.

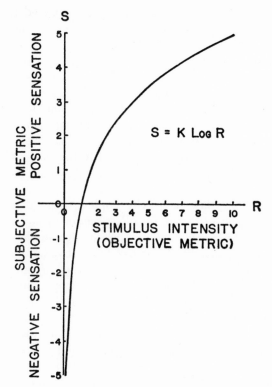

Figure 7. Fechner's law

anomalous in finding a few parks with negative scale values (or negative projected Kepler coefficients), for the analysis takes a psychometric framework.

It also happens that in the case of each of the five parks in Series C, one or more of the scale judges emphatically stated that national park status should not have been given to it. Nonpark considerations may provide the basis for the positive visitation rates at these places. One judge who gave Hot Springs National Park the lowest rating conceded that his evaluation might have been different if, for health reasons, he were interested in the mineral baths.

Gravitational Concepts Clarified

1 Proportionality

Newton had recognized a fact that had eluded the reasoning of his predecessors—that the orbital motion of planets consisted of two component motions: an unaccelerated forward movement, combined with a steady acceleration inward toward the sun. He decided that the sun exerted a force that continually bent each planet's inertially linear trajectory into an elliptical orbit. Centrifugal force is merely another name for the tendency an orbiting body has because of its inertia to depart from its nearly circular path and proceed outward on a tangential straight line. This force was exactly offset by solar gravitation. In accounting for orbital motions by a law of gravity, Newton made an assumption whose importance was not fully recognized until much later. He assumed that each planet's *gravitational* mass (which was a factor in the formula expressing the magnitude of that body's *centripetal* force) was linearly proportional to the planet's *inertial* mass (a factor in the formula expressing the magnitude of its *centrifugal* force).[26]

The empirical validity of Newton's law of gravity implied, then, that a body's *capacity to attract and be attracted by other matter* must be proportional to its *capacity to resist acceleration*. This implication has been termed the "principle of proportionality." The free fall of two bodies of unequal mass is the easiest demonstration of the principle of proportionality. The greater inertial mass of the larger body exactly compensates for the greater accelerating force of the earth's attraction for its larger gravitational mass. Thus the two bodies are accelerated equally. Any disproportion between inertial and gravitational mass would result in their being accelerated unequally.[27] Aristotelian thought assumed that heavier objects fell faster than lighter ones. This seemed intuitively correct and was accepted unquestioningly for centuries. Its plausibility was due to the fact that the concept of gravitational mass was intuitively appreciated (because it was involved in the notion of weight) while the concept of inertial mass was not comprehended.

I submit that a principle of proportionality must hold in regard to social accelerations as well as physical accelerations. If states which are located equally distant from a given national park tend to have equal visitation rates at that park, I think a principle of proportionality is implied just as truly as in the case of a marble and a baseball striking the ground together after being simultaneously released from a height. According to the value theory employed in this study, park visitation arises from an attractive force. The magnitude of the force depends on the characteristics of the park and on proximity to it. Presumably it also depends on the characteristics of the populations being attracted. But it apparently depends in some way that makes the populations' capacity to be attracted to the park proportional to their capacity to resist acceleration. Any disproportion between inertial and gravitational "social mass" would disrupt the pattern of visitation rates described by Equation 19.

[26] Cf. Chalmers W. Sherwin, *Basic Concepts of Physics.* New York: Holt, Rinehart and Winston, Inc., 1961, p. 53.
[27] *Ibid.,* p. 55.

2 Equivalence

A more fundamental principle has been asserted in physics which would "explain" the physical principle of proportionality. It is the principle of equivalence—an essential feature of the general theory of relativity. It not only recognizes that a gravitational field is not operationally distinguishable from a constant acceleration of the observer's frame of reference, but it asserts that a gravitational field and a constantly accelerating frame of reference are indistinguishable *in principle*.[28] The demonstrable proportionality of gravitational and inertial mass, then, is simply the result of the fact that they are the same thing! In other words, the capacity of matter to attract and be attracted by other matter *is* its capacity to resist acceleration.

Could a similar statement hold for sociology? Obviously it would not be sufficient to assert that it had to hold on the basis of analogy alone. It would not be naturalistic to say that since there appears to be a principle of proportionality in sociology as in physics, and since the physical principle is due to the more fundamental principle of equivalence, therefore the sociological principle must also be due to a principle of equivalence. It would not be inconsistent with naturalism, however, if a similar statement were offered which omitted "therefore" and substituted "may" for "must." Are there any independent, sociological considerations that point toward a sociological principle of equivalence? In the case of national parks' capacity to attract visitors, I think there are.

One of the early superintendents of Yellowstone National Park has been quoted as writing in his final report, 1889: "In the unsurpassed grandeur of its natural condition, it is the pride and glory of the nation; but if under the guise of improvement, selfish interests are permitted to make merchandise of its wonders and beauties, it will inevitably become a byword and a reproach."[29] A national park's capacity to attract is believed by many knowledgeable people to depend on (or perhaps be the same thing as) its capacity to resist change. A number of the comments written by the scale judges and cited in Chapter 6 indicated this. Our civilization could be considered an accelerating frame of reference, within which the relatively unchanging scenes in national parks seem to have a gravitational effect on us.

Bernard DeVoto said the entire National Park System could be justified by the opportunities the parks afforded "to be alone in the primeval." He said steadily increasing numbers of Americans were cut off by our civilization "from first-hand knowledge of nature—streams, plants, forests,

---

[28] Peierls, *op. cit.*, p. 142.
[29] Capt. Moses Harris, sixth superintendent of Yellowstone, quoted from p. 139, *The Yellowstone National Park*, by Hiram M. Chittenden, edited and with an introduction by Richard A. Bartlett. Copyright 1964 by the University of Oklahoma Press.

animals, birds, even the effects of storm—and yet their need of it can never be extinguished. . . ."[30] Even before the Grand Canyon was a national park, Theodore Roosevelt expressed the wish that it be kept unchanged, that no building of any kind be built there "to mar the wonderful grandeur, the sublimity, the great loneliness and beauty of the canyon."[31] A recent director of the National Park Service wrote that any change in the character of a park area destroys part of its ability to yield its cultural and inspirational benefits.[32]

3 Sacredness

Referring to what he called a "normative reaction to normlessness," Howard Becker noted a tendency for extensive secularization in a society to engender "sacralization."[33] This process endows certain cultural entities with the quality of sacredness. Things defined by the culture as sacred are things deemed unchangeable, and attempts to change them, or behavior which threatens to change them, are taboo. As cultural objects, the national parks have undergone a process of institutionalization by which they have been endowed with very nearly this quality of sacredness. It is noteworthy in this connection that the traditional campfire birth of the proposal to make Yellowstone a national park was itself an instance of sacralization as a reaction to an initially secular (mercenary) discussion.

One important function the national parks are sometimes expected to perform is the promotion of national solidarity and even the enhancement of family cohesion.[34]

Where else do so many millions of Americans, under such satisfying circumstances, come face to face with their government? How else can that government better promote the unity of the family than through experiences in which every member shares? Where else but on historic ground can Americans better renew the idealism that prompted the patriots to their deeds of diplomacy and valor? Where else do they have such opportunity to recapture the spirit and something of the qualities of the pioneers?

Abraham Lincoln said in 1864 at the dedication of the cemetery at Gettysburg that the brave men who had struggled on that battlefield had "conse-

---

[30] Quoted in John Ise, *Our National Park Policy: A Critical History*. Baltimore: The Johns Hopkins Press, 1961, p. 4.
[31] Quoted in Devereux Butcher, "Resorts or Wilderness?" *The Atlantic*, 207 (February, 1961), p. 48.
[32] National Park Service, *Mission 66 for the National Park System*. Washington, D.C.: U.S. Department of the Interior, January, 1956, p. iii.
[33] Howard Becker, "Normative Reactions to Normlessness," *American Sociological Review*, 25 (December, 1960), pp. 803–810.
[34] National Park Service, *op. cit.*, p. 119.

crated it, far above our poor power to add or detract." This battlefield, and many other historic shrines, are administered now by the same National Park Service vested with the guardianship of sublime scenic areas. One of the tasks of the Park Service has thus been to help implement Lincoln's wish that the living persons who visit the Gettysburg battlefield might "be dedicated here to the unfinished work" and would "take increased devotion to that cause" for which the troops had given "the last full measure of devotion. . . ." Lincoln's immortal words may, of course, be read from the walls of the Lincoln Memorial, in Washington, D.C., another of the products of sacralization assigned to the care of the National Park Service.

It has been suggested that, by means of accurate and inspirational exhibits interpreting them, the entire array of sacred places administered by the National Park Service—the geological and other scientific wonders, the historic remains of early man, and the buildings "that once rang to the footsteps of the founding fathers"—can have "value in holding America to her best ideals and traditions. . . ."[35]

The sociological concept of institutional sacredness, and an understanding of the mission of the National Park Service and the effects expected from the sacred places it administers, lend support to the notion of a sociologically applicable principle of equivalence. It might be stated in this form: A sociocultural element is valued to the extent that it is regarded as sacred and is surrounded by secular (i.e., changing) sociocultural elements. The husband who dislikes having his wife rearrange their furniture regards the existing arrangement as sacred and finds it attractive when he comes home from his day's business in the secular (changing) world. To his wife, whose world is less secular, the sacredness and attractiveness of an existing furniture arrangement is much less.

4 Other Interaction Types

It might be objected that Becker's linking of secularization and sacralization cannot properly be compared to Einstein's equating of gravitation and reference frame acceleration because men do strive for some desiderata that are not subsumable under sacred values. It seems to be not always the case that what we are drawn to is what resists secular change. Fad and fashion behavior, for example, seems to involve repulsion of people from old and established ways, rather than attraction toward them. The newest is taken to be the best; newness is a good in itself, supposedly.

[35] Joseph Wood Krutch, *Grand Canyon: Today and All Its Yesterdays*. New York: William Sloane Associates, 1958, p. 33. Cf. Emile Durkheim, *The Elementary Forms of the Religious Life*. New York: The Free Press of Glencoe, 1947, for a persuasive argument that ensuring group cohesion is a major function of the sacred objects of religion.

Even those people who want to see things in nearly their primeval condition when they get to a national park may wish to go there in a car that is the latest model. To some extent, of course, the lateness of the model is just an index of its newness and hence of the goodness of its mechanical condition. Preference for the latest model does not in this respect contradict preference for primeval scenery. But if the new model is preferred as a status symbol, rather than as a mechanically superior vehicle, this is a different sort of phenomenon.

In sociology as truly as in physics, then, the principle of equivalence merely says that there is one kind of interaction in which mutual attraction and resistance to acceleration are indistinguishable. There are other types of interaction, and their occurrence no more *contradicts* the sociological principle of equivalence than the existence of electrical and magnetic phenomena contradicts the physical principle of equivalence between gravitational and inertial mass. Bodies may be attracted to each other by electrical and magnetic forces as well as by gravitational forces. To say that a body's capacity for *gravitational* attraction is identical to its capacity to resist acceleration is not to say that its capacity for any kind of attraction at all must be identical to its inertial mass. Its electric charge may be quite different from its gravitational mass. Within certain ranges of variation, at least, these can be considered two orthogonal dimensions.

Physically, two bodies may simultaneously interact in both these ways. Their mutual gravitation toward each other may be offset by electrical repulsion. There is no *a priori* reason to exclude similar possibilities in sociological interactions. People might be "gravitationally" attracted to parks in proportion to their resistance to change, yet having visited a long-established park last year, a person might leave it out of his itinerary this year and prefer to spend his vacation visiting a newly created park or even some destination that has no connection at all with the sacralization process (e.g., a world's fair). I make no claim that *all* sociological interactions are gravitational and subject to a principle of equivalence. Moreover, I must emphasize once again that a sociological principle of equivalence relates two *sociological* concepts of mass to each other and does not link either of them to physical mass as such. The principle says that gravitational *sociocultural* mass is indistinguishable from inertial *sociocultural* mass. It does *not* say that an object's value (gravitational mass in the sociological sense) depends on its physical inertia.

Misuse of Gravitational Concepts

In Chapter 7, I showed how wide of the mark had been a number of previous attempts to formulate sociological equivalents of Newton's axioms. I tried to show also that these abortive attempts did not suffice to demonstrate the impossibility of genuinely naturalistic sociology. The study reported in the present chapter is likewise not the first attempt to use physical gravitation as a model for the analysis of human social interactions. It differs from earlier attempts, however, because of its greater concern for conceptual clarity, and a thoroughgoing reluctance to mistake analogy for proof. I have insisted on empirical tests of the utility of borrowed concepts, not just because they are borrowed (and therefore supposedly somehow illegitimate), but because empirical verification is a fundamental tenet of naturalism.

To emphasize the difference between naturalistic use of physical models and mere pseudo-scientific argument, it seems desirable at this point to contrast the present study with some of its less cautious predecessors. Perhaps those readers who look askance at *any* sociological use of physical models and are, therefore, inclined to dismiss all such attempts as equally unsophisticated will be reassured to find that this study of national park visitation differs from (at least as much as it resembles) the naïve social physics of the past.

First of all, consider Henry Carey's glib application of alleged gravitational principles to human behavior. He saw the relations among prices of land, corn, flour, and bread as dependent on "growth of the power of association" which makes "circulation" more rapid "as the attractive and counterattractive forces increase in their intensity." Far-fetched as it may seem for him to have done so, Carey saw this as analogous to Kepler's third law. Surely the use of that model in the present study has been far more enlightened. Carey said that the law by virtue of which "Venus moves through her orbit at a rate so much more rapid than that of Mars, or Jupiter" was "precisely the same" as the law governing "societary movement."[36] The forces tending to raise and lower prices were seen by Carey as "corresponding, precisely, with those which govern the movements of our solar system."[37]

It seems fair to say that Carey used analogy as an end in itself, or at least as a means of proof, rather than for the merely heuristic purpose of generating hypotheses. The need for empirical tests of the propositions he espoused by analogy seems to have escaped him. Perhaps it was because of this that he committed the error of identifying the social analogue of mass with the sheer quantity of people present in a place. He wrote:[38]

Man tends of necessity to gravitate towards his fellow-man. Of all animals, he is the most gregarious, and the greater the number collected in a given space the greater is the attractive force there exerted, as is seen to have been

[36] Henry Charles Carey, *Principles of Social Science*. Philadelphia: J. B. Lippincott Company, 1858, vol. 2, p. 269.
[37] *Ibid.*, vol. 2, p. 268.
[38] *Ibid.*, vol. 1, pp. 42–43. (My italics.)

the case with the great cities of the ancient world, Nineveh and Babylon, Athens, and Rome, and as is now seen in regard to Paris and London, Vienna and Naples, Philadelphia, New York, and Boston. Gravitation is here, *as everywhere else in the material world*, in the direct ratio of the mass, and in the inverse one of the distance.

The phrase I have italicized indicates that Carey was as unconcerned to distinguish sociocultural mass from physical mass as he was unaware of subtleties in the relation of gravitational to inertial mass. For him it was enough to assert triumphantly that as man becomes increasingly diversified, grows in his power to control the forces of nature, increases his numbers and his activity, "the more does man become subjected to the great law of molecular gravitation—local centres attracting him in one direction, while great cities, centres of the world, attract him in the other. . . ."[39]

Bad as was Carey's unconcern for careful quantitative verification, lack of empirical concern by those who criticize him would be at least as inexcusable. Yet Stark has written, "If Carey were right, if in society, as in space, 'gravitation' were in inverse ratio to the distance, then a town would have to be more attractive to those near to it than to those far from it. . . . This is complete nonsense."[40] Stark was wrong: this is not nonsense, it is fact. Stark seems to have been unaware of or unperturbed by the abundant findings of geographers and human ecologists who have investigated patterns of retail buying, newspaper subscribing, church attendance, etc., among residents of a community's hinterland. Distance gradients occur in all such phenomena. Moreover, Stark must have ignored the implications of even his own personal experience, for he could hardly have chosen at random among all the cities of the world each time he wished to go to a drugstore to buy a toothbrush. Voluntaristic convictions strong enough to make the hypothesis of distance gradients seem nonsensical could not altogether prevent their holder from exhibiting such gradients in his own actions.

Charles Fourier was another nineteenth-century writer who used the gravitational model. There are superficial similarities between his statement and the use of the model in the present analysis of park visitation rates, but I intend to make it clear that the resemblance was *only* superficial. Fourier wrote that "the laws of Passional Attraction were in all respects conformable to those of Material Attraction as explained by Newton and Leibnitz," and he argued that there was "unity of system between the movement of the material world and that of the spiritual world," as if *the same forces* accounted for both.[41] He did refer to the formal simi-

---

[39] *Ibid.*, vol. 3, pp. 467–468.
[40] Stark, *op. cit.*, p. 144.
[41] Charles Fourier, *The Social Destiny of Man* (tr. Henry Clapp, Jr.). New York: Calvin Blanchard, 1857, p. 13.

larity of laws of "passional attraction" and those of "material attraction" as an analogy, and said he "suspected" the analogy "must extend from general laws to particular laws; that the attractions and properties of animals, vegetables, and minerals, were perhaps distributed according to the same plan as those of Man and the planets. . . ." Then he said he was convinced of this "after making the necessary researches,"[42] but he evidently meant something quite different by "research" than the naturalistic sociologist would mean. "From the moment that I possessed the theory of Passional Attraction, and of the Unity of the Four Movements, I began to read in the occult book of Nature," he said, as if that were what constituted research.[43]

His "reading" led to the conclusion that nature comprises three "eternal, uncreated, and indestructible principles." They are: "1. *God, or Spirit;* the active and moving principle. 2. *Matter;* the passive principle, which is acted upon. 3. *Justice, or Mathematics;* the regulative principle of Movement." God had to act mathematically, according to Fourier, or else "he would not be in accord with a justice positive and independent of himself." As a result: "The properties of Friendship are calculated according to the properties of the Circle;—The properties of Love are calculated according to the properties of the Ellipse;—The properties of Paternity are calculated according to the properties of the Parabola;—The properties of Ambition are calculated according to the properties of the Hyperbola. . . ."[44]

It would have been more appropriate for Stark to have applied the epithet "nonsense" to Fourier's conclusions than to Carey's. Clearly, the resemblance to the park visitation study doesn't go very deep. Fourier did not understand the gravity model, and his laws of passional attraction were not stated in a form that could be put to quantitative test, nor was empirical research done to test them. If nature seemed occult, it was Fourier's own mystical turn of mind that made it so. His methodological rules were "the principle of Absolute Doubt of all existing theories, and Absolute Deviation from all existing methods."[45] No naturalist could subscribe to such rules.

One recent attempt to apply gravitational formulas to human events is the work of physicist John Q. Stewart. It has almost as much resemblance to Carey's ideas as it has to the national park study. Though Stewart hardly subscribed to rules such as those of Fourier, Stewart's pursuit of physical models did seem to lead him away from (rather than toward) comprehension of social phenomena. His formula for "demographic energy" is essentially the same as the formulas of Zipf and

---

[42] *Ibid.*
[43] *Ibid.*, p. 14.
[44] *Ibid.*, pp. 32–33.
[45] *Ibid.*, p. 4.

Dodd. It can be written as follows:

$$E = \frac{G(\mu_1 N_1)(\mu_2 N_2)}{d_{12}} \tag{22}$$

where G is a constant (analogous to the physical gravitational constant, though Stewart was not careful to select notation that would indicate it was *only* analogous rather than giving the impression it was identical in magnitude and dimensionality). N_1 and N_2 are numbers of people, μ_1 and μ_2 are "molecular weights," and d_{12} is the distance between the two population aggregates.[46] Stewart suggested that the weights, μ_1 and μ_2, might be "proportional to the available mass of goods per capita."[47] This suggestion had the merit of softening the error of Dodd and Zipf, who equated sociocultural mass with quantity of people, but it apparently commits the more egregious error of equating sociocultural mass with physical mass, for in the context the unit of measurement was tons (of artifacts).

Stewart's theory was severely criticized in a letter to one journal in which an article on it had appeared. It was called "balderdash" and "weird." The letter writer argued that the one most effective way of obstructing progress toward mathematical description of social behavior was to begin with the concepts of physical science and to insist on "jam-packing" social observations into these "usually quite irrelevant concepts." Such a procedure "represents a gross and unpardonable failure to approach the data of social behavior at their own level and in the terms which they themselves suggest."[48] It is in just this respect that I think my work with the national park data is most fundamentally different from Stewart's work on "demographic energy." I have tried to approach park visitation data "on their own level," while he did not approach his sociological data on a sociological level. I have not, on the other hand, assumed (as animistic sociologists would) that this meant no patterns in the data could legitimately resemble patterns in physical data and no social or psychological processes accounting for such patterns could resemble the mechanisms that account for physical patterns.

By approaching the data on their own level, I have avoided the need for absurdly mixing metaphors—a technique which Stewart resorted to of necessity. He construed the "molecular weights" in his formula as properties of populations. Thus it was, after all, *people* who attracted people gravitationally. But from this it seemed to follow that in the long run all people would tend to gravitate together into a single aggregate. Since real societies seem to remain structured into more or less discrete communities, Stewart had to seek a counterforce "to explain the resistance

[46] John Q. Stewart, "The Development of Social Physics," *American Journal of Physics*, 18 (May, 1950), p. 247.
[47] *Ibid.*, pp. 249–250.
[48] Walter H. Eaton, "Letter," *Scientific American*, 179 (July, 1948), p. 1.

of human beings to social gravitation." His answer was to make human populations analogous to a gas, whose molecules continually rebound from each other. "Were it not for the expansive force of the human gas," he wrote, "representing the need of individuals for elbow-room, the center-seeking force of gravitation would eventually pile everyone up at one place."[49] Carey had envisioned a similar end result.

This ploy reminds me of the legendary account by which Indians who used to live in the vicinity of what is now Devil's Tower National Monument explained the short ears and short tail of the grizzly bear. Unaware of the principles of volcanism, the Indians attributed the fluted sides of that great lava plug to the clawing of a giant grizzly which had chased some of their ancestors to its summit. The ancestral Indians ultimately overpowered the bear with magic, according to the story, and vindictively cut off his long ears and long tail before magically subdividing him into a number of ordinary-sized grizzlies. Hence the short ears and short tails on their present-day descendents. But no explanation was required for the short ears and tail of the modern grizzly until the Indians had assumed the shortness was a departure from a previous hypothetical pattern no one had ever observed.

Referring to Stewart's social physics, an anthropologist wrote that it "does not, alas, carry us into the post-Keplerian stage of social thinking. Rather he transports us to a pre-Heraclitean era where we are asked to believe in unexamined generalities like 'population potential' and the 'human gas.'"[50]

The faults of past attempts to apply gravitational models to social phenomena have constituted departures from naturalism. The foolish or insignificant results attained by such attempts have not, then, demonstrated that the cautious and enlightened use of physical models in a thoroughly naturalistic approach to sociological problems would be futile. On the basis of results obtained in the study of national park travel patterns, it seems to me that such concepts have a promising future.

Interaction Strength

In Chapter 5, empirical studies were described which confirmed the hypothesis that values influence human choices, but the apparent degree of influence values exerted on the behavior studied was slight enough to suggest that circumstances can easily attenuate their predictive power. The present chapter has shown that intervening distance can be a factor

[49] John Q. Stewart, "Concerning 'Social Physics,'" *Scientific American*, 178 (May, 1948), p. 23.
[50] Jules Henry, "Letter," *Scientific American*, 179 (July, 1948), p. 1.

in weakening the effects of values that pertain to goals that have fixed spatial locations. The conceptions of the desirable that seem to motivate travel to national parks have weaker effects on populations residing far from the parks than on those residing nearer to them. It should be noted, though, that even in the case of a population located quite close to a park with a large Kepler coefficient, the resulting visitation rate is a minor fraction. The largest rate shown in Table 6 represented entrance into Yellowstone by 9,290 out of every 100,000 Montana cars in 1940, or *less than one out of every ten,* despite the proximity of Montana to that oldest and largest national park. In a given year, the vast majority of residents of states quite near a park do not visit it.

Nowhere, I think, could it be said that park visitation is normatively required. On the other hand, despite the fact that in most communities only a tiny fraction of the population visits a given national park in a given year, it could hardly be argued that the normative system prohibits park visitation. People go to national parks or stay away from national parks for reasons other than normative prescriptions. Park visitation patterns are shaped by park *values* in conjunction with the travel-impeding effects of distance, and it would be unnecessary and misleading to invoke *norms* to account for these patterns.

American folkways do include the expectation that people who can afford it will take an annual vacation and that vacationing usually will involve leaving home to do something different from the routines of the rest of the year. Within the wide range laid out by such permissive norms, however, destinations can be chosen on the basis of values. It seems important, then, to distinguish between the concept of values and the concept of norms.

In making such a distinction, I am not merely suggesting that one is on a higher level of abstraction than the other. Sociologists sometimes speak of the values from which norms are said to "have arisen," or of the values "implicit in" certain rules, or "underlying" certain customs or laws. I am suggesting instead that there are some values involved in some interactions directly, without the intermediate influence of norms. Only when the norms which ordinarily preoccupy us are set aside, then, can the influence of such values be clearly discerned.

In national park travel, the values are manifested in behavior that can only occur on special occasions—during vacations, mostly. For the rest of each person's year, obligations toward other activities are prepotent. In some degree, values may be involved in the routine commitments people have to their occupational and familial roles and to their other activities in their home communities. But there are also, quite obviously, norms which prescribe and reinforce such commitment and the behavior that commitment entails. Any direct influence of the values is almost impossible to disentangle from the more obvious influence of the norms and the sanctions by which these are enforced. Most nonrecreational behavior is subject to constraints as well as to the attractions of sought-for desiderata. Only when the occasion calls for temporary suspension of these constraints can the force of nonobligatory values, such as those which impute sacredness to a primeval scene, cause people to journey to national park destinations.

The interactions of people and national park values are *weaker* than many of the other interactions in which those same people are involved. This fact is in accord with characterization of the park attraction as gravitational (as I shall explain in a moment), and it suggests an important difference between recreational travel and genuine migration. Migration patterns are shaped by employment opportunities and are more strongly subject to the impact of normative obligations than is recreational travel. The populations of various states are not attracted to the parks in proportion to "park populations" (even after controlling for distance), as has been shown, but the visitor population in a park *is* attracted to the various states in proportion to state populations (again, after controlling for distance). That is to say, nearly all park visitors return to the homes from which they came. Their trip to the park was influenced by park values rather than by any obligation or normative requirement to visit the park. But their trip home is subject not only to values which make home directly attractive, but also to obligations and normative requirements that regular activities be resumed when vacation ends. As our factor analysis showed, "park population" is hardly an index of park attractiveness. But state population is more closely indicative of the magnitude of a state's job market. This is why it could suffice as an index of "opportunities" either at a given distance or in the intervening space and could yield some confirmation of Stouffer's or Zipf's and Dodd's hypotheses when applied to actual migration from city to city or state to state. I contend, however, that residential relocation of persons responding to the structure of the job market or the housing market is not properly analogous to gravitational interaction.

In physics, four different kinds of interactions between particles have been distinguished. There are the *strong* interactions which take place between such particles as pions, K mesons, nucleons and hyperons in which "strangeness" is conserved.[51] On the average, the strong interactions are about a hundred times stronger than the *electromagnetic* interactions between charged particles. But these in turn are about a trillion times as strong as the so-called *weak* interactions, which involve neutrinos and strange particles in which strangeness is not conserved. But even the weak

---

[51] For an explanation of the "strangeness" concept, see Luis W. Alvarez, "Status Report on New Particles," chap. 2 in Louis N. Ridenous and William A. Nierenberg (eds.), *Modern Physics for the Engineer, Second Series.* New York: McGraw-Hill Book Company, 1961, esp. pp. 27, 28, 37.

interactions are about ten trillion trillion times as strong as *gravitational* interactions.[52] Gravitation is the weakest form of interaction yet known. It may be the weakest there is.

If there are distinct categories of interactions in the social world as well as in the world of matter, it would make sense to reserve the term "gravitational" for that class of social interactions to which the sociological principle of equivalence applies. That is, an interaction is to be called "gravitational" only if the capacity to attract and the capacity to resist acceleration are indistinguishable. By this conception, national park visitation could be described as a kind of gravitational interaction—possibly with some admixture of nongravitational types of interaction, as suggested by differentiation of the parks into three series and by the factor analysis of park attractiveness measures.

If each type of social interaction has a characteristic strength, as is the case for physical interactions, then it is at least plausible that in sociology as in physics the gravitational interactions would be the weakest. I say only that it is plausible, without asserting that it must in fact be so, because I have not done the elaborate research that would probably be required to demonstrate it conclusively. In the national park instance, the attraction which is gravitational by the above definition seems weaker than other interactions involving the same people, but there is insufficient evidence to prove that it is the weakest of all interactions in the sociologist's domain.

At any rate it seems clear that the early applications of ostensibly gravitational models to social phenomena were concerned chiefly with stronger kinds of interaction. If we take their work seriously, we would have to recognize that when Carey dealt with population aggregation and with the pricing of commodities in the open market, and when Fourier dealt with friendship, love, paternity, and ambition, each man was dealing with stronger interactions than those involved in the national park study. Whatever values might have been involved, the influence of normative considerations was more likely to obscure them in those studies than in the present one.

Had the work of Carey and Fourier shown adequate empirical sophistication, then, it might still have erred in failing to reserve gravitational concepts for very weak interactions. To neglect the principle of equivalence and to construe stronger forms of social interaction as sociologically gravitational may be quite misleading. If the sociologically gravitational interactions are indeed very weak, it would be little wonder that they had escaped careful analysis until now.

In regard to the material world, where gravity is the weakest known kind of interaction—by many orders of magnitude!—it is in some sense an amazing thing that science has made so much headway in its investigation.

[52] Sir Harrie Massey, *The New Age in Physics.* New York: Harper & Row, Publishers, Incorporated, 1960, pp. 241–242.

This has only been possible because the gravitational force exerted by a body is proportional to its mass and celestial bodies are so massive that their gravitational forces are appreciable.[53] Moreover, the fact that electric charge is both positive and negative and the two forms exist in equal abundance, thus canceling out the attractive and repulsive electromagnetic forces in macroscopic bodies, has enabled man to observe the unmasked effects of the vastly weaker gravitational force. Weak as it is, gravity is indeed the dominant force *for the gross structure* of the material universe.[54] Perhaps in a similar way the forces of sociocultural gravitation may be of considerable sociological importance despite the ease with which they can be masked by other forces. Not until the national park concept had emerged, perhaps, were there instances in which the effects of social gravitation could be isolated from the obscuring effects of stronger kinds of interaction.

The weakest of all the physical interactions was the first to be rigorously described in quantitative terms! Prerequisite to that achievement was the abandonment of Aristotelian conceptions and the substitution of the axioms of Newton. Such conceptual innovation would have been unlikely and would have borne little fruit had celestial phenomena not been so constituted that highly systematic observations could be made with relatively crude equipment. Suppose that the ratio of the sun's mass to the masses of the planets had been very much less than it is, so that the center of their mutual gravitation were not so nearly coincident with the center of the sun itself. Suppose that the sun had been not a single star but a binary, with the planets revolving around the center of mass of a pair of mutually gravitating luminous bodies—or even a cluster of several stars. Suppose the moon had more nearly the same mass as the earth, so that their common center of gravity was not within the body of the earth but somewhere around half way to the moon. Terrestrial observatories would not then have moved around the sun in paths so nearly elliptical. They would have described a more serrated figure, and the calculations required to control for terrestrial motion in organizing our observations of the heavens would have been more complicated. Tycho Brahe's tables would have been vastly more difficult for Kepler to reduce to lawful relations. If, likewise, the satellites of Mars, Jupiter, and Saturn had been more nearly commensurate in mass to their parent planets, the orbits of those planets would have defied simple geometric description, and their explanation in gravitational terms would surely have been delayed many generations. Or if the radii of the orbits of the different planets had not been so far from equal, each planet would have caused larger perturbations in the motions of the others, greatly obscuring the explanation that seemed so simple once Newton had stated it.

Now what I have done in the preceding paragraph is to describe a

[53] *Ibid.*, p. 295.
[54] Sherwin, *op. cit.*, p. 56.

hypothetical solar system having complications somewhat analogous to those confronting the sociologist. The social gravitational forces impinging on the tourist come from a variety of national park sources, no one of which is as predominant in most instances as the sun is in the solar system. Nongravitational forces in the sociological case are only temporarily and occasionally neutralized—and more precariously neutralized than in the physical case. To distinguish between perturbations and primary motions, the sociologist must make even bolder assumptions than were required of Kepler or Newton, but unless such distinctions are made, scientific explanations cannot be achieved. Equation 19 describes what I regard as the primary pattern in the tables of park visitation rates, accounting for over 90 percent of the variance. The remainder is due to what I would choose to regard as perturbations, assuming negligible errors of observation. Not only will this residual variance be much harder to account for than the nine-tenths of the variance attributed to the primary pattern, but it will probably require a far more complex explanation than that which suffices for the perturbations of planets. It will doubtless take a long time before this is achieved.

The barest beginning can be made by examining time series data showing how national park visitation rates have *changed* over the years, from 1929 through 1952. At least two events during that time could have been expected to reduce the rates sharply. Economic interactions may be assumed to be stronger than the social gravitational interactions of park travel, so the Great Depression of the 1930s should be expected to have reduced park visitation appreciably. Wartime curtailment of "nonessential" travel also resulted from the fact that military and industrial interactions were of a stronger type than recreational. Accordingly, drastic reduction of park visitation rates should be expected to have occurred in the war years.

Fluctuations in the visitation rates for one state (Washington) at one national park (Yosemite) are shown in Figure 8. The obvious expectation of a decline in response to depression and war is unsurprisingly confirmed. What is impressive, though, is the size of each decline. From 1931 to 1933, the visitation rate was cut about in half, in spite of what I take to be a long-run tendency for growth. The effect of the Depression may be expressed in these terms: one of every two of the Washingtonians who would have gone to Yosemite under ordinary circumstances was prevented by economic deprivation from doing so in 1933. The Depression lowered both mean income and percentage of labor force employed, but severe as the economic disaster was, neither of these variables was cut in half. Moreover, it is likely that the segment of the population ordinarily inclined to visit national parks was not the segment hardest hit by the Depression. It follows, then, that a great change in park visitation was caused by a proportionately small change in economic interactions. Vacation travel

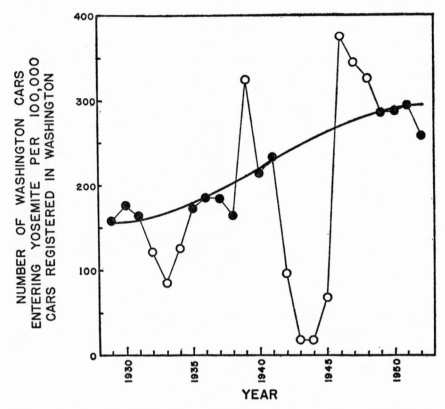

Figure 8.   Growth of visitation rate by Washington cars at Yosemite National Park

is in the luxury category; it can be given up more readily than some other activities. People's interactions with park values are weaker than their normatively regulated interactions with employers and creditors.

The Second World War, with its gasoline and tire rationing, its nation-wide 35 m.p.h. speed limit, and its suspension of civilian automobile production, curtailed pleasure travel even more drastically. In comparison with other behavior required by the war effort, national park visitation represented a very weak type of interaction. This time, of course, the curtailment was due to legal constraints rather than economic constraints, though park visits as such were not against the law. The Yosemite visitation rate by Washington residents was in 1943 only about one-twelfth what it had been just two years earlier. (It should be noted that the tabulations made by the National Park Service were for the "travel year"—from October 1 through September 30. Thus the 1941 visitation rates represent a period that was entirely prior to Pearl Harbor and the onset of wartime travel obstacles.)

It can be seen in Figure 8 that in addition to these two conspicuous travel deficits there was from 1938 to 1939 a sharp upsurge in visitation by Washingtonians at Yosemite. The rate nearly doubled in one year, though it subsided again the following year. In broad terms, I think this peak on the curve tends to support Hypothesis 6 in the value theory presented in Chapter 5, for it can be attributed to the temporary congruence of two desiderata. In 1939, a visit to Yosemite could be combined with a trip to San Francisco to attend the Golden Gate Exposition (one of two world's fairs being held in the United States that year). Many people from other states who would not otherwise have visited Yosemite did so because they were attracted to California by the fair. Not nearly all of the fair goers also went to the national park, however. The inference thus seems unavoidable that for Washington residents in general (and for residents of other states as well—represented in similar peaks on the time curves of other states), the secular fair on man-made Treasure Island exerted a stronger force than emanated from the sacralized scenes of Yosemite.

The other high point on the curve seems to represent "excess" visitation in the immediate postwar years, when travel restrictions were ended. Some portion of the park visitation in these years was probably due to a general restlessness characteristic of demobilization, rather than due to the social gravitational mass of the parks as such.

By making a judgment that certain years were "abnormal," and excluding their rates from consideration, we can form a rough image of the growth curve that might have been observed in the absence of such events as depression, world's fair, and war. To the black dots in Figure 8, which represent the years I deem "normal," I have visually fitted an S-shaped curve to represent what might have been a logistic trend. Similar curves can be fitted to the corresponding data for the other Western states and for other national parks. Not enough data were preserved in the records of some parks to permit calculation of the parameters of best-fitting logistic curves, but in the case of six parks this was done. These were Crater Lake, Lassen Volcanic, Mesa Verde, Mount Rainier, Rocky Mountain, and Yosemite. First, in each case, I estimated "normal" rates for the "abnormal" years by simple linear interpolation. Then from these artificially completed time series, I calculated logistic upper asymptotes. They can be taken as estimates of the "ultimate" visitation rates toward which each state's annual rates were tending (apart from fluctuations due to the obvious causes previously discussed). In a matrix of such "ultimate" rates, Equation 19 accounted for 90.1 percent of the variance. The Kepler model thus fits these "ultimate" rates about as well as it fits tables of actual rates for a single year. This suggests that no great violence has been done to the data by (1) discarding specified years' rates as abnormal, and (2) regarding the trend as logistic.

No Final Causes

Both the depression experience and the war experience demonstrate that the American social system is not "directively organized" with respect to park visitation as a goal variable. If the nation is a homeostatic system, there are other variables around which its equilibrating mechanisms are organized. Park visitation is one of the activities the system can give up as the price of stabilizing certain other variables, such as survival of either its constituent families or the system itself. If park visitation were one of the major goal variables of the system, the visitation rates would have been maintained somewhere near their normal magnitudes even in 1933 and 1943 by compensatory modification of some *other* rates of action (e.g., war production). If a tentative generalization can be made from this, it seems likely that actions which for individuals are consummatory are less likely than instrumental actions to constitute goal variables for the social system.

The postwar excess of visitation could imply a partial exception to what has just been said. If the system were *not at all* directively organized with respect to tourism and park visitation as goals, visitation rates at the end of the war would presumably have reverted merely to the approximate magnitude they would have attained by an uninterrupted trend. Any appreciable excess above that trend suggests that some people responded to the wartime regulations by postponing, rather than totally abandoning, intended trips to Yosemite (or elsewhere). The 1946–1948 rates are enlarged by the postponed visits superimposed on those which would normally have occurred. It should be pointed out, however, that this postwar surplus of visitation was a lot smaller than the wartime visitation deficit; more people abandoned than postponed their visits. Some of the postwar excess, moreover, may have been due to a push rather than a gravitational pull. That is, wartime deprivation of the use of automobiles, rather than deprivation of national park sightseeing, may have been what some of the postwar visitors were compensating. Their arrival at the national park might have been, then, in a higher than usual percentage of cases, incidental to other interests. For the travelers responding more to a push than to a pull, it could be said that wartime deprivation had temporarily blurred the distinction between Series A parks and those in Series B, or between national parks and other destinations not affected by the process of sacralization.

At least it seems safe to conclude that Equation 19 is not a "functional explanation" of park visitation patterns. This is made clear by observing how strange it would sound to assert that park visitation rates vary as they do *in order to* cancel out variations in the ratio of the $\frac{3}{2}$ power of D_{ij} to the square root of M_j. There is no basis for assuming that our social system requires that such variation be compensated or is directively organized to achieve such compensation. Visitation rates do vary in such a way that they do approximately cancel out variations in $D_{ij}^{\frac{3}{2}}/M_j^{\frac{1}{2}}$, but final causes need not be invoked. The sociologist can remain naturalistic and confine his attention to efficient causes, which in this instance include the travel-deterring effects of distance, the institutionalized sacredness of national parks, the phenomenon of value perspective, and the psychological linkage of stimulus and sensation. There is a persistent pattern in park visitation rates, but there is hardly an active process of homeostatic "pattern-maintenance."

Summary

The fact that there is an inverse distance pattern in national park visitation raises the question, "Why?" The travel-deterring effects of distance would tend to prevent park visitation unless balanced by some travel-fostering force. The effort to identify and measure that force is guided by recognition that it is with distance raised to a power greater than 1.0 that the visitation rates vary inversely. By excluding from consideration all visitation by residents of the state within which a park is located, we virtually eliminate weekend and nonovernight trips from the remaining data, permitting the assumption of a linear dependence of travel cost upon distance. The amount by which the exponent exceeds unity in the relation $R_{ij} = b/D_{ij}^d$ thus reveals the phenomenon I have called "value perspective," the dependence of a park's attraction on its proximity.

By making purely heuristic use of Kepler's third law and carefully following out the implications of a force-field model involving a value space reduced in this instance to the two dimensions of an approximately flat land surface, I have shown that a force F_{ij} would vary inversely with D_{ij}. Then, taking into account the pertinent principles of psychophysics, I have shown that this "mental force" arising from a value (or conception of the desirable) would have associated logarithmically with it a "social force" f_{ij}, which would thus vary inversely with D_{ij}^n. By letting

$$n + 1 = d$$

we get $R_{ij} = b/D_{ij}^d$ within what has thus been shown to be a naturalistic set of assumptions.

Empirically, by taking $d = \frac{3}{2}$, we can account for over nine-tenths of the variance in each of several matrices of visitation rates representing a dozen national parks and the 24 states in the Western culture area. It does not simply follow mathematically from this that the accelerating force emanates from the parks to which the people travel, but support for this additional conclusion is afforded by special analysis of visitation data separately tabulated at the five different entrances of Yellowstone National Park. By sorting the states into two sets for each entrance, distinguishing those for which that entrance is a front door from those for which it is a back door, we distinguished between two batches of travelers with differing proportions of merely incidental park visitation. The force-field model is most effective in reducing variance among the visitation rates in which the proportion of travel to ulterior nonpark destinations is minimal. This implies that in data fitting the model, it is the park destination as such which cultural values surround with a force field.

The passage of time has brought about improved fit between the data and the model, and I have interpreted this as reflecting a trend toward an equilibrium condition. Equation 19, then is a description of that equilibrium condition, in which variations in R_{ij} just about cancel out variations in $D_{ij}^{\frac{1}{2}}/M_j^{\frac{1}{2}}$. The fact that there has been such a trend suggests that for a time after the establishment of a national park, visitation rates will be less as distance is greater because of three considerations, not just two. In addition to the deterrent effect of travel cost, and the value-perspective phenomenon, there is the further process of spatial diffusion of park attitudes. At a given time (up until an area's status as a national park has been fully institutionalized), the probability of attributing park values to it is apparently dependent on the proximity of one's residence to it.

The voluntaristic assumptions which have led some sociologists to suppose that naturalism somehow distorts "reality" are incompatible with at least two of these considerations. Within a voluntaristic framework, there would be no value perspectives, nor would attribution of park values to a given site be dependent on proximity. If there has been distortion, it has resulted from animistic orientations, not from naturalistic ones. Defenders of animism in sociology must shoulder the burden of proof which they have too long tried to impose on naturalists.

I have assembled four different ways of measuring park attractiveness and subjected them to a factor analysis by the principal axis method. Almost two-thirds of the variance is accounted for by Factor I, recreational desirability, of which the Stouffer coefficients and Kepler coefficients are nearly pure measures. Most of the remaining variance is due to Factor II, wilderness-invasion with which the successive-intervals scale values and the park population figures are correlated oppositely. A third factor, popularity, makes a very small contribution. Apparently any tendency to perceive parks that many people do visit as parks one ought to visit is so latent that normative factors must be considered virtually neutralized in the case of national park visitation.

By taking account of their regression on the Kepler coefficients, we can convert the successive-intervals scale values to a true ratio scale with an absolute zero. This entails distinguishing Series A parks from Series B, with visitors to the latter parks presumably having proportionately more awareness of the national park idea. Since attractiveness scale values A_j could in principle be obtained for nonpark areas through comparison by knowledgeable judges with existing parks, predictions of future visitation rates for proposed new national parks could be made by the formula

$$R_{ij} = \frac{kA_j}{D_{ij}^{\frac{3}{2}}}$$

Five national parks turn out to have negative A_j, but this is in accord with previous psychometric experience and theory and only suggests that these areas fall below the limen of scalable attractiveness.

There is good reason to believe that for national parks the capacity to attract is proportional to the capacity to resist change. This is analogous to the physical principle of proportionality between gravitational and inertial mass, which is in turn due to the principle of equivalence. Using the sociological concept of institutional sacredness to describe the national park value, we find that a similar principle of equivalence seems applicable in sociology. The gravitational sociocultural mass of an entity would be, according to such a principle, indistinguishable from its inertial sociocultural mass. Thus a social or cultural element surrounded by changing (secular) social and cultural elements would be attractive insofar as it resisted change (was sacred).

If the term "gravitational" is to be used to describe any of the interactions studied by sociologists, it would be reasonable to reserve it for just those interactions to which such a principle of equivalence seems to apply. In physics, four different kinds of interactions have been distinguished, and the gravitational are the weakest category of them all, by many orders of magnitude. Perhaps in sociology, too, the interactions defined by the principle of equivalence as gravitational are much weaker than those to which normative and obligatory factors apply. The early attempts to import gravitational models into sociology may have been misapplications of the concepts partly because the studies were concerned chiefly with stronger kinds of interaction.

Previous attempts to use gravitational models to describe social behavior have not consistently approached sociological data on their own level and have sometimes been insufficiently concerned with empirical verification. Analogy has been mistaken for a means of proof rather than a merely heuristic device. Thus the faults of such past attempts have constituted departures from naturalism, and their foolish or worthless results have not demonstrated that a naturalistic approach to sociological questions is futile.

When careful attention is given to naturalistic requirements, a gravitational model seems to work in the case of national park visitation because the other, stronger social forces have been effectively neutralized in the vacation context. There are indications, too, that if the nation is a homeostatic system, it is not with respect to this very weak interaction that it is directively organized. National park visitation rates vary in such a way that they do approximately cancel out the variations in $D_{ij}^{\frac{1}{2}}/M_j^{\frac{1}{2}}$, but there is no basis for assuming that compensation of such variations is required by the social system. There is thus no warrant for, or advantage in, invoking final causes to explain this pattern.

The consummatory activities of persons are not the goal variables which a social system operates to maintain within a restricted range. Yet they are the very activities to which voluntaristic assumptions would seem most obviously applicable, if they apply to any behavior at all. If *these* activities are patterned in ways that are predictable within rigorously naturalistic terms, there is no remaining excuse for sociologists to cling to animistic thoughtways.

Chapter Nine
REDUCTIONISM: PRO AND CON

The Taboo against Reductionism

The main import of the previous chapters might be summed up in these words: naturalistic concepts and procedures are as applicable to sociology as to any other body of empirical knowledge. This has been claimed before, but the effectiveness of previous claims generally has been impaired by implicit or outright reductionism. I have sought to disentangle naturalism from reductionism. In the present chapter I will explore the topic of reductionism more explicitly in order to show why that disentanglement is required and to certify its accomplishment.

Social systems involve men. Men, as reasoning, responding, and socializing beings, involve psychological processes, and as organisms, men involve living tissues. Living tissues are composed of matter in organized structures capable of activity beyond the scope of matter that is otherwise constituted. "Reductionism" is a term sociologists use to refer to attempts to explain social behavior in psychological or biological terms. It could also refer to attempts to explain organic phenomena in molecular terms, or chemical phenomena in physical terms, etc. In short, it denotes any effort to account for collective phenomena exclusively through what is known of their constituent parts.

Starting with Comte's delineation of a hierarchy of sciences, with sociology at the top, sociologists have thought in terms of some natural assortment of phenomena into different levels. It has been argued that the concept of "emergent" levels of phenomena has helped suppress nonnaturalistic images of man by opposing the recurrent attempts to separate studies of human society from the sciences of the material universe. But the concept has been said also to have utility in resisting the reductionist tendency (or temptation) to squeeze social phenomena into the conceptual categories of the older sciences in some merely *a priori* manner.[1] It is therefore appropriate to ask, Why have naturalism and reductionism heretofore tended to be intertwined? Must defense against reductionist thinking lead to nonnaturalistic thoughtways? Conversely, must naturalism lead to reductionism? If it leads inevitably to reductionism, would this be too great a cost?

Reductionism has been taboo among sociologists for a long time—certainly since Durkheim so stoutly argued for sociological autonomy. Sociology, he said, must not be considered the mere auxiliary of some other science. Distinctly sociological training, rather than training in any older science, is necessary for the sociologist so that he may have an adequate appreciation of "the specificity of social reality" and may be prepared to "grasp social facts intelligently."[2] According to Timasheff's appraisal of the state of the discipline, by now it is commonly recognized among sociologists that social phenomena are *sui generis*. They are not reducible to such nonsocial facts as the psychological, the biological, or the physical. Accordingly, he said, biological and physical analogies are now commonly rejected by sociologists.[3]

It is one thing to reject analogies of a certain type as alleged proofs for sociological propositions. It is another thing to dismiss them as sources of sociological hypotheses subject to testing against sociological data. In the nineteenth century a whole generation of sociological effort was wasted because analogy was mistaken for proof. But the heuristic value of analogy should never be overlooked in our eagerness belatedly to recognize the empirical insufficiency of analogy. Some sociologists have discounted even the heuristic potential of physical or biological analogies. Read Bain, for one, wrote that explanation by reduction really does not explain simply because it changes the universe of discourse. Whenever we "reduce" phenomena to a lower level, we wind up talking about different aspects of the world than those with which we started, and thus fail to explain the phenomena originally confronting us as problematic. Bain

---

[1] See Abraham Edel, "The Concept of Levels in Social Theory," chap. 6 in Llewellyn Gross (ed.), *Symposium on Sociological Theory.* New York: Harper & Row, Publishers, Incorporated, 1959, p. 170.

[2] Emile Durkheim, *The Rules of the Sociological Method* (tr. Sarah A. Solovay and John H. Mueller; ed. George E. G. Catlin). New York: The Free Press of Glencoe, 1950, p. 145.

[3] Nicholas S. Timasheff, *Sociological Theory: Its Nature and Growth,* rev. ed. New York: Random House, Inc., 1957, pp. 303–304.

felt that the "arrested development" of sociology could be attributed in large part to reductionism.[4]

Various suggestions have been made as to *why* reductionism has made sociological analyses abortive. Lundberg, in his most systematic metasociological treatise, wrote that numerous sociologists had been "smitten" with the belief that sociological phenomena must be reduced to psychological phenomena if they are to be explained. In turn, however, by the same logic these would have to be reduced to biological, and thence to physicochemical terms, and if the chain is pursued all the way, he said, all events presumably would be reduced to actions of God, and explanation in any verifiable sense would have been abandoned.[5] In accord with a professional norm that seems to have become traditional, Lundberg went on to declare that sociological phenomena could be observed and described on their own level and in their own terms, regardless of any constituent physicochemical processes involved.[6]

Parsons has offered quite a different view of the disutility of reductionism. In his early opposition to sociological positivism, he wrote that it tends to obscure man's essential nature as an "active, creative, evaluating creature."[7] That is to say, reductionism is wrong for sociology because it discards basic, inescapable aspects of human nature. How do we know that activity, creativity, and evaluation are essential? Apparently, for Parsons, this was a premise rather than a conclusion, and was not an empirical issue.[8] Sociologists' apprehension that something vital is "left out" when sociological phenomena are "reduced" to a lower level is expressed, among other ways, in the predilection for the *Verstehende* approach.[9]

For sociologists who begin with the assumption that the social sciences are *sui generis* and have a logical and epistemological structure inherently different from those of the natural sciences, naturalism itself can seem tantamount to reductionism. According to Sorokin, for example, the fundamental difference between sociocultural phenomena and physicochemical and biological phenomena is basic and perhaps unbridgeable because of the component of *meanings* in sociocultural phenomena.[10] There is a strong Aristotelian tone in Sorokin's insistence that every empirical socio-

---

[4] Read Bain, "The Concept of Complexity in Sociology: II," *Social Forces*, 8 (March, 1930), pp. 375–376.
[5] George A. Lundberg, *Foundations of Sociology*. New York: The Macmillan Company, 1939, p. 128.
[6] *Ibid.*, p. 174.
[7] Talcott Parsons, "The Place of Ultimate Values in Sociological Theory," *International Journal of Ethics*, 45 (April, 1935), pp. 282, 286.
[8] Talcott Parsons, "An Outline of the Social System," in Talcott Parsons, Edward Shils, Kaspar D. Naegele, and Jesse R. Pitts (eds.), *Theories of Society*. New York: The Free Press of Glencoe, 1961, p. 32.
[9] Cf. Theodore Abel, "The Operation Called *Verstehen*," *American Journal of Sociology*, 54 (November, 1948), p. 214.
[10] Pitirim A. Sorokin, *Sociocultural Causality, Space, Time*. Durham, N.C.: The Duke University Press, 1943, p. 27.

cultural phenomenon has three components: (1) meanings, which are immaterial, timeless, and spaceless; (2) material vehicles, by which meanings are made external and objective; (3) human agents, who, by means of the physicochemical or biological vehicles, use or convey the meanings. Since (2) and (3) supposedly cannot be adequately understood without (1), there is a radical difference between sociocultural phenomena and physicochemical or biological phenomena as such.[11] Thus, in Sorokin's view, efforts to make sociology naturalistic are misleading because they are inherently reductionist.

I have suggested that MacIver was ambivalent on these matters. Studied in sequence, his writings reflect increasing affinity for naturalism, yet like Sorokin, he seemed to see naturalism as inseparable from reductionism, and like nearly all sociologists of the present century, he abhorred reductionism. He classified all phenomena into three great "dynamic realms"—the physical realm, the realm of organic being, and the realm of conscious being—and assumed fundamental differences between them.[12]

If these views were accurate, if reductionism retarded the empirical advancement of sociology, this would be good reason for avoiding it. If naturalism entails reductionism, we should be extremely cautious about adopting naturalistic concepts and methods unless the advantages clearly exceed the costs. It can be questioned, however, whether naturalism really does entail reductionism and would therefore include the latter in its price. In Chapter 5, I sought to show that naturalistic sociology did not have to overlook valuing as an aspect of human behavior. In Chapter 8, the gravitational model accounting for patterns of park visitation was naturalistic but was most emphatically not reductionist, as previous gravity models in sociology have sometimes been. It was not contended that tourists were drawn toward national parks by a force field generated by the physical mass of the mountains therein; the force fields invoked were not physical, but pertained to institutionalized values. Reductionism and naturalism can be distinguished from each other.

Ideology and Reductionism

It should be recognized that reductionism itself has not been resisted purely because it allegedly leads to empirically invalid results. It has also had opposition for reasons that might best be termed ideological. For example, no major sociologist completely accepted psychological behav-

[11] *Ibid.*, pp. 4–5.
[12] For comparison with Sorokin's listing of three components, see Robert M. MacIver, *Social Causation*. Boston: Ginn and Company, 1942, pp. 272–273, 289.

iorism (despite the favorable disposition some felt toward it). Some of
the resistance to behaviorism was apparently due to the fact that the inner,
mental, nonphysical aspect of human life was taken to be the ultimate
force in society and culture.[13] In American sociological thought, in particular, individualism has been a persistent assumption. Cultural limitations
on the feeling, knowing, and willing of individuals have been recognized,
but human interaction, social structure, and social change have been assumed to be ultimately rooted in individuals' volitions, desires, and actions. American sociology has interpreted human behavior as voluntaristic.
Nonvoluntaristic theories have been inimical to the American ethos.[14]

Charles Bolton has expressed alarm regarding a trend he has perceived
in contemporary American sociological theory toward energy models. Such
a trend would represent a drift away from voluntaristic assumptions. I
presume he would assign Chapter 8 of this book to that trend, in which
he also included the equilibrium concept, and input-output analysis. This
sort of trend is "inevitably reductionist," he said, because it conceives
social relationships in terms of what is "clearly a construction of the sociologist." He insisted there is nothing real that can be termed "social energy."[15] But it could be argued that Bolton himself has adopted a
construct—an image of man incompatible with the energy concept, which
thereby *makes* energy models reductionist. As I have noted earlier, it is
no criticism of a theory merely to point out that illata are included among
its concepts. It must be shown (not assumed) that the illata are either
superfluous or erroneous. If they are truly illata, with quantifiable relations
to concreta, they are different from mere fictions, even if they remain
beyond the reach of direct observation.

It is pointless, said MacIver, to apply the causal formulas of classical
mechanics to social systems. Knowing the state of a social system at a
given time in terms of some system of coordinates will never enable us,
as in mechanics, to calculate mathematically its past or future states.
Mechanics and sociology require two different frames of reference, he
insisted. In the sociological frame of reference, causes are *understandable;*
they can be perceived in our own experience.[16] This argument, in terms
of some kind of "direct" experience of causes, rejects all mechanistic illata,
but assumes there are unmeasurable aspects of human experience that
would be inexcusably omitted by adoption of a mechanical frame of reference. It begs the question whether these are illata or fictions. It asserts

[13] Roscoe C. Hinkle and Gisela J. Hinkle, *The Development of Modern Sociology.*
New York: Random House, Inc., 1954, p. 26.
[14] *Ibid.*, p. 73.
[15] Charles D. Bolton, "Is Sociology a Behavioral Science?" *Pacific Sociological Review,*
6 (Spring, 1963), p. 4.
[16] MacIver, *op. cit.*, pp. 263–264.

axiomatically that the mechanistic framework would be reductionist. But the argument is implicitly ideological, in that man's humanness is taken to be at stake in the asserting or doubting of his uniqueness.

This, I think, is what Lundberg had in mind when he wrote that the perennial attempt to declare social phenomena "different" from physical phenomena, so that sociology and the natural sciences must proceed by different fundamental methods, has been a desperate rearguard defense of the "dignity" of man. At least from the time of Darwin, naturalistic views have been eroding the notion of contrast between man and the rest of the animal kingdom and the universe.[17] The erosion is painful to some, and they fight it. Jules Henry, an anthropologist, rejected Stewart's social physics *in principle*, as well as for its theoretical crudeness. "Mechanistic treatment of social phenomena," he wrote, "distracts attention from the real problems of social living. The consideration of persons as particles paves the way for those who would treat them as assembly-line items, to be organized and handled as any political party wishes." Such thinking must be resisted *because it could be "the backdoor to tyranny."*[18]

An occasional antinaturalistic writer views all steps toward naturalistic sociology as "scientism," and imputes to them the illegitimate purpose of turning people into puppets so that they can be subjected to some sinister regime.[19] Reductionism has been viewed as a tool of regimentation. It has been condemned as a mask for ulterior motives, rather than on grounds of empirical inappropriateness. Defense of the free will notion sometimes has involved impugning the motives of the determinist instead of refuting his assertions. Stark, for example, has argued that Pareto distinguished between logical and nonlogical actions so as to facilitate a mechanistic theory of social life whose superficially clever distinction between residues and derivations would enable him to throw out freedom.[20]

Perhaps the taboo against reductionism has commanded more allegiance among sociologists than its scientific value would warrant because it has been linked to the defense of freedom and human dignity. Viewed in an ideological light, the issue of reductionism and the issue of naturalism have seemed to be the same issue. They ought to be considered as separate topics, however, for only in this way can each be explicitly understood. When they are not understood, sociological inquiry tends to remain abortive, because its lapses into animism are legitimated by the belief that they are required by the taboo against reductionism.

[17] George A. Lundberg, "Is Sociology Too Scientific?" *Sociologus*, 9, (September, 1933), p. 304.
[18] Jules Henry, "Letter," *Scientific American*, 179 (July, 1948), p. 1.
[19] See, for example, A. H. Hobbs, *Social Problems and Scientism*. Harrisburg, Pa.: The Stackpole Company, 1953, pp. 22–23, 254.
[20] Werner Stark, *The Fundamental Forms of Social Thought*. New York: Fordham University Press, 1963, pp. 129–132.

Temptations to Reductionism

No taboo would be required to prevent reductionism, of course, if there were no impulse toward reductionist analyses. There seems to be such an impulse, at least under some circumstances and in relation to some topics. Perhaps because they are older than sociology or psychology, such disciplines as physics and chemistry, or physiology and neurology, are more prestigious. It is thus tempting to explain human behavior in physical, chemical, physiological, or neurological terms, and to feel that no other mode of explanation really explains.[21]

Within the natural sciences, older disciplines or subdisciplines tend to be accorded greater legitimacy and reality than newer ones. However vast the array of experimental observations organized by a given theory, if the theory is novel and employs concepts unlike those of the old, established models, it is suspect. Its explanation of the facts is sometimes felt to be "unsatisfactory"—meaning that it doesn't relate new facts to familiar, comfortable concepts.[22] In social science, then, the temptation to formulate reductionist theories may be attributed at least partly to the wish to achieve explanation in terms of concepts that seem palpable. Familiar abstracta and illata seem less contrived than novel ones. The taboo against reductionism has been useful in the development of sociology insofar as it has weaned us away from an assumption that a concept's reality is proportional to its antiquity. The taboo may also have been as necessary to an infant science as protective tariff barriers are to an immature national economy; it may later become just as obsolete and dysfunctional.

Among the first generation or so of sociologists—Comte and Spencer, Ward in some ways, and certainly the Social Darwinists—the drive to assert that sociology was a science degenerated into a campaign to extend the science of biology to cover sociological problems. If biological principles were inadequate to account for social phenomena, the early sociologists failed to discover it because their preoccupation with the concepts and theorems of a recognized science was divorced from a concern for empirical verification. Sociology could not remain merely a branch of biology for empirical reasons. Additional concepts, besides those then known to biology, were required to organize sociological observations which differed from the biologists' data. Had the first generation been more concerned with observation, they might have discovered this. Sociology could not be reduced to biology. The attempt to generalize biological notions to cover social situations seemed to those who indulged in it to be scientific, but their misconception of science poisoned the conceptual

---

[21] F. V. Smith, *Explanation of Human Behaviour*, 2d ed. London: Constable & Co., Ltd., 1960, p. 29.
[22] Ernest Nagel, *The Structure of Science.* New York: Harcourt, Brace & World, Inc., 1961, p. 114.

atmosphere of sociology. To a later generation, the antidote has seemed to consist of a rigid taboo against reductionism.

If the error of the early sociologists lay in using imported concepts uncritically, rather than just in using them at all, then the required antidote does not consist of a rule proscribing all such concepts. It should consist of a rule that any concept (whether originated by a sociologist, or by a practitioner of biology or any other more venerable discipline) will be incorporated into the sociological lexicon only if it is useful in the formulation of verifiable propositions about sociological data. The rule should allow borrowing of hypotheses as well as concepts from older disciplines *if* they are tested in terms of sociological data. Verification of a proposition in biology (or physics, etc.) does not confirm the validity of its sociological version. Naturalism reminds us of this. The taboo against reductionism distracts attention from it, defines the issue in other terms, and has even been construed to mean that propositions true on "lower levels" *cannot* be true in sociology.

The early sociologists supposed certain propositions had to be true in sociology because they were true in biology. In this they were wrong, and revealed their ignorance of naturalistic tenets. But the taboo against reductionism seems to say that *their* failure to learn anything sociological from their study of biology proves biology has nothing to offer sociology. It no more proves this than a five-year-old's inability to learn from the Encyclopaedia Britannica proves that reference work has nothing to teach his elders. By the same token, it does not suffice to show that sociology has nothing to gain from conceptual interplay with other sciences such as physics, chemistry, etc. The early sociologists were not adequately naturalistic in their work. Their failure to produce useful sociological insights from their encounter with another science hardly demonstrates that naturalistic sociologists could not succeed in a similar quest.

Alleged Futility of Reductionism

Many sociologists have said that sociology *should* not be reductionist; some have said or implied that ultimately it *could* not be. Durkheim insisted that social facts were external to the individual and were coercive of individual actions. Because social facts consisted of collective representations and actions, they were not merely biological phenomena. Because they were external to the individual, social facts were not merely psychological phenomena.[23] As a science of social facts, sociology therefore had to be nonbiological and nonpsychological. To attempt to reduce social facts to the psychological or biological level was futile.

[23] Durkheim, *op. cit.*, pp. 3–4.

The reason sociologists should avoid reductionism, according to this view, was that reductionist thought constituted wasted effort. Social phenomena could not be *successfully* reduced to the categories and dimensions of a lower-level discipline and described by its principles. To MacIver, the effort to translate what he called "the data of consciousness" into physicalistic terms was sometimes done on metaphysical grounds, but because the result would be abortive, such metaphysics must be condemned. It seemed to MacIver that this kind of sociology would sidestep consideration of goals and motives, and would thus neglect something he assumed to be an important aspect of social phenomena. Real sociological problems would remain unsolved because of such misleading metaphysical predilections. For MacIver this was the reason to oppose reductionism.[24] Similarly, Stark felt that sociological models based on physics or physiology were spurious because they were addressed to phenomena men "find" rather than to phenomena men "create."[25] Reductionism was seen by both these men to be something to avoid because it rejects voluntarism. The conviction that reductionism must be futile and wasteful of intellectual effort thus arises out of animistic assumptions. From animistic premises, interhuman behavior, of course, seems irreducible to categories appropriate to a naturalistic framework.

Sorokin sought to "liberate" sociology from what he described as its "voluntary servitude" to naturalism. He said he wished to do this because of the futility of such bondage; if it had been fertile and fruitful he would have had no objection to it. In order to progress, sociology must declare its independence from the natural sciences, he insisted.[26] Radcliffe-Brown, too, regarded subordination of the science of society to the concepts of a lower-level discipline as an obstacle to progress, but for him the obstructive servitude was to psychology rather than to natural science as such.[27] Similarly, Madge has attributed the "slow growth" of sociology since Comte's time to inadequate recognition of the individuality of each science and the resulting wasted effort to create a sociology patterned after some other science dealing with phenomena of a different nature.[28]

It is not altogether clear, however, that reductionism has been futile because of fundamental differences between social and other phenomena. Part of the difficulty has been due to the distorted images of the other sciences which sociologists have sought to imitate. Counterarguments to the antireductionism taboo have been offered, including the view that any science which has been conspicuously successful deserves careful study

[24] MacIver, *op. cit.*, pp. 116–117.
[25] Stark, *op. cit.*, p. 12.
[26] Sorokin, *op. cit.*, p. vii.
[27] A. R. Radcliffe-Brown, *A Natural Science of Society*. New York: The Free Press of Glencoe, 1957, p. 147.
[28] John Madge, *The Origins of Scientific Sociology*. New York: The Free Press of Glencoe, 1962, p. 2.

by the practitioners of a less developed science to see if its procedures can be extended to their field. It is essential, though, that any such extension be based on a correct and undistorted understanding of the science one takes as a guide.[29]

I have already pointed out some of the gross distortions of physical concepts and axioms on which past versions of social physics have been based. The futility of this branch of sociology up till now is at least as much attributable to its misunderstanding of physics as to its reliance on physics. The same can be said for sociology styled after biology. The major fault of the Social Darwinists lay in their misconceptions of the principles of natural selection, not in their conviction that those principles might be generalizable beyond the borders of biology. Many of them supposed that Darwin had formulated an explanation of changes in organisms; society was an organism, therefore his formulations applied to society. They failed to see the difference between this and a theory accounting for changing frequency distributions of species traits from generation to generation—which is what natural selection meant.

To some extent, therefore, it must be concluded that the belief that reductionism is ultimately futile has grown out of the sloppiness of the early and most notorious attempts to build sociology in the image of another science. It is not self-evident that all such attempts must be equally crude.

Impossibility of Rigid Compartmentalization

The taboo against reductionism has not totally foreclosed exploration of cross-disciplinary uniformities. Different sciences may in some fashion stand on different levels, but the hierarchy of these levels is not incontrovertibly discontinuous. One level may shade into another. The boundaries between sciences may be hazy. The walls between conceptual compartments are often porous. In the face of these circumstances, continued reassertion of the taboo against reductionism has begun to be construed as a sign of sociologists' intellectual insecurity. Sociology has now and then been defended as sacred territory, to be guarded against trespass by the unwashed partisans of lower sciences.[30] Viewed in this light, resistance to reductionism—at least when it becomes excessive (and obsessive)—obstructs sociological discovery more than it fosters it. Whether intended as a barrier to stem the tide of naturalism or not, the taboo

[29] Cf. Abraham Kaplan, *The Conduct of Inquiry.* San Francisco, Calif.: Chandler Publishing Company, 1964, p. 11.
[30] Alex Inkeles, "Personality and Social Structure," chap. 11 in Robert K. Merton, Leonard Broom, and Leonard S. Cottrell, Jr. (eds.), *Sociology Today.* New York: Basic Books, Inc., Publishers, 1959, p. 249.

against reductionism functions as such when it is too rigidly enforced. Solution of some problems in sociology requires cognizance of data and laws of other sciences contiguous to the territory staked out by sociology. In particular, the study of social systems cannot wholly avoid concern for what social psychologists have learned about human personality, or what other categories of psychologists can tell us about the functioning of the human nervous system.[31]

We seem to be beginning to outgrow the taboo against reductionism. Sociology is reaching a stage of maturity in which it can afford to reassert Comte's conviction that the pursuit of its own problems requires familiarity with some of the less complicated phenomena already studied and explained by anterior sciences.[32] Even MacIver, drawn as he was by his animistic predispositions toward the antireductionist attitude, recognized the pitfalls in the departmentalism for which Durkheim had seemed to stand. In the study of social causation, he said, it would be necessary to "ignore all frontiers," at least between one *social* science and another.[33] To restrict our attention to the special domain of any one of the social sciences would obstruct solution of the problem of causation which was the common substratum of them all. The interdependence of institutions makes it impossible to explain legal processes entirely in legal or political terms, religious behavior entirely in religious terms, or economic phenomena entirely in economic terms.[34]

Martindale has suggested an apt metaphor with which to question the feasibility of rigid antireductionism. A research problem, he said, no more respects departmental boundaries than a vein of ore respects property lines.[35] Furfey, too, despite his apprehensive attitudes toward naturalism, has acknowledged the impossibility of delimiting the field of sociology with a perfectly immutable and impenetrable boundary.[36] The indefiniteness of sociology's boundaries is only a special case, he said, of the general rule that sciences merge imperceptibly into each other.[37]

At this point it is well to recall the goal Stouffer seemed to have in mind when he formulated the intervening opportunities hypothesis. He sought to substitute the properly sociological variable, intervening opportunities, for the unacceptably physical variable, distance. It is therefore interesting to note that in a recent publication, Parsons gave explicit recog-

[31] *Ibid.*, p. 251.

[32] Auguste Comte, *The Positive Philosophy* (tr. Harriet Martineau), New York: Calvin Blanchard, 1856, p. 31.

[33] MacIver, *op. cit.*, p. 76.

[34] Robert M. MacIver, "Social Causation: A Rejoinder," *American Journal of Sociology*, 49 (July, 1943), p. 58.

[35] Don Martindale, *The Nature and Types of Sociological Theory*. Boston: Houghton Mifflin Company, 1960, p. 44.

[36] Paul Hanly Furfey, *The Scope and Method of Sociology*. New York: Harper & Row, Publishers, Incorporated, 1953, pp. 146–147.

[37] *Ibid.*, p. 147.

nition to the involvement of physical variables as such in social interaction. Individuals perform their tasks, he said, in a physical environment; their behavior depends in part on physical location in space.[38] Especially in view of the source, such a statement is clearly a crack in the antireductionist dike. Further erosion of the levee may ultimately cause sociologists to be swept back to Comte's view that the various sciences are "not radically separate, but all branches from the same trunk."[39]

While some sociologists seem to be giving ground grudgingly in their commitment to the isolation of sociology from other sciences, an occasional philosopher of social science has already begun to move for repeal of the professional statutes forbidding reductionist thought. Kaplan has said there are no fixed boundaries in the domain of truth, there is but one world of ideas, and therefore utility is the final test of the propriety of borrowing concepts, data, laws, techniques, or models by one discipline from another.[40] Opposition to reductionism is becoming less adamant, less doctrinaire. Another generation of sociologists may regard it as a meaningless issue.

Decay of the Biological Prop for Antireductionism

It is ironic that part of the support for the notion that sociology is irreducible because social phenomena are *sui generis* comes from the linking of sociology to biology. In relation to inanimate matter, biological phenomena have been thought also to be *sui generis*. Accordingly, biology was supposed to be immune from reduction to physics or chemistry. It seemed to follow that sociology, which also studied "living" entities, must be immune too. It has turned out, however, that major advancements in biology were achieved through closing rather than preserving the gaps between that science and the "lower" sciences of chemistry and physics. Progress in the latter disciplines has facilitated this closure. In the state of physical and chemical knowledge which prevailed a generation ago it was true that biological phenomena defied physicochemical explanation. In a more advanced state of knowledge, this is no longer so.

There is a further irony. It was Comte who fostered this *sui generis* notion, in spite of his "positive" intentions for sociology. He wrote that biology would "always furnish the fundamental ideas that must guide sociological research."[41]

[38] Parsons, "An Outline of the Social System," p. 45.
[39] Comte, *op. cit.*, p. 30.
[40] Kaplan, *op. cit.*, p. 4.
[41] Comte, *op. cit.*, pp. 826–827.

But the irreducibility of one science to another is subject to change. Advancing knowledge in a given science can make it less reducible to another than it once was, and at the same time can increase its capacity to explain the principles of some "higher-level" science. When this is not borne in mind, issues in the strategy and tactics of research tend to be mistaken for issues in the ultimate nature of things.[42] At a time when what was known of biology could not be satisfactorily explained by what was then known of physics and chemistry, the inference was prematurely made that living phenomena constitute a domain of reality that is almost unconnected to the domain of inanimate matter.

This metaphysical conclusion neglected advances in biology that had already been achieved precisely through consideration of the common features of living and nonliving mechanisms. Harvey, for example, had conceived the heart as a pump, with far-reaching consequences.[43] The drift toward mechanistic biology, to which Harvey's insight contributed, was in competition with a vitalistic mode of thought in biology that would continue to attribute to life a special mystical character.[44]

Vitalism fosters questions that are simply not empirically answerable. It has all but died out in biology today, presumably for this reason. But there is still opposition to the drift toward mechanism, at least by a minority of biologists. It is an opposition that goes beyond pointing out that some biology has not yet been reduced to physical or chemical principles. It still contends that such reduction is impossible fundamentally. What is significant in the present context, however, is that in biology this attitude is vestigial; it is in retreat.[45]

In the light of these developments in biology, it is perplexing to find Parsons believing the early sociologists erred in ignoring cybernetic control patterns when they pointed out the parallels between metabolic processes in organisms and behavioral processes in societal systems.[46] If this is not criticizing sociologists for neglecting biological principles of which even the biologists in that day were incompletely aware, then it begs another question. Are those who today persist in regarding biology as the only permissible outside model for sociology the ones whose understanding of cybernetic mechanisms is most advanced? I doubt it. They seem to use these concepts as a last refuge for the Aristotelian notion of final causes, but as Floyd Allport has recognized, ecological studies of interdependent animal species show cycles of increase and decrease in their populations that imply "negative feedback." Such interspecies cybernetic action belies the teleological connotations of terms such as

---

[42] Nagel, *op. cit.*, pp. 363–364.
[43] William S. Beck, *Modern Science and the Nature of Life*. Garden City, N.Y.: Anchor Books, Doubleday & Company, Inc., 1961, p. 60.
[44] *Ibid.*, p. 63.
[45] *Ibid.*, pp. 148–150.
[46] Parsons, "An Outline of the Social System," pp. 37–38.

"servomechanism," or even "feedback" itself, plausible as those connotations might be in the case of the single organism.[47]

The important implication of cybernetic models is precisely that those processes which have heretofore seemed to require and justify teleological conceptualization and explanation can now be described in thoroughly mechanistic terms.[48] In this way as in others, the boundaries separating biology from other sciences have all but dissolved.[49] Modern genetics has thoroughly fused biology with chemistry. The most noteworthy progress in biology in the near future seems likely to occur in biophysics—where the methods and concepts of physics are brought to bear in explaining organic processes.[50] If so, the excuse which sociologists have until now supposed they got from biology for avoiding contact with "lower" sciences will be gone.

A few other arguments in opposition to reductionism remain to be briefly considered. First, any assumption that other sciences have flourished by jealously guarding their independence is mistaken. In addition to the undeniable success already achieved in explaining many biological phenomena in physicochemical terms, attempts to unify various special branches of physical science by integrating their several systems of explanation into a single comprehensive theory are generally encouraged.[51] Formulation of a more general theory subsuming several limited theories is regarded with favor by scientists.

Second, the property of "emergence" often attributed to so-called "collective phenomena" may be more a characteristic of current theories than a trait of the phenomena themselves. While some properties of collective phenomena may indeed be emergent in terms of a given state of knowledge (i.e., inexplicable by theories pertaining to the constituent phenomena), as knowledge of the constituent phenomena improves, the emergent character of the collective phenomena may be diminished.[52] This year's theories often explain what last year's theories couldn't.

Third, man's inability to manufacture a given object does not suffice to remove that object from the realm of natural science or make it inexplicable within a naturalistic framework. Even if it should remain clear that biology were irreducible to physics and chemistry, it would not be man's inability to assemble an organism from nonliving components that made this so. No man can assemble a carbon atom from its electrical components, but this is not taken as refutation of the theory of atomic

---

[47] Floyd H. Allport, *Theories of Perception and the Concept of Structure.* New York: John Wiley & Sons, Inc., 1955, p. 486.
[48] *Ibid.*, p. 495.
[49] Beck, *op. cit.*, p. 304.
[50] Sir Harrie Massey, *The New Age in Physics.* New York: Harper & Row, Publishers, Incorporated, 1960, p. 330.
[51] Nagel, *op. cit.*, pp. 398ff.
[52] *Ibid.*, pp. 369–371.

structure. Nor can a solar system or a galaxy be constructed by human enterprise from a stockpile of matter, yet physicochemical theories explaining such systems are reasonably good and have gained wide acceptance.[53] The mountains were not built by men, but geologists can symbolically reconstruct the mountain-building processes of nature. To recognize that nobody "invented" society does not justify rejection of naturalistic approaches in the investigation of societal phenomena.

Heuristic Use of Analogy in Natural Science

The various natural sciences seem not to have been so shy as sociology about using analogy to suggest promising and testable hypotheses to account for previously unexplained phenomena. There have been many instances in which theoretical breakthroughs were due to insights gained from analogy. For example, William Thomson (later Lord Kelvin) once called attention to an instructive parallel between gravitational theory and the theory of heat conduction. The uniform motion of heat in homogeneous media turned out to be described by mathematical formulae of the same form as those used in describing gravitational attraction. The heat source was the analogue of the center of attraction. At any given point, the flow of heat was analogous to the accelerating effect of gravity. Temperature was analogous to gravitational potential. The term "force," however, was not involved.[54] What must be emphasized is that gravitational theory was useful in *suggesting* such a theory of heat conduction, but the latter theory had to be independently verified by thermal data. James Clerk Maxwell, aware that there were obvious and significant limits to the resemblance of the two kinds of phenomena, nevertheless looked favorably upon the analogy and deemed it fruitful in stimulating appropriate mathematical ideas.[55]

In turn, Maxwell used the laws describing the motions of incompressible fluids as an analogy in developing his mathematical representation of electrical phenomena.[56] Other examples of the fruitful use of analogy in generating important scientific hypotheses can be cited. They include Lyell's inference from the dependence of present social structures on remote events in history that the present structure of the earth's surface might have resulted from ancient but specifiable geological processes. What made this analogy pay off was Lyell's conviction that similar geological processes were still operating and could be observed now. Thus, in keep-

[53] *Ibid.*, pp. 443–444.
[54] *Ibid.*, p. 109.
[55] *Ibid.*
[56] *Ibid.*, p. 110.

ing with naturalism, speculation could be checked by observation. And again, Darwin's confessed dependence on Malthus is an example. From Malthus's *Essay on Population* Darwin got the idea of the struggle for existence. He made important heuristic use of analogy when he extended that idea to imply the principle of nonrandom survival as a mechanism of biological evolution. Natural selection was analogous to common practices of stockbreeders. Yet another example comes to mind from astronomy. Despite the differences between sound and light, the recognition that both have the properties of wave phenomena, with fixed speeds of propagation through given media, made it reasonable to generalize the Doppler effect from sound to light and thereby to calculate the speed of recession of remote galaxies by measuring the shift of their spectral lines toward red.

Sociologists ought to keep such examples as these in mind, rather than letting the folly of the organismic sociologists and the Social Darwinists alienate them forever from the heuristic advantages of analogy wisely used. Of course a model may be a potential intellectual trap, but it can also be a powerful conceptual tool. It will be a trap if some inessential feature is overemphasized, or if similarities between phenomena are mistaken for identities.[57] There is no *a priori* way to know what is essential and what is not, so there is no purely logical safeguard to prevent a tool from becoming a trap. The security of the sociologist in this respect, as for investigators in any other field of inquiry, is in reliance on empirical tests of his hypotheses.

In the final analysis, then, the tenets of naturalism provide better protection from false identification of distinct phenomena than is provided by any taboo against reductionism. If we are truly naturalistic in our studies, the taboo is unnecessary, for inappropriate analogies will eventually be discarded when found empirically inadequate or misleading. If we conform to the taboo ritualistically, our naturalism tends to be obstructed.

Summary

"Reductionism" is a word that denotes any attempt to account for collective phenomena exclusively in terms of what is known of their constituent parts. In sociology, reductionist explanations have long been taboo. The taboo has been excessive in its scope, stigmatizing any reliance at all on knowledge of lower-level phenomena in the explanation of so-called "emergent" phenomena. This taboo has been one of the factors inhibiting sociologists from fully embracing the tenets of naturalism. It has been mistakenly supposed that naturalism is inevitably reductionist. Careful re-

[57] *Ibid.*, p. 115.

examination of reductionism and of the taboo against it should help to remove one impediment to naturalistic inquiry.

The taboo arose from belated recognition that the use of analogy as a means of proof by the nineteenth-century organismic sociologists had been abortive. Social phenomena had not been satisfactorily explained with biological principles, so these phenomena were declared *sui generis*. Overcorrecting the earlier error, subsequent generations of sociologists became reluctant to avail themselves of analogies drawn from sciences of lower-level phenomena even for heuristic purposes.

Various grounds have been cited in justification of the taboo against reductionism. It has been said that reductionist analyses really don't explain the phenomena they purport to explain. Consequently, preoccupation with reductionist thought is alleged to have arrested the development of sociology. Reductionism has also been criticized on the ground that it leaves out basic and indispensable aspects of human nature. Sociologists who begin with the premise that social phenomena are *sui generis* and believe that social science must accordingly have a logical and epistemological structure fundamentally unlike natural science tend to see naturalism itself as tantamount to reductionism. But reductionism and naturalism can be distinguished from each other; the distinction is an important step in augmenting sociological inquiry.

Some of the opposition to reductionism (and to naturalism) has had an ideological basis. Reductionism has been seen as a device for regimentation. The taboo against it may have been more rigidly observed than could have been warranted by scientific considerations alone because defense of freedom and human dignity appeared to be at stake. For sociologists caught up in this ideology, reductionism and naturalism were easily confused.

Impetus toward reductionism results from several causes. Age has lent prestige to such sciences as physics, chemistry, and biology. Social scientists are tempted to feel that only the concepts of those disciplines are tangible and afford genuine explanations of more intangible phenomena. On the other hand, prestige considerations aside, any science which has succeeded impressively would seem to deserve careful study by the practitioners of a less advanced science, to see if their field could employ some of its demonstrably effective procedures. The drive to learn from the successful sciences is not altogether foolish. Some who have followed that impulse have made foolish mistakes; nineteenth-century sociologists used borrowed concepts uncritically. But the antidote for their pseudoscience does not consist of an embargo on conceptual interchange with other sciences. Not all such conceptual borrowing need be so crude. Theirs would not have been so erroneous if they had more clearly understood naturalism's requirements. The tenets of naturalism—particularly the requirement of empirical verification—offer a better safeguard against erroneous conceptualization than is afforded by the taboo against reductionism.

Sociologists have begun to outgrow that taboo. There is increasing recognition that the boundaries of sociology, like those of any other empirical discipline, cannot be rigid and impenetrable. There are no fixed territorial limits in the domain of truth, and the ultimate test of the propriety of borrowing concepts, data, procedures, or even laws from other sciences has to be empirical.

The irreducibility of one science to another is subject to change. Classes of phenomena only seem *sui generis* because the state of knowledge at a given time is limited. Imputing to collective phenomena properties we call "emergent" does not explain them. There is no merit in reification of ignorance. Biologists have learned this and have found great intellectual profit in making common cause with chemistry and physics. Vitalistic notions have lingered in biology, but have lost their former vitality; they should be permitted to wither and die out in sociology, too. Modern biology, unlike the biology of yesterday, does not provide legitimation for Aristotelian notions in sociology.

As patriotism, for all its virtues, is the last refuge of scoundrels, so anti-reductionism among sociologists, for all its ostensible sophistication, is the last refuge of animism. It is a false issue. It should be extinguished.

Chapter Ten
CONCLUSION: THE USES OF DIVERSITY

Aids to Innovation

The conventional taboos forbidding sociologists to use scientific concepts that originated outside sociology have been shown to be unwarranted. But this is not the proper note on which to rest the case for naturalism. Instead, I want to conclude on a more positive basis by showing that important progress is likely to be made by sociology if it enlarges its conceptual contacts with other sciences. The reader will quickly see that by enlargement of conceptual contacts I have in mind something quite different from the usual plea for collaborative, interdisciplinary research.

The progress of a science, like any other kind of social change, depends in part on the occurrence of innovations. New instruments of measurement, new techniques of observation, new problems, new analytic procedures, and new concepts are essential ingredients of scientific advancement. Of course, the advancement of science must not be confused with processes of mere fashion or fad. The new is not superior just by virtue of its newness. With a thoroughgoing commitment to empiricism, however, a science ultimately sifts new wheat from new chaff. This being so, its advancement depends as truly upon the occurrence of innovations as it does on the empirical discrimination between sound innovations and ones that are unsound.

The essence of innovation, says LaPiere, is the creation of a unique and unprecedented mental construct.[1] The mere need for such creation does not guarantee that it will occur. Necessity cannot mother invention unless it is fathered by someone's asocial perception. Someone must redefine a recognized problem in a new way that may make it soluble, or define as problematic something not previously so regarded.[2] In earlier chapters, I have tried to show that sociologists have tended to regard social change as nonproblematic, and I have argued that the shift to naturalistic thoughtways in sociology would entail a fundamental modification of outlook in this respect. Instead of continuing to regard social continuity and stability as problematic, we would adopt the inertial axiom and take these for granted—defining change as the problem requiring explanation.

An asocial perception can be considered a necessary but not sufficient condition for innovation. Innovation is at least made unlikely by conventional preconceptions.[3] Emancipation from such preconceptions does not guarantee innovation; it only lowers some of the barriers that otherwise stand in its way. There are other prerequisites that must also be met if innovation is to occur.

Creative thinking can happen only if one possesses knowledge that is relevant to the problem. Such knowledge is ordinarily accompanied by the very kind of preconceptions that tend to inhibit innovation. For innovation to occur, the knowledge must somehow be available, divorced from the blinding preconceptions. In addition, the creative thinker has to have skill in manipulating symbols so that he can do something with the items of knowledge besides simply knowing them, yet if he is to innovate he must not be bound by habits that cause him to manipulate the symbols only in traditional ways. Perhaps even more important, creative thinking depends on conviction that a problem is soluble, but this conviction must not entail fixed ideas on the nature of the solution.[4] I submit that these combinations of requisite conditions are exceedingly uncommon even among intellectuals, and become a little more likely in the case of a person for whom disciplinary boundaries are of slight concern. I am suggesting that some degree of disciplinary marginality may enhance the probability that one will bring forth innovations.

One of the sources of innovation leading to social change in a society is cultural borrowing—the importation of culture traits from other societies. The imported trait is novel to the receiving society, and may be integrated into its culture if the trait can be adapted to perform some service that is performed not so well or not at all without it. For a scientific discipline, the ideas of other sciences are the analogues of such alien cul-

---

[1] Richard T. LaPiere, *Social Change*. New York: McGraw-Hill Book Company, 1965, p. 107.
[2] *Ibid.*, pp. 114–115.
[3] *Ibid.*, p. 117.
[4] *Ibid.*, p. 118.

ture traits. Cultural borrowing may serve as a substitute for indigenous invention. The novelty of the borrowed traits may also remove conceptual blinders and stimulate indigenous invention that would otherwise have been delayed or might not have occurred at all. The science that borrows concepts from other sciences and finds the borrowed concepts useful may be stimulated by them to invent still others.

According to Lewis Feuer, the greatest original thinkers in science have been persons whose thought was not completely socialized. The asocial element in creative thought has not been completely recognized by the sociology of knowledge, which has neglected the fact that original think-ing departs from traditional problem-solving paths and subverts traditional conceptual categories.[5] To succeed, such asocial thinkers have had to be intensely interested in a problem and have had to believe earnestly that it was amenable to solution and that they could solve it. One writer has applied the phrase "magnificent obsessions" to the great scientific theories.[6]

LaPiere has noted that innovation is inherently a discouraging activity, both because it is difficult in its own right and because society generally imposes sanctions that express social disapproval for such deviation. If he is to solve a problem, therefore, an innovator has to be exceptionally confident of the soundness of his own asocial judgment. He has to have enough self-confidence to surmount active discouragement of his efforts by his peers. His self-confidence must also be obsessive enough that he does not "learn" from repeated failures which he is likely to experience—i.e., does not conclude from recurrent failure that ultimate success is improbable.[7]

Reliance on an analogy from a more advanced science may sometimes be the basis for just such obsessive perseverence. The conspicuously suc-cessful use of certain concepts or procedures by an older science is no substitute for their empirical validation within one's own discipline, as I have repeatedly pointed out. To *some* people, however, it has *seemed* to suffice in lieu of empirical verification. Their self-confidence in using concepts which their peers avoid has been enhanced accordingly. The risk that a person will mistake analogy for proof may not be too high a price to pay for the hypermotivation by which innovative thought is pressed forward. So long as science remains a collective enterprise, others can supply the empirical tests which will correct this error, while apart from the motivation arising from the error there might not have been generated any hypotheses for them to test.

[5] Lewis S. Feuer, *The Scientific Intellectual.* New York: Basic Books, Inc., Publishers, 1963, p. 12.
[6] Ernest R. Trattner, *Architects of Ideas.* New York: Carrick and Evans, 1938, p. 3.
[7] LaPiere, *op. cit.,* pp. 134–138.

Irrelevance of Conventional Objections

Accepted ideas in a given time and place have an inertial aspect; they resist displacement. People absorb ideas in a process of socialization and often resent other ideas at variance with them.[8] This being so, there has to be provocation for a few individuals to pursue deviant ideas in an obsessive manner, or innovation would be even more rare than it is. If the deviant ideas are adorned with legitimacy and success in another science in which they are not deviant, this may provide the basis for the obsession though it may not reduce the antipathy or skepticism of one's peers.

Sorokin's criticism of theories of social mechanics seems to be a case in point. His antipathy to imported concepts is obvious and conventional. He conceded no possibility that such theories might stand on their own sociological feet if subjected to empirical test. To him they were no more than analyses of social phenomena "as purely physical manifestations." He assumed that these theories must exclude everything that was specifically sociocultural and everything that differentiates social facts from inorganic phenomena. Human beings and all aspects of their conduct, such as "heroism, crime, love, hatred, struggle, cooperation, organization, ethics, religion, arts, literature" were transformed by such theories, said Sorokin, "into a mere 'physical mass,' and a study is made of its transformation and its 'motion.'"[9]

Surely the content of previous chapters in this book, especially Chapter 8, has shown that the use by a sociologist of concepts first used in physics need not emasculate sociology. Yet that is what Sorokin seemed to fear. To say that a sociocultural entity has an inertial property—a measurable resistance to change—and to use the term "mass" in a rigorous way to denote the magnitude of that resistance does not reduce human beings and all aspects of their conduct to "physical mass." I have explicitly and insistently maintained the distinction between sociocultural mass and physical mass, while recognizing the similar parts to be played by these concepts in the theories of sociology and of physics, respectively. By insisting on injecting the adjective "physical," however, Sorokin refused to see that the distinction was possible.

Sorokin's apprehensions were apparently based in part on the supposition that if sociologists take over physical concepts, the physicists must take over sociology, leaving no sovereign domain for the sociologists. Since the laws of physical mechanics apply to all physical objects, including

---

[8] Cf. James Bissett Pratt, *Naturalism*. New Haven, Conn.: Yale University Press, 1939, p. 10.
[9] Pitirim A. Sorokin, *Contemporary Sociological Theories*. New York: Harper & Row, Publishers, Incorporated, 1928, pp. 33–34.

human bodies, Sorokin argued that there was therefore "no reason to insist on, or to create, a special theory of 'social gravitation' or 'social inertia,' or a 'law of social entropy,' or any special law of physical mechanics."[10]

He apparently supposed that "social gravitation" had to mean that human *bodies* were attracted to each other merely by the physical gravitational force dependent on their physical masses and proximity in physical space. But gravity is such a weak interaction that only an infinitesimal fraction of one human being's attraction to another could ever be attributed to the physical gravitational effects of their bodies. Sorokin was falsely accusing his naturalistic antagonists. Few of the mechanistically inclined sociologists who have used the phrase "social gravitation" or any near equivalent have meant merely the physical force of gravity operating between aggregates of physical mass that happened to consist of human flesh. Certainly it was no such notion that I employed in Chapter 8 of this book, so at least it cannot *henceforth* be said that every rigorous attempt to discover gravitational-type interactions among sociocultural entities is a disloyal act tending to subjugate sociology to cold, materialistic physics.

Antipathy to sociological use of concepts emanating from physics was plausible in the days when Sorokin could validly charge that no efforts had been made to *measure* social forces, or to *verify* propositions in social physics empirically.[11] Such sweeping charges can no longer be sustained, however. Nor can it any longer be said without contradiction that the principles of the natural sciences are inapplicable to meanings and to sociocultural phenomena. Sorokin asserted such inapplicability on grounds that sociocultural phenomena exist without reference to physical space and physical time, do not exhibit the causality of natural science, and lack such physicochemical properties as mass, etc. Meanings, he said, were the most important component of sociocultural phenomena. They have no physicochemical properties, and physicochemical principles are consequently inapplicable to them. "This syllogism is practically unimpeachable," he concluded.[12] But its irrelevance is sufficient ground for its impeachment.

Believing he had shown the utter futility of building sociology along naturalistic lines, Sorokin went on to claim for sociocultural reality a "supersensory, superrational, and metalogical aspect." He said this would have to be apprehended by way of a "supersensory, superrational, metalogical act of 'intuition' or 'mystic experience,' representing a type of cognition 'sui generis,' profoundly different from sensory perception and the logical activity of reason."[13]

[10] *Ibid.,* p. 32.
[11] Pitirim A. Sorokin, *Sociocultural Causality, Space, Time.* Durham, N.C.: The Duke University Press, 1943, p. 30.
[12] *Ibid.,* pp. 32–33.
[13] *Ibid.,* pp. 227–228.

Parallels in the History of Science

There are ways in which the history of sociological thought recapitulates the history of other sciences. It is instructive to examine some of these parallels. The tenacious conviction that sociology studies phenomena that are so different from any other phenomena that "metalogical acts of intuition" must constitute the essential core of its research procedures has been foreshadowed in other sciences. More than a century ago, for example, the geologist Sir Charles Lyell pointed out that geologists of an earlier day had been poorly acquainted with present processes of change in the surface structure of the earth. Accordingly, they had supposed that these processes could never suffice to explain the momentous transformations that apparently had occurred in the past. They thought it more legitimate, Lyell said:[14]

. . . to speculate on the possibilities of the past, than patiently to explore the realities of the present; and having invented theories under the influence of such maxims, they were consistently unwilling to test their validity by the criterion of their accordance with the ordinary operations of nature. On the contrary, the claims of each new hypothesis to credibility appeared enhanced by the great contrast, in kind or intensity, of the causes referred to, and those now in operation.

It was thus by no means unprecedented when Sorokin seemed to insist that the credibility of a sociological idea is enhanced by its contrast with ideas from natural science. Sociological ideas that resemble principles of natural science have been scorned, and the resemblance taken as prima facie evidence of their absurdity. From Lyell we learn, however, that the declaration that sociology is forever barred from membership among the natural sciences was presaged by a similar declaration about geology. He wrote:[15]

Never was there a dogma more calculated to foster indolence, and to blunt the keen edge of curiosity than this assumption of the discordance between the ancient and existing causes of change. . . . Geology, it was affirmed, could never rise to the rank of an exact science,—the greater number of phenomena must forever remain inexplicable, or only be partially elucidated by ingenious conjectures.

In sociology, the vestiges of animism likewise foster indolence and dull our scientific curiosity.

The parallel is striking enough to warrant pursuit a little farther. Lyell was substantially an "advocate" of ideas developed in the preceding century by an "innovator" named James Hutton, founder of "uniformitarian"

[14] Sir Charles Lyell, *Principles of Geology,* 9th ed. New York: D. Appleton & Company, Inc., 1853, p. 196.
[15] *Ibid.*

geology. Hutton, born in 1726, was the son of an Edinburgh merchant. He became a doctor of medicine in 1749, but never practiced. Instead he studied farming methods and operated his family's farm, traveled, and observed the features of the earth.[16] It is thus fair to say that he was marginal to the discipline in which he made his innovations, and it is possible that his marginality facilitated his innovating.

After presenting the first brief version of his geological theory in 1785, Hutton spent some years traveling and making further observations, and in writing on metaphysics and epistemology. Though he was compiling more materials for expansion of his geological theory, illness postponed the writing until he was finally stimulated by harsh criticism from a chemist, Richard Kirwan. He addressed himself to the errors contained in Kirwan's critique and wrote a two-volume revision of the *Theory of the Earth*, which was published in 1795.[17] It seems clear that Hutton was hypermotivated, as LaPiere says the innovator must be, and this motivation seems clearly to have been directed toward the solution of intellectual problems rather than toward the achievement of notoriety. Again, his marginality to the discipline in which his innovation occurred is notable as a possible cause.

Hutton's writing was not of a type that immediately won hordes of converts to his theory. His first effective advocate was John Playfair, born in 1748, educated for the ministry (his father's profession) in which he served from 1773 until 1782 as his father's successor. He had shown early distinction in mathematics, however, and in 1785, three years after moving to Edinburgh, he reverted to this interest and became professor of mathematics at the University of Edinburgh. Twenty years later he was made professor of natural philosophy. He was a friend and close associate of Hutton from the beginning of his years in Edinburgh until Hutton's death in 1797.[18] Like Hutton, Playfair was marginal to geology, but contributed importantly to its progress.

Playfair did research and writing in mathematics, physics, astronomy, meteorology, and geology. His friends, regarding him first as a mathematician and physicist, regretted his devotion of so much time to Hutton's theory.[19] But Playfair's *Illustrations of the Huttonian Theory* was important in keeping the theory alive in scholarly circles in the face of strong ideological opposition. It did not lead to immediate and general acceptance of the theory.[20]

In Hutton's own time, his theory (which explained present geological features by past operation of present processes of erosion, deposition, vol-

[16] George W. White, "Introduction and Biographical Notes," in John Playfair, *Illustrations of the Huttonian Theory* (Facsimile Reprint). Urbana, Ill.: The University of Illinois Press, 1956, p. x.
[17] *Ibid.*, p. xv.
[18] *Ibid.*, pp. xv–xvi.
[19] *Ibid.*, pp. xvi–xvii.
[20] *Ibid.*, p. vii.

canism, etc.) was associated with atheism. Later, Lyell's *Principles of Geology* provided a persuasive argument for Hutton's uniformitarianism at a time when the intellectual climate had become more receptive, "and soon all joined in the acclaim of Hutton, in the appreciation of his commentator Playfair, and in the approbation of his proponent Lyell."[21] Thus it is clear that among his contemporaries, opposition to Hutton's scientific theory had been legitimated by nonscientific considerations. These nonscientific objections were eventually overcome by the theory's scientific worth and by successful advocacy of the theory in a later and different intellectual climate. It will be interesting to see whether the ideological resistance to naturalistic sociology is correspondingly temporary.

As Playfair himself pointed out, one of the objections to Hutton's theory was that it ascribed to the earth a far greater antiquity than could be reconciled with the chronology derived from scripture. Playfair's ministerial background, which had not prevented him from embracing Hutton's ideas, apparently did alert him to a way of circumventing this specious objection. He conceded that it would have carried some weight "if the high antiquity in question were not restricted merely to the globe of the earth" and had been extended also to apply to mankind.[22] Since Hutton's theory was not meant to challenge the recency of the creation of Adam and Eve, it made no real theological difference that it portrayed the physical world as vastly more ancient than had previously been realized. Later scientific progress proved Playfair's counter argument spurious, too, but at the time it probably helped reduce the cognitive dissonance between geology and theology for others besides himself.

Such cognitive dissonance between the new scientific ideas and the traditional theological outlook has been a perennial problem. Sociologists have been by no means the first to experience it. Great scientific innovators in past ages have had to cope with it. According to Playfair, the aspects of Hutton's theory to which Hutton himself was most devoted and attached greatest value were the very features that contradicted the charges of atheism. Or, in other terms, Hutton was fondest of those portions of his theory in which the transition from animism to naturalism was least evident. In the Huttonian theory, Playfair wrote, "we see everywhere the utmost attention to discover, and the utmost disposition to admire, the instances of wise and beneficent design manifested in the structure or economy of the world." Playfair asserted that Hutton "would have been less flattered, by being told of the ingenuity and originality of his theory, than of the addition which it made to our knowledge of *final causes.*"[23]

Resolution of cognitive dissonance aroused by naturalistic innovations followed a similar path in the writing of Lyell. Wherever geologists pursue

---

[21] *Ibid.*, p. viii.
[22] John Playfair, *Illustrations of the Huttonian Theory*. Edinburgh: William Creech, 1802, p. 125.
[23] *Ibid.*, pp. 121–122.

their researches, he said, they "discover everywhere the clear proofs of a Creative Intelligence, and of His foresight, wisdom, and power." Lyell went on to display a curious vestige of animistic teleology, reversing the cause-effect sequence. By Lyell's time, enough knowledge had accumulated that geologists could recognize that life adapted to environmental circumstances was not unique to the present era. Various species of organisms now extinct were known to have existed in earlier times and to have been so constituted that they were adapted to the state of the physical world which had then prevailed. But this is not the way Lyell expressed it. He wrote that geologists had discovered "that many former states also have been adapted to the organization and habits of prior races of beings,"[24] as if it were the environment which adapts to organisms, rather than vice versa. Apparently the language of teleology has mass; it lingers on and constrains thought even after research on efficient causes has been well launched.

The problem of cognitive dissonance was acute for contemporaries of Newton, too. His description of celestial processes in mechanical terms was a drastic departure from the theologically sanctioned cosmologies which had preceded it. In a rejoinder to criticisms of the first edition of his *Principia*, Newton tried to steal some of the theological thunder of Berkeley and Leibnitz. He reverted to teleological expressions in spite of his own preeminent contribution to naturalism:

This most beautiful system of the sun, planets, and comets could only proceed from the counsel and dominion of an intelligent and powerful Being. And if the fixed stars are the centres of other like systems, these, being formed by the like wise counsel, must all be subject to the dominion of One; especially since the light of the fixed stars is of the same nature with the light of the sun, and from every system light passes into all the other systems. . . .

Here is a strange mixture of animism and naturalism! Then Newton added, ". . . And *lest the systems of the fixed stars should, by their gravity, fall on each other, he hath placed those systems at immense distances from one another.*"[25] Had Newton remained consistently naturalistic, he would merely have said that gravity has not brought the fixed stars together because their immense remoteness from each other makes their mutual attraction minute. There was no *scientific* need to impute final causes.

If their reversions to animistic and teleological expressions reveal the intellectual forces influencing these men's thoughts, the analogies they em-

---

[24] Lyell, *op. cit.*, p. 799.
[25] Florian Cajori (ed.), *Sir Isaac Newton's Mathematical Principles of Natural Philosophy and His System of the World*. Berkeley, Calif.: University of California Press, 1962, p. 544. (My italics.) The quoted passage is from the General Scholium which Cajori points out was, added by Newton to his second edition in 1713 as a rejoinder to criticism of the 1687 first edition.

ployed likewise reveal the productive effects of their scientific marginality. Here is the analogy with which Lyell began his presentation of geological theory: "As the present condition of nations is the result of many antecedent changes, some extremely remote, and others recent, some gradual, others sudden and violent; so the state of the natural world is the result of a long succession of events; and if we would enlarge our experience of the present economy of nature, we must investigate the effects of her operations in former epochs."[26] Broadly speaking, the foundations of modern geology were thus informed by an insight borrowed from the field of social science!

Some social scientists may be tempted to acknowledge the legitimacy of this kind of borrowing, while clinging to the conviction that borrowing in the other direction remains illicit. Viewing the sciences as arranged in a hierarchy (after Comte), I have seen it argued that lower sciences may appropriately borrow from higher ones, but higher ones must not borrow from below. It is difficult to defend such a thesis on either logical or empirical grounds, however, and it smacks of mere ethnocentrism on the part of a social science ingroup.

Lyell described geology as the study of the permanent effects of causes now in action, and regarded such effects as lasting monuments of transitory phases in the physical structure of the planet. Geological features can be regarded, he said, "as a symbolic language, in which the earth's autobiography is written."[27] This was not only a convenient metaphor by which to convey to his readers the geological knowledge already accumulated. It expresses the perceptual perspective in which geologists had learned to view the world so differently from the way it was viewed by nongeologists. They had indeed achieved a unique and unprecedented mental construct, an innovation. For the nongeologist, structural features of the earth were nonproblematic—traits that had simply existed since the original creation, except insofar as altered recently by man. For the geologist, new questions had become askable: How was this canyon formed? Or how did these remnants of marine life get into the rocks on this mountaintop?

The analogy between history and geology was extended by Lyell to point to similarities in the roles and the strategies of historian and geologist. Just as historians require assistance, he said, "from those who have cultivated different branches of moral and political science, so the geologist should avail himself of the aid of many naturalists, and particularly of those who have studied the fossil remains of lost species of animals and plants."[28] One might generalize: *any* science can use the aid of other sciences in probing its own domain.

[26] Lyell, *op. cit.*, p. 1.
[27] *Ibid.*, p. v.
[28] *Ibid.*, p. 2.

Then, despite the need which would cause him to end his book on the teleological note previously mentioned, Lyell pointed out an advantage the geologist has over the historian precisely because the geologist's data were laid down without purpose. Though often fragmentary, "the testimony of geological monuments" is at least "free from all intentional misrepresentation."[29] The sociologist who feels he must concentrate his research on "mystic experiences" and "intuitions" that are "supersensory, superrational, and metalogical" thereby abandons all defense against the deceptions his own psychic processes can perpetrate upon him. He drops his own guard against self-deception, and he erects insurmountable obstacles to the corrective effects of replication by others.

Lyell was an ardent empiricist, but he did not let his commitment to this aspect of naturalism mislead him into the categorical rejection of abstracta and illata. In his day, one of the tasks confronting geologists was to show convincingly that sudden geological convulsions and catastrophes need not be postulated to account for breaks in stratigraphic sequence, etc. This could be done, he maintained, by showing how regular and uninterrupted sequences of changes *could* give rise to unconformability of strata. But Lyell insisted that any order of events hypothesized to account for such problematic features must be in harmony with known facts of structure and current processes. The admissibility of illata was expressed in these words: "It may be necessary in the present state of science to supply some part of the assumed course of nature hypothetically; but if so, this must be done without any violation of probability, and always consistently with the analogy of what is known both of the past and present economy of our system."[30] The sins of the catastrophist theorists had consisted in violating this precept; they had introduced mere fictions rather than illata. Among sociologists, those who have insisted that sociocultural reality has essential aspects that are "supersensory, superrational, and metalogical" have been committing the same kind of offense.

Utility of Borrowed Concepts

I want to turn now to a few illustrations of the way the concepts presented in earlier chapters, whose origins lie outside sociology, may be useful for the clarification of sociological problems.

Sociologists agree today that human personality is an organization of the activity of an individual organism that is produced by the experiences of his interaction with others in a social process. The personal organization is based on the organized features of the surrounding social system. Per-

[29] *Ibid.*, p. 3.
[30] *Ibid.*, p. 181.

sonality is in large part an internalized version (somewhat idiosyncratic, of course) of the culture in which socialization has taken place.[31] But theories of personality development and change are far from finished. The things that have been said, for example, about the effects of prolonged isolation on personality have been somewhat ambiguous and are potentially misleading.

The language he has used in this connection has made Robert Faris, for example, seem almost to be taking the functionalist's position, with its excessive interest in so-called "pattern-maintenance." It is a position with which he has not intended to align himself, but he has written that personality is a kind of organization that is not simply "achieved in early life and perpetuated under its own power from then on. It needs to be sustained constantly by the same kind of organized social experience that creates it—constant regeneration is necessary to keep it alive."[32] Complete disorganization of personality, however, does not occur the instant an individual is cut off from society. It takes time. The issue is clarified, I think, by suggesting that the persistence of personality traits into the period of social isolation indicates the inertial property of personality. Personality has mass. Doubtless it also has homeostatic properties, but these need to be distinguished from mass. The distinction can be facilitated if the concepts are willingly used.

In isolation, the human personality is not merely deprived of exposure to the social experiences that normally sustain it. Because human beings have a propensity for activity (overt or covert, depending on circumstances), prolonged isolation from contacts with others exposes the individual to prolonged and uninterrupted self-interaction. It can just as well be argued that the personality disorganization that occurs when isolation is complete and lasting is a change brought about by the *force* of self-interaction despite inertial tendencies. It is not really necessary to regard social experiences as a force for continuity in the animistic sense. Ongoing social experiences subject the personality to forces, some of which produce personality change, development, or growth, and which offset the disorganizing force of self-interaction by interrupting and preventing soliloquies.

The amount of deterioration of personality apparently varies with the duration of isolation,[33] and it is plausible to suggest that Axiom II, the principle of proportionality, could be invoked to yield precise quantification of this generalization. If satisfactory measures of the extent of deterioration, the rate of self-interaction per unit of time, etc., were devised, important advances in the precision and clarity of understanding of the

[31] See, for example, Robert E. L. Faris, *Social Psychology*. New York: The Ronald Press Company, 1952, p. 365.
[32] *Ibid.*, see also pp. 339, 352, 366.
[33] *Ibid.*, p. 366.

effects of isolation might be achieved. The result just might turn out to be a sociological (or social-psychological) proposition of the same form as the equation relating traversed distance to elapsed time in the case of freely falling bodies: $s = \frac{1}{2}gt^2$. On the other hand, the social-psychological analogue of g in this equation might not be a constant (even for a given person); this "soliloquy force," as it might be termed, could conceivably vary with time, increasing with length of isolation up to some maximum and perhaps diminishing again after the capacity for interaction even with self had been destroyed.

Instructive analogies for extending the conceptualization of this problem might be drawn from other fields besides mechanics, of course. Faris has suggested that continued and careful investigation of the effects of isolation of varying types and durations and degrees has immense promise. Such research might make it possible, he pointed out, to list the sociological essentials on which normal personality depends "in the way that dietary essentials are revealed for the physiological organism."[34]

Forces producing personality change can, of course, be studied in other contexts besides complete isolation. Changes of position in a social structure, changed family relations (e.g., the addition of a member by birth or marriage, or the loss of a member by death or divorce), advancement through age-graded sequences of roles, the experience of social mobility, or geographic migration, and many other experiences of changed social relations expose individuals to personality-changing forces. From day to day, others react to one's behavior in varying ways. There is ordinarily enough stability of the self to prevent it from being modified by minor inconsistencies in the social mirror. Some individuals, however, never achieve a stable self-conception. They remain low in self-confidence because of deficiencies of socialization. Such persons are usually overly sensitive to the momentary responses of others. Excessive elation may result from minor items of favorable feedback, and unwarranted depression may be the consequence of an inadvertent slur or recognition of a minor *faux pas*. Such a hyperresponsiveness to momentary feedback seems to be associated with a general trait of indecision.[35] It would make good sense to sharpen the image of such a personality by saying the self-conception had an unusually low mass.

Reverting to the principle of equivalence discussed in Chapter 8, we should not be surprised to find that persons whose self-conceptions have low mass tend to be less attractive than the average person. Low inertial mass and low gravitational mass may be at least proportional and perhaps identical in sociology as elsewhere. Faris has suggested that this is so, but without having employed the physicalistic terms: "Persons with definite character are more interesting because of their differences from

[34] *Ibid.*, p. 395.
[35] *Ibid.*, p. 167.

others. The person who never asserts or disputes, but is completely agreeable to everything, has nothing to contribute to a conversation, and is likely to be overlooked, taken for granted, or even exploited."[36] Conversely, it might be hypothesized that when sociometric status or popularity is taken as the independent variable, it will be positively correlated with stability of self-conception (measured separately and taken as the dependent variable). If appropriately cardinal scales of these variables are devised and used, the principle of equivalence would imply that the relationship should be not only positive, but linear. And if true ratio scales were used in making the measurements, the hypothesis could be stated even more explicitly with the expectation that the intercept of the regression of one variable on the other ought to be zero, and the slope would be unity if both variables were measured in equivalent units. Valuable as is the qualitative expression of the hypothesis by Faris, it appears that more precise (and hence more unequivocally testable) versions of the hypothesis become possible when the borrowed physical concepts are deliberately and carefully employed.

None of the above is meant to imply that interpersonal attraction is exclusively gravitational—dependent on the masses of the interacting personalities and their proximity in value space. There may be other kinds of interactions between persons, giving rise to forces that will often obscure the force of this particular interaction, just as the electromagnetic interactions of small physical particles vastly overshadow their gravitational interactions. Any nongravitational interactions between persons would of course attenuate the correlation between the stability of self-conception and magnitude of personal attractiveness.

I think no violence is done to the qualitative hypothesis Faris had in mind when it is augmented as I have done above. The concept of inertial mass was all but named as such by him when he wrote, "The firm organization of a conception of self requires some resistance to certain social influences if there is to be any consistency of character."[37] And at least one empirical study inspired by his published comments has lent support to the notion that inertial mass and gravitational mass in sociology are at least proportional if not equivalent. Costner and Warne found that stability of self-conception was predictive of the degree to which subjects defined certain roles independently of the perceived expectations of others and in accord with their self-conceptions.[38] In other words, the more stable the self-concept (the greater its inertial mass), the greater its power (using their term) to "pull" role definitions toward itself and away from

---

[36] *Ibid.*, p. 168.
[37] *Ibid.*, p. 167.
[38] Herbert L. Costner and Nanci Warne, "Stability of Self Concept and Deviating Role Definitions," paper read at 1963 annual meeting of the American Sociological Association, Los Angeles.

contrary perceived expectations of others (i.e., the greater its gravitational mass).

In the studies of cognitive dissonance, additional hypotheses might be suggested, or existing hypotheses refined, by conscious use of such borrowed concepts. Festinger's principal hypothesis is that cognitive dissonance is uncomfortable and is therefore a source of motivation to strive for consonance.[39] People who experience cognitive dissonance will try to avoid situations which would aggravate it and will seek information or experiences which would reduce it. The strength of the dissonance-reduction pressure varies with the magnitude of the dissonance.[40] The avoidance of dissonance-increasing cognitions and the quest for dissonance-reducing cognitions are indications that dissonance acts like a drive, need, or tension—or a force.

But if two cognitive elements are dissonant, which one is more likely to be modified, or which will be modified more? The concept of inertial mass can be useful in clarifying hypotheses on this point. Festinger cited a study by Osgood and Tannenbaum in which attitudes toward communication sources and attitudes toward certain opinions were carefully distinguished and separately measured. Dissonance was introduced by attributing given opinions to oppositely valued sources. Prior measurements of the relative resistance to change (inertial mass) of the attitudes toward sources and attitudes toward opinions made it possible to predict the direction and sometimes the amount of change in evaluation resulting from the dissonance.[41] More research along these lines should be undertaken.

Without using the term, Festinger clearly had a close approximation of the concept of inertial mass in mind. Among his hypotheses were these: the magnitude of the dissonance between two contradictory elements of cognition depends on the importance of the elements; the amount of dissonance between one element and the remainder of a person's cognition depends on the proportion of other relevant elements that are dissonant with the one.[42] Arguing that dissonance can be reduced by obtaining social support for one's preferred views, Festinger used an interesting illustrative example. He suggested that a parent who happened to be a strict disciplinarian but was aware of many things (including his children's reactions) which cast doubt on the effectiveness of strict discipline and were thus dissonant with his awareness of his own practices, might seek to persuade others of the virtue of strict discipline. Success in such persuasion attempts would provide social support for his behavior and would thus reduce dissonance—even if his children's reactions continued to pro-

---

[39] Leon Festinger, *A Theory of Cognitive Dissonance*. New York: Harper & Row, Publishers, Incorporated, 1957, p. 3.
[40] *Ibid.*, p. 18.
[41] *Ibid.*, pp. 8–9.
[42] *Ibid.*, pp. 16–17.

vide evidence of strict discipline's ineffectiveness. And Festinger added that such a person might be able to influence the opinions of his childless acquaintances quite easily on this matter.[43]

His implication is that childless persons would have less strong convictions regarding the efficacy and rightness of strict discipline than would other parents; their opinions would have less mass and could be changed by the application of less persuasive force. Mere translation of Festinger's hypothesis into physicalistic terms is not an end in itself, of course. But it brings to light a further hypothesis which Festinger did not mention, namely, that the dissonance-reducing benefits of persuading others to accept one's preferred cognition would depend on the magnitude of the resistance by others that was overcome by persuasion. Like the man who demonstrated his chess-playing skill by defeating his dog three games out of four, one can hardly find it very dissonance-reducing to gain assent from a person whose contrary views were weak in the first place. Such a person's conversion is poor testimony to the validity of the persuader's views if the contrary convictions from which the opponent was converted were unimportant to him.

Festinger did not address himself to the question whether the dissonance-reducing effectiveness of P's changing O's opinion would depend on the mass of the opinion changed in O. He did address himself to the related question of whether P or O will change as a result of their interaction. If O does not change, their interaction (P's attempt to persuade O, and O's refusal to change) will have *increased* P's dissonance, perhaps to the point where P will change.[44]

The theory of cognitive dissonance has implications for the response to failure of prophecy, as Festinger has shown.[45] These implications are enlarged, however, when the above hypothesis regarding the mass of O's opinion is considered. For example, in the earliest days of Christianity, after the crucifixion (apparent defeat) of Christ, his followers were beset with cognitive dissonance. Active proselyting was a response Festinger's theory would make us expect. One of the non-Christians who changed his mind was St. Paul. His conversion has been widely regarded as a crucial event in the growth of the Christian religion. The theory of cognitive dissonance illuminates it. Because the Christians he had been persecuting remained steadfast in their faith, Paul found his own opinion had changed. The additional concepts introduced above would suggest, however, that his conversion was crucial for Christianity in more ways than one. Not only did he go on to play an important missionary role, but first, because he was an ex-persecutor of Christians *his* conversion was

[43] *Ibid.*, pp. 191–192.
[44] *Ibid.*, p. 192.
[45] Leon Festinger, Henry Riecken, and Stanley Schachter, *When Prophecy Fails.* Minneapolis: The University of Minnesota Press, 1956, *passim.*

more dissonance-reducing for the faithful than was the conversion of an *average* nonbeliever. For a whole decade after his conversion, Paul preached to Jewish audiences (presumably including many followers of Christ whose dissonance he helped reduce). Only when it had become obvious that most Jews would remain immune to conversion did he experience another vision and redefine his mission as preaching to the Gentiles. They proved to be more convertible, confirming thereby his redefinition.

Likewise, the receptivity of conservatives in modern America to the assertions of converted ex-Communists may be attributed to the greater dissonance-reducing service provided when a former enemy rather than a mere nonentity is persuaded of the rightness of the ingroup's cognitions.

Another example of the possible utility of bringing borrowed scientific concepts to bear on sociological problems is provided by findings of community disaster studies. When a severe earthquake struck the state of Alaska in 1964, for instance, the major physical facilities of several communities were almost totally destroyed. The surviving inhabitants would have to start over again, somewhere, building new roles as well as new homes. A superficial view of the matter might have suggested that there was little or nothing to motivate them to undertake the rebuilding process on or near the site of their former experiences. In many instances the simplest adjustment was to move elsewhere. Yet no community as such actually died. The question can be asked, Do such events indicate inertial tendencies in human behavior, or do they constitute the results of *active* pattern-maintenance processes by organic social systems?

It makes a difference, not only for the practical need to cope with future disasters, but also for the theoretical relations between disaster study findings and the findings of research in other settings, how much of this persistence of site attachment is inertial and how much is homeostatic. Existing evidence does not suffice for a clear apportionment, and further study of the problem seems desirable. But this is an issue that would not seem problematic apart from the concepts and axioms discussed in this book.

The issue bears upon human experiences of great importance. As Leo Grebler has noted, the Second World War reduced the city of Casino to rubble and scattered its inhabitants, but only temporarily. Very shortly after combat in the immediate area ended, people returned to live in caves and cellars. They lacked food or means of earning a living. The area was heavily mined, and malaria was prevalent. Even in the context of the Italian economy, the attraction of the site could hardly have been primarily economic. The wisdom of the returnees is questionable, but their action shows "the power of the city over people, even when all its physical features have disappeared."[46] If such power is a fact, its consequences

---

[46] Leo Grebler, "Continuity in the Rebuilding of Bombed Cities in Western Europe," *American Journal of Sociology,* 61 (March, 1956), pp. 463–464.

must surely depend on its nature and mode of operation. Is it gravitylike, depending on the mass of former spatially localized experiences and actions, or is it a kind of homeostatic pattern-maintenance? It would be useful to know.

The Casino experience was widely repeated. Despite the housing shortage, general disorder, and disruption of transportation, the great majority of heavily damaged or destroyed communities equaled or exceeded their prewar populations within a few years after the war. Evacuees and bombing refugees returned as soon as they could to their former homes. In addition, these cities, despite their devastation, continued to attract migrants from the surrounding area.[47] The fact that persons, as individuals and as families, had left and subsequently returned suggests that on the individual level their persistent residence in a given city was not altogether inertial. The persistence of their identification with the city was perhaps inertial, but the action of returning from refuge elsewhere suggests homeostasis. And yet, considering the process on the community level, the return of evacuees and refugees was probably more dysfunctional than functional; the devastation of facilities made their presence burdensome. Thus the return of these people would either have to be attributed to a malfunctioning of the allegedly directively organized system (the community) or else to what was on this social level a more purely inertial and gravitational process.

The above comments by no means resolve this issue. They suggest, however, that by focusing attention on the distinction between inertia and homeostasis, we might shed new light on traditional sociological distinctions between "levels." New (and possibly fruitful) ideas about the relations of persons to societies may thus eventually be generated. At any rate, the bombed cities of Europe turned out after the war to be less susceptible to rational reorganization than the dreams of community planners had led them to hope for.[48] There can be little doubt that improved knowledge of the nature of such resistance to change would be highly useful. It was at least not obviously all homeostatic.

The Crippling Illusion of Immanence

In studying social change from what he terms a "structural approach," Moore has said that the first requirement is to specify the *unit* to which change is attributed. Such a precaution is not so elementary as it might seem, he argued, for large-scale systems might exhibit essential constancy

[47] *Ibid.*, p. 464.
[48] *Ibid.*, pp. 467ff.

despite conspicuous change in their constituent small-scale subsystems, or vice versa.[49] This seems to have been so in the case of the bombed cities.

Parsons has at least partly missed this point in his own thinking, it seems to me. He has appropriately described empirical social systems as "open," engaged in elaborate processes of interchange with other systems that constitute their environment. These other systems include culture and personality, as well as the behavioral subsystems of organisms, and through them the physical environment. According to Parsons, this concept of society as an open system interchanging with environing systems "implies *boundaries* and their maintenance."[50] There can be no quarrel with his image of social systems as open and engaged in processes of interchange. But it appears that Parsons mentioned their openness only in order to bring up his notions of boundary-maintenance processes and "imperatives." He thus failed to make the more important point that the sociologist is *free to define* the scope of system he wishes to study. He is not bound by immutable rules to study only systems of a certain magnitude.

The sociologist can avoid all the age-long arguments over whether change is externally caused, or whether instead it is "immanent," by simply abandoning "total social systems" as his basic unit. Assertions that, unlike change in the physical world, social change is immanent—caused from within—have been one of the mainstays of resistance to naturalism in sociology. It is a form of the "something different" argument by which perpetuation of nonscientific thoughtways among sociologists has been legitimated time and again. The predilection for animistic concepts and images is reinforced by assertions of the immanence of social change, because these declarations seem to make social phenomena essentially unlike natural phenomena.

Sociological writers of animistic inclination see the issue I have defined in the preceding paragraph in similar terms, though they stand on the other side of it. Stark, for example, accused the sociologists who wanted to employ rational mechanics as their model of refusing to admit the reality of "developmental change" because to do so would have destroyed their hopes of success in the formulation of mechanicist theories.[51]

If change seems immanent or developmental, so that naturalistic approaches seem inapplicable, the unit under study as a system is thereby indicated to be too large. Selection of a smaller unit would dispel the appearance of immanence in the observed changes. This premise may be

[49] Wilbert E. Moore, *Social Change.* Englewood Cliffs, N.J.: Prentice-Hall, Inc., 1963, p. 28.
[50] Talcott Parsons, "An Outline of the Social System," in Talcott Parsons, Edward Shils, Kaspar D. Naegele, and Jesse R. Pitts (eds.) *Theories of Society.* New York: The Free Press of Glencoe, 1961, p. 36.
[51] Werner Stark, *The Fundamental Forms of Social Thought.* New York: Fordham University Press, 1963, p. 57.

used to evaluate the following statement by Parsons: ". . . Most empirically significant sociological theory must be concerned with complex systems, that is, systems composed of subsystems."[52] By itself, such a statement may be unobjectionable. In their interactions, subsystems may subject each other to change-inducing forces which could be described within a thoroughly naturalistic framework, but which would make the change in the total system containing them appear to be immanent (from within, an unfolding). Any insistence, however, that sociology must focus on the larger system and not on the interactions on the subsystem level is a mistake if it leads to the belief that social change is inherently developmental and cannot be studied naturalistically. Those who insist that sociology must focus on total social systems do so in the name of keeping its studies sociological. But they do so at the cost of keeping them also animistic.

Parsons's comment on the complexity of social systems would be equally applicable to chemical phenomena. The chemist would never insist that he must always have the largest system in mind as his ultimate frame of reference. Something like that insistence has been implicit in the sociologists' abhorrence of reductionism. The chemist would not construe all interactions between lesser systems as processes that had to be studied as endogenous or immanent change in some more inclusive system. He would simply avoid such issues, choosing for analysis that magnitude of system which permitted him to treat a given question in a completely naturalistic way. How far would the biochemist, or even the geneticist, have gotten if he had forbidden himself to shift his attention downward as necessary from the cell to the chromosome, and from the chromosome to the gene, and from the gene to the DNA molecule? How foolish it would have been for geneticists to have sought to defend the integrity of their science by insisting that the processes they studied must be regarded as immanent!

At various points in this book, I have quarreled with Parsons's term, "pattern-maintenance." It is a concept around which this confusion over the alleged immanence of social system change has precipitated, and it may be possible now to sort out the components of that confusion. Bredemeier and Stephenson, in an avowed attempt to use Parsons's concepts in an introductory textbook, have been (in spite of their purpose) extraordinarily and commendably lucid. Their book employed the phrase "mechanisms of pattern-maintenance" to refer to social control procedures that suppress deviant behavior *and* to socialization processes whereby motivation is so channeled that deviant behavior is made unlikely. They have defined socialization as the process by which *people are transformed into social system members.*[53]

[52] Parsons, *op. cit.*, p. 30.
[53] Harry C. Bredemeier and Richard M. Stephenson, *The Analysis of Social Systems.* New York: Holt, Rinehart and Winston, Inc., 1962, p. 61.

Thus, for Bredemeier and Stephenson, socialization is *a process that changes people in such a way that the social system remains unchanged.* One of the main trends in the development of sociology over the past fifty years has been a growing emphasis on social psychology, including such problems as socialization. This growing emphasis can now be seen as a part of the trend toward increasingly naturalistic sociology. Sociologists who work on a level where their attention is on small units (often as small as the individual person and rather obviously subject to outside forces) have less reason to insist on the immanence of change. They are thus potentially less susceptible to animistic temptations. The sociologist who insists that in order to be properly sociological he must focus primarily or exclusively on the total social system (delegating studies of smaller-scale—"lower-level"—phenomena to psychologists) is bound to see change as immanent, and may succumb to the traditional arguments for animism. The cosmologist who followed similar thoughtways would have to say that the cosmos must always be studied as an indivisible unity, any change in which is necessarily endogenous. Clearly, if he went on to conclude that the tenets of naturalism were therefore inapplicable to his subject matter, he would simply be written off as archaic and uninformed.

Studies of the socialization process are, in short, an integral part of sociology today, and in my view properly so. They can be pursued according to the tenets of naturalism. The results of even the most naturalistic studies of socialization may be misconstrued, however, if sociologists insist on applying to the socialization process a label which puts the spotlight on the total social system again. Unfortunately, this is what Bredemeier and Stephenson did in calling socialization a "mechanism of pattern-maintenance." The implication of this label is that socialization is a process that changes people *in order* to keep the social system unchanged. The possibility that persistent social patterns result from socialization that is not carried out *for the sake of* preserving those patterns is thus neglected.

The traditional functional interpretation of incest taboos can be cited again in this connection. It assumes that incest would often occur unless stringently forbidden. Finding that it is a relatively rare occurrence, the functionalist view must ask *why* it is universally forbidden. And in the terms of functionalism, the "why" means, What is its societal utility? It may be conceded that the rarity of incest is useful to society, yet its social utility is neither necessary nor sufficient to explain the avoidance of incest. Incest is rare because nearly everyone is socialized in such a way that he does not seek incestuous relations and is not usually driven into them. If we now ask *why* people are socialized in this way, it is not necessarily the case that the utility to be derived by society from the avoidance of incest is the reason socialization proceeds in such a way that people are produced who are disinclined to behave incestuously. Considerations of pattern-maintenance need not be invoked. Efficient causes suffice to account for the pattern of socialization, and no recourse to final causes is required.

This is shown by a careful study of mate selection in collective settlements in Israel, which found that even where there was no normative prohibition against marrying within the same kibbutz peer group, such endogamous marriages did not occur. Nor was there even a single case of an extramarital love affair or a publicly known case of sex relations between members of the same peer group. The irony is that despite the clarity of this evidence for the conclusion that cosocialization in the childhood years establishes nonsexual patterns of relations whose inertial character is sufficient to impede subsequent development of sexual attachments between the same persons, the author of the study struggled earnestly to achieve an interpretation in functional terms.[54] The commitment many sociologists have made to functionalist expressions seems to have considerable mass.

Whatever the ways in which exogamy might be said to be useful to the kibbutz, e.g., binding different peer groups together through marital ties, it was not this utility that had prompted the organizing of socialization of boys and girls in common living quarters and with a minimum of sex-differentiated activities. Intimate but quite nonsexual ties were thus established among the boys and girls of a given group, with the result that later in life they would establish erotic ties only with persons of the opposite sex who were not part of this group. Intergroup cohesion (the alleged function of exogamous patterns) is in this instance clearly a by-product, a result of the prior socialization and not at all a cause of it. But the tendency for sociologists to mistake functions for causes will persist.

Collective Aspects of Science

Not all sociologists are committed to functional interpretations, so there has always remained the possibility that the results obtained by those following other approaches would supplement or displace the conclusions of investigators whose thoughts were channeled by functionalist terminology. Sociology, like any science, is and must be a collective enterprise. All sociologists must share to some degree the commitment to empirical tests as the ultimate arbiter of theoretical disputes, or their efforts will not cumulate. But if there is substantial consensus on this, then disparities of theoretical predilection are both tolerable and welcome. On the essen-

[54] Yonina Talmon, "Mate Selection in Collective Settlements," *American Sociological Review*, 29 (August, 1964), pp. 491–508.

tial foundation, empiricism, the consensus among sociologists today *is* substantial. On less fundamental points, the wider the range of assumptions from which different investigators begin their inquiry, the greater the probability that their inquiries, taken together, will be productive.

The collective nature of the scientific enterprise is often overlooked. It is sometimes imagined that for sociology to be a science, each sociologist must fully "be a scientist"—possessing an assortment of personality traits appropriate to that title, including, especially, "objectivity." Those who speak of objectivity in this way misunderstand the term, or they misunderstand science as an endeavor. They speak of objectivity as if it were an *attitude* of cold disinterestedness. Some individuals are imagined to have this attitude and others to lack it. Individuals do vary, of course, in their ability to revise their ideas in response to observation and analysis. Those with high ability to do this may be expected on the average to make greater contributions to science than those lacking such ability, except that they may lack the obsessive quality so important to the innovator. But all sciences, not just sociology, have depended on contributions to knowledge that were made by people who were far from "objective" in this sense. The objectivity of science, as distinct from the so-called "objectivity" of the scientist, arises from its collective nature—from the replicability of an individual's research, rather than from his attitudes toward it.[55]

The dedicated researcher, as a human being, is likely to be dedicated to his hypotheses as well as to his discipline. Were this not so, the arduous and often discouraging labor involved in formulating the hypotheses, clarifying the concepts contained in them, devising techniques or instruments for measuring the relevant variables, contriving experiments or organized observations by which the necessary measurement can be brought to bear on the hypothesis, and interesting other people in the results, might seldom be carried through to completion. Yet if a person is dedicated to his hypothesis, his own research may not put it to sufficiently rigorous test. In every discipline that has become a science this paradox has been resolved by the collectivization of that discipline. It is the collectivity that is objective in the long run, not the individual scientist in the short run. The individual scientist may be little less prone than the nonscientist to seek to "prove" rather than to *test* his hypotheses. The collective effort to test rather than to reinforce ideas is the main distinction between science and nonscience, however, and the strongest incentive for the individual scientist to strive for the attitudinal kind of objectivity lies in the expectation that his work is subject to later verification or disconfirmation by others.

[55] Cf. Karl R. Popper, *The Poverty of Historicism.* Boston: Beacon Press, 1957, pp. 155–156; William S. Beck, *Modern Science and the Nature of Life,* Garden City, N.Y.: Anchor Books, Doubleday & Company, Inc., 1961, p. 14.

Whether the individual scientist succeeds in attaining an objective attitude, the collective nature of science ensures that ultimately his biases will be surmounted by evidence—collected, analyzed, and interpreted by other persons whose biases may be just as strong as his, but are different. Diversity of biases allows the scientific collectivity to achieve objectivity even when individual scientists fall short of the objectivity they could only attain by altogether eliminating perceptual selectivity.

If a discipline is naturalistic in its broadest outlines, its collective nature will overcome the errors that are committed from time to time by its individual practitioners under the impetus of special theoretical perspectives. Errors cannot be fatal in the long run, for subsequent research will eventually reveal that they *were* errors. In the short run, errors may be unfortunate for the discipline and insurmountable for the individual. As Charles A. Ellwood (a man with misgivings about naturalistic sociology) pointed out forty years ago, scientific and technological ideas are often based on tradition as truly as are the political, religious, or moral ideas people cherish. The difference, he noted, though he appreciated it too little, is that revision is more readily accomplished in the realm of science and technology than in the realm of politics, religion, or morality.[56] Unlike the political or religious collectivity, the scientific collectivity accepts or rejects ideas on empirical grounds.

According to Festinger, the major sources of resistance to change for a cognitive element that is subject to the pressure of dissonance with another cognitive element are these: (1) its responsiveness to reality—i.e., the extent to which it accords with observation, and (2) the number of consonant relations with other cognitive elements.[57] The latter may include consonant relations with knowledge that others share similar cognitions. In other words, a person tends to discard an idea that contradicts other ideas he holds if it lacks empirical support or if it lacks social support. A fundamental difference between scientific collectivities and political or religious collectivities is that the former are so organized as to ensure that the empirical criterion outweighs the social criterion for acceptance or rejection of an idea, whereas the latter give relatively greater emphasis to the social criterion. Even among scientists, ideas supported by agreement with many other well-established ideas may resist the pressure of evidence, but then it may turn out upon further investigation that the evidence was faulty.

In short, ideas acquire mass, but scientific inquiry is organized to ensure that their resistance to change derives principally from empirical validity. When concreta and illata collide, the latter must yield. Scientific work

---

[56] Charles A. Ellwood, *The Psychology of Human Society.* New York: D. Appleton & Company, Inc., 1925, pp. 199–200.
[57] Festinger, *op. cit.,* pp. 265–266.

is organized in ways that guarantee the eventual collective abandonment of illata that are superfluous or misleading, but it would be wasteful of effort to require this organization to be so overpowering that it could guarantee the prompt abandonment of inappropriate illata by each individual scientist. It is enough that those who cling to obsolete concepts are mortal; the obsolescence of an idea limits its longevity to that of its holders if others recognize that obsolescence, whereas empirically cogent ideas derive from their validity some degree of immortality.

Superfluous or misleading illata may persist through many generations if their flaws remain unrecognized, as will be the case when primary commitments are to arbiters other than observation—such as authority, public opinion, or religious sanctions. Thus, for example, it took the unusually perceptive Kepler a substantial part of his own scientific life to reach the conclusion that his predecessors for the previous twenty centuries had been insufficiently precise in describing celestial motions as circular.[58] It will doubtless be some time yet before we hear the last of the earnest assertions that the most important "fact" about change in social systems is that it is endogenous or immanent. The homeostatic connotations of the term "pattern-maintenance" will persist for some time even if evidence accumulates that many processes to which that label has been heretofore applied are more truly of an inertial character. And recognition of the serious error involved in emphasizing pattern-maintenance to the utter neglect of the pattern modification which Axiom III says pattern-maintenance must always entail will only diffuse slowly among sociologists.

There is reason to have faith, however, that the forces of naturalism will prevail in their encounter with the inertia of present concepts. To give due credit to a writer who may seem to have been too often singled out for criticism in this book, I must point out that Parsons has wisely recognized the transitory character of the "war of independence" which the "sciences of action" have fought for half a century in extricating themselves from their former subservience to misperceived biology. Now that the necessary autonomy of these sciences has been achieved, it should be increasingly seen, according to Parsons, that sociological and biological theories may still share a common conceptual scheme because sociological phenomena "are best conceived as in the broadest sense 'in nature' and not as set 'over against' nature."[59] I wholeheartedly agree with Parsons on this, and if I then discount his attachment of importance to the notion that biology is sociology's "nearest neighbor in the community of sciences,"[60] that is a dispute which I am sure will be resolved within the collective processes of scientific inquiry.

[58] Norwood Russell Hanson, *Patterns of Discovery: An Inquiry into the Conceptual Foundations of Science.* New York: Cambridge University Press, 1958, p. 74.
[59] Talcott Parsons and Robert F. Bales, *Family, Socialization and Interaction Process,* New York: The Free Press of Glencoe, 1955, p. 399.
[60] *Ibid.*

Summary

Empirical research is necessary, but it is not enough to ensure the advancement of scientific sociology. That depends in part on continued conceptual innovation. Innovative thinking depends on knowledge divorced from blinding preconceptions, on symbol-manipulating skills relatively unchanneled by habitual symbol sequences, on confidence that a solution to a problem is possible unencumbered with fixed ideas as to the nature of the solution, and on obsessive perseverence in pursuit of solutions that may long remain elusive. Use of concepts borrowed from other sciences is likely to enhance fulfillment of these combinations of characteristics. Some degree of marginality to the discipline may help the sociologist to be innovative. Not all conceptual innovations will be sound, but as a collective enterprise, science is organized to winnow the wheat from the chaff through empirical research.

Accepted ideas have mass and resist displacement. This is true of the allegation that sociocultural phenomena are "supersensory, superrational, and metalogical" and must be studied by "mystical" and "intuitive" methods. These and other objections to sociological theories embodying terms generalized from physics have lost their ostensible profundity in the face of recent contributions to naturalistic sociology. Similar obscurantist assertions have been made in past centuries about other sciences, and were unavailing. Sociologists' intellectual provincialism and vestigial animism will be comparably ephemeral.

Borrowed concepts can contribute to the extension of sociological theory. For example, the concepts of mass and force facilitate the quantification and clarification of hypotheses about personality degradation under the impact of isolation and personality persistence and change in response to role changes. The concept of mass also leads to additional hypotheses in the theory of cognitive dissonance. The principle of equivalence between inertial and gravitational mass suggests testable hypotheses relating stability of self-conception and degree of personal attractiveness. The contrast between inertia and homeostasis suggests new problems for investigation in the context of disaster studies.

The illusion that social change is immanent, and thus insurmountably different from processes in nature, arises from the fetishistic devotion of sociologists to the study of large-scale systems. This obstacle to naturalism can be bypassed if the unit of analysis is appropriately selected. It must be of small enough magnitude to permit the study of interactions among units, rather than so large as to require a vain attempt to describe "developmental" change within a unit. The trend in sociology toward increased emphasis on social-psychology has been a trend toward more fruitful choice of units for study. It has thus been almost as important as the trend toward reliance on data. It is a sociological equivalent to the rise of molecular studies in biology.

As a collective endeavor, sociology can be a science even when many individual sociologists are not truly scientists. Sociology can be objective by virtue of the intellectual diversity of its practitioners without awaiting their achievement of complete neutrality on theoretical issues. When empirical test is the final arbiter in theoretical disputes, unorthodox ideas can be tolerated because the valid ones will eventually be validated and the false ones will eventually be falsified. Individual devotion to misleading concepts or faulty hypotheses somewhat impedes but cannot wholly prevent this. It is not necessary that every individual adjust his beliefs immediately and fully to the findings of research. Individuals are mortal. Consequently, within the domain of a science useless concepts tend to die with their proponents, while concepts that are empirically cogent will be retained in the scientific culture handed down to posterity.

In the long run, therefore, whatever our theoretical follies as individuals, our work will have been cumulative, and recognition of the wisdom of embracing the tenets of naturalism as the basis upon which to build the science of sociology will inevitably spread.